D0620726

Health Policy Reform

Health Policy Reform

Competition and Controls

Robert B. Helms, editor

NATIONAL UNIVERSITY
LIBRARY   SAN DIEGO

The AEI Press

Publisher for the American Enterprise Institute
WASHINGTON, D.C.

1993

Library of Congress Cataloging-in-Publication Data

Health policy reform : competition and controls / Robert B. Helms,
   editor.
      p.   cm.
   ISBN 0-8447-3844-1
   1. Medical care—United States—Cost control.   I. Helms, Robert
B.
   RA410.53.H418   1993
   338.4'33621'0973—dc20   93-36870
                                                            CIP

1   3   5   7   9   10   8   6   4   2

© 1993 by the American Enterprise Institute for Public Policy Research,
Washington, D.C. All rights reserved. No part of this publication may be
used or reproduced in any manner whatsoever without permission in writing
from the American Enterprise Institute except in the case of brief quotations
embodied in news articles, critical articles, or reviews. The views expressed
in the publications of the American Enterprise Institute are those of the
authors and do not necessarily reflect the views of the staff, advisory panels,
officers, or trustees of AEI.

THE AEI PRESS
Publisher for the American Enterprise Institute
1150 17th Street, N.W., Washington, D.C. 20036

Printed in the United States of America

Contents

TABLES

CONTENTS

Foreword

The big game is about to begin. It has been talked about by the players, the media, and the spectators for years. The players have pregame jitters: they are excited about playing to win but unsure that they are fully prepared or that they can respond to whatever their opponents throw at them. Pregame television clips of "the thrill of victory" and "the agony of defeat" intensify the tension.

While this analogy is far from perfect, there is a certain similarity between the anticipation of a major athletic competition and the current health policy debate. Legislative action to reform the health care system has been discussed for most of this century: predictions call the coming legislative showdown "the toughest bill since the Social Security Act."[1] Public opinion polls have shown strong support for reform but substantial disagreement about how to accomplish it.[2] The media have devoted substantial time and space to the debate. Almost every state and national politician has emphasized health policy in recent campaigns. The various teams in this debate—individual politicians, political parties, the administration, all segments of the health care industry—are both nervous and excited about a legislative contest. Research is being conducted, facts are being collected, and consultants are being hired—all to make sure

[1]Representative Richard A. Gephardt on the NBC News program, "Meet the Press," as reported in the *New York Times*, April 2, 1993, p. A-20.

[2]For a summary of twenty-nine public opinion surveys on health care reform by the Center for Health Care Policy and Evaluation, see Sheila Leatherman, "Americans Don't Want a Heatlh-Care Revolution," *Wall Street Journal*, June 17, 1993, p. A10.

that each team's playbook is up to the challenge.

But the rules of this health policy contest differ radically from those of almost any organized sporting event. This is not an event designed just for its entertainment value. The outcome will have tangible effects on the users of our health care system, the millions of people who provide that care, and the economic performance of our economy. Further, there are no established rules about how this contest will be played. The event itself is not scheduled to begin or end at any certain time—it may not even be played if the major players do not see a good chance for victory. And, unlike many athletic events, there are many more than just two well-trained individuals or teams that will take part. Numerous political factions may or may not decide to join forces with each other. There will be no final buzzer in Congress to tell us that the debate on health policy reform is over, even if some provisions are ultimately enacted into law. This debate will probably extend for years, just as it has in almost all other countries, even those with substantially different approaches to health policy.[3]

The purpose of this volume is to help prepare for the debate by making information and analysis available to all sides about probable effects of the basic policy choices. The book concentrates on the economic effects of market competition and government controls, which are emerging as the two basic strategies for health policy reform. While no proposal so far relies exclusively on market competition or government controls, each proposal derives its primary impetus for change from one of these approaches.

Both approaches have been defended and attacked. The proponents of market competition contend that it is the only way to induce both consumers and providers to make more cost-effective choices about the use of medical resources. Its opponents say that it is an unproven strategy that cannot work in a market dominated by powerful physicians, uninformed consumers, and the distorting effects of tax policies and insurance. Conversely, government controls are defended as the only proven way to contain costs but attacked as ignoring the real causes of the cost problem and inflicting large hidden costs on consumers.

In providing evidence and analysis of these various effects, this volume offers twelve chapters, mostly written by academics, with commentaries by practitioners and others who have direct experience in these areas. Four sections look at the effects of controls, the concept

---

[3]See Robert B. Helms, ed., *Health Care Policy and Politics: Lessons from Four Countries* (Washington, D.C.: AEI Press, 1993).

of global budgeting, managed competition policies, and competitive trends in existing medical markets. A fifth section provides a political history of the health reform debate by a former congressman who participated in almost two decades of this debate.

Managed Competition and Global Budgets

The policies of competition and controls are discussed in this volume in the context of two emerging policy terms, managed competition and global budgeting. A short description of the two terms is presented here as background for that discussion.

"Managed competition" refers to a concept of reform deriving from the analytical works of Alain C. Enthoven of Stanford University and Paul M. Ellwood with Interstudy and the Jackson Hole Group. A specific proposal known as the Jackson Hole proposal was developed by a group of health policy analysts and health industry leaders meeting in the home of Paul Ellwood in Jackson Hole, Wyoming.[4] The proposal envisions a market where large, full-service health delivery organizations compete with each other on the basis of price and quality. Limits on the present tax-free nature of employer-provided health insurance and other regulations would give consumers strong economic incentives to choose among these competing plans. Comparisons among the plans would be simplified by requirements that each plan offer and quote prices for a defined set of benefits. Additional benefits could be purchased by the consumer with after-tax dollars. The process of certifying the competing plans and collecting and publicizing the information about each plan's performance and annual price bids would be carried out by health alliances (called health care purchasing cooperatives in the Jackson Hole proposal) at the state or substate level. A national board would define the basic benefit package, the standards for the operation of the health alliances and the competing health plans, and collect data

---

[4]For a recent account of the activities of Enthoven, Ellwood, and this group, see John Huber, "The Abandoned Father of Health Care Reform," *New York Times Magazine*, July 18, 1993, pp. 24–26, 36–37. For a description of the proposal, see Paul M. Ellwood, Alain C. Enthoven, and Lynn Etheredge, "The Jackson Hole Initiatives for a Twenty-first American Health Care System," *Health Economics*, vol. 1 (1992), pp. 149–68, and Alain C. Enthoven, "The History and Principles of Managed Competition," *Health Affairs*, vol. 12, supp. (1993), pp. 24–48. The Jackson Hole proposal is the basis for the Managed Competition Act of 1992, a bill developed by the Conservative Democratic Forum and introduced as H.R. 5936 in 1992.

on the cost-effectiveness of various coverages in the basic benefit package. Federal subsidies based on income would allow poorer consumers and employers to purchase health insurance from one of the competing health plans.[5]

Global budgeting, however, is not as well defined as any of the managed competition proposals. As both Patricia M. Danzon and Henry N. Butler point out in this book, the concept can mean different things to different people. The central concept, however, is a national, or top-down, system of expenditure controls designed to reduce aggregate health spending to a lower rate of increase. Following Stephen F. Jencks and George J. Schieber, global budgets differ from expenditure targets because they contain some formal mechanism to ensure that expenditures do not exceed the target amount during a current accounting period.[6] Some form of aggregate controls are used in several European countries and Canada. The prospect of adopting some form of global budgeting in the United States raises a host of issues about how the targets would be set, how they would be handed down to state and local areas, and how they would be measured and enforced. Several authors in this volume raise substantial concerns about the effects of such policies on the competitive incentives that are the backbone of all market-based and competitive health reform proposals.

Overview

As I stated in the introduction to *American Health Policy: Critical Issues for Reform,*[7] there is little disagreement that some kind of health policy reform could improve both the economic efficiency and the equity of the U.S. health care sector. The major disagreements involve how to achieve reform. All the essays and commentaries in this volume

---

[5]Alain Enthoven's definition follows: "Managed competition is a purchasing strategy to obtain maximum value for money for employers and consumers. It uses rules for competition, derived from rational microeconomic principles, to reward with more subscribers and revenue those health plans that do the best job of improving quality, cutting cost, and satisfying patients." Enthoven, "The History and Principles of Managed Competition," p. 29.

[6]Stephen F. Jencks and George J. Schieber, "Containing U.S. Health Care Costs: What Bullet to Bite?" *Health Care Financing Review*, Health Care Financing Administration, 1991 annual supp. (March 1992), p. 8.

[7]Robert B. Helms, ed., *American Health Policy: Critical Issues for Reform* (Washington, D.C.: AEI Press, 1993), p. 2.

attempt to answer two overriding questions: What have been the effects of various types of policies in the past, and what can we learn from these experiences about how specific policy prescriptions will affect different individuals? These chapters provide both conceptual analysis and empirical evidence about past attempts to control costs through government regulation or by changes in the competitive structure of the market. The volume is divided into four sections but with considerable overlap in the topics. This should not be surprising because almost every change in policy involves changes in both government regulation and the market's response to that change. The market changes examined in this volume (in California by Jack Zwanziger, Glenn A. Melnick, and Anil Bamezai; in Minnesota by Roger Feldman and Bryan Dowd; and the federal employees' health program by Walton Francis) are all changes that have been held out as examples of managed competition and have occurred in real markets where numerous market and regulatory forces have complicated our ability to measure the separate effects of change. These findings of the positive effects of market changes are reinforced by the analysis of private sector activities by Sean Sullivan, other market changes by Alain Enthoven and Mark V. Pauly, and the effects of the growth of managed care by Bernard Friedman and Rosanna M. Coffey. These analyses show clearly that some medical markets have become increasingly competitive over the past two decades. These relatively large market segments have responded in a predictable way to government policies that use some form of fixed capitated payment and give consumers a choice among plans. Such policies have forced providers to compete on the basis of service and price, have saved the sponsoring organizations money, but at the same time have illustrated the problems of biased selection that must be overcome if some version of managed competition is to work.

Health Policy Reform also looks at the probable effects of direct government controls. The more traditional tools of price controls and public utility regulation are analyzed by Stuart M. Butler and Charles Stallon, while Bernard Friedman and Rosanna Coffee study the effect of state rate controls. These chapters continue a long tradition of serious studies of government regulation showing that such attempts at direct controls are seldom enforceable in a way that can bring about the intended economic change. When they are enforced, such controls usually impose hidden costs on consumers and some producers while awarding other producers and their political allies larger than normal profits.[8]

---

[8]In addition to the references given in this volume, my earlier survey of

Although the policies are not new, global budgeting is the newest fad in the terminology of health care regulation. The probable effects on government health budgets, existing private health markets, and the proposed managed competition reforms are analyzed in part two by Patricia Danzon and Henry Butler. Patricia Danzon continues her excellent analysis of the hidden costs of government-provided health care in her analysis of global budgeting.[9] Her analysis shows the conditions under which a global limit on expenditures might achieve the objectives of reform. Achieving efficient results is substantially more difficult in private markets than in public programs such as Medicare. She reviews the experience of other countries with global budgets and concludes that such policies may discriminate against lower-income people, who might not be able to purchase supplementary insurance coverage. Her conclusions that "global budgets may control measured spending, but they cannot control the real social costs of medical care" illustrate the danger of believing that the real costs of a business can be controlled by assigning the task to the accountants who record the numbers. A concentration in the debate on recorded numbers, especially the crude estimates of health expenditures, confuses the real effects with less-than-perfect indicators.

Henry Butler uses the theory of public choice economics to analyze the effects global budgeting would have on the performance of markets based on managed competition. He concludes that such policies would substantially change the behavior of providers as they seek to reduce effort and service quality in response to limits on expenditures. Over time, such policies would ensure the failure of managed competition by destroying the incentives to compete for consumers on the basis of both quality and price. In Henry Butler's view, the failure of a competitive health reform policy would further erode the public's faith in a competitive health market and play into the hands of the proponents of government-provided health care.

Competition or Controls?

The research presented in these chapters warns that we should approach health policy reform with a strong sense of history. The

---

this literature illustrates the substantial body of evidence that was created on the economic effects of regulation in the 1970s, the last period of intense interest in government controls in health. See Robert B. Helms, "The Health Cost Problem: Is Regulation Our Only Hope?" *Bulletin of the New York Academy of Medicine*, vol. 56, no. 1 (January/February 1980), pp. 26–37.

[9] Patricia Danzon, "The Hidden Costs of Budget-constrained Health Insurance Systems," in Robert B. Helms, ed., *American Health Policy: Critical Issues for Reform* (Washington, D.C.: AEI Press, 1993), pp. 256–92.

market for health care can be made to work in a more efficient manner if we are willing to use what we know about competitive markets. Meanwhile, we should ignore the siren song of government regulation since we know from at least forty centuries of recorded history that such approaches have more to do with transferring political power than they do with controlling real costs.[10] Returning to the analogy of the major sporting event, in this case football, perhaps we should call the upcoming health policy debate the lemmings'super bowl. The offense should not try any wide runs to the left because the left sideline is not well defined and approaches a cliff above the sea. If both teams are too intent on the game and ignore the landscape, they both may suffer the fate of lemmings. What is not accurate about this analogy is that any legislative action to reform American health policy is unlikely to bring the health care system to the lemmings' sudden and catastrophic end. Policy reform based on direct government expenditure controls is more likely to produce something akin to a dull game played by lethargic and overweight players. Instead of a vibrant competitive market that rewards consumers with more cost-effective and higher quality care and the best providers with higher incomes, the diversion of attention to controls will place less emphasis on quality, service, and convenience to patients and on the search for new and beneficial technologies.

Acknowledgments

The American Enterprise Institute for Public Policy Research would like to acknowledge and thank two organizations, the National Committee for Quality Health Care and the Healthcare Leadership Council, for providing generous financial support to make this volume available. We would also like to thank the Principal Financial Group, the Travelers, the Association of Health Insurance Agents, and the Pharmaceutical Manufacturers Association for their support. None of these organizations necessarily agrees with the views of the editor or any conclusions reached by the authors or the discussants.

I would like to thank several individuals who provided valuable help in planning the volume and in selecting the authors and discussants. Among these were Pamela Bailey and Joan Simmons with the National Committee for Quality Health Care and the Health Leadership Council, Sam Mitchell with Marshfield Associates, Mark Pauly with the University of Pennsylvania, and Heather Gradison, Derrick

---

[10]Robert L. Schuettinger and Eaman F. Butler, *Forty Centuries of Wage and Price Controls* (Washington, D.C.: Heritage Foundation, 1979).

Max, and Christopher DeMuth at AEI. My assistant Elizabeth Baldwin deserves special thanks for the efficient and courteous manner with which she handled the large volume of correspondence with the authors, discussants, and AEI editorial staff. The help of these people and the cooperation of the authors and discussants made the editing of this volume a meaningful and enjoyable task.

ROBERT B. HELMS

Contributors

ROBERT B. HELMS is a resident scholar and director of Health Policy Studies at the American Enterprise Institute. He has written and lectured extensively on health policy, health economics, and pharmaceutical economic issues. Mr. Helms is the editor of AEI's newest publication on health policy, *American Health Policy: Critical Issues for Reform*. From 1981 to 1989, he was assistant secretary for planning and evaluation and deputy assistant secretary for health policy in the Department of Health and Human Services.

ANIL BAMEZAI is chief policy analyst at A&N Technical Services, Inc., a policy consulting firm. His research includes the assessment of government regulation in health and the environment, the impact of technological change on income disparity, water resource management, and economic and econometric modeling. He was a consultant to the World Bank and both a consultant and fellow at the RAND Corporation. A recent work (written with Glenn Melnick, Jack Zwanziger, and Robert Pattison), "The Effects of Market Structure and Bargaining Position on Hospital Prices," was published in the *Journal of Health Economics* (1992).

HENRY N. BUTLER is Koch Distinguished Teaching Professor of Law Economics at the University of Kansas. He was the associate dean and director of the Law and Economics Center at George Mason University and the John M. Olin Visiting Fellow in Law and Economics at the University of Chicago Law School. His research interests include law and economics, federalism, and regulation of financial services. Mr. Butler has written extensively on law and regulation.

He is a member of the American Bar Association and the American Economic Association, and director of the Virginia Council on Economic Education.

STUART M. BUTLER is a vice president and the director of Domestic and Economic Policy Studies at the Heritage Foundation. He plans and oversees the foundation's research and publications in all domestic issues. Mr. Butler is an expert on health, urban, and welfare policy and on privatizing government services. He has written numerous books and articles on a wide range of issues including his latest publication, *A National Health System for America* (cowritten with Edmund Haislmaier), which provides a blueprint for a national health system based on free market principles.

ROSANNA M. COFFEY is director of the Division of Provider Studies in the Agency for Health Care Policy and Research, Department of Health and Human Services. She also researches hospital costs associated with specific diseases and with clinical research, hospital reimbursement under alternative classification systems, and alternative treatments for specific medical conditions. Ms. Coffey has developed large national data bases linking discharge, patient, physician, hospital, community, and health program information.

ROBERT CRANDALL is a senior fellow in the Economic Studies Program at the Brookings Institution. He has specialized in industrial organization, antitrust policy, and regulation. His current research deals with the effects of the divestiture of AT&T and the changing regional structure of the U.S. economy. Mr. Crandall was assistant (late 1975–1977), acting (1977), and deputy director (1977–1978) for the Council on Wage and Price Stability. He is a member of the American Economic Association. Mr. Crandall has taught at Northwestern University, MIT, and the University of Maryland. He has written extensively on regulatory issues.

PATRICIA DANZON is the Celia Moh Professor at the Wharton School, where she is a professor of health care systems and insurance and risk management. She has held positions at the University of Chicago, Duke University, and the RAND Corporation. Ms. Danzon has been widely published in health care, insurance, and liability systems. She was recently elected to the Institute of Medicine of the National Academy of Sciences. She has been a consultant on international health care issues to the World Bank, the New Zealand government, the Asian Development Bank, and the U.S. Agency for International Development.

BRYAN DOWD is an associate professor in the Institute for Health Services Research, University of Minnesota. He is director of graduate studies for the master's of science program in health services research and policy. His primary research interests are markets for health insurance and health care services and evaluation of nonexperimental data. Mr. Dowd teaches advanced health services research methods in the doctoral and master's programs offered through the institute. He serves on grarnt review panels for major funding agencies, referees articles for major health services research and health economics journals, and is on the editorial board of *Medical Care*.

ALAIN ENTHOVEN is a professor of health research at Stanford University and the Marriner S. Eccles Professor of Public and Private Management at Stanford's Graduate School of Business. He is an authority on the economics of health care policy. Formerly an economist at the RAND Corporation, Mr. Enthoven was vice president for economic planning for Litton Industries and president of Litton Medical Products. He was instrumental in founding the Jackson Hole Group for health policy research and has been a consultant on health care policy to Congress and the executive branch. Mr. Enthoven has written many books and articles on health policy issues. His most recent book is *Theory and Practice of Managed Competition in Health Care Finance*.

ROGER FELDMAN is professor of health services and economics at the University of Minnesota. His major field of research is health economics. Recently, he has completed studies of competition among private health insurers, hospitals, and health maintenance organizations, including a study of health maintenance organization mergers. Mr. Feldman was a senior staff member of the President's Council of Economic Advisers. He is a regular contributor to professional journals in health services research and economics and is on the editorial boards of several journals, including *Health Services Research* and *Inquiry*.

WALTON FRANCIS is an economist and policy analyst in the Office of the Assistant Secretary for Planning and Evaluation at the Department of Health and Human Services, where he reviews regulatory proposals to analyze their economic costs and burdens. He has written on managed health care and retirement benefits and is a leading expert on the Federal Employees Health Benefits Program. Mr. Francis pioneered the systematic comparison of health insurance plans from a consumer perspective and continues as the author of the annual *CHECKBOOK's Guide to Health Insurance Plans for Federal Employees*.

BERNARD FRIEDMAN is an economist and senior research fellow at the Center for Intramural Research, Agency for Health Care Policy and Research. He was vice president at the Hospital Research and Educational Trust of the American Hospital Association. Mr. Friedman specializes in economic research with large national databases on hospital finances, patient discharge summaries, and market area characteristics in regard to responses of hospitals to financial risks and pressures; rationing of organ transplants and other expensive new technologies; and determinants of growth of cost and utilization for specific procedures, such as joint replacements.

BILL GRADISON is president of the Health Insurance Association of America. Before assuming his current post in February 1993, Mr. Gradison served in the U.S. House of Representatives for eighteen years where, most recently, he was ranking minority member of the House Budget Committee and the Health Subcommittee of the House Ways and Means Committee. Mr. Gradison is chairman of the Economic Roundtable of the American Enterprise Institute and was vice chairman of the U.S. Bipartisan Commission on Comprehensive Health Care (the Pepper Commission).

STAN JONES is a consultant to private foundations on competitive private health insurance markets and the role of public policy in improving these markets. He was a founding partner of the Washington consulting firm, Health Policy Alternatives, Inc., and has been vice president for Washington representation of the Blue Cross and Blue Shield Association and staff director of the Senate Health Subcommittee. Mr. Jones is a member of the Institute of Medicine. He has published numerous papers, most recently "Developing a Basic Benefit Package: Issues and Challenges." He is chairman of the Advisory Committee to the Robert Wood Johnson Foundation State Initiatives in Health Care Financing Reform Program.

MARVIN H. KOSTERS is resident scholar and director of the Economic Policy Studies Program at the American Enterprise Institute. He was AEI's director of the Center for the Study of Government Regulation. Mr. Kosters has served on the Council of Economic Advisers and as a consultant to the U.S. Department of the Treasury, the Department of Labor, and the Council on Wage and Price Stability. He has written numerous books and articles on labor economics, wages, and wage trends with regard to education levels. His latest article is "The Rise in Income Inequality," published in *The American Enterprise*, November-December 1992.

ARTHUR LIFSON is vice president of health policy and federal affairs at CIGNA Corporation. He was vice president of the Government Relations Department at EQUICOR and served in various capacities for more than fourteen years at the Equitable Life Assurance Society of the United States. Mr. Lifson serves on the Medicare Committee for the Group Health Association of America. He is a member of the National Academy of Sciences and a director of the National Health Council. Mr. Lifson was chairman of the Managed Medicare Working Group for the Health Insurance Association of America.

GLENN A. MELNICK is an associate professor at the UCLA School of Public Health and is a resident consultant at the RAND Corporation. Mr. Melnick has research, policy, and field experience in both domestic and international health care financing issues. Mr. Melnick has directed four major studies to determine the effects of competition policies and managed care on hospital efficiency, costs, prices, and access. An integral component of these studies was the development of hospital market structure measures. His current research involves investigating the relationships among the linked markets of hospitals, physicians, and insurers to determine to what extent the structure of related markets affects hospital and physician behavior.

NORMAN J. ORNSTEIN is resident scholar at the American Enterprise Institute, political contributor to the "MacNeil/Lehrer NewsHour," and election analyst for CBS News. He is codirecting the Renewing Congress Project, a comprehensive examination of Congress geared to the changes likely to occur with the 103rd Congress. Mr. Ornstein has worked on Capitol Hill as an American Political Science Association congressional fellow and as staff director of the Senate Committee to Study the Committee System, which reorganized the Senate. His books include *The People, Press, and Politics: The American Elections of 1982* and *The New Congress*. He is frequently interviewed on National Public Radio's "All Things Considered," ABC's "Nightline," and CBS's "Face the Nation."

MARK V. PAULY is the Bendhaim Professor, chairman of the Health

Care Systems Department, and professor of insurance and public policy and management at the Wharton School, University of Pennsylvania. From 1984 to 1989, he was executive director of the Leonard Davis Institute of Health Economics, and he is now its director of research. Mr. Pauly has analyzed Medicare and Medicaid financing, the behavioral impact of different methods of paying health care providers, and the role of employment-related group insurance. He has written extensively on health economics, public finance, and health insurance, and most recently was a coauthor of *Responsible National Health Insurance* (AEI Press).

MARTHA PHILLIPS is the executive director of the Concord Coalition, a nonpartisan grass-roots effort to break through political gridlock on economic issues. She was the Republican staff director for the House Budget Committee and, from 1977 to 1985, the deputy minority staff director of the Ways and Means Committee. In 1982, Ms. Phillips staffed the Impediments Committee of the President's Task Force on Private Sector Initiatives. She is a director of the Population Reference Bureau and served on the boards of the American Association for Budget and Program Analysis and of Women in Government Relations.

ROBERT RUBIN is president of Lewin-VHI. He joined Lewin-ICF Incorporated in 1984 as the executive vice president for health affairs and, with the company's reorganization, took primary responsibility for the health care branch. Dr. Rubin is a board-certified internist and nephrologist. He is clinical associate professor at the Georgetown University School of Medicine. Dr. Rubin was the first physician to be appointed assistant secretary for planning and evaluation in the Department of Health and Human Services. He consults with hospitals, physician associations, and pharmaceutical companies and has directed numerous studies on the impact of the prospective payment system on providers.

JACK SCANLON, JR., is senior vice president of research and analytic policy at HealthCare COMPARE. He is a health economist with an extensive background in data management and analysis in managed care environments. Mr. Scanlon cofounded AFFORDABLE Health Care Concepts in 1983, now a subsidiary of HealthCare Concepts. He was director of research of the California Governor's Office of Special Health Care Negotiations. Mr. Scanlon has developed a wide variety of data bases and computer models, as well as state-of-the-art workstations and management information systems.

STEPHEN C. SCHOENBAUM is associate professor of medicine and deputy medical director of the Harvard Community Health Plan. He supervises the departments for clinical quality management, clinical care assessment, health promotion and clinical publications, and risk management. Throughout the 1980s, he held positions in which he had oversight for HCHP's teaching programs and for software development and maintenance for HCHP's automated medical system, which serves more than 250,000 of its active members.

CHARLES STALON is director of the Institute of Public Utilities and a professor of economics at Michigan State University. For five years he was a commissioner on the Federal Energy Regulatory Commission and for seven years a commissioner of the Illinois Commerce Commission. During his twelve years as an economic regulator, he was active at the National Association of Regulatory Utility Commissioners.

SEAN SULLIVAN is president of the National Business Coalition Forum on Health, a movement of employer coalitions in more than fifty cities to get better quality health care for their workers while holding down costs. Mr. Sullivan attends meetings of the Jackson Hole East group and the Managed Competition Coalition and works with members of the Conservative Democratic Forum as well as Republican leaders. His recent work has examined the causes of rising health care costs and the development of private and public strategies for managing the cost and quality of care. He was executive vice president of New Directions for Policy, assistant director of the Council on Wage and Price Stability, and a scholar at the American Enterprise Institute.

HARRY SUTTON, JR., is senior vice president and chief actuary at R. W. Morey, Inc. He specializes in health care analysis and actuarial rating practices in governmental, prepaid, and insurance industries. He has also specialized in the development of prepaid health programs for Medicare and Medicaid. In the 1970s, Mr. Sutton became a leading consultant for the developing HMO movement. He was also involved with market valuations and the buying and selling of HMO corporations. He has been active in Minnesota and Massachusetts in helping to develop programs for universal health care at the state level.

ROBERT WALLER is president and chief executive officer of the Mayo Foundation and chairman of the Mayo Foundation for Medical Education and Research. He also is chairman of the board for Rochester Methodist Hospital Health Services and for Saint Mary's Hospital of Rochester, Minnesota. Dr. Waller is a trustee of the Healthcare Leadership Council and of the Principal Financial Group. He is a member of the American Medical Association and of the Society of Medical Administrators.

JACK ZWANZIGER is assistant professor of community and preventive medicine at the University of Rochester, a consultant to the RAND Corporation, and an independent consultant. He is investigating the effects of hospital competition and comparing hospital costs in the United States and Canada. Mr. Zwanziger is studying the effect of health care market structure on hospital costs, prices, quality and service intensity, and insurance premiums. He was a lecturer at the UCLA School of Public Health, a manager of the Telecommunications Policy Office of the Ontario Ministry of Transportation and Communications, and a senior policy analyst in the Policy Analysis and Coordination Office in the same department.

PART ONE

The Evidence of Spending Controls

1

The Fatal Attraction of Price Controls

Stuart M. Butler

In the debate over health care reform in the United States, there is significant support for the imposition of some degree of price controls in the health care industry. Controls often are advocated either as a short-term measure during the transition to a restructured universal health care system or as a permanent feature of a reformed system on the grounds that the nature of the health care economy means that market pricing necessarily leads to inflation and unacceptable inequities.

Resorting to price controls is nothing new for policy makers, in the United States or elsewhere. Indeed, the imposition of price controls as a national economic policy stretches at least as far back as the Code of Hammurabi, established some 4,000 years ago in Babylon.[1] More recently, price controls have been imposed by many countries during periods of international conflict or, like the controls introduced by several industrial countries in the 1960s and 1970s, as a strategy to tackle unusually high inflation.

The purpose of this chapter is to review international experience

---

[1]For a history of controls, see Robert L. Schuettinger and Eamonn F. Butler, *Forty Centuries of Wage and Price Controls* (Washington, D.C.: Heritage Foundation, 1979). See also Schuettinger, "The Historical Record," in Michael Walker, ed., *The Illusion of Wage and Price Control* (Vancouver: Fraser Institute, 1976).

with price controls. Since this necessarily must be selective, given the widespread use of controls, the review focuses on the modern era and on experiences that appear to have most relevance to the sophisticated U.S. health care economy. Particular attention is paid to potential side effects of controls that have significance to health care policy making.

Why Price Controls Are Introduced

Controlling General Inflation. Of the many justifications for price controls, perhaps the most controversial is their effectiveness as a tool for bringing down general inflation. This rationale stems from the notion that inflation is generated by cost-push factors, in other words, that inflation is due to a general rise in costs, passed on as higher retail prices. This theory has provided the intellectual underpinning for numerous price-control policies. Many health care policy makers in the United States today talk of extraneous "cost drivers" in the system, implying that rising health care prices stem from increases in input costs. (Many of these do see the dynamic more as costs in one sector forcing a switch in consumer spending from other sectors, not as a contributor to a general rise in consumer prices.)

The cost-push view of inflation has become far less fashionable among Western policy makers in recent years because of the widespread acceptance of theories of inflation based on total demand in an economy, and in particular demand made possible by an expansion in the stock of money. According to this view, a general rise in retail prices occurs because of an increase in total money supply, and a rise in "costs" (which are merely other prices in the production chain) is facilitated by consumer acceptance of higher retail prices thanks to the rise in the money supply. Thus, the cost-push theory confuses cause and effect. This makes price controls as worthless and irrelevant to controlling inflation as mechanically holding down a thermometer reading would be to reducing the heat in a room. As we shall see, the "monetarist" criticism of price controls seems to explain the ineffectiveness of price controls as a tool to combat general inflation.

Ensuring Fair Prices. A second argument for price controls is that an objective, just, or fair price can and should be applied to a good or service. This view, common in medieval times but still lingering today, holds that relative prices ought to correspond with the relationship between the supposed objective values of the items. Thus, medieval government officials often would determine the legal prices

4

for items based on a fixed mathematical relationship between products and their component costs and between different products.

The idea of objective values and prices is entirely rejected in market economics, which forms the basis of Western economies. Instead, flexible prices, reflecting supply and demand amid the differing subjective valuations attributed to goods and services by individuals, are key to efficient production, distribution, and exchange in an economy. Ironically, then, the whole basis for physician fee payment in the Medicare system (known as the resource-based relative value scale) is the notion that the value of physicians' services can be compared according to an objective standard of value, and fees set accordingly.[2]

Unusual Market Conditions. A third rationale for controls is to address peculiar market conditions. A typical example is wartime, when sudden changes in demand or supply can mean rapid increases in some prices. In addition, controls have been applied in peacetime to certain sectors of the economy or in particular localities to combat prices deemed unduly high—or beyond the reach of certain citizens. Examples include rent controls in the United States and many other countries, as well as health care fee and treatment schedules in the U.S. Medicare system and more general health care controls in numerous countries. In other cases, price controls are seen as a way of maintaining short-term stability while other far-reaching measures are being introduced. The use of controls is advocated for this reason by some in the current context of health care reform to avoid large economic gains to some suppliers during the transition to a universal health system. In still other cases, certain industries or firms are believed to have an effective monopoly in certain circumstances. This has led to the regulation of prices for certain utilities. It is also an argument used today by advocates of price controls for pharmaceuticals.

In addition to controls on prices themselves, most price-control policies in recent times have companion measures. One is wage controls, seen as necessary to check the major internal cost faced by firms subjected to price control, and thereby easing undue pressure on profits. The other is some system of rationing. Because holding a price below the market-clearing level necessarily will lead to shortages, there must be some form of allocation to willing buyers other than simply price.

2See Robert Moffit, "Comparable Worth for Doctors," *Backgrounder* no. 855 (Washington, D.C.: Heritage Foundation, 1991).

The Macroeconomic Experience

In the United States, price controls have been imposed on several occasions, with varying degrees of severity, since the American Revolution. Generally, the controls have been introduced during wartime to address potentially severe disruptions in domestic markets. In other cases, such as the voluntary system of controls introduced during the Carter administration, the aim has been to break a spiral of unusually rapid inflation. Even though the Nixon administration controls (1971–1974) coincided with the Vietnam War, the aim was to curb inflation rather than to deal with a typical wartime situation.

One of the great ironies in the current debate over health care price controls is that today's health care system for working Americans, which seems so prone to rapid cost increases, is a byproduct of wage controls introduced during World War II. During the war, employers in the controlled, tight labor market added larger fringe benefits, including health care, to compensation as a way of evading wage controls. Later, the IRS ruled these benefits to be tax-free without limit. Many analysts now contend that the tax subsidy for employer-sponsored group health insurance (as opposed to out-of-pocket expenses) and the third-party payment system operated through employers encourage heavy overdemand for medical care by insured Americans and is the principal cause of health care inflation.[3]

Without exception, the modern U.S. experience with price controls to curb inflation has been, to say the least, disappointing. While wage and price controls are credited, for instance, with keeping inflation lower during World War II than might otherwise have been the case, the impact of controls appears to have been the temporary suppression of rising prices rather than a real tapering of inflation. Observes Robert L. Schuettinger:

> After the war was over, however, the pent-up inflation burst and the controls broke down completely. From August 1945 to November 1946 wholesale prices rose over 32 percent and consumer prices over 18 percent. It is entirely possible, therefore, that the end result would have been almost the

[3]See Stuart M. Butler, "A Policy Maker's Guide to the Health Care Debate, Part 1," in Heritage Foundation, *Talking Points* (Washington, D.C.: 1992). See also Edmund F. Haislmaier, "Why America's Health System Is in Trouble," in Stuart M. Butler and Haislmaier, eds., *A National Health System for America* (Washington, D.C.: Heritage Foundation, 1989).

same by the year 1946 if controls had never been introduced in the first place.[4]

On the face of it, the experience during and after the Korean War controls is more heartening for advocates of price controls. Launched in earnest in early 1951 in the form of a wage and price freeze, controls remained in force until early 1953. In the six months before the price and wage freeze, prices rose at an annual rate of 11.2 percent and wages at 11.8 percent. During the next two years of tight controls, prices rose at an annual rate of just 2.1 percent (the rate for wages was 5.6 percent).[5] Thereafter, when price controls gradually were lifted, inflation slowed further.

Did the controls work? It seems not. Herbert Stein maintains that the Korean War controls were an "overreaction" to a temporary price surge as the war broke out. Prices in any case were softening, notes Stein, and this situation "seems not to have been the result of the wage-price controls, as there were few if any shortages and many prices were below their ceilings."[6]

What of other explanations? Significantly, 1950–1953 was a period of tight monetary control. The money stock per unit of real production *fell* at an annual rate of 6.4 percent during the last six months of 1950 and contracted at a rate of 0.4 percent between January 1951 and February 1953.[7] Given the typical lag between a decline in money growth and the easing of prices in the monetarist theory, monetary policy appears a far more likely explanation of the course of prices in the early 1950s than price controls.

The Nixon wage and price-control program produced even more disappointing results. In August 1971, Richard Nixon introduced a mandatory control system in an attempt to deal with a deteriorating balance-of-payments situation combined with an inflationary recession. The program consisted of a ninety-day freeze (known as phase 1) initiated in August, followed by mandatory controls on price and wage increases (phase 2) lasting until January 1973, a period of "voluntary" controls (phase 3) until June 1973, followed by another

---

[4]Schuettinger, "Historical Record," p. 91.

[5]Hugh Rockoff, *Drastic Measures: A History of Wage and Price Controls in the United States* (Cambridge: Cambridge University Press, 1984), p. 186.

[6]Herbert Stein, "Fiscal Policy: Reflections on the Past Decade," in William Fellner, ed., *Contemporary Economic Problems* (Washington, D.C.: American Enterprise Institute, 1976), p. 68.

[7]Rockoff, *Drastic Measures*, p. 186, using figures from Milton Friedman and Anna Schwartz.

TABLE 1-1

AVERAGE ACTUAL AND QUALITY-CORRECTED
INFLATION RATES, UNITED STATES, 1970–1975
(percent)

Periods	Government Data	Corrected for Quality Changes
1970:1–1971:2	5.2	5.2
1971:3–1972:4	3.2	5.4
1973:1–1974:3	9.0	7.0
1974:4–1975:1	11.4	11.4
1975:2–1975:3	5.1	5.1

NOTE: Compounded annual rates of change over previous quarter in GNP deflator (percent per annum). Corrected data for periods not affected by Economic Stabilization Program are identical to the government data.
SOURCE: Michael R. Darby, "The U.S. Economic Stabilization Program of 1971–1974," in Michael Walker, ed., *The Illusion of Wage and Price Control* (Vancouver: Fraser Institute, 1976), p. 149.

freeze, and then mandatory controls lasting until April 1974 (phase 4). Phase 4 incorporated a system of decontrol.

As table 1–1 indicates, inflation was at a declining annualized rate of just over 5 percent in the fifteen months before the initial freeze. It held at an average of just over 3 percent until the middle of phase 2 but then began a rapid rise until just after decontrol, when the rate fell sharply to just over 5 percent.

This could hardly be considered a glorious success for price controls. But the results are even worse than they initially seem. Michael Darby points out, for example, that the raw numbers do not take into account the effect of producers trying to live within price limits by reducing quality (a typical result of controls, which is discussed later). Refining the figures to account for quality, Darby found that "the apparent sharp decline in the rate of inflation during the first two phases was a statistical illusion." And the rise in the inflation rate in the third and fourth phases was somewhat exaggerated in the official figures. Concludes Darby, after adjusting the entire period and comparing inflation with the underlying trend during the whole period of controls, "The trend of the corrected price level appears little affected by the [Nixon controls]."[8] That trend, says

8Michael R. Darby, "The U.S. Economic Stabilization Program of 1971–1974," in Michael Walker, ed., *The Illusion of Wage and Price Control* (Vancouver: Fraser Institute, 1976), pp. 149, 152.

Darby, was influenced mainly by the lagged effects of monetary policy. Money creation accelerated during most of the 1960s, before a slowdown in 1969. The slowdown was followed by recession and then by decline in the rate of inflation. The money supply increased sharply once again from 1971 through June 1973, followed by another deceleration.

Other economists, using a variety of econometric models, draw similar conclusions. Among these, Otto Eckstein remarks that "the striking conclusion . . . is that the inflation experience would not have been substantially different in the absence of price controls."[9] And Robert Gordon found that "price controls worked temporarily, with a decline in the price level followed by a rebound, but wage controls had if anything a perverse effect."[10]

The recent experience of Canada has been similarly disappointing. Canada introduced wage and profit controls in October 1973 (these ran until late 1978) in an effort to reduce inflation without any increase in unemployment. Significantly, the program was not intended as a sharp shock to break inflationary expectations but as a classic cost-push anti-inflation strategy. Prices were not directly controlled. The main target was labor costs.

Yet after a dip from 10 percent inflation to just over 6 percent in the first year, inflation rose to nearly 9 percent in the final years of the program, more than double the target. Various econometric studies have failed to detect any benefit from controls instituted by the Canadian government.[11] And the Canadian Anti-Inflation Board, responsible for managing the program, began in the second year to question the effectiveness of its own program. "As time passes," the board commented in its 1977 annual report, "there is increasing room for debate about the amount of separate impact the controls are having on prices and incomes."[12]

Wage and price controls in some form or other were in force in

[9]Otto Eckstein, *The Great Recession* (New York: North Holland, 1978), p. 55; also quoted in Martin Lefkowitz and Cheryl Nikaos, *Wage and Price Controls: The Answer to Inflation?* (Washington, D.C.: U.S. Chamber of Commerce, 1979), p. 28.

[10]Robert J. Gordon, "Can the Inflation of the 1970s Be Explained?" *Brookings Papers on Economic Activity*, vol. 1 (1977), p. 276. For a summary of several studies, see Rockoff, *Drastic Measures*, pp. 217–21, and Jack Meyer, *Wage-Price Standards and Economic Policy* (Washington, D.C.: American Enterprise Institute, 1982), pp. 48–56.

[11]Lefkowitz and Nikaos, *Wage and Price Controls*, pp. 43–44.

[12]Quoted in ibid., p. 44.

Britain throughout the postwar period, up to 1978. Imposed by both major parties, these programs included freezes, statutory measures, and voluntary wage and price agreements.[13] In almost every case, the programs failed to come close to achieving their objectives. "What is striking about [a comparison of years with and without controls]," notes Michael Parkin,

> is the lack of any systematic tendency for controls to be associated with a reduction in inflation. Indeed, in broad terms, the reverse is true. As controls have become more severe (with statutory controls replacing voluntary guidelines) and more prolonged, so the pace of inflation has accelerated.[14]

As in other countries and periods, comments Parkin, the pattern of inflation in modern Britain is best explained by trends in money growth.

The postwar use of wage and price controls in other industrialized countries has been just as disappointing. From France[15] to the Netherlands[16] to Australia,[17] the record is one of controls failing to have any significant or lasting effect on the general trend of prices. At best, controls provide a temporary check on prices, chiefly by dampening public expectations of future price rises. At worst, controls merely suppress or hide inflation, while producing damaging side effects or dislocations on the economy. It is to those side effects we now turn.

How Price Controls Disrupt the Economy

Price controls appear to be ineffective as a tool to control general inflation. But as discussed, other reasons are put forward for introducing controls. One is that price controls may be necessary to hold

---

[13]For a summary of the programs, see Samuel Brittan and Peter Lilley, *The Delusion of Incomes Policy* (London: Temple Smith, 1977), pp. 154–55, and Michael Parkin, "Wage and Price Controls: The Lessons From Britain," in Michael Walker, ed., *The Illusion of Wage and Price Control* (Vancouver: Fraser Institute, 1976), pp. 105–8.

[14]Parkin, "Wage and Price Controls," p. 108.

[15]See Lefkowitz and Nikaos, *Wage and Price Controls*, pp. 45–46.

[16]Brittan and Lilley, *Delusion*, pp. 113–24.

[17]U.S. Congress, Joint Economic Committee, *Wage and Price Policies in Australia, Austria, Canada, Japan, the Netherlands, and West Germany*, 97th Congress, 2d session, 1982, pp. 1–11.

down the "high" cost of a good or service considered essential for lower-income individuals or to reduce "excessive" spending in one sector so that more resources can be devoted to other sectors. Another is to deal with the contention that relative prices do not accurately reflect the "real" or "objective" value of certain products. These arguments are particularly relevant to the current debate over health care. Neither argument actually requires controls to hold down the general level of inflation in an economy—only that they succeed in holding down prices in one sector and in shifting resources and spending to another.

To be sure, if a government succeeds in holding the price below the market-clearing level of supply and demand, it will reduce total spending in the sector (since production will fall to some degree). Consumers of the controlled product also will enjoy a lower price. But theory suggests, and practice indicates, that trying to circumvent the laws of economics in this way necessarily leads to a host of damaging, even bizarre, side effects. These should give pause to policy makers contemplating controls in the health care sector, since there is plenty of evidence to indicate that health care is as subject to these effects as any other sector.

Effect 1. Shortages appear amid underutilized productive capacity. When a price is held below the market level, demand is higher than it otherwise would be, while some producers calculate that it is no longer worthwhile to supply the market. The result, inevitably, is shortage—often amid plenty. History is replete with examples. When the Spanish army laid siege to the city of Antwerp in 1584, food in the city became scarcer, and prices rose. The city fathers responded with price controls. Food was plentiful outside the city, and the Spanish military grip was not sufficiently tight to prevent supplies reaching Antwerp. But at the controlled price, merchants were not prepared to accept the added cost and risk of running the blockade. And in the city, the controlled prices meant "nobody felt it necessary to economize. So the city lived in high spirits until all at once provisions ran out."[18]

Closer to home for Americans, the Pennsylvania legislature in 1777 imposed price controls on goods supplied to George Washington's army, then wintering in the commonwealth, to reduce the cost of supplying the force and to thwart profiteering. But many farmers and merchants held back their goods, feeling the prices to be too low. Some even sold their surplus to the British. The American army

---

[18]John Fiske, quoted in Schuettinger and Butler, *Forty Centuries*, p. 33.

almost starved. Next summer the Continental Congress passed a resolution citing the "very evil consequences" of price controls and asked states to repeal or suspend them.[19]

Shortages and underutilization due to price controls is just as evident in more modern economies. Severe shortages of rental housing, with a reluctance of property owners to supply the controlled rental market, is pronounced in cities with rent control, from New York to Stockholm to Moscow. More generally, shortages and a low utilization rate in manufacturing have been a distinct feature of price-control programs. During World War II, for instance, shortages appeared in several U.S. industries.

More significantly, given that the Vietnam War did not cause such direct disruption to the U.S. economy, numerous shortages appeared during the Nixon controls. Aluminum producers, for instance, announced production cutbacks in 1973, which in turn caused manufacturers using aluminum, such as refrigerator makers, also to slow production. The latter companies then pleaded with the Cost of Living Council to allow them to pay more for aluminum.[20] Also during 1973, as domestic oil producers responded to the Arab oil embargo, drillers complained that they could not obtain the steel needed for new rigs. Similar shortages appeared in other industries, from fertilizer to chemicals to newsprint.[21] The most politically explosive was the shortage of beef following a ceiling price imposed in March 1973. After the freeze, the rate of cattle slaughter abruptly fell, many smaller slaughterhouses faced bankruptcy, and retail supplies became scarce. The government compounded the problem that July, when in response to public anger over the shortages, it announced the ceilings would be lifted in September. With the prospect of higher prices in two months, the slaughter rate plummeted, returning to normal only after the ceiling was lifted.[22]

When such control-induced shortages appear, governments normally institute some form of rationing to distribute controlled products and services among consumers. This can include earmarked allocations, such as preferential distributions of gasoline to businesses and emergency services during the gasoline price controls of

---

[19]Robert L. Schuettinger, "Survey of Wage and Price Controls," in Michael Walker, ed., *The Illusion of Wage and Price Control* (Vancouver: Fraser Institute, 1976), p. 76.

[20]Lefkowitz and Nikaos, *Wage and Price Controls*, p. 31.

[21]Ibid.

[22]Rockoff, *Drastic Measures*, p. 223.

the 1970s. Rationing cards became a feature of daily life in early post–World War II Britain. But more commonly, rationing is accomplished by the crude tool of queuing.

Besides the usual public irritation with waiting lines, especially in the context of the health care debate, there is a hidden economic cost associated with queuing. Say an hourly worker earning $5 per hour must take two hours off work to wait in line for his allocation of five gallons of gasoline at a controlled price of $1 per gallon. Then the effective cost of each gallon to the worker actually is $3; meanwhile, the economy has "lost" $10 of production by the idled worker.

This is an important consideration if health care price controls are intended as a device to reduce total spending in the health sector. Rationing and waiting lines are a politically explosive matter in themselves. In addition, if patients are forced to wait for controlled services, let alone do without some, there is a real economic cost that is not included as an offset in official estimates of "savings" from controls. Calculating the cost of waiting is no easy task, but in the case of health care this hidden cost is likely to be large. In Canada an estimated 250,000 people (about 1 percent of the population) at any time are waiting for medical care.[23] In Canada, as in Britain, waiting time can stretch into years for certain procedures. The direct cost to the economy (ignoring the subjective cost to the patients themselves) includes any worker absenteeism and underperformance during the waiting period.

Effect 2. Price controls lead to a decline in quality. Another often hidden effect of price controls is that producers have an incentive to reduce their costs, and thereby maintain profit margins, by cutting the quality of their goods or services. Anyone who has lived in (or owned) a rent-controlled apartment is familiar with the constant battles over maintenance between landlords and tenants. And the declining quality of candy bars during World War II is well remembered by those who were children then.

The maintenance of quality is of particular concern regarding price control in medical care. Quality is even harder to measure and police in health care than in candy bars, and there is much evidence that physicians and hospital administrators are inclined to reduce quality when prices are restricted. There are, for example, the so-called Medicaid mills, in which doctors see a patient every few

---

[23]Michael Walker, Joanna Miyake, Steven Globerman, and Lorna Hoye, "Waiting Your Turn: Hospital Waiting Lists in Canada," *Fraser Forum* (Vancouver: Fraser Institute, 1992).

13

minutes, prescribe several quick tests, and then bill Medicaid. And under the uniform fee schedule in Japan, tight price controls on office visits simply lead to shorter visits for patients, making incorrect diagnoses and treatment more likely. Naoki Ikegami notes that "in outpatient care, a clinic physician sees an average of 49 patients per day; 13 percent see more than a hundred."[24] A recent international survey of health services for the elderly found that the average length of an office visit in Japan was just twelve minutes, compared with about thirty minutes in the United States.[25]

Effect 3. Controls inhibit investment. Another unpleasant side effect of price controls is that tighter profit margins discourage new investment. Investment in the housing rental market, as mentioned, has stagnated in cities with rent control. Similarly, price controls on oil during the 1970s undercut the investment needed to find new domestic sources of oil.

A decline in investment would be a potentially serious side effect, if widespread price controls were introduced in the U.S. health care system. At present, the United States is in the vanguard of medical technology innovation. And thanks in part to heavy investment, the pharmaceutical industry, apparently a top target for price controls, is one of America's most internationally competitive industries. Between 1975 and 1989, almost half of all major new drugs originated in the United States.[26]

Effect 4. Suppliers turn to less-regulated markets, or to relatively attractive controlled markets. Faced with a generally rigid structure of price controls amid a constantly changing general market, suppliers understandably respond by seeking out the most attractive available market. As Rockoff notes, during the American Revolution "controls were regional and local efforts; there always existed an incentive to divert desperately needed supplies to uncontrolled markets."[27] He adds that a similar pattern emerged during the Nixon

---

[24]Naoki Ikegami, "Japanese Health Care: Low Cost through Regulated Fees," *Health Affairs*, Fall 1991, p. 103.

[25]Diane Rowland, "A Five-Nation Perspective on the Elderly," *Health Affairs*, Fall 1992, p. 211.

[26]P. E. Barral, *Fifteen Years of Results of Pharmaceutical Research in the World (1975–1989)* (Paris: Rhone-Poulenc Sante, 1990). See also Edmund F. Haislmaier, "Why Global Budgets and Price Controls Will Not Curb Health Costs," *Backgrounder* 929 (Washington, D.C.: Heritage Foundation, 1993), pp. 23–26.

[27]Rockoff, *Drastic Measures*, p. 225.

controls. The 1973 freeze, for example, encouraged copper scrap dealers to shift to the export market, leading to a domestic shortage of the metal. And in the housing market, lighter controls or no regulation in certain categories of housing has in various countries led to rapid changes in the sector. Many landlords in Britain, for example, shifted their units into the luxury or furnished sector in the 1960s, to avoid the more heavily regulated unfurnished sector. Similarly, high U.S. housing inflation in the 1970s and early 1980s led to a spate of conversions to condominiums for sale in rent-controlled cities.

This effect already is seen in Medicare. Hospital administrators and physicians routinely adjust their activities in response to the government's fee schedules. When the federal government introduced in 1983 the prospective payment system, which set fixed payments for categories of in-hospital treatments, many hospitals responded by establishing "outpatient" clinics within the hospitals to take advantage of better rates intended for facilities outside a hospital setting.

Effect 5. Price controls lead to widespread evasion. Price controls trigger honest actions by consumers and producers that lead to perverse results. The effects described above are examples. But controls also unleash widespread evasion, in which both buyers and sellers of goods and services try to subvert the intent of the law. Explains Marvin Kosters, who was chief economist for Nixon's Council on Wage and Price Stability, "It would be a mistake to underestimate the ingenuity of people in the private sector to take advantage of discrepancies in a system of price controls."[28] Evasion takes many forms:

Political connections. One of the most common ways to evade price controls is to use political connections to secure a supply of controlled goods or to manipulate the rules themselves. Special supplies of controlled goods to politicians and their friends were a hallmark of the Eastern European economies. And in nationalized health systems, such as those of Canada and Britain, maintaining good relations with a politician is a simple and effective way of avoiding waiting lines. In a national system with price controls in the United States, politicians doubtless would expand their current range of "constitu-

---

[28]Quoted in "Price Controls: Past as Health Care Prologue," *Washington Post*, March 14, 1993, p. H1.

ent services" to include quick access for the favored to health services in short supply.

In addition, firms subject to price regulation invariably seek a cozy relationship with the regulators, trading freedom to adjust prices for other benefits, such as restrictions on new entrants into the industry. The result can be a price ceiling that in reality is above the level that would prevail in a free market. The Civil Aeronautics Board, for instance, was largely a creature of a small number of major airlines. The deregulation of the industry, and the abolition of the price-controlling CAB, generally reduced the price of air travel.

Brokers and gray markets. Controls limiting markups or setting prices directly usually lead to creative and often elaborate trading schemes to evade the intent of the controls (hence gray rather than black markets). During the Nixon controls, the revenues of chemical brokers doubled to $600 million between 1972 and 1973.[29] Some lumber producers sold their product to brokers in Canada (at controlled prices) and then imported it back for resale at import prices exempt from controls.[30] Rockoff describes multiple series of "daisy chain" brokers during the Korean War. These bought and sold steel and other metals. With a series of trades, the individual markups were moderate and the amounts small. So the process did not attract the close scrutiny of controllers, but the cumulative markup between producer and end user could exceed the regulated amount.[31] Rockoff reports domestic brokerage deals for oil during the Nixon controls:

> Oil was bought and then resold, often in swap agreements, not because such sales were necessary to distribute the product, but simply because each dealer was allowed to add his normal markup. Thus daisy chains were created, where ordinarily the fuel would have changed hands only a few times.[32]

While there is little or no scope for brokers in the medical services market, there is plenty in equipment, supplies, and pharmaceuticals. In fact, novel trade arrangements would likely mushroom in a regime of price or markup controls. Price controls on pharmaceuticals in Europe have already led to parallel markets. In these, brokers buy prescription drugs in countries with low controlled prices and resell

---

[29]Lefkowitz and Nikaos, *Wage and Price Controls*, p. 34.

[30]"Price Controls," p. H1.

[31]Rockoff, *Dramatic Measures*, p. 196.

[32]Ibid., p. 229.

them in countries allowing higher prices (in some cases, the country in which the drug was manufactured).[33]

Black markets. In addition to quasi-legitimate gray markets, black markets invariably appear whenever prices are controlled. Consumers desperate for goods during shortages and suppliers seeking profits find it in their mutual interest to invent devices to exceed the official price. Key money and other under-the-table payments are commonly made by tenants wishing to obtain a rent-controlled apartment. Schuettinger notes that in New Zealand during World War I, farmers evaded price controls on wheat by selling wheat only in combination with an equal load of unregulated oats and then overcharging for the oats. Alternatively, wheat was packed in "special" sacks, for which there was a fee.[34] Black market fees were also common after gasoline price controls were introduced following the 1979 oil supply limits of the Organization of Petroleum Exporting Countries. To evade controls, while satisfying customers tired of lines,

> some station owners tried to evade the problem by offering to fill up one's gas tank before the station's regular opening hours, if one would park in the station lot the night before— for a minor "parking fee" of, say, $10. Drivers tried to help, too, by offering to buy one-gallon gas cans at four times their regular price—if they were full of gas.[35]

Medicine is not immune from black markets. Balance billing refers to the practice of physicians charging extra amounts to patients beyond the fees set by government. This has been banned in Canada and the United States with respect to fees reimbursed by the government in an attempt to put tighter controls on fees. But for some doctors, this simply means the extra billing takes place off the books. Because of long waiting lists due to price controls in Japan,

> a black market exists for those who can afford it. Using the channel of a monetary gift in the range of one to three thousand dollars to the attending physician in a Tokyo university hospital . . . a patient choosing a private room can

---

[33]M. L. Burstall and I. S. T. Senior, *Undermining Innovation: Parallel Trade in Prescription Medicines* (London: Institute of Economic Affairs, 1992), pp. 16–17. See also Haislmaier, "Global Budgets and Price Controls," p. 25.

[34]Schuettinger and Butler, *Forty Centuries*, p. 61.

[35]Roger L. Miller and Daniel K. Benjamin, *The Economics of Macro Issues* (St. Paul: West Publishing Co., 1992), p. 73.

17

be admitted sooner and can be treated by a senior specialist.[36]

Redefining the product. To control the price of something, that something itself must be defined. This opens two huge opportunities for evasion, especially in the case of health care. The first concerns the product; the second, the individual who does the defining.

When controls are based on profit margins, or regulated prices are adjusted on the basis of cost, trying to determine the basis for cost can be a daunting undertaking. Rockoff explains that controllers during the Korean War faced enormous problems with multiproduct firms, since manufacturers "would load overhead costs on those products for which they were challenging the price ceilings."[37] The prospect of price controls on pharmaceuticals raises similar problems over what is a legitimate cost; that is, what is the product? To what extent should research costs on drugs that do not lead to a marketable product be added to the price of other drugs?

Even more daunting for price controllers can be the issue of who determines the product. When price controls are applied, businessmen quickly figure out that making small changes in their product—probably of no consequence to the buyer—can allow them to obtain a better price. During the Nixon price controls, for example, butchers developed new cuts subject to higher ceilings. Some lumber firms even drilled holes in plywood and filled them in again, so that the product would qualify for higher prices allowable on "customized" work.[38]

The issue of who defines the product is particularly problematic in health care, because in practice the supplier (the hospital or physician) has a wide scope in making a diagnosis and determining the treatment. U.S. hospital administrators, and the software writers developing programs for them, have become adept at figuring out how to exploit Medicare by changing their internal guidelines for diagnosis and treatment to maximize their reimbursement. Describing a condition slightly differently, for instance, may qualify for a higher reimbursement. The same is true in other countries. German hospitals, for instance, receive a payment for each treatment based on the number of days a patient remains in the hospital (U.S. hospitals serving Medicare patients receive payment based on the

---

[36]Ikegami, "Japanese Health Care," p. 104. See also Haislmaier, "Global Budgets and Price Controls," p. 21.

[37]Rockoff, *Drastic Measures*, p. 183.

[38]"Price Controls," March 14, 1993, p. H1.

diagnosis). Not surprisingly, Germans experience far longer hospital stays than Americans with the same ailment.[39]

Increasing the volume. A related problem in medicine, where in practice it is the supplier who determines how much service will be purchased, is evasion of controls by increasing volume. Between 1972 and 1984, for instance, the Canadian provinces cut physician fees by an average of 18 percent in real terms. But the number of billings rose by almost exactly the same percentage. Japanese doctors have responded to reduced fees for office visits simply by bringing in their patients more often.[40] In the U.S. Medicare system, reports the *New York Times*, "today, Medicare administrators assume that every dollar saved by binding fee limits is offset by a 50-percent increase through volume, upcoding and unbundling."[41]

Medicare has responded to this problem with "volume standards." Under this arrangement, the government determines the total acceptable level of expenditure in the program. If the total volume of services has risen faster than appears reasonable, fees are reduced the following year to curb total spending. Thus, the physicians who exploit the system by steadily increasing their volume can maintain their incomes. Physicians who do not try to cheat the system see their incomes fall.

Effect 6. Controls lead to increasing bureaucracy. Price controls lead to mushrooming bureaucracy in the public sector operating the controls and in the private sector trying to comply with them or evade them. By 1945, for instance, the U.S. Office of Price Administration had become the largest civilian agency in the government, with more than 64,000 employees.[42] These civil servants were supplemented by more than 300,000 volunteer price watchers.[43]

The cost of such controls can be enormous. John Dunlop, head of Nixon's Cost of Living Council, estimated that the program cost $200 million in administrative expenses. But the cost to the private

---

[39]Haislmaier, "Global Budgets and Price Controls," p. 23.

[40]Ibid., pp. 19, 21.

[41]"The Dangers of Declaring War on Doctors," *New York Times*, March 21, 1993. Upcoding refers to the practice of giving an illness a slightly different diagnosis or treatment that qualifies for higher reimbursement. Unbundling refers to "splitting" a diagnosis into two components eligible for reimbursement at a higher total than the single diagnosis.

[42]Lefkowitz and Nikaos, *Wage and Price Controls*, p. 24.

[43]Miller and Benjamin, *Economics of Macro Issues*, p. 74.

sector may have been several times that. The National Association of Manufacturers put the average annual compliance costs for firms with revenues above $50 million at $175,000. Five of 186 firms responding to the association's survey put their annual costs at more than $1 million.[44]

Controls tend to become more complex, requiring a growing bureaucracy, as government struggles to combat evasion and to address the technical details. Even voluntary guidelines evolve into a web of complexity. During the Carter administration's controls, for instance, the government was called on to define one subjective term, such as "substantial," after another. And common-sense exemptions merely added to the complexity. Notes Meyer, "Each new ruling, each new exception, set a precedent that others tried to exploit, leading to difficulties no matter where and when the line was finally drawn."[45] Significantly, the Carter administration found the process of setting wage and price ceilings for thousands of procedures and charges so complicated in the case of hospitals that it exempted them from wage and price guidelines. "It was just too damn complicated," says Barry Bosworth, who was director of Carter's Council on Wage and Price Stability.[46]

Conclusion

Governments through the ages have been lured by the idea that enacting laws to set maximum prices can reduce inflation or hold down expenditures in one sector relative to another. But the history of price controls is little more than a dismal catalog of painstaking failure. To the extent that price controls hold down inflation, the effect is temporary, and the economic costs heavy. Controls lead to misallocation and inefficiency, as well as evasion, outright cheating, and a growing sense of injustice. Controls also lead to shortages and reductions in quality for the consumer. And although improving technology seemingly increases the ability of government to regulate complex sectors, such as health, that same technology, combined with private ingenuity, always enables those wishing to avoid controls to stay at least one step ahead.

---

[44]Lefkowitz and Nikaos, *Wage and Price Controls*, p. 33.

[45]Meyer, *Wage-Price Standards*, p. 37.

[46]"Price Controls," p. H6.

Unfortunately for Americans, there is one other lesson to be drawn from the history of price controls. No matter how often they fail, there always seems to be politicians who believe that—this time—they can be made to work.

2

Regulatory Limits in a Process-oriented Society

Charles Stalon

Because price and service quality regulation will apparently have some role in the health industry reform proposals of the Clinton administration, it is useful to examine essential characteristics of U.S. regulatory traditions. Proponents of new or expanded forms of health industry regulation will not be writing on a clean slate. Economic regulation has strong traditions, which will not be easily set aside. The objectives embodied in these traditions may be more deeply embedded in American society than are the objectives embodied in the health industry reform proposals. Clearly, they have been demonstrated to be more deeply embedded in American society than are many market traditions.

The Problem of Multiple Regulatory Objectives

Regulation is a pervasive part of American society: the many courses about regulation in economics, business, and law curricula in American universities support that conclusion. Paradoxically, a large role for regulation can be seen as a necessary complement to the nation's heavy reliance on private enterprise. As other nations privatize former government-owned enterprises, they too discover a need to increase the breadth of their regulatory activities. One important American export in recent years has been American regulatory knowledge and experience.

An Initial Statement of the Problem. Despite the diversity of regulatory responsibilities, the core responsibility of regulators is always the same, namely, to prevent rational, self-interested decision makers from making decisions they would otherwise make and induce them to make decisions they would otherwise not make. To design regulations with desired constraints and inducements it is necessary to have:

- a supportable hypothesis of the objectives of the regulated entity, an understanding of the constraints imposed on it by forces and agencies other than the regulator, and a theory predicting decisions the entity would make in the absence of regulation
- a defined objective, or set of objectives, for the regulatory agency that allows it to (1) separate the regulated entity's goal-seeking actions into those that the regulator needs to constrain and those that are consistent with the regulator's objectives,[1] and (2) construct rules, enforcement actions, and decision procedures to implement its objectives

The objective of firms in a private enterprise economy is usually easy to describe: it is to maximize profit, often translated as to maximize the value of the firm. Furthermore, economics textbooks provide plausible models to predict the behavior of rational, profit-maximizing firms under a broad range of circumstances. If the targets of regulation are other governments or consumers, the formulation of objectives is much more difficult.

The problem that plagues much American regulation is that the objectives of regulatory agencies are many, tend to conflict, and are seldom well defined. When regulators do state their objectives, they are seldom stated in operational terms, that is, in terms that allow agency staff members and affected parties to predict how the agency's key decision makers will respond to new or altered circumstances.

Multiple Objectives in American Utility Regulation. The seriousness of the problem of multiple regulatory objectives can best be illustrated by current problems of utility regulation. On the surface, utility regulation, at least regulation of some of the more technologically

---

[1]The tendency of regulators to create and to enforce rules to require regulated firms to do what they want to do or to prohibit them from doing what they have no incentive to do gives rise to the joke that "regulators are people who build fences over bull pens to keep bulls from flying away."

familiar utilities, seems about as simple as serious regulation is ever likely to be.

The grand compromise that defined utility regulation. Utility regulation, with its fundamental characteristics, was created in a grand compromise in the opening decades of this century. This compromise has proved to be durable, although procedural embellishments have been added in the past decade or so. The nation, consequently, has a long record of experience of this form of regulation. The grand compromise has four crucial characteristics:[2]

1. Private ownership of utilities with broad monopoly powers, powers protected and frequently enhanced by government, was accepted as a desirable form of economic organization when economies of scale and scope could be more efficiently exploited by regulation than by unregulated market rivalry.[3]

2. Control of utility prices, quality of outputs, and financial structures were lodged in independent state agencies.

3. Independence meant, and still means, that the agency is multi-membered and that its members (usually called commissioners but occasionally called board members or judges) are given fixed, moderately long terms (four to six years), often staggered, to provide them with some protection from short-term political pressures. Independence also means that the agency has a staff of technical experts who are directly responsible, subject to civil service and due process limitations, to the direction of the commissioners.

4. The agency's discretion is limited by enabling legislation and constitutional interpretations to: (a) ensure that each utility has extensive opportunities to present evidence and arguments to persuade the regulator to the utility's view of its interest and of the public interest; (b) require the regulator to permit the utility, if efficiently managed, to earn a just and reasonable rate of return on assets devoted to public services; (c) ensure the right of utilities to appeal to state and federal courts for review of key elements of regulators'

---

[2]Despite almost continual attacks on utility commissions in the 1970s and 1980s, including attempts to convert elected regulators to appointed ones and appointed ones to elected ones and to change otherwise the method of selecting appointed commissioners, there were surprisingly few attacks on the fundamentals of the compromise.

[3]In early utility industries, emphasis was on exploiting economies of scale rather than economies of scope. In contrast, in the health care industry, economies of scope may be the principal source of potential cost reductions.

decisions. This right of appeal has been of great importance in the regulatory process. In practice, utility regulation has been a joint operation of regulators and courts, as have other forms of U.S. regulation.

Economic efficiency as an objective of utility regulation. Because arguments for utility regulation almost always emphasize that regulation improves the economic performance of firms, one clearly understood objective of utility regulation has been to improve economic efficiency.[4] It would be misleading, however, to describe economic efficiency as the principal objective of U.S. utility regulators.

The persistent refusal of utility regulators to pursue economic efficiency vigorously contains valuable lessons for students of American society. The efficiency objective is relatively easy to understand (compared with other objectives that are vigorously supported), it is moderately well described in textbooks, it is usually supported in agencies' enabling legislation, it is supported by courts,[5] and it is vigorously supported and articulately defended by proponents of efficiency-pursuing regulation.[6] Still, it is an unusual agency that

---

[4]The position was well stated by Richard Schmalensee: "The defining characteristics of natural monopoly are economic, and the only coherent justification of which I am aware for singling out natural monopolies for special treatment rests on economic analysis and argues that economic performance in the absence of control may be unacceptable." Schmalensee, *The Control of Natural Monopolies* (Lexington, Mass.: Lexington Books, 1979), p. 19.

[5]Compare, "[T]he basic goal of direct governmental regulation through administrative bodies and the goal of indirect governmental regulation in the form of antitrust law is the same—to achieve the most efficient allocation of resources possible." *Northern Natural Gas Co. v. FPC*, 399 F .2d 953 at 959.

[6]Compare,

> Pursuit of economic efficiency in natural monopoly industries may, of course, conflict from time-to-time with other legitimate social goals, just as pro-competitive antitrust policy may conflict with a legitimate social interest in fostering small business. But there is a fundamental and importance sense in which economic efficiency is consistent with almost all imaginable basic social goals. If policy B promotes more efficient resource utilization than policy A, society's options are generally greater under B than under A. In particular, there will generally exist a policy C that only redistributes income such that if B and C are adopted together, all affected parties will be made better off than they were under A. Attainment of economic efficiency implies a potential improvement in the well-being of all (Schmalensee, *Control of Natural Monopolies*).

pursues efficiency with any consistency. In contrast, experience does support the observation that one important objective of utility regulators is to avoid economic inefficiencies so gross as to embarrass the regulatory agency and the administration of which it is a part.

Fairness as an objective of utility regulation. If economic efficiency has not been the principal objective of utility regulation, what has been? A common answer is that fairness is the principal objective. Fairness is a frequently used term in the decisions of regulators and in arguments of most parties to regulatory proceedings. In many uses, it is merely a label to express approval of positions, but the term is not vacuous. Over the years, it has gained several well-understood meanings. Some fairness objectives are imposed on agencies by lawmakers and courts, and others are accepted by regulators as proper and necessary objectives for their agency. Because fairness is such an important objective of utility regulation and it is a slippery and ill-defined term, it is useful to distinguish the more important meanings of the word, especially between procedural and substantive fairness.

• Correct decisions and legitimate decisions as objectives of regulation. A useful platform on which to build a discussion of the role of fairness contains three propositions. First, utility regulators are expected to make decisions that are both substantively correct and legitimate. While a substantively correct decision sometimes adds legitimacy to the decision, the principal tool for creating legitimacy when the subject matter is complex and politically sensitive is due process. Due process here is defined not as the minimal process guaranteed by the Constitution but as elaborate procedures designed to grant parties to agency proceedings substantial powers to influence the substantive content of regulatory decisions.

Second, because the substance of regulation is almost always complex, regulators can make many decisions that well-informed observers would call incorrect without seriously damaging either the regulatory agency or the reputations of regulators. Third, procedural standards tend to be moderately clear, and transgressions easy to discover. A single failure to respect a procedural standard can seriously damage the agency and the reputations of regulators.

Not surprisingly, in light of these observations, regulators tend to be more attentive to the necessity of legitimate decisions than they are to the necessity of substantively correct decisions. One of the more important consequences of this search for legitimacy through procedures is a widespread emphasis on courtlike adjudications when making decisions.[7] The heavy reliance on courtlike procedures seems, in part, an attempt by regulators to gain legitimacy by imitating courts and, in part, an attempt by lawmakers to ensure that regulators are especially sensitive to the interests of parties directly represented in agency proceedings.

Furthermore, regulators know they must defend their decisions not only before courts and knowledgeable critics, but also in the court of public opinion. If they fail, the public will take its complaints to legislators. Since one objective of legislators is that utility regulators persuade the public of the legitimacy and correctness of their decisions, strong and multiple complaints to legislators are a sign of regulatory failure. Utility regulators, consequently, find it necessary to be attuned to popular standards of fairness and to respect them. The substantive fairness standards, in particular, define in large part acceptable standards of correctness.

• Edward Zajac's fairness propositions. Because these fairness standards will define key elements in the decision environment of health care regulators as they do the decision environment of utility regulators, surveying them is worthwhile. One of the most persuasive surveys of public standards of fairness as revealed in records of utility proceedings is Edward E. Zajac's.[8] He summarized his findings in six propositions:

> *Proposition One:* It is now accepted that every individual has basic economic rights to adequate food, shelter, heat, clothing, health care, education, and, in the United States, basic utility service. Deprivation of basic economic rights is considered unjust.

---

[7]Compare, regulatory agencies and other government agencies of control are "a form of government but they are not 'democratic' in the sense of representing anyone or anything except procedure for its own sake." J. R. T. Hughes, *The Government Habit: Economic Controls from Colonial Times to the Present* (New York: Basic Books, 1977), p. 235. Compare also, "It is procedure as much as the ultimate outcome that matters. Or rather, the procedure *is* the outcome." Bruce Owen and Ronald Breautigam, *The Regulation Game: Strategic Use of the Administrative Process* (Cambridge: Ballinger, 1978), p. 26.

[8]Edward E. Zajac, "Perceived Economic Justice: The Example of Public Utility Regulation," in H. Peyton Young, ed., *Cost Allocation: Methods Principles Applications* (New York: Elsevier Science Publishers, 1985), pp. 137–48. These propositions were first presented by Zajac in "Toward a Theory of Perceived Economic Justice in Regulation," Bell Laboratories Economic Discussion Paper 235, January 1982.

This standard of substantive fairness has had an enormous impact on regulatory practices in the past decade or so. In state after state, utilities have been deprived of the ability to deny service to customers merely because they do not pay their bills. Customers threatened with a shut-off of utility service today have a myriad of procedural safeguards that they can invoke to block or to delay shut-offs.

Clearly, this standard of fairness is more potent in the health care industry than in utility industries. One can persuasively argue that the principal thrust of the Clinton administration's reforms follows from an acceptance of this fairness standard. Health care regulators, therefore, will find it necessary to respect proposition one.

> *Proposition Two:* Equal treatment of individuals is seen as a just basis for policy, especially when common measurements, such as dollars or time, of individual gain or sacrifice are at hand. Unequal treatment of individuals is considered unjust.

This standard puts a heavy burden of justification on regulators for new and unfamiliar forms of discrimination. Evidence suggests that this fairness standard is assigned even greater importance by the general public for health care than for utility services.[9]

> *Proposition Three:* The beneficial retention of a status quo is considered a right whose removal is considered unjust.

This standard of fairness has probably had a more profound impact on utility regulation than any of the others. Bruce Owen and Ronald Breautigam, in *The Regulation Game,* describe regulation as granting "individuals and firms some legal right in the status quo."[10] The act of imposing regulation on a set of economic activities tends, in the United States, to be an affirmation of this fairness standard.[11]

---

[9]This fairness standard was illustrated in a recent report of an Associated Press poll showing "a strong theme: American won't buy any health plan that allows the wealthy to have wider options for medical care than the poor or lower-middle class. . . . Health reform finds an audience: Clinton needs to build a consensus for entire package." *Chicago Tribune,* March 28, 1993, sec. 1, p. 5.

[10]Compare, "[A] major effect of the administrative or regulatory process is to attenuate the rate at which market and technological forces impose changes on individual economic agents: . . . The result is to give individuals and firms some legal right in the status quo." Owen and Breautigam, *Regulation Game,* p. 2.

[11]Compare, "If there is a widely noted consequence of the operation of

Owen and Breautigam elaborate on this standard and emphasize a dilemma that all regulators must recognize, namely,

> Market forces, particularly those associated with innovative activity, necessarily pose a threat to human beings with less than instantaneous adaptive capabilities. It is not merely that investment in physical capital with few alternative uses may be threatened, but also investments in human capital, specialized skills, knowledge of an industry or a firm and the like. . . . In a sense, then, regulation is not much different from unemployment insurance and agricultural price supports, both are intended to protect human as well as financial interests from shocks and blows of market forces.[12]

The bias of this fairness standard toward resisting "harmful" changes is suggested by Franklin Tugwell: "The most ubiquitous and binding rule of the game in American politics is this: there shall be no costly, visible redistributions."[13] Also pertinent to the current discussion is Tugwell's observation that "the enlargement of political participation in general, and the mobilization of stakeholder groups in particular, has only made this rule more sovereign over the last two decades."[14]

> *Proposition Four:* Society is expected to insure individuals against economic loss because of economic changes. Failure to insure is considered unfair.

In the past three decades, the United States has seen rapid growth in what is sometimes called social regulation, often contrasted with economic regulation. More descriptive yet is the term *protective regulation,* because it focuses on protecting workers and consumers from hazards of daily life, those created by market and consumption activities, and from many of the hazards of nature. Decades earlier, utility regulators were forced to use their limited powers to provide similar forms of protection. The distinction between economic regulation and social, or protective, regulation has always been more clearly drawn in textbooks than in practice.

Zajac summarizes the context of this fairness standard:

---

pluralist democratic decision making, it is that it overwhelmingly favors the status quo." Franklin Tugwell, *The Energy Crisis and the American Political Economy: Politics and Markets in the Management of Natural Resources* (Stanford: Stanford University Press, 1988), p. 199.

[12]Owen and Breautigam, *Regulation Game*, pp. 23–24.

[13]Tugwell, *Energy Crisis*, p. 204.

[14]Ibid.

It is impossible to protect oneself against all contingencies. No matter what level of disaster or misfortune we provide for, something worse is possible. So, it is common in almost all societies to provide shelter and food when natural disasters such as earthquakes, floods or volcanic eruptions destroy homes, or medical care when an unexpected, grave illness strikes. Likewise institutions that in economic disasters shift the responsibility for economic burdens from the individual to someone else are also common. The idea that such a shift is only fair is, of course, behind the notion of economic rights. But it is also behind the notion of society protecting the individual against the fickleness of the marketplace.[15]

Proposition Five: The existence of numerous and significant economic inefficiencies is considered unjust, especially if their existence is seen as conferring benefits on special interest groups who oppose their removal.

This fairness standard explains in part the eagerness of utility regulators to avoid gross inefficiencies, not because they value efficiency but because they value public standards of fairness.

Proposition Six: The fewer the substitutes for a regulated firm's output, and the more the output is considered an economic right, the more the public expects to exert control over the firm. Denial of control is considered unjust.

Legislators and utility regulators, responding to this fairness standard, have gone to great lengths to support the active participation of more and more groups in regulatory proceedings in the past decade or so.[16] Because health care has even fewer substitutes than utility services, a regulatory program that suppresses rivalry among health care providers must be expected to lead to intense public demands for citizen inputs into the regulatory process.

With so many objectives being pressed on regulators and decision procedures that require due consideration of the positions of so

---

[15]Zajac, "Perceived Economic Justice," p. 141.

[16]Commonly in regulatory proceedings, a consumer advocate is financed directly by the legislature, a second one represents the governor's office, and a third is supported by the state's attorney general. Sometimes these consumer advocates are joined by a division of the regulatory agency explicitly designated for that role and by a second and third advocate from the attorney general's office providing special representation for selected groups of consumers. And these are only the publicly funded consumer advocates.

many parties, it is an unusual agency that escapes, even temporarily, the tendency to allow fair decision procedures to become the principal outcome of the process.

Direct versus Indirect Consequences of Regulatory Decisions. In regulation, as in all areas of political life, fairness to some is more important than fairness to others. Many years ago, Charles Schultze noted,

> Over the years the American political system has developed a set of formal and informal rules about losses associated with political decisions. First, we tend to subject political decision to the rule, "Do no direct harm." We can let harms occur as the second- and third-order consequences of political action or through sheer inaction, but we cannot be seen to cause harm to anyone as the direct consequence of collective actions.[17]

Schultze further noted that although there are good reasons in a democracy for respecting such rules, it is also correct to observe that "because the direct harm is minimized, not by compensation arrangements or by general income-redistribution techniques but by placing limitations on the nature of collective actions, the overall efficiency of collective action is sharply reduced."[18]

In recent years, legislators and courts have placed many constraints on decision procedures of utility regulators. The constraints are often described, correctly, as designed to suppress illegitimate channels of information flow and to affirm the legitimacy of other channels.[19] These constraints do, however, have a second effect, and probably a second objective: they tend to encourage, almost coerce, regulators to respect the rule of no direct harm when making decisions that affect those who appear before them.

The Schultze rule manifests itself in regulatory agencies by inducing regulators to focus on the direct consequences of their

---

[17]Charles Schultze, *The Public Use of Private Interest* (Washington, D.C.: Brookings Institution, 1977), p. 23.

[18]Ibid., p. 24.

[19]Utility regulators today often have even less control over the content and timing of information flows to, from, and within the agency than do courts or legislators. Courts, for example, are not burdened with government-in-sunshine acts and separation-of-function rules, and legislators are not burdened with separation-of-function rules and ex parte rules. More important, legislators are not burdened with a tradition of great respect for judicial passivity and legal precedent.

decisions and to weigh heavily indirect effects only to the extent that parties to their proceedings insist that they do so and provide evidence that will allow the regulator to justify doing so. One way of describing this decision bias is to say that regulators are under intense pressures to pursue local fairness at the expense of global fairness.

Regulatory Objectives in a Process-oriented Society. This analysis demonstrates why regulators have such a difficult time specifying their objectives in operational terms, in fact why they seldom try to do so. Economic efficiency is important, but the need to respect widespread standards of fairness forces trade-offs between efficiency and fairness. Because of the many standards of fairness, trade-offs must occur among the fairness standards and between each standard and efficiency. There are also direct and indirect fairness and efficiency consequences of regulators' decisions. Above all, procedural fairness standards imposed by legislators and courts demand that regulators be especially respectful of effects on those directly involved in their proceedings.

Simple logic, consequently, leads us to expect what we see in regulatory agencies, namely, a tendency to emphasize process rather than substance, and to see the solution of most problems as the creation of a decision process in which key parties of direct interest can negotiate mutually beneficial outcomes, often at the expense of parties not represented in the proceeding, and can have the agency approve that outcome.[20] When substantive issues are greatly influenced by decision procedures, it is not surprising that substantive debates are often submerged in elaborate debates about procedures.[21]

Adjudication, not surprisingly, becomes more a vehicle for negotiated settlements than a tool to inform regulators. Although the professional staff of the regulatory agency may be an active party in the negotiation process, separation-of-functions requirements in most large regulatory organizations do not permit duly appointed regulators to have much control over the work of the staffs.[22] The task

---

[20]An attorney for the Federal Power Commission asserted once that the FPC ought not to have objectives other than procedural ones. In his view, "whatever comes out of the decision procedure is the public interest."

[21]Compare, "[J]udicialization . . . masks real policy disputes and problems with an ephemeral debate over procedure and the structure of government decision-making. In some ways, this result may be comforting to political leaders and voters who cannot make up their minds on the policies they wish to follow." Loren A. Smith, "Judicialization: The Twilight of Administrative Law," *Duke Law Journal*, 1985, no. 2, p. 430.

[22]One brief submitted to the Federal Energy Regulatory Commission

of regulators is to reject or approve proposed settlements, although they sometimes approve them with conditions and modifications.

Coherent economic policies are not to be expected from such decision practices in a rapidly changing economy. In this regard, regulation is a reflection of a long-standing problem in the American economy. J. R. T. Hughes, in *The Governmental Habit*, eloquently described this problem in American economic policy: "Our . . . control tradition has a basic weakness which derives from its history, and that is the belief in the efficacy of piecemeal supervision, . . . Our methods amount to an ad hoc structure, and function accordingly."[23]

The Unfair Consequences of a Vigorous Pursuit of Direct Fairness

In a world of decentralized decision making, one lesson economists have to teach is the importance of distinguishing between individual actions and systemic results, that is, results that are produced by individual participants in a complex social system but are not intended by them. Counterintuitive systemic results, that is, results quite different from—and sometimes in direct conflict with—those intended by individual participants, occur so often in complex economies that recognition of them is the beginning of intelligent decision making.

One counterintuitive lesson that should be stressed is that the single-minded pursuit of local fairness can produce serious global unfairness.[24] This possibility gives rise to a paradox of fairness. The idea is simple.

First, the economics profession has provided regulators a set of guidelines that, if followed in the many thousands of government proceedings around the nation each year, will tend to induce regulated firms, interacting with firms disciplined by competitive markets and consumers exercising free choice, to create the maximum economic pie for the nation. Taxation, spending, and redistribution and

---

asserted, in effect, "The FERC decision process works well as long as FERC commissioners stay out of it."

[23]Hughes, *Government Habit*, p. 239.

[24]Compare, "If all public programs concentrated on fairness to the exclusion of efficiency, the result could make most people worse off and would surely produce a crazy quilt of special-purpose benefits that would be difficult to justify." Susan Rose-Ackerman, *Rethinking the Progressive Agenda: The Reforms of the American Regulatory State* (New York: Free Press, 1992), p. 18.

compensation policies that are internally consistent and taken with the intent to maximize fairness for the minimal harmful impacts on the size of the pie can add substantial elements of fairness to the system.

Second, no profession has provided regulators with a set of guidelines for determining which fairness decisions in local proceedings add to total fairness in the system. The economic theorems just described do, however, make clear that many actions taken in pursuit of fairness at the local level tend, *ceteris paribus*, to shrink the size of the pie. The smaller pie makes it politically difficult to continue or to expand global fairness policies that can have minimal harmful impact on the size of the pie.[25]

In summary, the vigorous pursuit of fairness in local decisions without central coordination should shrink the pie available for compensation and income-redistribution programs by the national government. An alternative way of stating the same conclusion is to use the language of fairness. A vigorous pursuit of fairness to parties directly involved in regulatory proceedings leads to unfairness to nonparties, who experience the indirect effects of the decision.

Lessons for the Health Care Industry

Because the health care industry has complexities beyond the utility industries, one must be cautious in drawing lessons from other regulatory experiences. More persuasive deductions can be drawn once the details of the coming grand compromise in health care regulation are known. Still, there are lessons of value in the utility experience. Three, in particular, deserve to be recorded.

First, health care regulators will be required to respect the same set of public fairness standards that utility regulators do. Some of these fairness standards are driving the restructuring of the health care industry, and they will, in part at least, mold legislative charges to regulators. The diversity of these standards will make it unlikely that health care regulators will be any more successful in defining their objectives than utility regulators have been. The expected con-

---

[25]An extreme form of this problem is illustrated by policies of some third world nations that underprice energy and telecommunications services in the name of fairness to consumers and simultaneously expand connections to smaller and smaller users. They sometimes find that (1) the utilities cannot finance their growth and (2) the central government itself is required to cut back on social welfare programs in order to finance such growth.

sequence of that failure will be a strong emphasis on fair decision procedures for making and legitimizing the agencies' decisions.

Second, health care regulators will be regulated. Congress will not write special procedural rules for health care regulators. Regulation, of necessity, will be a cooperative effort of administrative agencies and courts, with the courts deciding what constitutes an adequate defense of an administrative action. Furthermore, many decision procedures imposed on utility regulators will be imposed on health care industry regulators. In particular, these decision procedures will limit the discretion of regulators and will force them to rely heavily on regulated entities and customers for needed information. The regulators, consequently, will find it difficult to avoid extensive reliance on adjudication. And regulators will be encouraged to, or find it necessary to, induce regulated entities and their customers and suppliers to use the proceedings of regulators to negotiate solutions to their problems rather than require the regulators to solve them. Publicly held standards of fairness will play a large role in such decisions, and the focus will be on the direct effects of decisions rather than on the systematic effects.

Third, utility regulators learned early in their history that large firms with substantial monopoly powers are much easier to regulate than are small, financially insecure firms. Substantial monopoly powers allow a regulated firm to tolerate decision delays, costly decision processes, and regulatory mistakes without serious threat to the profitability of the firm. Regulators also learned that to regulate a monopoly, sometimes they had to create one. Health care regulators, making decisions in a society that values highly beneficial interests in the status quo, will soon become respectful of the benefits of monopoly power. Furthermore, a monopoly with an obligation to serve is easier to regulate than one without such an obligation, because it must create a record of losses rather than withdraw services. This record of losses eases the task of raising prices.

Utility regulation as practiced in the United States has lasted almost one hundred years. During that period, there have been dramatic reductions in the real unit cost of service in many utility industries. Regulatory success stories are hard to find; a few do exist. But, as William G. Shepherd reminds us, "Regulation is like growing old: we would rather not do it, but consider the alternative."[26]

---

[26]Quoted in Douglas F. Greer, *Business, Government and Society*, 3d ed. (New York: Macmillan, 1993), p. 274.

35

3

The Effectiveness of State Regulation of Hospital Revenue in the 1980s

Bernard Friedman and Rosanna M. Coffey

Policy makers are actively seeking methods of slowing the growth of expenses for hospital and health care services. Some bills in the 102d Congress (for example, H.R. 5502) proposed to limit total health care spending in accord with national targets. This approach is criticized by advocates of a strategy to foster competition. They argue that "managed care" is emerging as a route to more cost-effective health care.[1] Other analysts argue that strong regulatory programs might be effectively combined with competitive strategies.[2]

The views expressed in this chapter are those of the authors, and no official endorsement by the sponsor, Agency for Health Care Policy and Research, or Department of Health and Human Services is intended or should be inferred. We thank Leif Karell and Migdalen Eley of Social and Scientific Systems, Inc., for computer programming assistance.

[1]See Donald W. Moran and Patrice R. Wolfe, "Can Managed Care Control Costs?" *Health Affairs*, vol. 10 (Winter 1991), pp. 20–128, and Alain C. Enthoven, "The History and Principles of Managed Competition," *Health Affairs*, vol. 12, supp. (1993), pp. 7–23.

[2]See Paul B. Ginsburg and Kenneth E. Thorpe, "Can All-Payer Rate Setting and the Competitive Strategy Coexist?" *Health Affairs*, vol. 11 (Summer 1992), pp. 73–86; Paul Starr and Walter A. Zelman, "A Bridge

These policy debates have been influenced by the apparent success of some states during 1975–1982 in controlling hospital expenses with mandatory regulation of hospital rates and budgets. Eight states have had substantial experience with such programs since 1970. Brian Biles and others described favorable experiences of six states between 1975 and 1978.[3] As of 1982, it was widely accepted that state regulation of hospital revenue slowed the growth of hospital expenses per admission and per capita.[4] A rigorous econometric study for 1970–1982 supported the positive view of state regulation of hospitals.[5] The study allowed for the possibility that the states enacting regulation had begun with unusually high hospital expenses and that these high expenses would descend over time even in the absence of regulation. Even so, the effect of state regulation on hospital expense per capita was significant.

In this chapter, and in the citations above, the effectiveness of state regulation of hospitals is defined in terms of state-level aggregates of hospital expenses per capita or hospital expenses per admission. Expenses per admission ("cost per case") may be a fairer measure of performance of state regulation than expense per capita, because state programs have not attempted to control the number of cases per capita. In addition, there are reasons to think that a state regulatory program could survive even if it was not effective for cost containment. Katherine G. Bauer observed in case studies that enactment of state regulation of hospitals was driven by a political coalition of insurers, hospitals, and state leaders with differing objectives: commercial insurers wanted to reverse the success of Blue Cross plans in negotiating double-digit discounts from charges; hospitals were concerned about discounts and about redistribution of the burdens of uncompensated care; and states were concerned about

---

to Compromise: Competition under a Budget," *Health Affairs*, vol. 12, supp. (1993), pp. 7–23; and Stuart Altman and Alan B. Cohen, "The Need for a National Global Budget," *Health Affairs*, vol. 12, supp. (1993), pp. 194–203.

[3]Brian Biles, Carl Schramm, and J. Graham Atkinson, "Hospital Cost Inflation under State Rate-setting Programs," *New England Journal of Medicine*, vol. 303 (1980), pp. 664–65.

[4]D. Crozier, S. Mitchell, H. Cohen and J. Colmers, M. Drebin, F. Sloan, C. Buck and M. Gold, and R. Davidson, Forum Section, "The Rate-setting Model: Long-Range Solution or Short-Term Expedient?" *Health Affairs*, vol. 1 (Summer 1982), pp. 65–128.

[5]David Dranove and Kenneth Cone, "Do State Rate Setting Regulations Really Lower Hospital Expenses?" *Journal of Health Economics*, vol. 4 (1985), pp. 159–65.

the growth of their Medicaid spending.[6]

Joyce A. Lanning and Michael Morrisey found a significant effect of the size of Medicaid budgets, as well as several other political variables, on enactment of state regulation of hospitals.[7] As a result of federal legislation of the Medicaid program in 1981, states were allowed to depart from "reasonable cost" reimbursement principles and to reimburse on the basis of "reasonable cost of an efficiently run institution." As a consequence, many state Medicaid programs now limit payments per admission to hospitals below the amount paid by any other third-party payer and use selective contracting to exclude some hospitals with high prices. It is probably not coincidental that after the federal rules for Medicaid changed in 1981, not a single new state has instituted a hospital regulatory program.

Regardless of initial motives for regulation, some economic theories deriving from Milton Friedman and George Stigler (the Chicago School) would predict an eventual capture of the regulators by the industry itself. These theories have been applied in such areas of regulation as professional licensing, telephone communication, transportation, and drug safety.[8] Their point is that regulation may eventually be of greatest benefit to the established industry members—maximizing their profits or utility by restricting entry, enforcing list prices, and limiting competition.

Not only is there a theoretical possibility that the effectiveness of state regulation of hospitals might dissipate over time, but also in the 1980s other policies and pressures may have restrained hospital expenses in nonregulated states. In particular, the federal government initiated a new policy to restrain its payments to hospitals in 1983. Moreover, enrollment in health maintenance organizations (HMOs), organizations that use fewer hospital services, grew substantially during the decade. Private insurers began to require prior approval of procedures and to contract selectively with providers on the basis of price.

Figures 3–1 and 3–2 show growth rates of hospital expenses by year for the group of eight states with hospital regulatory experience

---

[6]Katharine G. Bauer, "Hospital Rate Setting—This Way to Salvation?" in M. Zubkoff, I. Raskin, and R. Hanft, eds., *Hospital Cost Containment* (New York: Prodist, 1978).

[7]Joyce A. Lanning, Michael Morrisey, and Robert L. Ohsfeldt, "Endogenous Hospital Regulation and Its Effects on Hospital and Non-Hospital Expenditures," *Journal of Regulatory Economics*, vol. 3 (1991), pp. 137–54.

[8]See, for example, Samuel Peltzman, "Toward a More General Theory of Regulation," *Journal of Law and Economics*, vol. 19 (1976), pp. 211–40.

FIGURE 3–1

HOSPITAL EXPENSE PER ADJUSTED ADMISSION FOR EIGHT REGULATED
STATES AND FOR OTHER STATES, 1976–1990
(percent change from previous reporting year)

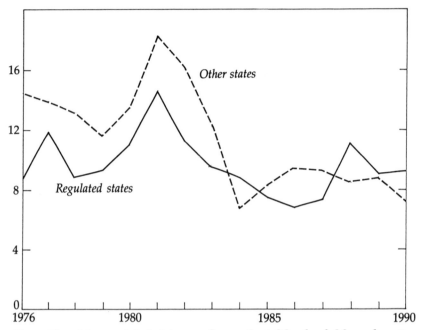

NOTE: The eight regulated states are Connecticut, Maryland, Massachusetts,
New Jersey, New York, Rhode Island, Washington, and Wisconsin.
SOURCE: American Hospital Association surveys and other sources described
in text.

versus other states. These charts support the general observation of
earlier studies that regulated states performed more favorably than
other states through about 1983. They also indicate a change after
that year, suggesting a waning effectiveness of state hospital regulation or the impact of confounding factors that slowed the rate of
growth of hospital expenses in nonregulated states.

Purpose

This chapter has two purposes: first, to examine trends in state-level
aggregate hospital expenses in relation to state regulation since 1980,
and, second, to assess the effectiveness of state regulation while

FIGURE 3–2

Hᴏsᴘɪᴛᴀʟ Exᴘᴇɴsᴇs ᴘᴇʀ Cᴀᴘɪᴛᴀ ꜰᴏʀ Eɪɢʜᴛ Rᴇɢᴜʟᴀᴛᴇᴅ Sᴛᴀᴛᴇs ᴀɴᴅ
ꜰᴏʀ Oᴛʜᴇʀ Sᴛᴀᴛᴇs, 1976–1990

(percent change from previous reporting year)

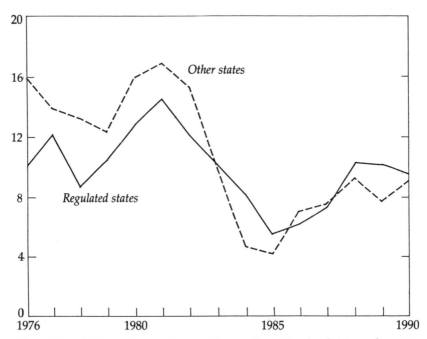

Nᴏᴛᴇ: The eight regulated states are Connecticut, Maryland, Massachusetts, New Jersey, New York, Rhode Island, Washington, and Wisconsin.
Sᴏᴜʀᴄᴇ: See source for figure 3–1.

controlling for other confounding factors that may be related to hospital costs.

The main outcome variables are hospital expenses per capita and expenses per adjusted admission.[9] We also describe some trends that may reveal hospital responses to regulation. These include trends in employment compensation, capital investment, use of intensive care units, staffing, and use of outpatient services. Examination of trends in patient selection, use of particular treatments, or quality of care was reserved for future research at the hospital level rather than state aggregate level.

---

[9]Adjusted admissions are a weighted sum of the number of admissions and outpatient visits, using relative revenues as weights.

40

In the multivariate analyses, we include effects of state regulation and other changes in the health care delivery system. We consider types of state regulatory programs, the length of experience with regulation (allowing for "depreciation" of that experience), the advent in 1984 of the first full year of the Medicare prospective payment system, and the garnering of market share of state populations by HMOs. At the same time, we control for the differential cost of providing health services in different states.

Data and Methods

Data on hospital expenses (the cost of producing hospital services, including operating costs and capital allowances) are derived from the Annual Survey of Hospitals conducted by the American Hospital Association. Surveys for various years were combined to create calendar-year data for each hospital and then for each state. HMO market share was taken from reports of Interstudy, Inc.[10] Data on the generosity of Medicaid programs are from reports of the Health Care Financing Administration.[11]

Measures for both temporal changes in prices and geographic differentials were used to deflate hospital expenses. The consumer price index is used for the annual deflator. A payroll cost index by state was derived from a series produced by the Bureau of Labor Statistics estimating average annual pay by state for about 90 percent of the labor force (excluding agricultural workers on small farms, domestic workers, and others not covered by federal workers' compensation programs). For each year, the state index is the ratio of the state average to the national average. Deflation of expenses precedes any other calculation.

Most of the variables to be compared between regulated and unregulated states are ratios such as hospital expense per capita. For any such ratio, the group aggregate of the numerator is divided by the group aggregate of the denominator, so that larger states are weighted appropriately in the comparison of groups. For multivariate statistical tests across the states, such as regression analyses, ratios are calculated specific to each state. Therefore, the within-group

[10]Group Health Association of America, "Patterns in HMO Enrollment, 1992" provides comparable data in 1990 to the results of the Interstudy survey for that year.

[11]Health Care Financing Administration, *Program Statistics, Medicare and Medicaid Data Book, 1986*, p. 125.

variation of the ratio plays an important part in tests for statistical significance.

Eight states have had substantial experience with regulation of hospital revenue since 1970. That experience is summarized in table 3–1. There is no simple and compelling way to categorize these programs. We classify them by the proportion of hospital patients for whom reimbursement is directly regulated. All-payer regulation includes the federal Medicare payments, as well as state Medicaid programs and payments to all private payers. Some states regulate only Blue Cross and Blue Shield payments, leaving charges to other private payers unregulated.

This categorization is simplistic because the mechanism of payment also varies. States may review each hospital's budget in determining allowable charges or use a fixed formula. "Rebasing" for actual costs may occur as frequently as every year, or much less frequently.

States are ranked in table 3–1 by the length of experience with all-payer regulation, because all-payer regulation is the policy currently of interest to federal policy makers deciding structures for health care reform. Currently, only Maryland retains all-payer regulation.[12] Previous research, confirmed by the present study, finds that the length of experience with regulation is a more important variable than the typology in explaining hospital expenses, markups, and other outcomes. This is not to dismiss the point that particular features in particular states (for example, the disallowance of expenses within peer groups used by New York during 1983–1986) may be particularly powerful tools.

Multivariate Analysis of Trends. The dependent variable for state s in year t, C_{st}, represents either expenses per adjusted admission or expenses per capita. This variable is deflated by the CPI and transformed into log values. The log transformation is convenient for several reasons: errors in the transformed dependent variable are more suitable to a normal distribution, coefficients are easier to interpret, and the coefficient on the time trend becomes approximately equal to the average annual percentage change in the dependent variable.

---

[12]New Jersey lost its federal waiver, apparently because the federal government thought it would pay less with normal Medicare reimbursement. Other states may have dropped all-payer regulation after 1984 because they expected to take in more Medicare revenue under PPS than under the state regulatory program.

TABLE 3–1
YEARS OF EXPERIENCE OF STATES WITH REGULATION OF HOSPITAL REVENUE, 1970–PRESENT

State	First Year	All-Payer[a]	Private, Medicaid[a]	Blue Cross, Medicaid[a]	Cumulative Experience through 1990	Final Year
Maryland	1974	11	N.A.	N.A.	17	Continuing
New Jersey	1975	9	2	N.A.	16	1992
Washington	1975	5	4	N.A.	14	1988
Massachusetts	1971	4	5	N.A.	18	1988
New York	1970	3	8	N.A.	21	Continuing
Connecticut	1973	N.A.	11	N.A.	18	Continuing
Rhode Island	1971	N.A.	N.A.	11	20	Continuing
Wisconsin	1972	N.A.	N.A.	5	13	1984

N.A. = Not applicable.

a. Years of regulatory experience in the 1980s.

SOURCE: Intergovernmental Health Policy Project of George Washington University and personal communications with officials in the states.

A reduced form model is

$$C_{st} = C_0 + \alpha t + \Sigma_k \beta_{kst} X_{kst} + U_{st} + \epsilon_{st} \qquad (3\text{--}1)$$

where α is the constant proportional trend. The X_k vector consists of the state payroll cost index, the proportion of the population below poverty covered by Medicaid, length of the state's experience with regulation, and the proportion of the population enrolled in HMOs. Clearly, important demand and cost determinants such as insurance coverage would improve the specification. The variable U_{st} represents all the unmeasured state-specific variables that do not change over time or change very slowly. We assume a fixed autocorrelation or "persistence" rate for this unmeasured state-specific error: $U_{st} = \rho^* U_{st-1}$. Because of the importance of unmeasured state-specific differences, panel data with multiple observations on the same state are essential to unbiased estimation of any of the parameters. The panel used here includes observations from 1980 through 1990 for fifty states and the District of Columbia.

Consider the difference calculation $C_{st} - C_{st-1}$. Let Δ indicate a difference from the previous year. Taking differences from the first equation, we have

$$\Delta C_s = \alpha + \Sigma_k \beta_{ks}^* \Delta X_{ks} + (\rho - 1) U_{st-1} + \Delta \epsilon_s \qquad (3\text{--}2)$$

Now α becomes the intercept.

Changes in the X variables become the relevant independent variables. We began by allowing an annual proportional depreciation in the length of experience. Let E_t be the number of years of experience in year t, then $E_t = (1 - \theta)E_{t-1} + R_t$, where $R_t = 1$ if the state continued with regulation and θ is the rate of depreciation. Note that $\Delta E_t = -\theta E_{t-1} + R_t$. We set θ at 5 percent, 10 percent, and more. The best fit was found with no depreciation. The result is that experience can be defined as the cumulative number of years of experience.

We tried two approaches to the importance of HMO enrollment. In one approach, only the change in enrollment is used in the second equation. In another approach, we assume that HMO enrollment has a gradual effect on hospitals so what matters in any year is the cumulative experience. But the change in the cumulative experience is just the level of current enrollment. We allowed the empirical fit to pass judgment on these approaches with the result that a much better fit was found by using the cumulative approach.

The method of ordinary least squares (OLS) should not be used to fit the Δ equation due to the assumed autocorrelation of the unmeasured variable U_{st}. We used a well-known iterative method. First, a cross-section model was fit for 1980, including some state-

TABLE 3–2

ACTUAL HOSPITAL EXPENSES PER ADJUSTED ADMISSION FOR THE
UNITED STATES AND THE EIGHT REGULATED STATES, 1980–1990

	Dollars			Percent Increase		
	1980	1984	1990	1980–84	1984–90	1980–90
United States	1,971	3,086	5,102	57	65	159
Maryland	2,294	3,042	4,764	33[a]	57[a]	108[a]
New Jersey	1,933	2,815	4,688	46[a]	67	143[a]
Washington	1,602	2,794	4,721	74	69	195
Massachusetts	2,649	3,934	5,843	49[a]	49[a]	121[a]
New York	2,631	3,823	6,625	45[a]	73[a]	152[a]
Connecticut	2,129	3,343	6,351	57	90	198
Rhode Island	2,250	3,496	4,897	55[a]	40[a]	118[a]
Wisconsin	1,934	2,868	4,315	48[a]	50[a]	123[a]

NOTE: States are listed in decreasing order by years of experience with all-payer revenue regulation.
a. Denotes growth rates less than the national average.
SOURCE: American Hospital Association surveys, and other sources described in text.

specific variables not available over all years, for example, Medicaid recipients in relation to the population in poverty. The residuals for that model, along with an assumed value for ρ, were used to build up the time series U_{st}. Then an OLS fit of the Δ model gives a new estimate of ρ that is used to iterate until the estimated value of that parameter stops changing.[13]

Results

The actual levels and growth rates of hospital expenses for each regulated state and for the United States are shown in tables 3–2 and 3–3. Considering expense per adjusted admission, six of the eight states achieved a rate of increase for the entire decade that was below the national average. While this result suggests effectiveness of state regulation, note that in the period 1984–1990, only four of the eight

---

[13]If we were not interested in the change in C as a dependent variable, the first equation would be fit with a fixed-effects design, and then a second step would be an iterative method to estimate the autocorrelation of the residuals. The fixed-effects model would use up just as many degrees of freedom and therefore would not be any more efficient.

TABLE 3–3

ACTUAL HOSPITAL EXPENSES PER CAPITA FOR THE UNITED STATES AND
THE EIGHT REGULATED STATES, 1980–1990

	Dollars			Percent Increase		
	1980	1984	1990	1980–84	1984–90	1980–90
United States	378	549	873	45	59	131
Maryland	343	467	729	36[a]	56[a]	113[a]
New Jersey	326	493	871	51	77	167
Washington	267	423	692	58	64	159
Massachusetts	494	744	1,163	51[a]	56[a]	135
New York	473	688	1,136	45	65	140
Connecticut	352	534	919	52	72	161
Rhode Island	366	538	859	47	60	135
Wisconsin	370	501	749	35[a]	50[a]	102[a]

NOTE: States are listed in decreasing order by years of experience with all-payer revenue regulation.
a. Denotes growth rates less than the national average.
SOURCE: American Hospital Association surveys and other sources described in text.

states were below the national average. One state, Wisconsin, which had a "weak" regulatory program and dropped regulation early, had slow growth of expenses per admission throughout the decade. Maryland, with the most experience in all-payer regulation, had a relatively slow rate of growth of hospital expenses per case.

Only two states, Maryland and Wisconsin, had favorable experience with expense per capita, compared with the national average rate of growth. This suggests that in four of the regulated states, increases in volume of services provided to patients may have offset the successful control of expenses per case. State regulators may not have targeted the volume of services and expense per capita. In current national policy debates, however, hospital expenses per capita may be the relevant measure of the effectiveness of policies to contain health care costs.[14] It is therefore important to assess whether the trends suggested by tables 3–2 and 3–3 are confounded by other variables.

Figures 3–3 and 3–4 provide deflated expense trends for the

[14]A better measure is health care cost per capita, but such data are not readily available at the state level.

FIGURE 3–3

DEFLATED HOSPITAL EXPENSES PER ADJUSTED ADMISSION FOR EIGHT
REGULATED STATES AND FOR OTHER STATES, 1980–1990

(1984 dollars)

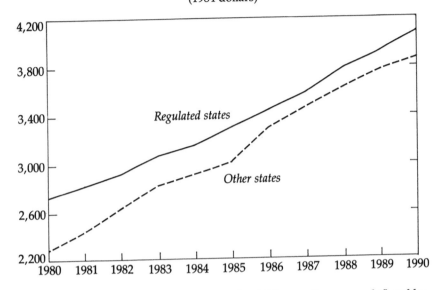

NOTES: Total expense deflated by year using CPI; payroll expense deflated by
state using a BLS index.
The eight regulated states are Connecticut, Maryland, Massachusetts, New
Jersey, New York, Rhode Island, Washington, and Wisconsin.
SOURCE: See source for figure 3–1.

regulated states as a group compared with other states. Expenses are
deflated as described earlier. Figure 3–3 indicates again that the
regulated group had slower growth per case than the other states
through as late as 1987, with parallel trends thereafter. Figure 3–4
shows that growth per capita was less for the regulated states through
1982. Then, through 1985, growth was less for the unregulated states.
Thereafter, the trends are essentially parallel (we are checking for a
possible data problem in 1989). These charts suggest that differences
in input costs among the states do not alter the picture that emerged
from the raw data.

Figure 3–5 compares the volume of adjusted admissions over
time for the two groups of states. Clearly, volume was falling in the
nonregulated states in comparison with the regulated states through
1987. If there are returns to scale in the production of hospital services
as many time-series studies have found, a decline in volume leads to

47

FIGURE 3–4

DEFLATED HOSPITAL EXPENSES PER CAPITA FOR EIGHT REGULATED
STATES AND FOR OTHER STATES, 1980–1990
(1984 dollars)

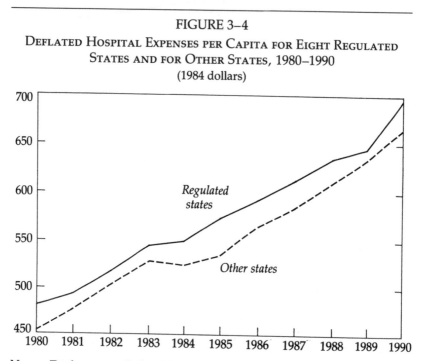

NOTES: Total expense deflated by year using CPI; payroll expense deflated by state using a BLS index.
The eight regulated states are Connecticut, Maryland, Massachusetts, New Jersey, New York, Rhode Island, Washington, and Wisconsin.
SOURCE: See source for figure 3–1.

an increase in average cost. Under that assumption, the volume trends could help explain why costs per case grew more rapidly in the nonregulated states before 1987. That possible explanation raises the question of why volume declined more rapidly in the nonregulated states.[15] In the multivariate analysis below, we find that volume change did not have a significant, independent effect on cost per case.

Figures 3–6, 3–7, and 3–8 address group differences in some

_____

[15]This might reflect a more "protective" effect of regulation—that is, hospitals in the nonregulated states may have been more concerned about accepting patients without health insurance and competition from freestanding ambulatory care centers. If volume changes turned out to be important for the econometric analysis, it would be desirable to allow for simultaneity in the relationship between volume and cost per case over time.

FIGURE 3–5

ADJUSTED ADMISSIONS PER CAPITA FOR EIGHT REGULATED STATES
AND FOR OTHER STATES, 1980–1990

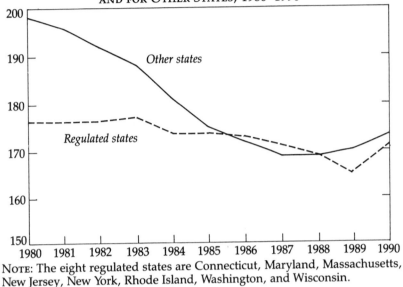

NOTE: The eight regulated states are Connecticut, Maryland, Massachusetts, New Jersey, New York, Rhode Island, Washington, and Wisconsin.
SOURCE: See source for figure 3–1.

possible hospital responses to regulation: payroll expense per full-time equivalent employment, depreciation per bed, and use of intensive care units as a proportion of total days of care. Both payroll expense and depreciation are deflated by the average pay index for the state in any year. The trends were tested for significant differences between regulated and unregulated states in the following manner. Let Y_{st} be the behavior outcome variable for state s in year t, and let R_{st} be 1 if the state is regulated in year t and 0 otherwise. We fit the following equation across all states and years:

$$\text{Log } (Y_{st}) = \alpha + \beta R_{st} + \gamma R_{st} * t + \delta (1 - R_{st}) * t + \epsilon_{st} \qquad (3\text{–}3)$$

The null hypothesis of equal proportional trends is $\gamma = \delta$. In each figure, the trend for regulated states appears to be flatter, but the test takes into account the variation within groups. The null hypotheses are rejected at the levels of $P<.01$, $P<.06$, and $P<.01$ for the three variables, respectively. We also examined trends in the proportion of surgery performed on an outpatient basis and the supply of outpatient visits in total. Neither of these variables had trends that differed between the regulated and the nonregulated states. A more careful analysis of behavior would require an investigation of the

49

FIGURE 3–6

DEFLATED PAYROLL EXPENSE PER FULL-TIME EQUIVALENT EMPLOYEE
FOR EIGHT REGULATED STATES AND FOR OTHER STATES, 1980–1990
(thousands of 1984 dollars)

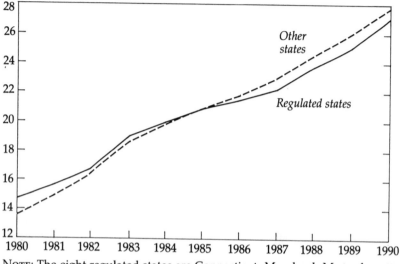

NOTE: The eight regulated states are Connecticut, Maryland, Massachusetts, New Jersey, New York, Rhode Island, Washington, and Wisconsin.
SOURCE: See source for figure 3–1.

hospital, allowing for changes over time in demographics of the population, services available outside hospitals, and other market area characteristics.

Results from multivariate analyses are presented in table 3–4. Note that all three equations are dominated by strong constant growth rates of about 6 percent above the CPI. The equation reported in the first column separates the significant effect of the advent of the prospective payment system (PPS) from the effect of state regulation of hospitals. The coefficients for PPS and state regulation are about the same. The persistence of unmeasured state differentials, ρ, was estimated to be about 95 percent. The effect of volume change was not significant.

The second specification of table 3–4 indicates that aside from any general effect of experience with regulation, there is still the Maryland differential of 2 percent off the general growth rate. Clearly, the Maryland success is not just longevity of regulation (or a formula using diagnosis-related groups), or one would expect a separate New York differential also.

FIGURE 3–7

DEFLATED DEPRECIATION ALLOWANCE PER BED FOR EIGHT REGULATED STATES AND FOR OTHER STATES, 1980–1990
(thousands of 1984 dollars)

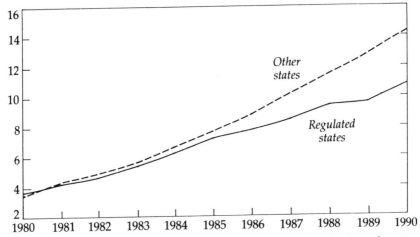

NOTE: The eight regulated states are Connecticut, Maryland, Massachusetts, New Jersey, New York, Rhode Island, Washington, and Wisconsin.
SOURCE: See source for figure 3–1.

Finally, the third specification in table 3–4 reports a significant effect for HMO enrollment, overshadowing federal and state payment policies. The HMO variable was multiplied by 100, so that the coefficient implies that a change in HMO enrollment from 10 percent to 20 percent would take 1 percent per year off the growth rate. The coefficient of experience with regulation changes by only a small amount in this equation, but the coefficient becomes insignificant ($p = .07$). The negative estimated effect of HMO enrollment is unexpected and probably reflects a wide range of competitive developments in health insurance. HMOs and utilization review should reduce expenses per capita, but one would expect the effect on expense per case to be positive, as discretionary care is moved from inpatient to outpatient settings with cases remaining in the hospital causing hospital case mix and cost per case to rise. The negative effect of HMO enrollment on expense per case appears more consistent with selective contracting and price competition. If the negative HMO effects were capturing in some part an indirect response to Medicare PPS (insurers acting to reduce cost shifting), then the importance of PPS may not be adequately reflected in the final equation.

51

FIGURE 3–8

PROPORTION OF INTENSIVE CARE UNIT DAYS TO TOTAL HOSPITAL
DAYS FOR EIGHT REGULATED STATES AND FOR OTHER STATES,
1980–1990

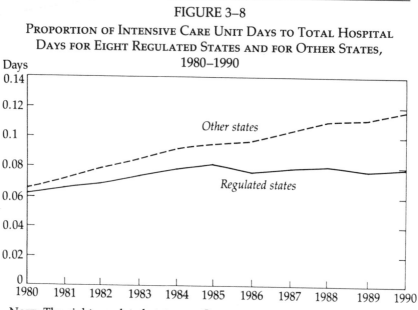

NOTE: The eight regulated states are Connecticut, Maryland, Massachusetts,
New Jersey, New York, Rhode Island, Washington, and Wisconsin.
SOURCE: See source for figure 3–1.

To assess the change in behavior of hospital expenses within the
decade, the final equation of table 3–4 was estimated separately for
the periods 1980–1984 and 1985–1990, dropping the dummy variable
for the advent of Medicare PPS. The new results are presented in
table 3–5. Note first that the constant term is lower by about one
percentage point, presumably because of PPS. We find clearly that
the effect of regulation was significant in the first part of the decade
(a lower growth rate by two percentage points) but not significant in
the second half. Just the opposite pattern is shown for the HMO
market share variable. Volume changes had a positive association
with changes in cost per case in the early period, but a negative
relationship in the second period. This altered relationship of volume
and cost is not readily explained, but it is not crucial to the issues
under discussion. When volume is dropped from the equations, the
other results are not substantially changed.

We applied the same models and variables to analysis of expenses per capita. The results are not reported because they are not
credible. None of the exogenous variables considered here could help
explain trends in expenses per capita, including state regulation of
hospital revenue.

TABLE 3-4

REGRESSIONS ON HOSPITAL EXPENSES PER CASE ACROSS STATES, 1981–1990
(dependent variable: change in the log of real expenses per adjusted admission)

Independent Variables	Equations including Particular Variables		
	Coefficients (t-statistics)		
Intercept (constant rate of increase)	.058 (26.68)	.059 (26.83)	.061 (27.41)
Medicare PPS in force after 1984 (for states without all-payer regulation)	−.008** (−3.06)	−.009** (−3.32)	−.004 (−1.29)
Change in experience with regulation	−.011** (−2.97)	−.008* (−2.03)	−.007 (−1.79)
Change in log of adjusted admissions per capita	−.054 (−1.67)	−.051 (−1.57)	−.042 (−1.32)

(Table continues.)

TABLE 3–4 (continued)

Independent Variables	Equations including Particular Variables		
	Coefficients (*t*-statistics)		
Lagged hospital-specific residual persisting from 1980 fitted equation[a]	−.045** (−3.58)	−.042** (−3.26)	−.030** (−2.51)
Lagged share of population belonging to HMOs			−.0010** (−4.412)
Dummy variable for Maryland		−.020* (−2.07)	
Dummy variable for New York		.003 (.28)	
R-squared	.07	.07	.10
Residual d.f.	485	483	484

*P<.05; **P<.01; df. = degree of freedom.
NOTE: Expenses are deflated by the consumer price index.
a. Equation regressed hospital expenses per adjusted admission for 1980 on a state payroll expense index, Medicaid generosity, type and duration of regulation, proportion of population in HMOs, and adjusted admissions per capita.
SOURCE: Division of Provider Studies, Center for Intramural Research, Agency for Health Care Policy and Research.

TABLE 3–5

REGRESSIONS ON HOSPITAL EXPENSES PER CASE ACROSS STATES, WITH
SPLIT TIME PERIODS, 1984–1990

(dependent variable: change in the log of real expenses per adjusted
admission)

Independent Variables	1980–84	1985–90
	Coefficients (*t*-statistics)	
Intercept (constant rate of increase)	.066 (24.23)	.057 (24.18)
Change in experience with regulation	−.024** (−4.44)	.004 (.97)
Change in log of adjusted admissions per capita	.147** (2.78)	−.127** (−3.28)
Lagged hospital-specific residual persisting from 1980 fitted equation[a]	−.049** (−2.86)	−.014 (−.96)
Lagged share of population belonging to HMOs	.000 (.02)	−.001** (−5.01)
R-squared	.14	.11
Residual d.f.	191	290

*P<.05; **P<.01; d.f.; = degree of freedom.
NOTE: Expenses are deflated by the consumer price index.
a. Equation regressed hospital expenses per adjusted admission for 1980 on a state payroll expense index, Medicaid generosity, type and duration of regulation, proportion of population in HMOs, and adjusted admissions per capita.
SOURCE: Division of Provider Studies, Center for Intramural Research, Agency for Health Care Policy and Research.

Conclusion

The analyses above challenge some accepted thinking on the effectiveness of state regulation of hospital revenue since the late 1970s. It appears that effectiveness of regulation in restraining cost per case eroded after 1984, coincidental with the advent of Medicare PPS. No effect of regulation in restraining cost per capita can be detected,

55

although two states with regulation experience, Maryland and Wisconsin, had favorable outcomes. In addition, HMO market share, perhaps reflecting a wide range of intense market forces, should be considered as one of the determinants of the growth rate of state-level hospital expenses since 1984.

This study has many limitations and could be improved in many ways. More data on demographic changes should be included in future analysis. Studies with data from individual hospitals would be required to clarify responses to regulation and market forces. Attention should be given to changes in case mix that are beyond the control of hospitals.

Our purpose in providing these updated trends is twofold: first, to enlighten health policy makers, who are weighing alternatives for changing the health care system, and, second, to stimulate better studies of the effectiveness of regulation and market forces for cost containment.

The results here show that the effects of state regulation of hospital revenue waned in the mid- to late 1980s. Furthermore, the measured effects of state regulation over the entire decade are diluted when the implementation of Medicare PPS is taken into account. Reactions to Medicare payment policy may have been stronger among the unregulated states because hospitals in unregulated states were permitted to retain more of the savings on Medicare beneficiaries than they could retain under state regulatory programs. Effects of PPS might have been even larger if hospitals were not able to boost prices to other payers to offset declines in Medicare payments.

From this finding it is clear that federal regulation of health care spending will confound and be confounded by regulation and experimentation in the states. The perceived benefits of one payment system compared with another will influence the response of health care providers. For purposes of evaluation, state programs should be isolated from federal programs rather than allowing the interactions of differing payment systems to affect the same providers, as Medicare and most state regulatory programs do now.

A tentative but potentially more interesting result is that the significant measured effects of state regulation over the decade disappeared when HMO enrollment differences among the states were controlled. This suggests that the effectiveness of state regulation may be confounded by the growth in HMOs and their restraining influence on medical practice. The HMO effect on hospital expenses per admission was unexpectedly negative, however, suggesting that unmeasured factors other than HMO enrollment, such as the age and health of the populations in different states or the strength of selective contracting and negotiated discounts of private payers, may be underlying the HMO effect in our findings. The puzzle of the HMO results certainly begs for better specification and further study.

Finally, state regulatory programs were probably not effective in controlling the growth in hospital expenses per capita. Maryland and Wisconsin clearly had better than average outcomes, but it was not possible to attribute that success to regulation per se. Although we did not present these results, the absence of effects of state regulation of hospital revenue on hospital expenses per capita suggests that programs aimed at one level cannot be expected to succeed at another. Policies aiming to constrain total health care costs require programs aimed at total spending, not piecemeal programs aimed at one type of health care provider or sector.

Commentary on Part One

Robert Crandall

Let me remind you that I come from the Brookings Institution, where some liberal noneconomists are wont to argue, first, that some goods and services are just too important to be left to markets. Education, shelter, and health care are three of them. It is acceptable to shop for Redskins' tickets in the black market, but not to provide for one's basic needs there. A second popular maxim is that long-term health insurance is too expensive for individuals to afford and so the government should provide it. Obviously, there is a fallacy in such a view.

A third belief is that because Americans have relied on private health insurance for so long, too many competitors have emerged, leading to excessive administrative costs. My colleagues' intensive experience in the government suggests to them that the government is more efficient as a collection mechanism. That is an interesting theory. Finally, some even argue that our current health care market works so badly that no attempted remedy, such as price controls, could make it any worse. That is a tough standard by which to judge anything. Would abolishing health care altogether be no worse?

I was particularly interested in Stuart Butler's comments about the United Kingdom. I have always sensed that the British like to queue up, and I almost expected Stuart Butler to have kind things to say about price controls. At my supermarket in Washington, if three people are in line, the manager will open a new register or else the supermarket will pay for a portion of the customer's groceries. I cannot imagine that happening in the United Kingdom, where the experience of price controls have been so long-lived. Who knows, perhaps these interventions in the economy have so reduced the wage rate that the opportunity cost of waiting is negligible.

No economists in the health care arena really believe that price controls will work, but some argue either that they will not make things any worse or that they are a temporary expedient to promote fundamental reform. One often hears that view attributed to the Clinton administration: it wants to employ price controls only for a short time, as a transition. Why we need a transition to the next, unknown proposal is never explained.

The explanation, however, is clear. Our current president is increasingly reminiscent of Jimmy Carter. He wants to get involved in absolutely everything at all times. He wants to arbitrate the spotted owl dispute in person. He wants to deliver something to every constituent group in Washington, D.C., without imposing costs on anyone. Clearly, price controls are one way to conceal the cost of broadening a health insurance system by government mandate. Thus, the price controls will be temporary as we phase in the expanded coverage, if that is to be the first order of business in the health care program. I agree with Stuart Butler that distortions will creep in slowly whenever the government turns to price controls. If price controls do not work for meat or steel, how can they work in health care, given the enormous potential variations in service quality?

A distinguished, older journalist at Brookings once commented on how poorly the health care sector performs and how badly we need price controls. He spoke about receiving a particular treatment under Medicare for which the government was being billed $50. Suddenly, that treatment was redefined, and the government was billed $100. "You see," he said, "we need price controls." But the reason for the redefinition of the service is that there *are* price controls on the $50 service and that redefinition of the service is the only way to avoid them. Here is an example of an economic journalist in Washington who still does not understand how price controls work after watching them in action during the Korean War and the Nixon administration.

In a visit to Budapest, before all the tumultuous changes occurred in Eastern Europe, I was surprised to learn that in a socialist country, where health care was provided by the state, it was almost impossible to see a real physician for most maladies. The average citizen would see someone less trained than a physician, unless he wished to pay a bribe. And bribes were widespread, accepted openly by physicians. People did not call their politician friends to get to the head of the line—they just paid their way there. That is how a "socialist" system worked.

Regarding the Friedman and Coffey chapter, one of the advantages of having fifty states is the opportunity they provide to experiment and to provide data points to estimate the effects of state regulation. Such estimates are more difficult to effect in Canada, where there are far fewer provinces. What troubled me about Friedman and Coffey's approach, though, is their attempt to determine the cost per admission to a hospital where admission per capita is an independent variable on the right-hand side of the equation, and HMO participation is the right-hand variable. It seems likely that regulation affects both and that a more complete model might therefore give different results. Friedman and Coffey conclude that regulation might affect the expenses per admission but not the number of admissions per capita. That is, if a patient has a serious illness, the hospital might remove him from the intensive care unit, and the patient might check back in again.

Consider the example of mine safety regulation. Proponents of safety regulation point out that the number of fatalities per man-hour in the coal mines has shown a sharply downward trend since regulation. Regulation might even have had a statistically significant effect on the number of accidents or fatalities *per hour of labor* in the coal mines. The problem is that regulation has caused a huge increase in the number of hours per ton of coal mined, and the fatality rate has not come down per ton of coal mined. Such results cannot fairly be trumpeted as evidence of success unless success is measured by having more people to watch the accidents. Regulation creates many effects, and one has to decide what is exogenous and what is endogenous to the regulatory system.

Finally, I agree with Charles Stalon that the notion of procedural fairness permeates all regulator processes, and it does not necessarily translate into equity. I do not know of a study that shows that regulation has caused the redistribution of income from wealthy people to poor people. Environmental regulation, one of the most costly forms of regulation, is shown by almost every study to be quite regressive in its effect on the distribution of income.

In the case of telephone regulation, enormous pressure was raised by the defenders of the poor and the struggling—namely, the Consumer Federation of America and the American Association of Retired Persons—for a repricing of telephone system services toward costs. For decades, regulators had been subsidizing local connection costs from long-distance service revenues. In the early 1980s, the Federal Communications Commission began to raise the price of local service so that the price of long-distance service could come down and both would move closer to cost. Given that the demand for long-distance service is more price-sensitive than the demand for connection to the network, this repricing would have beneficial effects on economic welfare. The populist opposition to the FCC's repricing quickly formed, arguing that raising the price of local telephone service by a putative $6 per month—it turned out to be $3.50 a month, $42 a year—would force 6 million people to disconnect their telephones because they could not afford service. In fact, since that time penetration of telephones in the United States has gone from about 91 percent of all households to between 93 and 94 percent.

The *increase* in telephone subscriptions obviously cannot be attributed to increasing the cost of a local connection. Real incomes have increased over this period, and demand has correspondingly increased for telephone service. But more important, a recent study shows that the demand for telephone service is related not only to the monthly connection charge but to the cost of *using* the telephone. This study concludes that repricing of service increased welfare without inducing anyone to disconnect his phone.

The repricing may not have been inequitable either. Poor people do use long-distance service, intensively in some cases. The distribution of long-distance calling is dramatically skewed, and many poor people, because of where they live, have to use long-distance service frequently to communicate with their friends and families or to conduct business transactions. As a result, it is not clear that equity in the repricing of telephone service is adverse to equity in the distribution of income.

In numerous areas of regulation, the loss in total social welfare, total economic output, is sufficiently great that even if such regulation is skewed to favor poor people, they may end up with less total income. One would rather be poor in Florida, for example, than middle class in Cuba today.

Consider the area of broadcasting. Does anybody believe that limiting the number of spectrum allocations so that politically powerful people can earn enormous rents—rents that almost approach those earned by owning a taxicab in New York City—will redistribute income from rich to poor? Might it be relevant that when the major decision was being made about spectrum allocation, the majority leader in the Senate, Lyndon Johnson, owned several broadcast licenses in Texas? Of course, the excuse was that his wife managed them, so there was no conflict of interest.

I will conclude with some hopeful thoughts about regulation. My colleague Clifford Winston and I have done research on the political effects on presidential elections of changes in regulatory policy, looking as far back as 1900 and also looking across states to observe many degrees of freedom. We find that after World War II, economic regulation was extremely unpopular. As a result, politicians eventually moved to reduce economic regulation. Social regulation, however, was quite popular: that is, health, safety, and environmental regulation. Perhaps for that reason, Richard Nixon was the most vigorous social regulator in history. One can only hope that political sentiment catches up with reality in this area as well.

Now that the Clinton administration is supervising the reregulation of cable television, perhaps it will create political opposition to further exercises in regulation. The failures in cable regulation may become apparent before Clinton takes on health care, a sector that represents 12–14 percent of gross domestic product. In the 1992 election, for example, the increase in social regulation offset some of the effects of the economy on George Bush's reelection bid, but it could not save him. If Clinton persists in increasing *economic* regulation, however, our results predict a sharp decline in his returns in 1996. Given that he starts from a base of 43 percent, he may want to think twice about imposing the heavy hand of government on the health care sector.

Robert Rubin

From 1981 to 1984 I spent a great deal of time traveling around the country and debating whether regulation or competition was the best way to control costs in the health care arena. I debated with such people as Karen Davis, Rashi Fein, and Joe Califano. The question is, Who was right and who was wrong? The answer is, All of us were right under certain circumstances.

In the short term, a sincere regulator can control health care costs. But the unintended consequence of regulation is a diminishing capacity to control costs. Market mechanisms are the preferred way to go in the long term.

The preceding chapters by Stuart Butler and Charles Stalon clarify several issues. The concept of rights and the status quo is really the Achilles' heel of the Clintons' developing health care reform program. We are now told that when Hillary Rodham Clinton talked about never taxing employees' health benefits, she really meant that they would never tax currently negotiated union contract benefits. When a contract expires, however, everything will be up for grabs.

Ira Magaziner tried to explain Mrs. Clinton's comment on the tax cap by saying she was really talking about basic benefits, not extraneous benefits. Past a certain level, the increment can be taxed. This is a distinction without a difference: Hillary Clinton meant all along that they were going to tax health care benefits. But it took her a while to get to the point.

The second problem with the Clintons' program is the benefit package. Many people believe in the possibility of a uniform minimum benefit package, or a basic benefit package, or a comprehensive benefit package.

The *New York Times* reports that the Clinton plan may include a package as generous as 80–90 percent of the employee packages around the country. This suggests that virtually everything is going to be in the package, except perhaps treatment for infertility—but most people manage to get around the insurance regulations for that through manipulating the way the tests are coded—and perhaps limitations on treatment for substance abuse, although Mrs. Gore is trying to guard against that.

Some of the mental health benefits may be covered, based on diagnosis. Since some of them are hard to diagnose definitively, one can well imagine how to get around restrictions. I am reminded of an experience I had as chief of nephrology at a Boston hospital. The utilization review nurse would not let one of my patients be admitted to the hospital with the diagnosis I had written. Clearly, the patient needed to be hospitalized. I did not know what was wrong with her, and I said, "How about unexplained chest pain?" They said, "Oh, yes, that will get you three days." I said, "Fine, she has unexplained chest pain."

This brings me to Stuart Butler's chapter, about the fatal attraction of price controls. In the mid-1970s I was a member of a charitable trust known as the Faculty Practice Plan at a major New England university. Some smart lawyers from distinguished Boston law firms had advised us that as a charitable trust, we would be exempt from wage and price controls. Our salaries went along merrily, and we thought this was an interesting blip on the national economic scene, proving that smart professionals will usually figure out a way to get the job done.

Concerning regulation and its effect on hospital costs, we recently did a study in Maryland using regression equations. For those who think the Lewin/VHI position is that Maryland rate setting is a good thing, I quote Gilbert and Sullivan's "H.M.S. Pinafore": "Things are seldom what they seem, and skim milk does masquerade as cream." John Sheils and I agree that Maryland's ability to control health care costs has eroded over time.

In our study we tried to answer the questions, Did the average annual growth in Maryland differ substantially from that of the rest of the country? Was there a trend difference? And were there significant year-to-year differences? When Maryland began their hospital rate setting, admissions were 30 percent lower than in the rest of the country. Length of stay, however, was 10.8 percent higher. By 1990, admissions per capita were 5 percent lower in Maryland than nationwide. That is to say, Maryland's position relative to the rest of the country decayed dramatically over the decade. This was due mainly to the decline in admissions nationally, but also to the increase in the building of hospitals in the Washington, D.C., area. And by 1990, length of stay was 5 percent below the national average; Maryland went from 10.8 percent above to 5.5 percent below.

It is reasonable to conclude that most of the savings effect of Maryland rate setting was achieved through decreasing length of stay. The Friedman-Coffey chapter suggests that this cannot be sustained, and in fact the effect is already attenuating.

How significant are the savings? We first looked at the average annual rise in cost and came up with 1.2 percent; virtually every other researcher has found 2 percent, and one found 1.8 percent. We used the trans-log regression model.

In doing econometric analyses, one frequently looks at alternative measurement methods. We used something called the difference model, which limits hospital-specific variation. Using this test, the statistical significance totally disappears. So at the very least, it is not a robust statistical finding. Furthermore, the differences in each year were not statistically significant, except for 1983. Finally, using the polynomial equation, we showed that Maryland's success in controlling its costs was decaying over time. While the statistical tests may be interesting to some, I think the common-sense approach is the issue. Maryland was able to decrease length of stay, and the state therefore continued to save.

Did Maryland pay a price for this? Not as great a price as has been paid in other places. But as the Friedman and Coffey chapter shows, one can contain the rate of growth in regulated or unregulated states. The issue is, What are we building for when we go to that next level? What will New York have to do to get its hospitals into shape, to provide the care that people in New York demand and expect? In New York, for example, there is "supercapacity" of hospitals. It is not uncommon for hospitals to be filled at more than 100 percent of their capacity; that means people are sleeping in the emergency rooms for two or three days. What does that do to the quality of care?

The regulatory effects are not clear-cut. From a practical, clinical basis, the regulatory effects can diminish the quality of care. As a former policy maker, I believe there are other ways to control costs, as was shown in the Friedman-Coffey chapter.

Marvin H. Kosters

The chapters in this section provide insights on what might follow if we impose a full-fledged system of price-and-fee controls on the health care sector. I will use them as a springboard for my comments, comparing controls on health care costs with the Nixon wage-and-price controls, with which I became familiar twenty years ago.

In the first part of his chapter, Stuart Butler discusses the cost-push rationale for controls. He is probably correct that this rationale is less fashionable now than twenty years ago. But it was much more popular in business and media commentary then than it was among those planning and managing the controls system. Nevertheless, the logic of the system at that time was consistent with a cost-push rationale for inflation.

The logic of the 1970s controls system was that prices should be raised only to reflect increased costs; of course, increased costs were generally regarded as justification for raising prices. It was basically a cost pass-through system, with a continually expanding set of regulations to accommodate particular circumstances. The more closely one examines the economy, the more differentiated all those particular circumstances appear. During my time on a committee to consider exceptions and appeals, I found that it did not seem difficult to design general rules, but that making a specific decision that seemed most sensible was tantamount to throwing overboard the logic of the entire controls system. Nevertheless, the basic idea of the system was that cost increases could be passed along. The wage standard of 5.5 percent was the anchor to this system.

The cost pass-through logic of the controls was connected with the idea that the controls would be temporary. If the system was previously close to equilibrium, price-and-wage misalignment would build up only gradually. Furthermore, only limited misalignment under cost pass-through principles would allow decontrol without a big price bulge. This meant that the general standards were intended to be roughly in line with the market, and serious misalignments should be avoided or remedied.

Because of the way they were designed and a reluctance to lean heavily on the controls, major examples of harm were not prevalent. The absence of good horror stories from the early 1970s may be a disappointment to critics, who must reach all the way back to World War II. It was not our idea to give controls a good name, however, but rather to make it easier to get rid of them. Distortions are worth avoiding in any case because they are costly.

The controls were discredited mainly because inflation began to surge in 1973. This was the price paid for a controls system that tried to avoid disruption when demand threatened to overwhelm the controls. The public was not glad to pay this price, at least not initially. The price surge in 1973 was blamed on loosened controls; there was a reversal of policy, followed by a new freeze. Problems under this second freeze became so obvious so quickly that gradual and selective decontrol was preferable to the public, despite the inflation that came with it.

The conviction that the controls should be temporary highlights an important difference between those of the early 1970s and prospective health care cost controls. Twenty years ago the devaluation and the import surcharge were causes for some concern, but in the common view, inertia was at least partly responsible for price increases, and especially wage increases, at rates that were coming down quite slowly. Aggregate supply and demand were not viewed as being out of balance—or at least not much—because the economy had some slack when the controls were imposed.

In the health care sector today, ceilings would be imposed at the same time that demand is increased perhaps by 10 or 20 percent. This is a formula for serious suppressed inflation, with all the problems Butler describes. The idea that controls could be temporary under these circumstances, or could be removed gracefully without a price explosion, is dubious. Strong pressures would build up under health controls if they were used to supplant market-determined prices, not just to nudge them in a direction consistent with market pressures.

The failure of controls in any particular case is usually blamed on external, uncontrollable events. In 1973, for example, food price increases were blamed in part on El Niño—because the warm ocean currents off the coast of Peru reduced the anchovy catch and put pressure on the U.S. soybean market, a source of protein-rich feed supplement. This perception led to the soybean export embargo, of which the Japanese have been reminding us ever since. Less emphasis was placed on the Soviet wheat deal, because this would implicitly criticize another action of government. Besides, the wheat sales were a reflection of the customary "unusually" poor harvest in the Soviet Union.

Activities to evade controls that pinch are always numerous and ingenious. This keeps rule writers busy. Regulations always proliferate over time, because even the most dedicated and ambitious policy wonks cannot possibly foresee all the arrangements that emerge in response to controls. Activities to evade controls are not usually developed with malicious intent—one party trying to take advantage of another by engaging in price gouging, for example. Although customers always prefer buying at a lower price, a buyer often willingly pays a price above the ceiling because he needs the good or service and cannot afford to wait.

Successful evasion of controls can reduce some of their costly side effects, but evasion itself is costly. The line between different kinds of evasion is sometimes blurry. Some types are completely legal, such as buying a business to get access to its products. Some types of evasion are not explicitly illegal, but their sole motivation is to evade controls—for example, absurd tie-in arrangements. Finally, there are explicitly illegal transactions, such as prices above ceilings or bribes. Ironically, proliferating regulations impede those methods of getting around controls that are most obvious and would be least costly.

One adverse side effect of controls that is likely to be particularly serious for health care is discouragement of investment in research and development. This effect is not easy to measure, and cutting back on research and development would have little effect on currently provided services. Such cutbacks would be still another way of exchanging less improvement in the future for more current consumption.

Since producers cannot always get the relief from controls they think they need or deserve from a regulator, they often turn to the political marketplace. A regulator might prefer to give relief but feels politically constrained. A strategy the producers can adopt is to convert themselves from the presumed beneficiaries of some action to the innocent victims of an unresponsive bureaucracy. In one case, service-station operators wanted an increase in their retail margin on gasoline. Giving it to them would have been unpopular, so we stalled while they made their case on Capitol Hill and on television. By the time we relented, the increase was viewed by the public as long overdue.

The notion that the goals of regulation are seldom as simple as keeping rates or prices down is one of the themes of Charles Stalon's chapter. His discussion highlights a striking difference between the traditional approach to the so-called regulated industries and the likely goal of health care cost controls. Traditional regulators have not been charged with reducing the share of the gross domestic product spent on air fares, railroad transportation, telephone communication, or electricity. Health care cost regulation would presumably be quite different, if it is to reduce its share of total output.

Cross-subsidies have often been sanctioned or even encouraged in regulated industries. But, with some exceptions, regulators have not tried to keep prices below full costs. They recognize the need to allow firms to earn enough profits to attract capital. Promotion of the sector and its growth has often been a part of their mission, as in the air transportation system, universal service in telephones, and electricity use. Producers in the health care sector are not likely to be receptive to the idea that their share of GDP should shrink. They can be expected to work hard to get their interests taken into account, some of which might also be in the interest of health care consumers.

The Stalon chapter's discussion of due process and procedural fairness shows how legal and political issues that can usually be avoided in analyses of unregulated markets are critical in regulatory decision making. From the perspective of economic efficiency, much of this process seems like an elaborate charade. What price regulators really do is usually quite simple. In response to requests for price increases, they say no, not so much, or not yet. Often procedures, the hearings, and the legal rationale for decisions provide a legitimacy for such decisions that would otherwise seem substantively arbitrary.

Regulators, of course, need to prevail in the court of public opinion. Hearings can provide information and generate publicity that helps regulators make a case for their decisions to the public. This arena always contains a great deal of competition. Many parties can organize events, supply information, and sometimes lead demonstrations to call attention to their point of view.

This role of regulators and their procedures does not come cheap. Process-oriented decision procedures are generally expensive if the stakes are high. Lawyers, experts, and public relations talent are costly. Economies of scale imply that large producers are in a much better position than small ones to play this game effectively, and the health services industry could be expected to adapt to reflect these circumstances.

Many observers are concerned about health price-and-fee controls, believing they will fail. My worry is that they will seem to succeed for a while, based on data like those for the early years in the Friedman and Coffey study. Later, they may seem irritating, inefficient, and ineffective but absolutely indispensable.

Even obvious problems do not always lead to early abandonment of controls. In spite of the shortages and gas lines of 1973, oil-price decontrol did not occur until 1981. People were even willing to cope with rationing devices without much common-sense justification. For a while, people could fill up their cars with gas only on odd or even days, for example, depending on their tag numbers. Theoretically, we could use such devices for health care based on people's social security numbers. For patients for whom the most useful advice would be "take two aspirins and call back in the morning," this might reduce costs with little adverse effect on outcomes. For others, the effects could be more serious than postponing a trip.

Although public attitudes toward price controls can be fickle, as we saw in 1973, I was amazed by the results of a *Wall Street Journal/* NBC News poll reported in early 1993. Among the sample polled, 87 percent found "government limits on doctor and hospital charges" acceptable as part of a revamped health care system. I wonder whether the remaining 13 percent understood the question—or whether they might all be employed in the health care services sector.

When we were removing wage-and-price controls in late 1973, John Dunlop emphasized that "it's easier to get into controls than it is to get out." This seems particularly likely in the case of health care. It looks particularly easy to get in because of devices already developed, such as the prospective payment schedule, diagnosis-related groups, and the resource-based relative value scale, which have been used for government reimbursement formulas. Once controls are imposed, it will be extremely difficult to remove them if they are applied in a serious way to suppress health care cost inflation. Price pressures will seem even bigger than they are, because it would be unclear to what extent demand or supply would respond if controls were removed. The worst fear when controls are threatened or imposed is "to get caught with your prices down." Market institutions also disappear or become weakened when controls are in force. These institutions need not recede as far into the background as they did in Eastern Europe and the Soviet Union before questions are raised about what we might rely on other than controls.

Full-fledged controls on health services will be a disaster if they are imposed. My concern is that this might not be apparent for a while and that it would be extremely difficult to remove health care price controls after we came to rely on them and on the administrative rationing decisions that would inevitably come with them.

PART TWO

Will Global Budgeting Work?

4

Global Budgets—
Why, What, How?

Patricia Danzon

This chapter evaluates the contribution of global budgets to achieving the goals of health care reform in the context of a competitive strategy such as managed competition. I assume that the goals of health care reform are:

- universal insurance coverage for a basic set of medical services
- affordability, that is, the cost of core services should not exceed some reasonable fraction of income for all citizens
- an efficient allocation of resources to and within the health care sector
- control of total government spending on health care[1]

These four goals subsume a potential fifth goal: equity or solidarity, defined as universal access to basic medical care at an affordable price.[2] The status quo in the U.S. health care system violates all four of these objectives.

Competitive strategies for health care reform, including managed competition (hereafter MNC)[3] and responsible national health insur-

---

[1]This could be considered one component of an efficient allocation of resources to health care.

[2]Equity defined as uniformity in access to all services is an additional and less widely accepted goal. It would violate the dimension of equity defined as equal freedom to spend after-tax income.

[3]Alain Enthoven, "The History and Principles of Managed Competition," *Health Affairs*, vol. 12, supp. (1993), pp. 24–48.

ance (hereafter RNHI),[4] outline a structure of changes designed to achieve these goals. The common ground shared by market-based reforms is reliance on competition in private insurance markets to achieve efficiency. Efficiency has two components: (1) provision of the level, quality, and mix of medical services and insurance that consumers prefer and (2) use of least-cost methods of producing these services. The belief that the incentives and information generated by competitive markets are the best guarantor of efficiency distinguishes competitive strategies from a single payer, public monopoly approach.

Competitive strategies also assign a role for government: to define the medical services and financial protection that are guaranteed for everyone; to ensure that coverage for these core services is universal; to implement subsidies where necessary to make coverage affordable; and to apply the minimum regulations necessary to ensure availability and efficiency in insurance markets. The presumption is, however, that efficiency in setting the level and mix of health care spending and in the production of insurance and medical services can best be achieved through voluntary choices in competitive markets, provided that incentives reflect true social costs and benefits.

A key change in the status quo—and a necessary condition for efficiency—is a cap (or total elimination, under RNHI) of the tax exclusion of employer contributions from taxable income of employees.[5] The amount of coverage chosen by consumers when faced with the full marginal cost for coverage above the cap is presumed to yield the efficient level of spending on health care, assuming that consumers are reasonably well informed (with no systematic bias) and that there are no external costs or benefits if some people buy more than core coverage. Competition then creates incentives for insurers to act as cost-conscious purchasers on behalf of policyholders, which in turn creates incentives for (second-best) efficient control of moral hazard and of noncompetitive pricing by providers.[6]

---

[4]Mark V. Pauly, Patricia M. Danzon, Paul J. Feldstein, and John Hoff, *Responsible National Health Insurance* (Washington, D.C.: AEI Press, 1992).

[5]MNC also limits the amount that an employer can contribute to the least costly of the subset of plans offered.

[6]The competitive approaches differ in other dimensions. RNHI uses an individual mandate to ensure universal coverage. MNC plans usually include an employer mandate and also require an individual mandate if coverage is to be universal (for example, Paul Starr and Walter Zelman, "Bridge to Compromise: Competition under a Budget," *Health Affairs*,

The Clinton administration's proposals for health care reform are expected to adopt the MNC approach to insurance regulation and to use both an employer mandate and an individual mandate. Unlike the original MNC proposals, however, the open-ended employee tax exclusion for employer premium contributions may be retained; a limit on the tax deductibility of contributions for employers appears more likely. Either because this key demand-side incentive for cost control has been rejected, or because of lack of faith in its efficacy, some variant of a global budget is being proposed. The question to be addressed here is, How does a global budget contribute to achieving the goals of health care reform, assuming that other features of the MNC approach are adopted?

This chapter considers three possible spending limits: on government spending, total core spending, and on total spending, including supplementary coverage. I conclude that a global budget defined as a limit on government spending, including tax expenditures, is a necessary component of efficient cost control under any competitive strategy, including MNC and RNHI. A global budget defined as a limit on *total* spending on core benefits is operationally equivalent, under certain conditions, to a limit confined to *government* spending and therefore *may* also be consistent with efficient cost control. A

---

vol. 12, supp. [1993], pp. 7–23). To achieve affordability, MNC uses a set of income-related subsidies for those obtaining coverage outside employment. RNHI replaces the current tax subsidy to employer contributions with a system of income-related tax credits that apply regardless of source of coverage—employment-based or individual. The two approaches also differ in their strategies for insurance regulation and risk pooling. Under MNC, health plans (AHPs) are required to use community rating and open enrollment, but then the health insurance purchasing cooperative (HIPC) makes risk-adjusting transfers across plans. This contrasts with the simplest version of RNHI, which permits plans to charge risk-rated premiums but makes risk-adjusted subsidies to individuals. Alternatively, insurers could be required to community rate within broad categories (for example, age or location); voluntary risk pooling among insurers can be implemented through a reinsurance facility, without the regulatory structure of an HIPC. Thus, RNHI implicitly pools risk between low and high risks nationwide, whereas the risk pool under MNC is confined to the HIPC population. HIPCs are a new regulatory structure in every locality, which increases administrative costs. HIPCs may reduce costs of informing consumers about prices and outcomes of alternative plans and the costs of enrolling individuals and small groups, relative to the status quo. The information dissemination, however, could easily be performed by existing insurance departments. If HIPCs are selective among plans, approving only a preferred subset, this could have important implications, as discussed later.

necessary condition for this equivalence is that individuals are free to purchase supplementary coverage. But if supplementary coverage is banned or implicitly or explicitly taxed, then a global budget defined as a limit on premiums for core coverage is a binding constraint and generates a dead-weight loss. Even if supplementation is nominally free, a global budget for core services implemented through all-payer rate regulation also generates a dead-weight loss, since all-payer rate regulation constrains prices and copayments for individual services, leading to distortions in quantities and qualities of different services.

While global budgets may control measured spending, they cannot control the real social costs of medical care, which is what matters in determining health care's total contribution—positive or negative—to economywide productivity and consumer well-being. Real social costs under a spending cap could exceed the level that would have occurred without constraint on observable spending. The proponents of global budgets might argue that these dead-weight cost conclusions presuppose the existence of a perfect market and that spending limits or all-payer rate regulation is necessary precisely because markets for health insurance and medical services are not competitive. But if market imperfections exist, these are unlikely to be eliminated by spending limits or fee controls, which in turn add other distortions.

There are two possible coherent rationales for a global budget that restricts individuals' rights to spend their own aftertax income on health care. The first is based on a strongly egalitarian definition of equity, that the universal minimum should also be a universal maximum. This is a value judgment that should be debated before being assumed. The second is to impose a constraint on interest group pressures that might otherwise expand the definition of covered core services.[7] This goal might be achieved by other, less costly means. Thus a convincing case for global budgets on total spending remains to be made.

Why, What, and How of Global Budgets

An evaluation of the costs and benefits of global budgets begs the question, What problem is the global budget designed to address? This section considers rationales for each level for which a spending cap has been proposed—government spending, total core benefits spending, and total spending (including supplementary coverage)—

---

[7]This is analogous to the Gramm-Rudman-Hollings limit on federal spending.

and the likely effects of such limits.

A Limit on Government Spending on Health Care. A fixed budget for government spending on health care is essential to control the federal deficit and potentially consistent with an optimal allocation of resources to health care, assuming that the budget is set at the "right" level. A limit on government subsidies to health care, including tax expenditures, is a key component of competitive models for health care reform, including MNC and RNHI. The open-endedness of the current employee tax exclusion distorts incentives by subsidizing marginal spending, thereby contributing to excessive insurance and to excess health care cost inflation. Closing this subsidy is an essential component of market-based reforms that seek to constrain excess cost growth by facing consumers with the full marginal cost of coverage beyond the level that is subsidized by the government.

Limiting government spending is relatively simple. Assume that the government has defined the mandatory core benefits plan, including a set of medical services X and an upper limit on out-of-pocket expense, f, which ideally should vary by income. Since core coverage will be subsidized for low-income families, core benefits should include those services that taxpayers are willing to buy for everyone, including those too poor to pay for themselves. This is not necessarily the same as the services they may want to buy for themselves with their own after-tax income. Health plans compete to provide core benefits in a managed-competition environment with community rating.[8] In each ith locality, the health insurance purchasing cooperative (or some government agency) determines a benchmark cost of core benefits, $P_i(X,f)$, defined as either the minimum cost plan, the median, or any other percentile of the distribution of premiums for plans offering core benefits. The government determines the fraction s_j of this benchmark cost that it wishes to pay for consumers in each jth percentile of the income distribution. The government may wish to pay the full cost of coverage for those below the poverty line, for example, with subsidies declining at higher incomes, so that no family contributes more than x percent of its income to the premium cost of health care. The government budget B_g is then:

$$B_g = \sum_i \sum_j s_j w_{ij} P_i(X,f) \qquad (4\text{--}1)$$

---

[8]This assumes a noninterventionist HIPC that monitors the rules governing competition, including open enrollment, community rating, and outcomes reporting, but with no direct or indirect regulation of rates and no selective discrimination between plans that seek to be offered as qualified plans.

where s_j = the government share of benchmark cost for income group j

w_{ij} = the number of persons in group j in locality i

$P_i(X,f)$ = benchmark premium for core benefits in locality i

Defining and implementing this government budget is simplest if subsidies take the form of refundable tax credits, defined as a percentage of the cost of the benchmark premium. If the tax exclusion of employer contributions is retained, a global cap on government tax expenditures can be achieved provided that the tax exclusion is capped at the cost of the benchmark plan. Simply capping the exclusion rather than replacing it with a system of refundable tax credits, however, retains the regressive distribution of federal subsidies and requires higher total tax expenditures for any given level of subsidy to low-income people, since tax expenditures also accrue to high-income employees. Thus, government expenditures are capped but at a higher level, so that whatever the budget deficit is, total tax revenues and hence total dead-weight loss from raising taxes must be higher.[9]

Some recent proposals favor capping the employer's tax deduction for premium contributions, leaving the current open-ended tax exclusion for employees. These two approaches can have very different effects. A cap on the employer's deduction can leave an open-ended subsidy for individuals in high tax brackets. To show this, appendix 4-A develops a simple model of a firm that determines the mixture of cash and noncash benefits to minimize cost, subject to the constraint that the total compensation package is sufficient to attract the desired number of employees. An open-ended employee tax exclusion combined with a cap on employer tax deductibility implies a subsidy or a tax to health benefits, depending on whether the employee's marginal tax rate t^p exceeds or is less than the employer's marginal tax rate t^c.[10] An employer tax cap thus reduces but does not

---

[9]Starr and Zellman ("Bridge to Compromise") propose a limit on the employer's contribution to 7 percent of wages, a limit on the employee's contribution to 2 percent of income, and federal subsidies to make up the difference, with implementation through adjustment in the employee's tax withholding. This is operationally similar to the system of income-related tax credits proposed in RNHI, also implemented through an adjustment in the employee's tax withholding. Under the Starr-Zelman proposal, however, an individual with income just above the poverty line would contribute 9 percent of wages if employed (assuming that the employer contribution is passed on as lower wages) but only 9 percent of *income above the poverty line* if unemployed. Effectively, this plan imposes a tax on working.

[10]The optimal mixture of cash wages W and health benefits K satisfies the following marginal condition (see appendix 4–A):

eliminate the marginal subsidy if $0 < t^c < t^p$. The regressivity of the tax exclusion, defined as the marginal change in the subsidy at higher wages, is also reduced but not eliminated if $t^c > 0$. Further, a cap on the employer's tax deduction does not cap the government's tax expenditures, which depend on the joint distribution of corporate and personal marginal tax rates. Of course if the employer's contribution is also capped at 100 percent of the cost of the benchmark plan, this effectively limits government tax expenditures even without a limit on the employee's tax exclusion.

One objection to a limit applied only to government spending is that the cost shifting that now allegedly occurs as a result of Medicare and Medicaid reimbursement controls would worsen. But if Medicaid and ultimately Medicare beneficiaries as well are enrolled in competing private health plans along with everyone else, and individual consumers enroll in large groups through the intermediation of either large employers or HIPCs, then no single plan need necessarily have disproportionate market weight relative to the others. Although competing plans may use different forms and scales for reimbursement, such variation occurs in any competitive market in which products are differentiated to meet the heterogeneous preferences of consumers. Even within the status quo, the extent of cost shifting per se remains an open theoretical and empirical question.[11] Price differences certainly exist, possibly because of unmeasured differences in quality—for example, longer visits for higher fees. The differences could also reflect appropriate charging of joint costs to those market sectors that generate the marginal demand for higher-quality services, just as peak load users of public utilities are charged higher rates because their demand generates the need for larger capacity.

A Limit on Total Core Spending.

A market-determined cap. A second possible target of a global budget is to limit total spending on core benefits, excluding copayments and premiums for any supplementary coverage. A "bottom-

---

$$U_k / U_w = (1 - t^p) / (1 - t^c).$$

If $t^c > t^p$, the employee's effective marginal tax rate on K above the limit is different from the marginal tax rate on cash wages, so marginal choices remain distorted, although the distortion is less than under the status quo with unlimited employer deductibility.

11David Dranove, "Pricing by Non-Profit Institutions: The Case of Hospital Cost-Shifting," *Journal of Health Economics*, vol. 7 (1988), pp. 47–57. Although cost shifting is not consistent with profit maximization, it may be consistent with utility maximization by not-for-profit entities.

up" approach to setting the cap is to use the market-determined cost of the government mandated core coverage:

$$B_c = \sum_{ik}\sum m_{ik} \, P_{ik}(X,f) \tag{4-2}$$

where B_c is the total national cost of core benefits, m_{ik} is the population in state i that buys core benefits plan k with premium cost $P_{ik}(X,f)$.

The main rationale given for such a cap on total core spending is the belief that the United States spends too high a percentage of gross national product on health care, at the expense of other, more productive investments such as education (as Starr and Zelman mention). Although spending 13 percent of GNP on health care is not bad per se, the grain of truth in this argument is that the current structure of open-ended subsidies to public and private insurance does encourage consumers and providers to ignore the full social cost of their spending decisions and thus probably contributes to excessive use of "low-benefit care," with marginal benefits less than costs. This situation may be exacerbated by the low level of public investment, until recently, in providing information about costs and effectiveness of alternative medical technologies. The MNC approach, however, is designed to correct these problems of distorted incentives and inadequate information. By contrast, a crude spending limit that restricts supply without addressing the underlying stimulus to excessive demand will necessarily result in inefficient forms of rationing.

A cap on total spending on core benefits may be unnecessary, assuming that the other key features of a competitive strategy are adopted: a defined core benefit plan, correct marginal incentives for consumers, and a limit on government spending. A cap on total core spending may, however, be innocuous under certain conditions. In particular, this form of global budget does not constrain private choices,[12] provided that (1) $P_i(X,f)$ is market determined (for example, the minimum or median premium charged by approved health plans for basic coverage in locality i); (2) supplementation is unconstrained: that is, insurers can freely offer plans with more comprehensive benefits, higher "quality," or greater choice, without facing any implicit tax or constraint, but without any public subsidy; and (3) prices for medical services are market determined, that is, without price regulation.

Under these conditions, a global budget applied to total spending

---

[12]The mandate that everyone obtain minimum basic benefits inevitably constrains private choices, but there is no additional dead-weight loss due to the global budget.

on the benchmark plan may be operationally equivalent to applying the limit to government spending, which, it has been argued, is a necessary component of an efficient market-based approach to health care reform.[13] To see this, assume that competition forces all plans to be similarly efficient in the long run, although in the short run there may be random errors or temporary mistakes, as in any competitive market. Then differences in the cost of benchmark coverage across plans reflect either more comprehensive medical benefits, lower co-payment, better amenities, or higher quality along some other dimension. To be able to charge for these additional features, the plan would presumably advertise them and classify itself as providing "supplemental" coverage. Supplemental refers here to quality dimensions of coverage, as well as number and types of services covered. Since the government-mandated core plan cannot conceivably define all the quantity and quality dimensions of coverage, the distinction between core and supplemental coverage is intrinsically fuzzy. Thus a plan offering higher "quality"—for example, shorter waits, more choice of specialist—might designate itself as supplemental, reporting the benchmark cost as its cost of core coverage, although this might not be available as a stand-alone policy. The global budget for total core spending would simply be

$$B_c = \sum_{ik}\sum m_{ik}P_i(X,f) = \sum_{ij}\sum w_{ij}P_i(X,f) \qquad (4\text{-}3)$$

where $P_i(X,f)$ is the benchmark cost of core coverage in state i. Thus, under the maintained assumptions (that premiums for core benefits are competitively determined and supplementation is unconstrained), B_g in equation (4-1) is proportional to B_c in equation (4-2); that is, the cap on total core spending differs from the cap on government spending only by a factor of proportionality, which reflects the weighted average government subsidy to lower-income subgroups. Such a cap is not a binding constraint on total health care spending. It is innocuous, except to the extent that it entails administrative cost.

Such an estimate of total spending on core benefits could enhance efficiency if used, not as a binding constraint, but as a planning tool to guide the proposed National Health Board. The NHB would need to calculate the total cost implications of adding or deleting benefits from the core, since this would affect government expendi-

---

[13]Whether the limit includes copayments on core services or just insured spending on core services is also irrelevant if copayments are capped as part of the definition of core services.

tures. Since core benefits are services that will be made available to all, at taxpayers' expense for a significant fraction of the population, taxpayers (or their public representatives) should be able to make informed choices about how much they want to spend on health care versus other distributional transfers. Estimating the total cost of the core benefit package is thus an essential input into defining the optimal set of core benefits. The efficiency-enhancing use of this measure of total spending, however, is as a planning tool for determining government transfers through the health budget, not as a binding constraint on how individuals spend their own money.

An arbitrary cap on core spending. Proponents of caps on total spending on core benefits often argue that the cap should be imposed "top down," rather than derived "bottom up" from market prices. Thus, the cap would not be derived from the market-determined cost of providing mandated benefits $P_i(X,f)$; rather, it would be based on some arbitrary target, for example, 10 percent of gross domestic product. The common rationale for such spending constraints is doubt that managed competition will quickly reduce the present rate of cost increase. If all the provisions of MNC are enforced, including the employee tax cap, the level of spending should reflect consumer preferences as revealed by informed choices in competitive markets. It is unclear why this should be nonoptimal or how government, in imposing a limit on private spending, could make socially preferred choices.[14]

In some discussions, it appears that global spending caps are a supply-side substitute that is preferred politically to removal of the demand-side distortion of the tax exclusion. A complete analysis of the distributional effects of these two approaches is beyond the scope of this chapter. Clearly, the spending cap gives more power to bureaucrats. The losers are likely to be similar groups under either approach—those willing to pay for higher quality or greater choice of health care, particularly those in high tax brackets, and those with a high value of time. But the global spending cap is inherently less efficient. Thus, it seems unlikely that it would be preferred by taxpayers, if the implications of each approach were clearly understood.

If an arbitrary global budget limit for core spending is implemented through binding regulation of insurance premiums for core benefits, insurers must somehow cut costs below the market-

---

[14]One possible concern is market power of insurers and providers, which is addressed later.

determined level to break even. Since services are covered and copayments are regulated but many other dimensions of insurance policies cannot be regulated, the likely response of insurers is to reduce one or more of the unregulated aspects of "quality," such as delayed access to services (more restrictive triage), longer waits, and reduction in choice of specialists.

Even such an arbitrary cap on core spending, however, may in practice not be a binding constraint, provided that it is implemented through regulation of insurance premiums rather than through regulation of prices for medical services and provided that supplementation is unconstrained. If both these conditions are met, then those who are willing to pay for higher "quality" coverage than insurers can provide, given the regulated premiums for core coverage, will choose plans designated as supplemental. Again, the constraint is nonbinding.

A Limit on Total Spending plus a Ban or Tax on Supplementation. A cap on total health care spending, over and above a cap on government spending, constrains consumer choices if either (1) there is an implicit or explicit tax or ban on supplementary coverage or (2) the spending limit is implemented by a system of all-payer rate regulation. This section evaluates a tax or ban on supplementary coverage; rate regulation is discussed in the next section. It is probably impractical to attempt to limit direct out-of-pocket spending for medical services. The relevant issue is therefore an implicit or explicit tax or ban on plans that offer either more comprehensive benefits or higher "quality" than the benchmark plan.

Most likely is an implicit tax rather than an outright ban on supplementary insurance. Implementing such a tax is easiest when the constrained core services are publicly provided. Supplementation then entails buying access to unconstrained, privately provided substitute services, and the implicit tax arises if there is no credit for forgoing the use of public services. Private insurance in the United Kingdom and New Zealand is subject to such an implicit tax, since those who buy private coverage get no credit for either their tax contributions to the public system or for forgoing use of some public services. Similarly, education policy in the United States mandates an implicit tax on private supplementation, since those who pay for private schools get no credit for forgoing their entitlement to free use of public schools. Although Germany is often cited for its success in implementing global budget constraints, it in fact does not tax supplementation; an individual who meets the income criteria can assign his or her payroll tax contribution to a private insurance fund rather than to the mandatory sickness fund.

More generally, when supplementary insurance covers services that are substitutes for those provided under core benefits, there is an implicit tax on supplementation if those who buy it get no credit for their contribution or for forgoing their right to use the publicly provided core benefits. The voucher systems proposed for education eliminate this tax on supplementation. Such "vouchering out" is permitted in the Medicare health maintenance organization (HMO) option and has been proposed for New Zealand's health care reform.

Optimal public policy toward supplementary insurance should distinguish between supplementation that covers services that are complements to the publicly provided or core alternative and supplementation that is a substitute for the public alternative. In the United States, supplementary "medigap" coverage covers copayments and ancillary services (such as outpatient drugs) that tend to be complements to services covered under basic Medicare.[15] By contrast, policies sold as supplementary in New Zealand or the United Kingdom cover both complements and substitutes for the public alternative. Coverage of private hospital care, for example, tends to reduce the use of public hospitals, but coverage of copayments for drugs and physician visits (also called gap insurance) tends to increase use of these services and hence increase public sector costs.[16] Since supplemental policies that cover complements to publicly provided services tend to increase public costs, such policies should be taxed to reflect this cost increment, to correct consumers' incentives to purchase this supplementary coverage. This logic applies to Medigap insurance in the United States. In the context of managed competition, however, plans referred to here as supplemental simply offer more or higher "quality" services than the benchmark core plan. Since such supplemental plans are substitutes for not complementary to the bench-

---

[15]One service A is a complement (substitute) for another service B if a reduction in the price or increase in coverage of A tends to increase (decrease) the use of B. Empirical evidence shows that Medicare beneficiaries who have medigap coverage generate higher expenditures for basic Medicare, although the amount of the induced usage is hard to measure because the increase in use induced by supplementation (moral hazard effect) may be exacerbated by biased selection; that is, those who anticipate high health care costs are more likely to buy Medigap insurance.

[16]Patricia M. Danzon, "Gap and Supplementary Insurance in New Zealand: Theory, Evidence and Policy Options," unpublished report to the New Zealand Health Reform Directorate.

mark plan, the standard rationale for taxing supplementary gap coverage does not apply.

In the context of managed competition, costless supplementation means that the tax credits or subsidies to which individuals are entitled do not depend on the type of plan that they elect. Taxes on supplementation are implicit in MNC models that advocate an interventionist HIPC that approves only a subset of health plans as eligible for tax preference or other public subsidies. Taxes on supplementation are explicit in proposals that would tax plans that charge more than the benchmark plan in the area.[17]

Even without an explicit ban or tax on supplementation, all-payer rate regulation is likely to result in an implicit discriminatory tax on plans that offer supplementary coverage in the form of freer consumer choice, of both providers and services.

Efficiency effects of premium constraints. The efficiency effects of a binding cap that either bans or taxes certain types of health care spending or plans depend on the market failure in the absence of a cap. Discussions of global budgets seem to envisage two possible rationales.

• *Equity and merit goods.* One rationale for banning or taxing supplementary coverage presumes that equity requires everyone to have the identical insurance coverage or choice from only the same limited set of options. Thus, the universal minimum is also a universal maximum, in the hope of ensuring a "single tier" health care system. This requires taxpayers to pay for the same coverage for the poor as they would like for themselves. If this conforms to taxpayers' preferences, then such a cap entails no efficiency loss: the government would simply be the enforcer of a universally accepted choice. But such a limit imposes a real utility loss on any taxpayer who is willing to contribute to ensure that everyone has access to a basic core benefit package but who is not willing to forgo spending his or her own money on supplementary medical services. This definition of equity is more restrictive than that applied in Canada, Germany, the United Kingdom, or France; it is also more restrictive than that applied to

---

17In the Jackson Hole initiative, small-group participation in the HIPC would be a condition for the tax exclusion of employer contributions. This is nondiscriminatory only with a noninterventionist HIPC that offers all plans that meet the terms of competition, including coverage of at least core services, community rating, open enrollment, dissemination of price and outcome information, and participation in the risk-transfer mechanism.

other publicly subsidized goods and services in the United States. If a preference by some people for this definition of equity underlies the pressures for binding spending constraints, the issue should be clarified to taxpayers and explicitly debated before choices are made.

• *Inefficiencies in insurance and health care markets.* A second rationale given for a binding spending cap is to attempt to increase efficiency in markets for insurance and medical services. The presumption is that although MNC would correct the status quo distortions to demand, by providing more information about prices and outcomes of health plans and correct marginal incentives for consumers, some distortions would remain. The presumption is that binding regulation of insurance premiums for core coverage and a ban on supplementation will increase efficiency. Presumably, the hope is for a reduction in cost per unit of services (increase in production efficiency); a more aggressive bargaining stance toward providers that results in lower fees (elimination of quasi-rents); or more efficient control of moral hazard, to eliminate services with benefits less than cost.

Since premium regulation does not change either the demand or the cost conditions facing insurers, however, such potentially efficient responses are not guaranteed and in fact seem quite unlikely. A simple model of insurer choice of the various dimensions of an insurance policy, assuming net revenue maximization, shows that a binding premium cap affects the mix of benefits and cost controls included in the plan *only* to the extent that relative preferences or costs differ at different levels of total expenditure (see appendix 4-B). An insurer expands each dimension of coverage to the point where the marginal revenue (which reflects consumers' valuation or willingness to pay for that dimension) is equal to the marginal cost. This balancing of cost and consumers' valuation applies to cost-enhancing characteristics (more services, more choice, and nicer amenities) and to cost-reducing features (higher copayment, tighter utilization review, and other controls on moral hazard). A premium cap does not eliminate any distortions in the underlying insurance demand and cost conditions that determine the response to premium constraints. There is, therefore, no guarantee that a cap affects only those coverage dimensions inappropriately provided or priced in the absence of the cap or even that the effects of the cap are positive in general. If efficiency in medical markets is distorted because of imperfectly informed consumers or imperfectly competitive markets for medical services—as presumed by this rationale for government constraints—then premium regulation alone will not eliminate or even necessarily reduce these distortions.

Some global budget proposals discriminate among plans and

target constraints only at those plans presumed inefficient. The California MNC proposal, for example, would limit premiums for plans that charge more than the benchmark. The presumption is that higher premiums reflect lower efficiency and that regulation will force the inefficient plans either to become more efficient or to go out of business. But discriminatory premium regulation is a blunt instrument for eliminating production inefficiency, since it cannot distinguish between plans that are truly inefficient and those that provide higher "quality" services—for example, fewer restrictions on access to specialists or lower time costs for patients—that are valued by consumers at their actuarial cost. Since quality of medical care is multidimensional and partly subjective, true inefficiency is impossible to measure. It is not necessarily inefficient for a patient to pay more for a provider in whom they have greater trust, or who offers greater convenience, even if measurable health outcomes are no different from those of other providers who charge less. Moreover, even if the perceived utility difference is based on consumer ignorance, regulation will not necessarily eliminate this inefficiency.

Many discussions of MNC presume that free choice, fee-for-service indemnity plans are inherently less efficient than plans that restrict choice to a limited set of providers, as in a staff-model HMO. More generally, the presumption is that the strategies used by indemnity plans to control moral hazard, primarily copayment and utilization review, are less efficient than the strategies used by HMOs, including restrictions on choice of providers or provider-targeted reimbursement incentives, such as capitation and prospective payment. Since copayment imposes financial risk on patients, whereas provider-targeted strategies do not, this assumption might be generally true if providers were perfect agents.[18] If providers are not perfect agents, however, then provider-targeted strategies may expose patients to other types of loss, including loss in utility (if they must use providers they do not trust); health risk (if providers who are personally at financial risk restrict access to higher-cost but lower-risk or less painful options); increased patient time costs (if gatekeeper triaging requires two visits rather than one visit to see a specialist); and forgone productivity and utility (if there are delays in access to nonemergency services).

If consumers are imperfectly informed and at least some providers are imperfect agents, then the choice among types of health plans is a choice among imperfect alternatives. At one extreme are

---

[18]Randall Ellis and Thomas McGuire, "Combining Demand and Supply-Side Cost Sharing," *Inquiry*, vol. 26 (Summer 1989).

plans that cover a large, informal network of providers paid fee-for-service, with freedom of choice for patients and autonomy for providers; cost control is through copayments and utilization review. At the other extreme are tightly integrated HMOs in which patients are tied to an exclusive panel of providers who are paid a capitation or salary; cost control is through informal and formal controls and by transfer of financial risk to physicians. These HMOs are often characterized as more cost conscious because they are prepaid, but this is misleading. All insurance plans are prepaid: they receive fixed premiums for the policy period and are at risk for the cost of covered services incurred by policyholders, net of copayments. From the perspective of the consumer or plan, HMOs are more "prepaid" only to the extent that they charge lower copayments at point of service.

The important distinction is that physicians in HMOs are usually partially prepaid or financially at risk. This creates incentives to provide too few services if consumers are imperfectly informed, whereas fee-for-service plans may create incentives to provide too many services. Thus, neither arrangement is perfect. Requirements under MNC that plans report data on cost, outcomes, and consumer satisfaction may improve information and thereby mitigate incentives to underprovide or overprovide. But given the limitations of data on both the objective and the subjective dimensions of quality, information is likely to remain imperfect for the foreseeable future.[19] Thus although integrated health plans can be designed that reduce costs to any desired level, there is no assurance that such cost reductions enhance efficiency, since too little (on quality and quantity dimensions) may be as inefficient as too much. Integrated systems cannot be evaluated solely by reference to the market leaders, such as the Harvard Community Health Plan or Kaiser Permanente, which are preeminent precisely because they are above average. There are similarly outstanding individual doctors, group practices, and hospitals in the fee-for-service sector that practice cost-conscious, high-quality medicine. But the preeminent few are by definition above average. Valid generalizations about average provider performance and average consumer satisfaction under alternative plan types are

---

[19]Inferring quality of care from data on outcomes requires accurate controls for other contributing factors, such as the patient's initial health status, lifestyle, compliance with recommended regimens, and the like. Even with hospital data, where the potential for unobservable contaminating influences is much less than in ambulatory care, experience suggests that accurate inference on the effects of care versus underlying condition is difficult.

more reliably based on the survivor evidence from the market.

In theory, the optimal use of copayments versus provider incentives and other forms of moral hazard control depends on the consumer's preferences between these alternatives, on the elasticity of demand for the specific medical service, and on the consumer's income or ability to bear financial risk.[20] It also depends on the extent to which integration of providers into closed-panel networks in practice reduces the costs of information transfer and coordination of care. The structure provided by an HMO or other integrated delivery system may in theory increase information flows, but the reality often falls short of the theory. Similarly, fee-for-service physicians coordinate care through referral networks and direct information transfers, even if they are not formally linked in a preferred provider organization (PPO) or HMO. Thus the advantage of HMOs in practice, relative to looser, fee-for-service networks, is an empirical question.

Regulations may have originally obstructed the growth of closed-panel HMOs.[21] But now their relatively static market share reflects consumer choices. Market evidence shows that the majority of consumers prefer plans with higher copayments but more freedom of choice of provider (traditional free-choice plans or the hybrid point-of-service HMOs) to staff model HMOs that offer lower copayments but control costs through provider incentives, to limited choice of provider and limits on access to specific services through triage, delay, or outright denial. These status quo choices may be distorted by the tax subsidy to insurance and to copayments sheltered through flex-benefit plans. Once these distortions are eliminated, however, there is no efficiency reason for preferring a priori one form of moral hazard control over another or for doubting that informed choices in competitive markets will lead to the mix of plan types that consumers prefer.

It is also not necessarily true that free-choice plans are more

---

[20]In simple theory of demand for insurance by informed consumers with no external effects, optimal copayment depends on risk preferences, which may be related to income but need not be. If, however, the rationale for mandating universal coverage is that some people would buy suboptimal coverage, if the choice is voluntary, either because of underestimate of risk or intentional free-riding, then the optimal maximum allowable copayment for the mandated coverage varies positively with income.

[21]Lawrence Goldberg and Wallace Greenberg, "The Emergence of Physician-sponsored Health Insurance: A Historical Perspective," in W. Greenberg, ed., *Competition in the Health Care Sector: Past, Present and Future* (Germantown, Md.: Aspen, 1978).

costly, provided that they can design their own copayment structures (within limits). The RAND Health Insurance Experiment showed that copayment, subject to a reasonable stop-loss, can be as effective as a staff model HMO at limiting total expenditures, with no significant differences in health outcomes. Since similar costs were achieved by the fee-for-service plan without utilization review, with utilization review the copayment necessary to achieve equal expenditures would be lower, and the relative advantage of HMOs, using closed panels and provider incentives, would be reduced. The rate of increase of costs in HMOs is similar to that in indemnity plans.[22]

Although theory and evidence suggest that free-choice plans could compete with integrated closed-panel plans, the design of core benefits may discriminate against plans that rely disproportionately on copayments. If the mandatory core plan includes a comprehensive set of services with a low limit on out-of-pocket cost for those services—for example, comparable to the copayments in a staff-model HMO such as Kaiser Permanente—this limit is likely to be a binding constraint on many plans that place greater reliance on copayments to control costs. This imposes a discriminatory tax on such plans and on consumers that prefer such plans. Of course, the design of core benefits must include an upper limit on out-of-pocket expense for covered services, to protect against catastrophic expense. The permissible stop-loss, however, should vary with income and should recognize that copayments may for some people be a pre-ferred approach to moral hazard control.

The implicit tax from setting the copay limit below the optimal level is greater the more comprehensive the range of services included in basic benefits is. Services with high demand elasticity optimally have a higher copayment rate than services with inelastic demand; for some services the optimal coinsurance may be 100 percent: that is, these services are excluded from coverage. Thus, if the mandate requires coverage of services with elastic demand, which would optimally be excluded or limited by competitive indemnity plans, such plans may be unable to compete if the mandate also requires a stop-loss below the level that such plans (and their consumers) would have chosen if unconstrained. The implicit tax on indemnity plans is

---

[22]Fee-for-service plans are also sometimes criticized for having "airgaps." Any insurance plan, however, must define covered and uncovered serv-ices. Details may be more explicit in indemnity plans, more hidden in HMOs that directly control availability and use of services. In any case, since all plans will be required to offer core services, any such differences would be curtailed under proposed reforms.

heavier if the premium cap is reinforced by rate regulation with a ban on balance billing.

Efficiency effects of all-payer rate regulation. Regulation of prices for medical services (either instead of or as well as regulation of insurance premiums) is sometimes advocated as a device for controlling market power of providers and sometimes as a device for controlling total expenditure. As a device for controlling total expenditure, service-specific price regulation combined with service-specific expenditure caps (volume performance standards) is likely to be even more inefficient than premium regulation, since it entails the added distortion of discouraging efficient substitution among medical services, in addition to arbitrarily constraining total spending.

The argument that price regulation is necessary as a device for controlling market power of providers is based on the overly narrow view that price differences among providers necessarily reflect market power rather than real service or quality differences. Consumers choose fee-for-service plans that permit balance billing in part because these plans provide partial insurance coverage for services of higher-cost providers who are outside of PPO or HMO networks. Since unlimited coverage would make consumers indifferent to prices charged by providers, indemnity plans control this dimension of moral hazard by reimbursing only up to a limit, but they permit providers to balance bill above the limit. Indemnity coverage with balance billing thus gives consumers partial insurance protection for use of high-quality, high-priced providers; by contrast, a closed-panel PPO or HMO would require 100 percent out-of-pocket payment for use of nonnetwork providers.[23]

If patients perceived no difference in quality among providers, this arrangement would in the long run drive out providers that do not accept assignment, that is, payment at the insurer's reimbursement limit, with zero balance billing. The fact that this has not occurred suggests that patients do perceive differences for which they are willing to pay some out-of-pocket fee. Of course, the counter argument is that patients do not know beforehand that a provider does not accept assignment, so the survival of physicians who balance bill is attributed to consumer ignorance about fees. This hypothesis may have some short-run validity, but as a description of long-run equilibrium, it requires implausible ignorance and inability to learn from experience.

---

[23]As noted earlier, the growth of point-of-service plans that provide partial coverage for out-of-plan providers is evidence of consumers' willingness to pay for the additional freedom of choice.

Another reason for fee differentials between physicians of apparently similar competence is specialization in serving patients who differ in their value of time. Patients who value time highly would be willing to pay more for a physician who offers a shorter expected wait and a longer visit, with more services performed in the single visit. The hypothesis that physicians in competitive markets optimally adjust the mix of money prices and time prices to patients is confirmed by empirical evidence for primary care markets.[24]

The fact that PPO plans use fee schedules supposedly below market rates and ban balance billing is sometimes interpreted as evidence that more efficient insurers use their buying power to constrain market power by physicians. Prima facie this would be inconsistent with the hypothesis that physicians operate in reasonably competitive markets and have incentives to trade-off between money price (fee) and time price (length of visit and expected wait) to maximize consumer utility. The cosurvival of PPOs with binding fee schedules and indemnity plans that permit balance billing, however, can be explained as efficient sorting and matching of heterogeneous consumers to insurance plans that are better tailored to their preferences. If consumers differ in their willingness to trade off between money and time price, a PPO option that constrains fees self-selects patients who prefer a lower money price and a higher time price. Such segmentation and product diversity permits greater satisfaction of heterogeneous consumer tastes.[25]

To interpret the higher fees or balance billing permitted under an unconstrained indemnity plan as evidence of inefficient insurers or market power of physicians is to neglect the importance of patient

---

[24]Thomas McCarthy, "The Competitive Nature of Primary Care Physicians' Services Markets," *Journal of Health Economics*, vol. 4 (1985), pp. 93–118.

[25]Enthoven, "The History and Principles of Managed Competition," suggests that any market segmentation based on differences among plans is bad. Segmentation based on risk selection might be undesirable in the absence of some other mechanism such as risk-related subsidies to make coverage affordable to higher-risk individuals. There is no reason, however, why product differentiation on other dimensions of quality, such as services covered or mixture of moral-hazard controls, should be any less desirable in health insurance than in markets for other goods and services. In general, we let markets determine the optimal trade-off between diversity of product offerings and economies of scale to preserve producer incentives for innovation. There is no reason why health insurance should be treated differently, provided that other features of the regulatory structure ensure universal coverage of core services.

time in the production of medical care. As a rough but reasonable illustration, assume that a fifteen-minute physician visit entails at least two hours of patient time, including travel, in-office wait, and "interruption" time (to get back into the activity that was interrupted). Thus, if the average value of patient time is at least one-eighth the value of physician time, the real social cost of patient time in the production of physician services is at least equal to the measured cost of physician time. If so, health care "reforms" that constrain budget payments for physicians but generate higher patient time costs are likely to increase, not reduce, the real resource cost of health care, correctly measured as total forgone productivity in other activities for patients as well as providers.

All-payer rate regulation that requires all plans to use Medicare rates for all providers imposes a tax on patients with a relatively high value of time and those who would prefer to pay more to see a provider of their own choice. It may be objected that rate regulation does not preclude free choice of provider. But those providers who currently work their preferred number of hours at higher rates will face excess demand at lower rates. They may substitute more shorter visits to the extent feasible within volume controls. If a 20 percent cut in fees is offset by a 20 percent reduction in visit length and a 20 percent increase in visits, there is no saving in the health care budget costs. But there is an increase in patient time costs of roughly 20 percent because of the additional travel and waiting time required to make the extra visits. To the extent that these providers face excess demand, because the lower money price attracts more patients than are deterred by the increase in time price, then some other form of rationing must occur. If "gifts" (as in Japan) are deemed inappropriate, nonprice rationing mechanisms will become more widespread, including longer waits for appointments, preference to friends and colleagues, or a further increase in time prices to clear the market.[26]

In theory, a lower-bound estimate of the willingness of consumers to pay for the greater freedom of choice and time savings offered by indemnity plans can be obtained by measuring the difference in out-of-pocket payments (plus any premium differential) paid by those who elect indemnity plans over HMO options when faced with an unbiased choice (including employer contribution). This is a lower

---

[26]For further discussion of the hidden costs associated with nonprice rationing in Canada, see Patricia M. Danzon, "Hidden Costs of Budget-Constrained Health Insurance: Is Canada's System Really Cheaper?" *Health Affairs* (Spring 1992).

bound because indemnity plans entail patient time costs to file for reimbursement.

Another argument for price controls is that population density is too sparse in some areas to support competing health providers and plans, implying significant market power to providers in rural markets. The evidence that prices for medical services are generally lower, not higher, in rural areas than in urban areas with more competitors is prima facie inconsistent with this hypothesis. Again, however, the data are generally inadequate to determine how far these urban-rural price differentials reflect unmeasured quality differentials.

Global Budgets for Short-Run Cost Control? Some proponents advocate regulation of insurance premiums or medical prices as a temporary measure, to control costs until MNC becomes operational and effective at controlling costs.[27] This seems unnecessary and is likely to obstruct the efficient evolution of the health care system for the long run. Short-term price regulation is unnecessary because providers who anticipate the introduction of MNC have every incentive to adopt strategies to strengthen their own competitive position, cutting costs and prices to increase their bargaining position with health plans that will bid for consumer enrollees through HIPCs. Thus, whereas the expectation of a price freeze in some industries leads to an anticipatory price increase, a short-run price increase in anticipation of MNC would be a perverse, shortsighted strategy that few providers would be likely to adopt—and those that did would be unlikely to survive.

A temporary price freeze would be not only unnecessary but also counterproductive, since it would hamstring providers in preparing for the new environment. All-payer rate regulation at Medicare rates, for example, would constrain plans that wished to adopt new fee levels or relativities. If there is an HMO exemption, all-payer rate regulation might lead some plans to adopt capitation or salary forms of reimbursement to avoid the regulations, whereas their optimal unconstrained strategy might be a mixed reimbursement system, with fee-for-service subject to various withholds. All-payer rate regulation would necessarily add administrative costs for providers and insurers, which would be particularly wasteful if the controls are only temporary. Experience with prior price control programs shows that

---

[27]Another variant of this is that price regulation is a bargaining strategy to force providers into accepting system reform.

implementation and enforcement costs could be significant, particularly if the program permits appeals for exceptional circumstances.

Evidence from Other Countries

The experience of countries such as Germany and Canada is often mistakenly cited to support the argument that global budgets can control costs and increase efficiency. The hidden costs of these systems are considerable.[28] More generally, the potential costs and benefits of a spending limit depend on the context, in particular, on the extent to which the underlying system uses other competitive controls on moral hazard and incentives for efficiency.

No other country has attempted to superimpose aggregate spending limits on a system of competing private insurance providers. Spending caps in other countries have been applied to total spending on all core services only where the government is a monopoly insurer and provider, as in the United Kingdom and Sweden—and even there supplementary private insurance is outside the limit. A global budget for total core spending, when applied to a monopoly public system, is analogous to a limit on government spending. It is an essential component of efficient government budget allocation and does not rest on presumptions about failures of competitive private markets. In the absence of such a limit, providers and consumers would spend without any budget constraint, which violates the fundamental conditions necessary for efficient resource allocation. As argued above, a limit on health care spending *by the government* is an integral part of competitive reform proposals for the United States.

The spending limits often referred to as global budgets in other countries are more commonly limits on spending on either particular services—for example, physicians or inpatient hospital services—or particular providers—for example, global budget reimbursement for individual hospitals in Canada or France. Such service-specific spending limits distort incentives for efficient substitution among medical services that are included in different budgets. The German physician subject to a personal spending limit that includes drugs but not hospital care, for instance, has incentives to hospitalize a patient rather than use drug therapy, even if the drug therapy entails lower total social costs. The Canadian hospital subject to an annual spending limit has little incentive to maximize output, since increasing output raises costs but not revenues.

If there is a policy decision to forgo use of information or

---

[28]Danzon, "Hidden Costs of Budget-Constrained Health Insurance."

incentive-based restraints on moral hazard, it is possible that provider-specific or service-specific budgets may reduce the potential dead-weight loss from moral hazard. In fact, countries that have applied global budgets typically make very little use of copayments, information-based controls, or provider incentives to restrain incentives for overuse that are created by insurance. Global budgets for hospitals in France, for example, may be less inefficient than the per diem reimbursement system that they replaced. Global budgets for physician services in some Canadian provinces may reduce inefficiency, if judged against a status quo that paid unconstrained fee-for-service reimbursement, with a low fee schedule and no copayment or utilization review. Although provider-specific global budgets may be better than no controls on moral hazard, however, they are likely to be less efficient than the information and incentive-based strategies that have been developed in competitive insurance markets. A global budget is a very blunt instrument with perverse side effects; it is unnecessary and counterproductive if some of the more efficient moral hazard control strategies are adopted, as would be the case under a well-designed MNC structure.

Conclusion

A global budget applied to government expenditures on health care is perfectly consistent with and a necessary part of efficient health care reform. A cap on total spending on core benefits is unnecessary in a well-designed MNC system but may be innocuous if derived from a market-determined cost of core benefits and applied without constraints on supplementation. But a global budget that includes supplementary coverage and applies either an absolute ban or an implicit or explicit tax on supplementation is not innocuous. Such a limit on total insured health care spending lacks a convincing equity or efficiency rationale; it entails potentially high dead-weight costs, and it is likely to discriminate disproportionately against lower-income people who lack the means to pay for additional services out of pocket but who would have purchased supplementary coverage if it were available at actuarially fair rates. Similarly, a global budget in the form of all-payer rate regulation entails discrimination against consumers who prefer copayment to control moral hazard over restrictions on choice and provider-targeted incentives such as capitation. In particular, all-payer rate regulation discriminates against consumers who place a relatively high value on their time.

This analysis suggests that there is no strong efficiency rationale for a limit on total spending or for all-payer regulation of medical prices—indeed such policies entail significant consumption and production inefficiencies. If issues other than efficiency underlie the motivation for global budgets, then these issues should be clarified so that taxpayers can make informed choices. If a global budget is a supply-side attempt at cost control, adopted as a substitute for a cap on the employee tax exclusion, then the issue is, Would higher-income taxpayers prefer to pay a bit more for after-tax health insurance or have their access or choices rationed through an arbitrary limit that leaves real rationing power to the discretion of bureaucrats, managers, and providers, and entails higher time costs? If the spending cap is intended to be imposed over and above a cap on the employee tax exclusion, is it adopted because the majority of the public prefers and is willing to pay for a concept of equity that constrains everyone to the same level of health care, restricting the freedom of those who wish to purchase different or higher-quality care? If not, and the rationale is a belief that a cap can increase efficiency in insurance and health care markets, would people prefer to be denied the freedom to choose plans that offer more choice for higher copayments (subject to a stop-loss)? Until these questions of why a global budget cap is necessary or desirable have been clearly posed and answered, the discussions of how to implement a cap seem premature.

Appendix 4–A: Effects of a Cap on the Deductibility of Employer Contributions to Employee Health Insurance

The effects of changing the tax treatment of employer contributions to health insurance can be analyzed in the context of a standard model of labor market equilibrium with noncash job attributes. Assume that workers' utility depends on after-tax cash income $W(1-t^p)$ and health coverage K, where K is the monetary equivalent of a given health benefits plan. Workers choose among jobs based on the compensation packages offered. Employers select the mix of cash wages and health coverage to minimize their after-tax total labor cost. Market equilibrium involves the sorting of workers among firms.[29]

---

[29]Sherwin Rosen, "Hedonic Prices and Implicit Markets," *Journal of Political Economy*, vol. 82 (1974), pp. 34–55; G. S. Goldstein and Mark V. Pauly, "Group Health Insurance as a Local Public Good," in Richard N. Rosett, ed., *The Role of Health Insurance in the Health Services Sector*, (New York: National Bureau of Economic Research, 1976); and Patricia M. Danzon, "Mandated Employment-Based Health Insurance: Incidence and Efficiency Effects," mimeograph (1989).

With a sufficiently large number of firms, market equilibrium involves sorting of workers into groups that are homogeneous with respect to their preferences over W and K. With heterogeneous employee preferences within a single firm, the number of plans offered depends on fixed costs.

To keep things simple and without loss of generality for showing effects of tax changes, consider a firm that hires workers with homogeneous preferences for W and K and offers only a single health plan. The representative worker's utility function is additive in W and K. The objective function for the firm is to minimize total labor cost, subject to the constraint that the compensation package must provide the level of utility necessary to attract the required number of workers, $\overline{U}$:

$$\operatorname*{Min}_{W,K} C = W(1-t^c) + p\overline{K}(1-t^c) + p(K-\overline{K})(1-t^c)$$
$$- \lambda[U[W(1-t^p) + K] - \overline{U}] \tag{4--A1}$$

where C = employer's total after-tax labor cost

t^c = corporate tax rate

t^p = personal tax rate

$\overline{K}$ = mandatory minimum health coverage (core benefits)

U = utility of representative worker

p = price per dollar of coverage ≥ 1

The Status Quo—No Taxation of K. The first-order conditions for cost minimization are:

$$C_W = (1-t_c) - \lambda U_W (1-t^p) = 0$$
$$\text{or} \qquad (1-t^c) = \lambda U_W (1-t^p) \tag{4--A2}$$

$$C_K = p(1-t^c) - \lambda U_K = 0$$
$$\text{or} \qquad p(1-t^c) = \lambda U_K \tag{4--A3}$$

Rearranging equations (4–A2) and (4–A3) yields

$$\frac{U_K}{U_W} = p(1-t^p)$$

The tax exclusion for K implies that the marginal rate of substitution is equated to the private cost of coverage, which is less than the real social cost if $t^p > 0$. If $p(1-t^p) < 1$, the effective loading charge is negative.

A Cap on Employer Tax Deductibility. If contributions $K > \overline{K}$ are not tax deductible for the employer but are tax exempt for employees, the first-order condition if $K > \overline{K}$ is

$$p = \lambda U_K \tag{4-A4}$$

Substituting from (4–A2),

$$\frac{U_K}{U_W} = \frac{p(1-t^p)}{(1-t^c)} \tag{4-A5}$$

Thus, a cap on the employer tax deduction, combined with an open-ended exemption for the employee, implies a marginal effective subsidy for $K > \overline{K}$ if $t^p > t^c$.

Appendix 4–B: Effect of Premium Regulation on Mix of Insurance Benefits

Assume that an insurance plan can provide a vector of medical services X, where the xth component of X could be an additional service, an amenity, or other dimension of quality. The plan can employ a vector of cost-control strategies Z, where the zth component could be a coinsurance rate, a more stringent utilization control, or a provider incentive to reduce services. The insurance inverse demand function is $P(Q, X, Z)$, where Q is the number of policies sold, with P_q, $P_z < 0$ and $P_x > O$. The insurance cost function is $C(X,Z)Q$, with $C_x > 0$, $C_z < O$. The insurer selects the mix of X and Z to maximize net revenues or profit. The insurer's objective function is:

$$\underset{X,Z}{\text{Max }} R = P(Q, X, Z)Q - C(X, Z)Q + \Gamma[\overline{P} - P(Q, X, Z)]$$

where Γ is a Lagrange multiplier. In the absence of a premium cap, $\Gamma = 0$ and the first-order conditions are:

$$R_x = Q(P_x - C_x) = 0$$
$$\text{or} \qquad P_x = C_x \tag{4-B1}$$
$$R_z = Q(P_z - C_z) = 0$$
$$\text{or} \qquad P_z = C_z \tag{4-B2}$$
$$R_Q = P_Q Q + (P - C) = 0$$

With a binding premium cap $P = \overline{P}$, $\Gamma > 0$ and the Lagrangian yields the first order conditions:

$$R_x = Q(P_x - C_x) - \Gamma P_x = 0$$
$$\text{or} \qquad P_x(Q - \Gamma) = QC_x \tag{4-B3}$$
$$R_z = Q(P_z - C_z) - \Gamma P_z = 0$$
$$\text{or} \qquad P_z(Q - \Gamma) = QC_x \tag{4-B4}$$

From equations (4–B1) and (4–B2), the unconstrained equilibrium mix of X and Z equates consumers' marginal rate of substitution to the marginal rate of transformation:

$$\frac{P_x}{P_z} = \frac{C_x}{C_z}$$

From equations (4–B3) and (4–B4) with the total premium constraint, this equilibrium condition is preserved:

$$\frac{P_x(Q - \Gamma)}{P_z(Q - \Gamma)} = \frac{P_x}{P_z} = \frac{C_x}{C_z}$$

Thus a cap on premiums does not affect the relative mix of services and controls if preferences and cost functions are homothetic.

If preferences and cost functions reflect true social values, then premium regulation does not distort efficiency in the mix of insured benefits, although it does affect the total level of spending. If preferences or cost functions do not reflect true social values, however, then premium regulation will not necessarily reduce the resulting distortions in the mix of insured services, since premium regulation does not correct any distortions in the underlying demand and cost functions.

5

Rent Seeking, Global Budgets, and the Managed-Competition Cartel

Henry N. Butler

One of the most dramatic statistics used to demonstrate the need for health care reform in the United States is the rapid increase in the percentage of gross domestic product devoted to health care. In 1950, Americans spent only $12 billion or 4.4 percent of GDP on health care, most of which was paid by private insurers or patients themselves. By 1990, expenditures had climbed to $653 billion or 11.9 percent of GDP. Health care expenditures approached 14 percent of GDP in 1992 and, unless some change occurs, may exceed 18 percent of GDP in the year 2000.[1] These statistics have helped move health care reform to the forefront of public policy debates.[2] Concern about

---

[1] Congressional Budget Office, "Projections of National Health Expenditures" (October 1992).

[2] Some health care economists suggest that the health care cost-containment crisis may be overstated. See Joseph P. Newhouse, "An Iconoclastic View of Health Care Cost Containment," *Health Affairs*, vol. 12, supp. (1993), pp. 152–71. Of course, equally dramatic figures about the large numbers of uninsured measures have been used to add fuel to the debate. The Department of Health and Human Services estimates that 37 million Americans can no longer afford even the most basic health insurance. The vast majority of these uninsured individuals (78 percent) either work for themselves or live in families with a full-time worker. Most of the uninsured (60 percent) work in small businesses with fewer than 100 employees.

the percentage of GDP provides the impetus for a potential policy solution: if we believe that we are spending too much on health care, government policy should mandate that we halt the increase in health care expenditures. One way to achieve that goal is to have the government order a cap on total expenditures, which would be implemented through an enforceable "global budget."

Thus, the idea of a global health care budget is appealing for its simplicity and head-on approach to what is perceived as the major problem with our health care system—too much of our nation's income is spent on health care. Unfortunately, the aggregate problem results from the complex interaction of numerous forces—the adjustments of a dynamic market in health care, income tax policies, federalism and the interaction of state and federal government policies, changes in the legal system, the influence of special-interest groups, and so forth. On this basis alone, we should all be skeptical about the prospects for success of such a simple-sounding solution.

Proponents of a global budget to control health care expenditures, however, recognize that it is not a simple solution, but rather a simple goal. They propose the creation of an elaborate managed-competition system to plan from the top down the control of health care expenditures. In general, managed competition within a global budget appears to be a technocratic, bureaucratic dream come true. Much attention has been paid to what the organization of the health care system would look like but little attention to how it would work in daily practice. Those with a lot of faith in bureaucrats to solve problems and to act for the common good may not be worried. A large body of evidence about bureaucratic incentives and bureaucratic behavior, however, suggests that managed competition within a global budget would create bloated bureaucracies that would stifle any possibility of meaningful competition and, consequently, lead to either higher expenditures or lower quality or both.

On top of the internal bureaucratic problems of the global budget system is the apparent disregard of the political realities of setting the global budget. The dynamics of interest-group politics cannot be ignored. Because seemingly minor bureaucratic decisions can have enormous impact on the wealth of various well-organized interest groups, these groups will lobby Congress and state legislatures to adjust the expenditure allocations within the budget limits to benefit themselves. The health care regulators, no matter how benevolent, will be unable to divorce their decision making from the political process.

The political activity of interest groups seeking special favors from legislators and other government decision makers is referred to as rent seeking, and the excessive profits earned by interest groups as a result of their political activity are referred to as rents.[3] The annual global budget-setting process, for example, would involve vigorous lobbying as various provider groups attempted to increase the size of their slice of the health care budget. Not only is this expensive in terms of real resources wasted on political rent seeking (and, of course, these wasted resources are not counted in any version of a global budget), but, as this chapter demonstrates, the combination of political and bureaucratic direction of resources dooms global budgeting—and its attendant managed-competition scheme—to failure.

This chapter considers the political economy of a fully implemented global-budgeting program in the United States. The first part summarizes the arguments in favor of a global budget, speculates about how a global budget would be made operational through managed competition, considers how global a global budget would be, and raises some general conceptual problems with the global budget concept, ranging from simplistic treatment of symptoms instead of the causes of escalating costs to concerns about price controls and the allocation of resources.

The second part introduces the public choice perspective adopted in this chapter—the view of a skeptical cynic informed by numerous economic studies of the behavior of bureaucracy and the influence of interest groups. Emphasis is placed on the political forces that might come into play if an industry representing more than 14 percent of GDP is suddenly subjected to government-imposed spending limits. In general, we should never underestimate the creativity and entrepreneurial ability of interest groups, politicians, and bureaucrats to

---

[3]Rent seeking is harmful to society because it results in two types of social costs. First, the political allocation of special privileges harms society through the misallocation of resources and the resulting deadweight loss of monopoly. Second, the potential for government-conferred rents leads interest groups to use resources to capture those rents through the political process. Such rent-seeking expenditures attempt to transfer wealth from one group to another. This use of scarce resources represents a social loss, because the resources could have been used for productive purposes instead of merely dividing up the economic pie. Gordon Tullock, "The Welfare Costs of Tariffs, Monopoly, and Theft," *Western Economic Journal* (June 1967); Richard A. Posner, "The Social Costs of Monopoly and Regulation," *Journal of Political Economy*, vol. 83 (1975), p. 807; and, generally, James Buchanan, Robert Tollison, and Gordon Tullock, eds., *Toward a Theory of the Rent-Seeking Society* (College Station: Texas A&M University Press, 1980).

exploit every conceivable opportunity for profit created by health care reform.

The third part offers a unified rent-seeking interpretation of the proposal for managed competition within a global budget. It is argued that the political determination of the benchmark benefits package, the mechanism set up for pricing the package, and the role of the states in administering the managed competition and a global budget can be viewed as an elaborate rent-seeking and rent-extraction system.

A final part offers some thoughts on the political viability of managed competition within a global budget. In general, and without endorsing the concept of managed competition, the combination of managed competition and global budgeting is a bad idea because a global budget will necessarily short-circuit the competitive pressures generated by managed competition. A global budget forces competition out of health care markets and into the political arena. The primary implication of the analysis in this chapter is that a global budget will not work, will kill managed competition, and will cause health care costs to increase. The stakes are high because if managed competition within a global budget system fails, it is likely to be replaced by a system with even more government control. The bottom line is that those who like managed competition should abhor the global budget.

Global Health Care Budgets

The basic case for a system of global health care budgets is that controlling total expenditures is the only effective way to control costs. Thus, a global health care budget is a statutorily imposed expenditure ceiling on the nation's total health care outlays.[4] This

---

[4]The concept of a global budget appears to have different meanings to different policy analysts and certainly has different meanings in different countries. Some proponents of global budgets, for example, refer to the application of global budgets to specific aspects of the health care delivery system such as a single hospital or all hospitals within a particular region. Other proponents of global budgets, though, clearly suggest that adoption of their plan would mean one big budget for all health care expenditures in the United States. These definitions of global budgets are not necessarily inconsistent because a comprehensive global budget for the United States would include specific "global" budgets for states and perhaps smaller areas. Nevertheless, whatever the precise meaning of a global budget, the common denominator is the presence of binding aggregate spending limits.

part summarizes and offers a critique of the case for a global budget and how it could be made operational through managed competition:

- First, the model of "managed competition within a global budget," based on the work of Paul Starr and Walter Zelman, is explained.[5] Although their model of managed competition builds on the one developed by Paul Ellwood and Alain Enthoven,[6] it differs in a number of respects because of Starr and Zelman's emphasis on the global budget.
- Second is a consideration of just how "global" (or inclusive) the global budget contemplated by global budget advocates is likely to be. An analysis of this area suggests that the goal of implementation of a global budget is often used to justify expanded government control of health care.
- Third is a discussion of some general conceptual problems with the model of managed competition within a global budget.

Managed Competition within a Global Budget. The definitive proposal on global budgeting has been put forth by Paul Starr and Walter Zelman. They envision a global budget system that is made operational by managed competition.[7] The imposition and administration

---

[5]See Paul Starr and Walter A. Zelman, "A Bridge to Compromise: Competition under a Budget," *Health Affairs*, vol. 12, supp. (1993), pp. 7–23, and Paul Starr, *The Logic of Health-Care Reform* (Knoxville, Tenn.: Grand Rounds Press, Whittle Direct Books, 1992).

[6]P. M. Ellwood, A. C. Enthoven, and L. Etheredge, "The Jackson Hole Initiatives for a Twenty-First Century American Health Care System," *Health Economics*, vol. 1 (1992), pp. 149–68.

[7]Starr and Zelman summarize their proposal: "Managed competition under a cap, as we envision it, involves new relations between the federal government and the states, between the public and private sectors, and between health care finance and health service delivery. The federal government would establish the framework of the new system but allow the states the flexibility in implementing it. Under federal law, all American citizens would be guaranteed the right to a comprehensive set of benefits, defined in general terms by legislation and interpreted and adjusted over time by a National Health Board. The federal government would require all individuals and employers, except perhaps the very smallest, to share the cost of health insurance. All—except, most likely, employees of large firms—would obtain coverage through new regional health insurance purchasing cooperatives (HIPCs).

"These purchasing cooperatives—the central innovation of the model—would neither deliver health care nor pay providers. Rather, they would contract with varied health plans, including health mainte-

of the budget constraints would be through state governments and intrastate networks of health insurance purchasing cooperatives. The HIPC, a public authority set up under a state commission, would contract with various health maintenance organizations and other managed-care plans. Under most plans, HIPCs would collect all revenue that had previously been paid as insurance premiums or, in the most inclusive plans, had been paid as Medicaid and Medicare payments. The pooling of the risk would be communitywide, and everyone would get health insurance through the same system. The managed-care health plans would be owned and run by insurance companies, provider groups, other businesses, and consumer cooperatives. All HMOs and other managed-care plans would be required to offer a standard benefit package, determined by a national health board, and the HIPC would pay the plans the lowest price charged by a plan for a given risk pool.

The competition in this plan comes from the proposition that consumers would be allowed to choose among different health plans at different prices. Although all plans would provide the standard benefit package, there could be price and nonprice competition among plans over selection of providers, convenience, and quality. The managed part of this plan is that each HIPC would have an expert staff to manage the competition through negotiation with the plans over price and quality. The most important part of the management of the competition would be the negotiation with the plans for the price of the standard benefits plan and the monitoring of the allocation of HIPC payments to health plans according to the risk of a particular plan's pool of insureds.

The central role of HIPCs in the managed-competition scheme provides the basis for imposition and administration of a global budget. The Starr-Zelman proposal, for example, would focus on per

---

nance organizations (HMOs), preferred provider organizations (PPOs), and one free-choice-of-provider option. The plans would be paid by capitation (although many plans would pay their physicians by other methods, including both salary and fee-for-service). Once a year, the HIPC would give every consumer the opportunity to choose a plan under the following principles of managed competition.

(1) *Open enrollment.* . . .

(2) *Standard, comprehensive benefit package.* . . .

(3) *Routine quality measurement.* . . .

(4) *Contribution pegged to the low-cost benchmark plan.* . . .

(5) *Community-rated premiums charged to the enrollees, risk-adjusted premiums paid to the plans* . . ." (Starr and Zelman, "Bridge to Compromise," pp. 9–10).

capita rates for health care coverage, as established by the HIPCs. Those rates would be set in the marketplace created by the HIPCs and would be largely paid by employers. The government would then determine a maximum allowable rate of increase in benchmark premiums each year. HIPCs that failed to keep their rate of increases under control would come under scrutiny by either the state or the federal government. Poorly performing HIPCs would be subject to strict regulatory controls or could even be disbanded if they were not able to keep prices in line.

Most of the policy discussions of global budgeting in the United States are theoretical discussions dealing with allocation of authority within newly designed managed-competition systems or institutions. Unfortunately, there is little systematic literature about the experiences of other nations with global budgets and their daily operations.[8] Although the theories are well developed, in the sense of addressing most obvious policy questions and challenges, the actual implementation of a global budget is sure to have numerous surprises and administrative difficulties.

How Global Is It? The phrase *global budget* has many potential meanings, but one would expect that some precision about the meaning of the phrase could be determined from its use in the current policy context. Much of the debate over the need for health care reform has focused on the larger percentage of GDP that is being spent on health care—where health care expenditures include both public and private expenditures. Thus, for a global budget to address that immediate policy concern, it must cover private as well as public expenditures on health care. That is, an effective global health care budget would limit the growth of all health care expenditures to some predetermined rate. And, of course, to reduce the rate of increase of such expenditures as a percentage of GDP, the global budget's growth rate must be held to the growth rate of the economy.

At first sight, the idea of an inclusive global budget for all health care expenditures may not seem extraordinary. Perhaps we should impose a global budget on health expenditures because it is good public administration to have such a budget. After all, we have budgets for all publicly provided services, such as education, national defense, and so forth. The problem with this reasoning is that most

---

[8]See Patrice R. Wolfe and Donald R. Moran, "Global Budgeting in OECD Countries," prepared for the assistant secretary for planning and evaluation, Department of Health and Human Services (draft, August 1, 1992), p. 24.

health care spending is outside the government's control, and it would be very difficult to decide where to draw the line on what goes in the budget (should we include the costs of running health clubs?). Moreover, there are tremendous data collection problems. Data on national health expenditures, geographical expenditures, or individual physicians or hospitals are not sufficient to set realistic budget target amounts to providers. Since the U.S. health care system contains a large component of private nongovernmental spending, even the often-quoted statistics on national health expenditures are a collection of estimates based on a large variety of data sources. Under an all-encompassing global-budgeting system, the estimation of these statistics would become a contentious issue, subject to both political and special interest manipulation.

In implicit recognition of these types of problems, Starr and Zelman have opted for a less ambitious and less inclusive global budget:

> The budget for a region could be defined in at least four ways: (1) the benchmark premium times the total number of enrollees; (2) total premiums paid to all plans, including out-of-pocket premium payments for higher-cost plans; (3) total spending on covered benefits for all eligible individuals (that is, premiums plus out-of-pocket payments for services); and (4) total spending on health care for covered and uncovered services. Of these four budget alternatives, the first has a special significance because it identifies government, employer, and individual obligations. All other spending would be with out-of-pocket (preferably after-tax) dollars. Thus, if a global budget cap were interpreted as limiting the growth of benchmark premiums, it would focus policy on the mandated core of health spending.[9]

This "mandated core of health spending" falls short of one of the primary goals of health care reform—reducing or controlling the increase in total health care spending as a percentage of GDP.

Controlling a portion of total health care spending could conceivably reduce the rate of increase in total health care spending, provided that cost shifting and other forms of cross-subsidization can be

---

[9]Starr and Zelman, "Bridge to Compromise," p. 19. Alain Enthoven, a harsh critic of global budgets, appears to offer his support of such a limited global budget in a recent article. See Enthoven, "The History and Principles of Managed Competition," *Health Affairs*, vol. 12, supp. (1993), p. 43: "These would be market-determined global budgets and would encompass all publicly supported and tax-subsidized national health expenditures."

prevented (presumably, by more regulation). Concentrating on controlling the mandated core of health spending, however, presents two problems (in addition to not addressing the problem as advertised). First, it is not at all clear that the mandated core of health spending is the area of health spending where most savings can be realized. Second, the pursuit of a more effective global-budgeting program may become a goal rather than the means to health care cost containment. That is, global budgets tend to get a life of their own. The fact that the global budget envisioned by its leading proponents does not include all health care expenditures means that the mandatory extension of managed competition to businesses is necessary for global budgeting to have a better chance of controlling health care costs: "The higher the proportion of health expenditures passing through the HIPCs, the easier global budgets will be to set and enforce."[10] Mandating participation in the HIPCs reflects Starr and Zelman's lack of faith in the ability of managed-competition plans to attract most employers to the managed-competition plan voluntarily.[11]

General Conceptual Problems. Many policy analysts are skeptical of

---

[10]Starr and Zelman, "Bridge to Compromise," p. 14.

[11]But this observation does not stop them from penalizing firms that want to purchase health care through an HIPC: "If larger firms can join HIPCs voluntarily, the firms that do so will tend to have higher-than-average costs. The problem of adverse selection will be especially severe if these firms are offered the purchasing cooperatives' community rates. Hence, if the purchasing cooperatives are voluntary for some class of employers, any employer from that class that wants to join must be given a risk-adjusted rate" (ibid., p. 15).

This statement reflects some interesting reasoning. First, the authors ignore several explanations totally unrelated to risk for why an employer might voluntarily join an HIPC: (1) an employer might use the HIPC as an opportunity to scale back the benefits provided to employees; (2) the HIPC per employee premium might be less than the employer's previous premium because of the higher administrative costs of the employer's plan (compared with the heralded and great administrative cost savings that accompany managed competition). Second, the rationale for charging a higher risk-adjusted rate for firms that voluntarily enroll in an HIPC suggests that firms that are mandated to enroll in an HIPC should be given a lower risk-adjusted rate on the ground that they had to be forced to join because they could receive lower premium rates without the HIPC's assistance. Surely, an HIPC would not want to be accused of cherry picking! Obviously, attempts by policy analysts to anticipate and solve every problem in advance leads to extreme micromanagement of the programs.

the fundamental concept of global health care budgets. Some of the more important objections are summarized below.

Treating symptoms. The adoption of a global health care budget is intended to solve our health care problems. Unfortunately, the superficial treatment of the symptoms will do nothing to address the underlying inefficiencies and perverse incentives that have caused the explosion of health care expenditures under the current system.[12] Moreover, because some of the underlying causes are the result of ill-conceived federal and state policies that have priced many workers out of the market for health insurance, it would seem reasonable to address these underlying problems directly before addressing them indirectly with a global budget.

Global health care budgets fail to address at least six important areas.

• First, expensive technological advances have surely caused some of the increase in health care costs. Expensive equipment is used to conduct tests that result in the diagnosis of problems that would not have been spotted at a treatable stage in the past. The increased expenditures save many lives and thus result in a higher standard of living.

• Second, the demographics of the American population point toward higher health care expenditures in future years as our population ages. Thus, a global budget will probably be faced with increasing costs from sources beyond the control of mere budgetary magic.

• Third, the federal tax code contributes to the increased cost of health care by permitting employers to provide employees an unlimited package of health benefits tax free. Many companies give complete first-dollar coverage and a wide array of benefits tax free to their employees. This generosity takes away employees' incentives to act as consumers of health care.[13] As a result, employees with extensive

---

[12]For a critique of the conventional arguments about the causes of escalating health care costs, see Newhouse, "An Iconoclastic View of Health Cost Containment."

[13]Paul Starr recognizes that lack of direct consumer involvement in buying health care has caused part of the explosion in costs: "Imagine that no money were taken from Americans' paychecks and taxes to pay for health care and instead each family received an annual, lump-sum bill for its prorated share of the nation's health expenditures. For 1991, with per capita costs at nearly $2,700, the bill would have been more than $10,000 for a family of four. Under such a system, it is inconceivable that health costs would have been allowed to grow to their present scale" (Starr, *The Logic of Health-Care Reform*).

coverage have little incentive to price shop or economize on health care expenditures, placing additional inflationary pressure on the system.[14]

• Fourth, the federal government placed additional burdens on states during the 1980s by expanding Medicaid coverage for the poor without voting the funds to pay for the expansion.

• Fifth, medical malpractice costs—both the direct costs of insurance, litigation, and settlements and the indirect costs of defensive medicine—are alleged to play a significant role in the rapid growth of health care spending.

• Sixth, the proliferation of state mandates on health insurance coverage also contributes to rising costs and helps price health insurance beyond the means of many Americans.[15] State mandates are simply concessions to special interests to force consumers to buy coverage for specific diseases or medical practices whether it is needed or wanted.

Finally, the explosion of health care costs is not a result of market failure but rather the direct result of major government-imposed distortions of basic market forces. For years, government policies have subsidized demand through tax incentives and restricted supply

---

Instead of using this logic to argue that health care costs can be contained by making consumers feel more of the pain, Starr argues that there should be even greater separation from consumers' pocketbooks through the imposition of a global budget and managed competition.

The favorable tax treatment of health insurance benefits also protects physicians from price competition for their services. See Peter Zweifel, "Protecting the Medical Profession," in H. E. Frech III, ed., *Regulating Doctors' Fees: Competition, Benefits, and Controls under Medicare* (Washington, D.C.: AEI Press, 1991), pp. 91–96.

[14]A RAND Corporation study found that people who had access to free health care used about 50 percent more health care services than those who had to pay the bill out of their own pocket. Remarkably, with the exception of vision care and high blood pressure, there were no discernible differences between the two groups with respect to health outcomes. Moreover, using insurance to pay for small health bills is wasteful, costing physicians an average of $8 per insurance claim. Insurance companies spend another $8 average for each reimbursement check written. Insurance policies with low or no deductibles are not really health insurance, but a prepayment plan for the consumption of routine medical care. See Robert Brook et al., *The Effect of Coinsurance on the Health of Adults* (Santa Monica, Calif.: RAND, 1984).

[15]Gail A. Jensen, "Regulating the Content of Health Plans," in Robert B. Helms, ed., *American Health Policy: Critical Issues for Reform* (Washington, D.C.: AEI Press, 1993), pp. 167–93.

through licensing regulations. The combined effect of these distortions is unambiguous—higher prices.

The specter of price controls. The conceptual criticism that global budgets treat the symptoms instead of the causes of escalating costs harks back to President Nixon's wage and price controls in the early 1970s, which were designed to stop inflation by simply commanding that the symptoms go away—that is, commanding that prices could not increase. In general, such efforts cannot possibly succeed in the long run (which may not be far off). In this regard, a global budget will likely result in price controls.

A binding global budget ceiling on total health care spending would impose lower total spending under the restraints than in the absence of the restraints. This reduction would come from a combination of at least three sources: lower prices, reduced use of services, and substitution of alternative, lower-cost services. Initially, to the extent that some of the current use of medical services is distorted by problems in the system, this response might be preferable to the existing bundle of health care services preferred by American consumers. This best-case scenario, however, is unlikely to prevail over successive years of effective global budget ceilings—there is a limit to how much fat or inefficiency can be squeezed out of the system, and surely the potential savings are subject to diminishing returns in subsequent budgets. In other words, it would be a mistake to assume that the savings generated by the initial imposition of effective ceilings could be found again in the future. Nevertheless, the pressure to keep the growth of health expenditures below some prespecified level will require the global budget to impose successively tighter grips on total spending.

As a consequence, there will not be sufficient flexibility in spending to attract the right combination of quantity and price for many services. That is, either prices will be too high, or prices will be held down so that the quantity of services supplied will be too low. In either case, some insureds will have to go without the care. Over time, a global budget will necessarily result in the same problems caused by explicit, direct price controls. The arbitrariness of this approach suggests that a global budget will be incredibly unpopular. At some point, for example, the global budget decisions will affect individual decision makers and, in effect, tell them that they cannot spend their own money on something they want.

Price controls are condemned because they are superficial and worse than ineffective.[16] The standard microeconomic effects are well-

---

[16]For a good summary of the adverse effects of price controls and global

known—the imposition of a price ceiling below the market-clearing price will result in excess demand, because consumers will demand quantities greater than producers are willing to supply. The excess demand will be relieved through nonprice rationing such as queuing or illegal side payments or political favors. Thus, although they appear to solve a problem, price controls involve numerous hidden costs as suppliers search for creative ways to meet consumer demand while complying with the letter of the law.[17]

Global budget proponents appear to be sensitive to these criticisms of price fixing, and they go out of their way to claim that a global budget will not result in price controls.[18] This has led to some

---

budgets, see Edmund F. Haislmaier, "Why Global Budgets and Price Controls Will Not Curb Health Costs," *Heritage Backgrounder* (March 8, 1993). For a historical examination of price controls, see Robert L. Schuettinger and Eamonn F. Butler, *Forty Centuries of Wage and Price Controls: How Not to Fight Inflation* (Washington, D.C.: Heritage Foundation, 1979).

[17]See, for example, C. Jackson Grayson, Jr., "Experience Talks: Shun Price Controls," *Wall Street Journal*, March 29, 1993; Republican Staff Report, "A Global Budget Fix for U.S. Health Care?" House Committee on the Budget, vol. 2, no. 8 (July 21, 1992); and from a study of price controls by Jon Gabel and Thomas Rice: "During previous periods of U.S. price controls, health care providers responded by increasing the volume of services. The services provided after controls are imposed are frequently not comparable to those supplied before. Office visits may be shorter, more tests may be undertaken for a given ailment, care may be provided in a less efficient but more remunerative manner. As a result, *price* controls do not translate into *cost* control" (emphasis in original) ("Reducing Public Expenditures for Physician Services: The Price of Paying Less," *Journal of Health Politics, Policy, and Law* [Winter 1985], pp. 595–609).

[18]For example, Paul Starr has stressed that global budgeting need not result in price controls: "The federal role in health care can be less extensive than it is today. My view is that the federal government should prescribe broad minimum criteria for acceptable universal insurance programs to be organized by the states and offer part of the financing to help carry out the programs. In addition to continuing to pay for Medicare beneficiaries, the federal government would subsidize the inclusion of low-income consumers in a mainstream standard of coverage. As the new system was phased in, the federal government would abolish Medicaid and provide support for universal coverage in fixed per capita contributions, graduated according to income. The funds might go to the states or directly to consumers in the form of vouchers redeemable through HIPCs. Unlike entitlement programs, the cost to the federal government would not depend on the volume or type of health services used. *Under this system, the federal government would have no relation with the specific providers; it would not set hospital rates or physician payment policies*" (emphasis added) (*The Logic of Health-Care Reform*, pp. 68–69).

disingenuous arguments. Paul Starr, for example, has attempted to deflect the price-controls criticism by arguing that a federally imposed global budget would not result in federal price fixing, although the states should have the power to regulate rates and prices if necessary for them to comply with the federal global budget.[19] In spite of this delegation to states of the option of imposing price controls, the states will be hard pressed to avoid rate and price ceilings once they are faced with a federally imposed global budget. Thus, a binding global budget constraint—with attendant price controls—will necessarily result in some nonprice rationing of health care services.

Starr and Zelman also attempt to disguise the price ceiling aspect of their recent proposal. Under their proposal, HIPC per capita rates would be set in the "marketplace," but the government would then determine a "maximum allowable rate of increase in the benchmark premiums each year."[20] Limiting the rate of increase in the premiums is a price control. If the limit is effective—that is, if it prevents rates from rising as fast as the market-determined rates would rise—then all the well-documented problems with price controls will become the overriding characteristics of our health care system. If the budget controls actually reduce health care expenditures, for example, then political battles will erupt as plans lobby to reduce costs by changing the definition of the benchmark benefits plan.

In fact, the potential for a global budget to result in all the distortions normally associated with price controls implies that bureaucratic management of price and quantity are a necessary part of any global budget.[21] In this regard, the managed-competition propos-

---

This is a clever way to address the concern that a global budget might result in some type of price controls.

[19]Ibid., p. 69: "Together, the federal and state governments would determine the revenues available to the HIPCs, which would then contract with the various health plans. In effect, this puts the health care system on global budgets (although, again, it does allow consumers to put in extra money to buy an option more expensive than the low-cost plan). Except for Medicare, which would necessarily have to be phased into the new system over time, the federal government and the states could get completely out of the business of determining reimbursement levels, leaving them to be negotiated privately by the plans and the providers. The federal government would neither regulate the rates of providers nor bar the states from doing so; whether to deregulate provider prices is a choice the states should make based on their varied circumstances."

[20]Starr and Zelman, "Bridge to Compromise," p. 19.

[21]Two global budget proposals introduced in 1992 rely on the price-setting methodology currently used under the Medicare programs. See,

als when coupled with a global budget necessarily become methods to counteract the disincentives created by the budget constraints. Given the unambiguously sorry history of price controls, a global budget would quite likely lead to highly bureaucratic controls on each state's spending and on each type of medical procedure. The result will be one huge bureaucratic nightmare, with competition managed out of the health care system and into the political arena.

Misallocation of resources. Market forces provide accurate and reliable signals about the relative value of resources and their highest-valued uses. Market forces currently guide some of the allocation of resources devoted to health care, and the general presumption should be that they guide those resources to their most highly valued uses. Although health care prices are distorted by a large government presence and tax-induced perversions of insurance policies and health care markets could work much better if consumers were better informed and had stronger incentives to act as consumers do in other markets, it would be a grave mistake to ignore or destroy the valuable information provided by health care markets. But the requirement that a politically determined global budget must supersede market prices has enormous consequences for the allocation of resources.[22]

The idea of a global health care budget implicitly assumes that the government—whether a commission of experts, a regulatory agency, or even elected officials—can somehow determine the cor-

---

for example, bills proposing the Health Care Cost Containment and System Reform Act of 1992 (H.R. 5502) and the Health Choices Act of 1992 (H.R. 5514). Under Medicare, hospital fees are based on diagnosis-related groups, and physician fees are based on the resource-based relative value scale.

[22]See Newhouse, "Iconoclastic View," p. 167. Richard Kronick offers the following assessment: "Insisting on the imposition of federally determined targets for expenditure growth may result in welfare losses. If the targets are too high, then they may serve as a floor as well as a ceiling and result in greater expenditure growth than would have occurred without them. If the targets are too low, the result may be fewer resources devoted to health care than might be optimal. Further, an insistence on rigid targets in the short run will lead in many states to the introduction of controls on the unit prices charged by physicians and hospitals; the political, bureaucratic, and provider attention that imposing and implementing these controls will require will inhibit the development of organized delivery systems and result, in the medium run, in a health care system that only slowly, if at all, produces increased value for money spent ("Where Should the Buck Stop: Federal and State Responsibilities in Health Care Financing Reform," *Health Affairs*, vol. 12, supp. [1993], p. 92).

rect, or optimal, amount that should be spent on health care. But this determination can be made only by fiat, since it is impossible for policy makers to take account of the variety of factors that influence aggregate health care expenditures—the size and age of the population, the services demanded by patients, and the technological possibilities for new products and procedures.

It is impossible to know the efficient allocation of a total budget across patients, geographical areas, and types of services. In addition, if a national target were selected, the total amount would have to be allocated by giving a budget for total expenditures to each state; each state would then have to allocate its budget to HIPCs and then down to individual hospitals, physicians, or managed-care or insurance plans. Finally, even if some miracle occurred and national policy makers selected the exactly correct total for the aggregate spending under the global budget system,[23] the time the national edict would take to work its way through the system would allow for numerous misallocations caused by errors of commission and omission and by political manipulation.

Too much management, not enough competition. Because some type of managed-competition system is at the heart of a global budget, the concept of managed competition must be analyzed in the context of conceptual concerns about the global budget. Alain Enthoven and others have spent a great deal of time designing and thinking their way through the managed-competition model of health care delivery. They are confident that managed competition will work:

> All of the pieces of the managed care/managed competition model are in actual successful practice somewhere. The challenge is to put these best practices together into one complete managed competition system. The rest is extrapolation based on generally accepted principles of rational economic behavior.[24]

The problem with this logic is that it commits a fallacy of composition—the pieces of the managed-competition model that work in isolation may not work when combined with the other pieces. As an example, Enthoven states that "we know that HIPC-like arrangements work well."[25] But we have no real basis for believing that they will work well when most of the health care expenditures in the

---

[23]It is important to recognize that the policy makers would never know that they got it right!

[24]Enthoven, "Managed Competition," p. 45.

[25]Ibid.

United States are channeled through them.

The combination of a global budget with managed competition suggests a lack of faith by global budget proponents in the ability of managed competition to control costs.[26] That is, it would seem that if the competition part of managed competition can do its job, then a global budget is unnecessary to constrain costs. In fact, Starr and Zelman appear to view managed competition as a way of administering the global budget, rather than as a source of cost savings:

> Moreover, we see the purchasing cooperatives not only as managers and promoters of competition but as a source of countervailing power and a mechanism for carrying out national spending limits. In these respects, too, we differ from advocates of managed competition who oppose any national budget setting. Some may ask why, if we believe competition will work, we also see a need for global budgets. One might as soon ask the designers of a new airplane if their specification of a second engine demonstrates a lack of confidence in the first. Good designs often build in redundancy. If competition is a complete success, the provisions for global budgets will turn out to be superfluous. But, if employers are going to give up control of health benefits they are going to expect strong guarantees of cost containment. Global budgets are that guarantee.[27]

Nevertheless, unlike a second engine for an airplane, it is not at all clear that the imposition of a global budget improves the likelihood that managed competition will fly.

In fact, the leading proponents of managed competition, Paul Ellwood and Alain Enthoven, are adamant in their opposition to a global budget because they believe that a global budget will doom managed competition.[28] Specifically, Enthoven views a global budget

---

[26]The proponents of managed competition within a global budget do not put much stock in the value of the competition side of managed competition: "Unlike some other proponents of managed competition, we do not expect the purchasing cooperatives to rely exclusively on competitive forces. To be sure, where competition exists, the purchasing cooperatives should manage it. Where competition can develop, the cooperative should promote it. But where the potential for competition is limited or absent, the states and the purchasing cooperatives must be able to use other means to guarantee universal coverage, control costs, and improve quality (Starr and Zelman, "Bridge to Compromise," p. 13).

Bureaucrats will find a lack of competition every time. Where they find it, they will love it to death.

[27]Ibid., pp. 13–14.

[28]Consider their letter to President-Elect Clinton: "The Jackson Hole

as a government control and a very real threat to his version of managed competition: "Competition is the way to achieve a system that is driven by the informed choices of consumers who are responsible for the costs consequences of their choices. *A government-controlled system is driven by political forces.*"[29] In other words, the combination of a global budget and managed competition will force competition out of the market and into the political arena. The

---

Group, as well as non-health care organizations such as the Business Roundtable, The American Business Conference, and the National Governors' Association, are skeptical of the feasibility of applying price controls or global budgets imposed by central government on the massive and diversified health sector. We have technical, economic, and political concerns.

"First, while some argue that global budgets and associated price controls are simple, effective, and can be quickly implemented, we have no evidence that these claims are correct. American health care is an enormously complex and unstructured system with wide geographic variations in costs and practice patterns. Its many components have a history of compensating for regulatory controls by manipulating service volumes, treatment settings (e.g., emergency rooms), and rationale for therapy. The sheer number of services and patient encounters, of diseases, procedures, technological advances, and providers, will require a vast Federal bureaucracy as well as absurdly complex formulae for pricing services and allocating resources. We believe the advocates of spending limits will not be able to deliver a practical, fair, and acceptable program within a shorter time frame than managed competition.

"Second, global markets will undermine the formation of a competitive market for health care services. Provider organizations, HMOs, and insurance carriers will see no benefit in making the enormous investment in corporate restructuring, service expansion, and performance reporting if the government threatens to set prices. The government's attempt to control fees, hospital budgets, and suppliers' prices will lock in the old fragmented health delivery system.

"Finally, global budgets will generate substantial political opposition from private sector organizations and from moderate and conservative legislators inevitably delaying the initiation of true cost-savings. Health care organizations will defer internal reforms during the political debate, irresponsible parties may increase prices in anticipation of coming limits, and the broad spirit of collaboration that could now be exploited will instead be corrupted. Health care reform can only deliver rapid benefits if the President and other national leaders speak with one voice, offering a single consistent direction for all to follow" (letter from Paul M. Ellwood, M.D. [President, Jackson Hole Group] and Alain C. Enthoven, Ph.D. [Marriner S. Eccles Professor of Public and Private Management, Stanford University] to President-Elect Clinton, January 11, 1993).

[29]Enthoven, "Managed Competition," p. 41 (emphasis added).

analysis presented in this chapter suggests that politics will be the undoing of managed competition within a global budget constraint.

Summary. In summary, the global budget is a very blunt and crude instrument[30] for solving our health care problems, when we can point to numerous underlying problems that can be corrected to help make the health care market function better. A global budget necessarily involves government and bureaucratic decision making about the total amount of resources allocated to health care as well as about very specific allocations within the confines of the global budget. In many instances, the effect of a detailed budget will be bureaucratic micromanaging of an entire industry. The decisions will run counter to the market signals produced by the interaction of supply and demand—and thus lead to shortages and nonprice rationing. Shortages demand political solutions, which means political battles—the next topic.

Political Decision Making and Rent Seeking

Public choice economics applies the methodology of economics to political decision making.[31] In other words, to borrow a phrase from Alain Enthoven, it applies "generally accepted principles of rational economic behavior"[32] to decisions made by politicians, bureaucrats, and interest groups. The basic assumption of public choice economics is that political decision makers behave just like consumers and businesses—they attempt to maximize their own self-interest. This is hardly startling to long-time observers and participants in the Washington public policy arena, but these incentives are important to take into consideration in the design of new political institutions such as

---

[30]See Haislmaier, "Global Budgets and Price Controls," p. 2: "Some lawmakers believe government-imposed national health budgets would lead to a more careful allocation of medical resources, reducing costs and improving efficiency. But the real effect has been bluntly but accurately summed up by Stanford University Professor Alain Enthoven as more similar to 'bombing from 35,000 feet, where you don't see the faces of the people you kill.' "

[31]For an introduction to the literature and methodology of public choice economics, see David B. Johnson, *Public Choice: An Introduction to the New Political Economy* (Mountain View, Calif.: Bristlecone Books, Mayfield Publishing, 1991). For an application of public choice economics to markets for physicians' services, see Zweifel, "Protecting the Medical Profession."

[32]Enthoven, "Managed Competition," p. 45.

those created by managed competition within a global budget. In this view, interest groups, lobbyists, politicians, and bureaucrats have one thing in common—they all are entrepreneurs. They are constantly looking to exploit opportunities for gain within the political system. This part of the chapter offers some general observations about the incentives political decision makers face when a scheme of managed competition within a global budget plan is adopted. The first section discusses the role of interest groups under a global budget. The second section discusses the incentives of bureaucrats within the managed-competition bureaucracy.

Interest Groups and the Global Budget. The interest-group perspective on legislation suggests that these groups compete against one another for the passage of favorable legislation. In this view, legislation is the result of a rent-seeking process in which legislation is "sold" by legislators and "bought" by the highest bidders. A large body of empirical research supports interest-group explanations for the emergence of economic regulations that apply to specific industries. Interest groups demand—and all levels of government supply—protective regulation, monopoly, and other special privileges.

The current health care reform movement is not immune to rent-seeking pressures. The imposition of a truly global budget would, in effect, turn almost one-seventh of the U.S. economy into one big interest group. Although all segments of the American health care industry have maintained their presence in Washington for decades, a global budget with its attendant bureaucratic controls would make it imperative for all health care providers to be politically active. Basic decisions, such as what is included in the benchmark benefits package, not only involve picking winners but also involve making political decisions about how to divide a fixed health care budget. *When every winner is chosen at the expense of a loser, all interest groups must play the game.*

The creation by the government of a new design for managing an industry that represents such a large segment of the U.S. economy will result in a system far removed from the anonymous decision making that characterizes market transactions. Although markets appear to be chaotic, they guide resources to their highest-value uses when allowed to work. In contrast, government is personal and political, and it is a serious mistake to talk about "the government" or "the federal and state governments" as if they are benevolent despots—for example: "Together, the federal and state governments would determine the revenues available to the HIPCs, which would then contract with the various health plans."[33] When "the govern-

---

[33]Starr, *The Logic of Health-Care Reform*, p. 69.

ment" guides the allocation of resources, every decision becomes a political decision. Moreover, it is naive to view government decision makers as merely benign agents of the people, carrying out the people's will.

Interest-group battles are bound to accompany decisions about the financing of any new health care system. It is not surprising that most proposals based on government management of some portion of the health care industry seek to avoid associating their proposals with new taxes. Instead, they tend to advocate maintaining a system similar to the current employer-based system of insurance premiums. Because many employers who are currently not insuring their employees would be required to pay all or a portion of their employees' insurance costs, however, these additional costs imposed on businesses will force some firms out of business or cut back employment.[34] The realization of potential problems with this type of financing has led Starr and Zelman to suggest ways to lessen the blow:

> This approach can easily be modified either to reduce needed revenue or to make the plan more attractive. For example, instead of providing subsidies to all firms to keep their premium obligations within 7 percent of payroll, we could limit the subsidies to small employers (or to those employers who enter the HIPCs). Alternatively, without increasing the subsidies required, we might graduate the cap—say, from 9 percent on larger firms down to 4 or 5 percent on the smallest. And, for small firms only, we might exclude some fixed amount of payroll in calculating the cap—say $5,000 per employee—thereby reducing premium obligations only for small firms with low average wages.[35]

---

[34]The requirement that all employers pay a certain percentage of payroll to an HIPC is likely to have disastrous dislocative effects on small businesses. The impact would be similar to play-or-pay proposals that involve a 7 percent payroll contribution. The Urban Institute has studied this proposal and concluded that "under a 7 percent payroll tax rate, the percentage of non-elderly Americans enrolled in the [government] plan would increase to 52 percent. . . . As many as 99 million Americans would switch health insurance plans. . . . Employers' insurance cost (in 1989 dollars) would increase [by] $29.7 billion. . . . Insurance costs for firms with fewer than 25 employees would increase by 71 percent. . . . The government's share of costs . . . would be $64.4 billion. This represents an increase of $36.4 billion over the 1989 Medicaid costs for the non-elderly, non-institutionalized population (see "Study Says Democratic Health Care Plan Would Boost Annual Costs by $66 Billion," *Wall Street Journal*, January 10, 1992).

[35]Starr and Zelman, "Bridge to Compromise," pp. 17–18.

This ad hoc approach is an open invitation to rent seeking. Once it is clear that special concessions and variances can be made to the plan, interest groups will run wild.

On a related point, Starr has recognized the importance of a global budget in forcing political leaders to consider the budgetary costs of health care explicitly:

> A key source of high costs in the United States is their fragmentation and obscurity. Reform that proposes to bring them into the clear light of day, therefore, represents a fundamental move toward cost containment. Western countries with national health insurance have lower health costs than the U.S. partly because their expenditures are more visible. To be sure, consolidated financing provides the leverage for cost control, typically through global budgeting. But fiscal arrangements not only raise money; they also help focus opposition. Where health care is wholly financed by general revenues, it has to compete with other national needs such as education and defense and other strong incentives that mobilize to keep health spending in check. And where health care is financed by a separate tax, political leaders have to summon the courage and build the support necessary to raise that tax. The difficulty of doing either tends to retard the growth of health spending.[36]

In contrast, other proponents of global budgets envision them as a mechanism for responsive legislators to increase the resources available to health care: "If the citizenry desires health care expenditures to grow at a rate faster than the economy, it can pressure the legislature to raise tax rates or mandate higher employment premiums."[37] Both perspectives on global budgeting are based on great faith in government actors to "do the right thing." But the entire process is surely subject to political manipulation. The quoted sentence, for example, could more accurately be rewritten: "If *organized groups of health providers* desire health care expenditures to grow at a rate faster than the economy, they can pressure the legislature to raise tax rates or mandate higher employment premiums."

In general, public choice interpretations of the impact of global budgeting reach a conclusion opposite to the one desired by global budget proponents. Where health care is wholly financed by general revenues, a well-organized industry of health care providers and

---

[36]Starr, *The Logic of Health-Care Reform.*

[37]James C. Robinson, "A Payment Method for Health Insurance Purchasing Cooperatives," *Health Affairs*, vol. 12, supp. (1993), p. 74.

insurance companies is ready to lobby and fight for a bigger slice of the budgetary pie provided by taxes on dispersed, unorganized individuals. Well-organized groups of beneficiaries, such as the elderly and the American Association of Retired Persons, or parents of children with special needs also have strong incentives to get involved in the process and try to increase the size of the pie. Where health care is financed by a separate tax, special-interest groups have a similar incentive to lobby for higher taxes, and all beneficiaries will be told that the higher taxes are necessary to maintain quality health care.

One aspect of the Starr-Zelman financing proposal does have some beneficial effects on political incentives. The capping of employers' and employees' contributions at a certain percentage of payroll means that Congress will have to come up with financing for any additional benefits that it includes in the basic benefits package. Thus, on the margin, Congress will have to fund whatever benefits it authorizes or requires. This stipulation is in stark contrast to the Medicaid program through which Congress imposes tremendous costs on the states when it expands the federal mandates.[38] Nevertheless, Congress will have much to say about whatever program emerges, and Congress is unlikely to prohibit itself from buying votes with other people's money.[39]

In the end, it is a huge leap of faith to assert that government control of aggregate health care expenditures will necessarily lead to lower health care costs. In fact, an understanding of interest-group politics suggests that the exact opposite effect is likely. Moreover, if a global budget is set and actually adhered to, then political activity by all actors in the health care market is imperative. With a global

---

[38]In criticizing the funding incentives under Medicaid, Newhouse points out that the "general principle is that the decision-making authority should face full costs at the margin," "Iconoclastic View," p. 168.

[39]Paul Starr notes: "Under any comprehensive proposal, some federal financing will certainly be required, at least if Medicaid and Medicare are integrated into the plan. But it is not clear to me that the federal government should raise all or even most of the revenue for health insurance. Under the Kerry proposal, the responsibility for controlling costs would lie primarily with the states. Yet because the federal government would provide nearly all the funds, the states might not have a strong enough incentive to be vigilant. To ensure the proper balance of fiscal responsibility, therefore, the states should have to raise much of the revenue (*The Logic of Health-Care Reform*, p. 68).

Of course, all the plans call for most of the revenue to come from private payments from businesses and individuals.

budget, political activity is a zero-sum game—one group's gain is another group's loss. Interest groups cannot afford not to play the game. Thus, the politicalization of an entire industry will result in tremendous social losses as health care providers invest millions of dollars in trying to influence the distributional decisions.

In designing a new health management system, policy analysts must pay attention to the impact of institutions and decision-making processes on the final result. The managed-competition reformers, whether within or without a global budget, have not convincingly addressed the political economy of their new systems.

Bureaucratic Incentives and Regulatory Capture. The proponents of managed competition—whether within a global budget or not—envision the creation of a vast new health management bureaucracy. The lead organization would be a national health board—an independent agency dedicated to keeping us financially solvent and, we hope, physically healthy. The board would delegate much authority to the states, which would charter the HIPCs and, presumably, set up state boards to monitor them. All these new bureaucracies are supposed to act to keep costs down and quality up. A major challenge facing the planners of these new bureaucracies, however, is how to insulate them from the institutional pressures that typically lead to ineffective and unresponsive bureaucratic bloat.

The history of economic regulation shows that industry-specific regulatory agencies often lose sight of their public-interest mission over time. That is, although an agency may be created to control a particular industry, most regulatory agencies eventually adopt the perspective of the regulated industry. This is referred to as regulatory capture. Thus, eventually, the regulated industry frequently benefits from the regulation.[40]

---

[40]This observation has led some students of the regulatory process to suggest that one should look to the beneficiaries of the regulation in attempting to identify the parties that demanded and procured the regulation. See George J. Stigler, "The Theory of Economic Regulation," *Bell Journal of Economics*, vol. 2 (1971), p. 3. The Interstate Commerce Commission, for example, was created to control price discrimination by railroads. Some customers complained that price cuts were helping large shippers at the expense of small shippers. The primary effect of price discrimination, however, was the destruction of the railroads' cartel, which tried to raise prices above competitive levels. The railroads were competing for the large customers through price cuts and rebates, and the cartel was crumbling as a result. This socially beneficial competition was eliminated by the government's imposition of fixed rates, which

It is not unusual for administrative agencies to act in the interest of the regulated industry rather than in the so-called public interest. One explanation often given is that the selection of board or commission members is biased toward individuals from the industry—hiring the fox to guard the henhouse. The hiring of industry insiders, though, may be necessary, because they may be the only available individuals with the special knowledge required to make a meaningful contribution to the agency. Such knowledge is rarely found in outsiders. Further, it is not clear that selecting board and commission members from outside the industry would change the result, because as outsiders become aware of the special problems facing an industry, they are likely to become sympathetic and supportive.

For other reasons, too, the regulated industries will tend to have relatively more impact on the regulations than representatives of the public interest. The regulated industry has the greatest interest in the rules and regulations promulgated by the agency. Thus, in administrative hearings on proposed rule makings, their perspective is likely to be better articulated than the public interest. This bias is not surprising, because individual citizens do not have the incentive to voice their positions on public policy issues because of free-rider problems. Thus, the interests of dispersed citizens are underrepresented in the political process in general and in the administrative process in particular.

The economics of regulation has revealed many instances when public-interest-sounding regulations passed (or cloaked) in the name of public safety and health have turned out to be well-disguised restrictions on competition, especially in fields where licenses and board certifications are required. When proponents of managed competition talk about federal certification of accountable health plans and state certification of health plans, we have good reasons for being suspicious of the long-term consequences of such programs—especially in light of the potential for regulatory capture.

The behavior of a new health care bureaucracy will ultimately be determined by the incentives of individual bureaucrats interested in

---

effectively enforced the cartel. Consumers, who presumably represented the public interest, did not benefit from the regulation. Instead, the benefits flowed to the railroads through the higher prices that resulted from the elimination of competition. In fact, some scholars have argued that the railroads engineered (pun intended) the creation of the ICC. See Gabriel Kolko, *Railroads and Regulation: 1887–1916* (Princeton: Princeton University Press, 1965), and Robert Spann and Edward Elickson, "The Economics of Railroading: The Beginning of Cartelization and Regulation," *Bell Journal of Economics and Management*, vol. 1 (1970), p. 227.

advancing their careers. The literature on the economics of bureau-cracy suggests that bureaucrats advance their careers by building empires, maximizing their budgets, and avoiding risks.[41] At first glance, the imposition of an effective global budget constraint appears to control the first two impulses—empire building and budget maxi-mization. An ambitious bureaucrat, however, may view the annual global budget review as an opportunity to expand coverage by the managed-competition plan, increase the benefits included in the benchmark plan, and argue for more money to keep interest groups quiet and to avoid the tough choices that must be made in the private sector. Moreover, risk-averse bureaucrats may be hesitant to make changes in response to market conditions, new technologies, and so forth, especially when the introduction of new technology threatens an existing set of providers. Risk-averse bureaucrats, for example, may be reluctant to approve the use of a new drug that reduced the need for surgery out of concern for the political wrath of the affected group of surgeons. Thus, the incentives facing health care managers under a global budget are likely to be as perverse as under any other bureaucracy.

Finally, it is no answer to say that the problems of bureaucracy and regulatory capture can be thwarted by the appointment of an independent regulatory agency or board: the same bureaucratic in-centives to advance one's career are present in independent agencies, and independent agencies are subject to political pressures. In fact, it is not clear that it is desirable to insulate independent boards from political pressures. Walter Zelman, for example, has considered the independence of a national health board and regional HIPC boards under a system of managed competition within a global budget:

> At national and state levels, longer terms and some protec-tion from removal by appointing authorities may make some sense. But granting these boards too much insulation from political forces would reduce accountability to an inappro-priate level. That national board will not be like the Federal Reserve Board, which makes decisions, however important, that most people know little about and do not understand. A national board and its actions would be highly visible and would affect everyone. Under such circumstances, the public has at least as much to fear from capture by the interest groups (all too common in independent agencies) as it has to fear from inappropriate interference by politicians.

---

[41]See, generally, William Niskanen, *Bureaucracy and Representative Govern-ment* (Chicago: Aldine, 1971).

At the regional HIPC level, where appointees are likely to be less visible and perhaps of more uneven quality, too much political insulation might be particularly unwise. Government leaders who are ultimately responsible for making HIPCs a success must have the capacity to shape policy, especially early on.[42]

Thus, even the proponents of managed competition within a global budget recognize that interest-group politics and bureaucratic incentives should be considered in evaluating the organization of their new health care management system. The perspective of this chapter, however, assumes the presence of much more pervasive, entrepreneurial efforts by legislators, health care plans, planners, providers, and even consumer advocates to exploit the system for private gain.

Summary. Managed competition under an effective global budget constraint will force competition out of the health care market and into the only place left for competition—the political marketplace. If the current jockeying among interest groups in the health care industry is any indication, then there will be plenty of competition in the political marketplace if such a scheme is adopted. Moreover, because the proposed plan involves reliance on new institutions such as HIPCs and a national health board, the fact that bureaucrats are not independent of politics or the influence of interest groups must be considered in analyzing how the system would function.

The interest-group and bureaucratic incentive issues raised here have been recognized by other global budget opponents. Alain Enthoven, for example, has stated:

> Top-down global budgets . . . would focus the whole health services industry on political efforts to raise or maintain the ceiling as a percentage of gross national product (GNP). The British refer to the likely behavior as "shroud waving." Regulatory authorities are held responsible for the economic survival of the regulated entities. Hospital rate regulators are notoriously unwilling to force unneeded or inefficient hospitals to close. Insurance rate regulators are responsible for the solvency of insurers. So such regulation becomes cost reimbursement. Only impersonal market forces can close down unneeded, inefficient activities. Thus, the history of such regulation is that it does not really lower cost to consumers.[43]

---

[42]Walter A. Zelman, "Who Should Govern the Purchasing Cooperative?" *Health Affairs*, vol. 12, supp. (1993), pp. 49–57, 56–57.

[43]Enthoven, "Managed Competition," p. 43.

The next part analyzes the functioning of managed competition within a global budget from the public choice perspective developed here.

A Unified Rent-seeking Theory

The consolidation in Washington of the decision on how much to spend on health care each year is bound to create an annual interest-group battle over the size of the annual increase in the global budget.[44] Lobbyists for various sectors of the health industry will be more prevalent than defense industry lobbyists in the 1980s. In general, the combination of managed competition and a global budget creates an ideal institutional setting for lobbyists to ply their trade. This part demonstrates that lobbyists and politicians would be hard pressed to design a system that requires more constant, vigilant political activity by all interest groups than the proposals for managed competition within a global budget.

Determining the Benchmark Benefits Package. The Starr-Zelman proposal would require that "under federal law, all American citizens would be guaranteed the right to a comprehensive set of benefits, defined in general terms by legislation and interpreted and adjusted over time by a National Health Board."[45] Although most policy analysts have avoided discussing the details of what would be included in such a package,[46] Starr and Zelman have offered their view of how it should be characterized:

Another difference in our approach is the conception of the benchmark plan. Other proposals have emphasized the low-

---

[44]Starr and Zelman call for an annual budget-setting process: "Under . . . benchmark budgeting, the federal government would determine a maximum allowable rate of increase in benchmark premiums each year and set a target for discretionary, after tax spending. The cap and the target might be set by the president and Congress on the advice of economic advisers and the National Health Board, which would evaluate demographic and technological factors and recent changes in interpretations of benefits. The board might then translate the overall national spending limits into caps and targets for the states, taking account of changes in population and other variables ("Bridge to Compromise," p. 19).

[45]Ibid., p. 9.

[46]For a discussion of benefit options, see Linda A. Bergthold, "Benefit Design Choices under Managed Competition," *Health Affairs*, vol. 12, supp. (1993), pp. 99–109.

cost plan as the point of reference. That term gives rise to misunderstanding; most people assume that the low-cost plan would offer less coverage when, in fact, the coverage would be the same. In addition, because people judge quality by price, the term *low-cost* may carry some stigma; *benchmark*, on the other hand, avoids that stigma and promotes a concern for quality. Indeed, HIPCs should have authority to evaluate whether a low-cost plan has sufficient capacity and quality to serve as the benchmark in its region.[47]

One needs to be only a realist, not a cynic, to recognize that this benign-sounding framework is an open invitation to rent seeking— both at the inception and throughout the implementation of a system of managed competition within a global budget.

It is unlikely that the Congress would miss the opportunity to draw some fairly clear lines about what is included in (or excluded from) the benchmark plan. In considering the initial enabling legislation, Congress will be positioned to extract substantial payments from every provider group that is not obviously included or excluded from the benchmark plan. Chiropractors, optometrists, dentists, podiatrists, and allergists, for example, should be willing to invest substantial sums to make sure that their services are covered as part of the benchmark plan. Moreover, inclusion or exclusion from the plan could be a continuing rent-seeking battle as circumstances change, new interest groups or coalitions emerge, and budgets come up for renewal.

Ample evidence supports the notion that the deliberative legislative process over the content of the benchmark plan is likely to become a congressional rent-seeking feeding frenzy. To begin with, the definition of the benchmark plan has distributional effects that approach the magnitude of reform of the income tax code. But more important, evidence comes from an analogous area of health care legislation—state legislative mandates for what services must be included in the basic health insurance policies in many states. As mentioned above, the proliferation of state mandates on health insurance coverage also contributes to rising costs and helps price health insurance beyond the means of many Americans. State mandates are simply concessions to special interests to force consumers into buying coverage for specific diseases or medical practices whether or not they are needed or wanted. If the decision on what is included in the benchmark plan becomes centralized, the rent seeking that occurs in state capitals will occur in Washington.[48]

---

[47]Starr and Zelman, "Bridge to Compromise," p. 13.

[48]It is worth reiterating that the results of these state mandates have been

Moreover, the experiences from the congressionally mandated increases in Medicaid benefits suggest that members of Congress will be more than willing to meet the demands of interest groups, because most of the costs of additions to the benchmark plan will be paid for by employers, employees, and state governments. As mentioned earlier, during the past decade the federal government has placed further burdens on states by expanding Medicaid coverage for the poor without voting the funds to pay for the expansion. The Medicaid program, much like the Starr-Zelman proposal, requires the federal government to determine the level of Medicaid coverage nationally with each state administering the program within its borders. States' Medicaid costs are shared, with the federal government picking up an average of 55 percent. Thus, like Medicaid, managed-competition with a benchmark plan presents Congress with an irresistible moral hazard—Congress can sell interest-group legislation, can satisfy constituent calls for more benefits, and does not have to worry about most of the cost.[49]

Pricing the Benchmark Benefits Plan under a Global Budget. Supporters of managed competition believe that effective competition will emerge from the rivalry among plans in the determination of the price of the benchmark benefits package. All plans would then be compensated by the HIPCs at a capitation rate determined by the lowest price for a satisfactory benchmark plan.[50] Proponents place

---

disastrous. John Goodman estimates that one-quarter—that is, 9.3 million—of persons currently uninsured could afford basic no-frills health insurance if some or all these state mandates were repealed. The stakes are higher when the rent seeking is centralized in Washington.

[49]One reason that global budgets are politically appealing is related to the vagaries of federal budgetary politics, through which projected reductions in mandatory health care spending can be used to justify increased expenditures for additional health care programs. In particular, the Budget Enforcement Act of 1990—the results of the infamous Bush budget deal—encourages the exaggeration of savings as a way to increase spending. Thus, if global budgeting is projected to save, say, $10 billion in federal outlays in 1995, then an additional $10 billion could be spent on expanded federal health care programs without violating BEA restrictions. See, generally, Republican Staff Report, "A Global Budget Fix for U.S. Health Care?"

Global budgets present politicians with a great opportunity—the opportunity to increase federal benefits to some groups without charging higher taxes. The catch, however, is that the projected savings may not be realized, and the new federal spending will go on despite the failure.

[50]Starr and Zelman, "Bridge to Compromise," p. 10: "*Contribution pegged*

great faith in the ability of HIPCs, when faced with budget constraints, to force plans to minimize prices.[51] They believe that, after the pegging of the benchmark contribution, competition would focus on price and nonprice characteristics as plans attempt to attract subscribers. In stark contrast, the analysis presented in this section suggests that managed competition within a global budget is an anticompetitive price-fixing system.

Several issues must be addressed with respect to the bidding or bargaining for determining the capitation rate for the benchmark plan. First, the strength of the incentives to be the lowest-priced plan is not clear. With respect to pricing the benchmark plan, Enthoven concentrates on the price elasticity of demand for the lowest-priced plan.[52] Little consideration has been given, though, to how the pricing mechanism would actually work. Enthoven seems to suggest an annual bidding process:

> An essential component of managed competition is that it must always be possible for the lowest-priced plan to take

_____

to the low-cost benchmark plan. For any given enrollee, the purchasing cooperative would pay no plan more than it pays the benchmark plan—that is, the plan providing the uniform benefit package at the lowest price and a satisfactory standard of care. Consumers who choose other plans would pay the marginal difference in cost."

[51]For example, Starr and Zelman have stated, "With these [global budget] constraints in mind, the HIPCs would then bargain with the health plans.

"HIPCs would have various means at their disposal to bring in plans with sufficient capacity at the allowable rate of growth and to achieve the overall target for out-of-pocket spending. Clearly, by virtue of their dominant role as purchasers, they would be in a position to jawbone the plans and effectively impose a rate. But they would also have other means. They could work with the plans to reduce the costs of covered benefits by using those with the lowest costs and best results as models for the others. They could 'carve out' some high-cost benefits from all of their contracts and seek competitive bids for a single, globally budgeted provider. They could enter into a state-administered arbitration process with the plans" ("Bridge to Compromise," pp. 19–20).

[52]Enthoven states: "For there to be an incentive for the health plans to cut price, demand must be so elastic that the additional revenue gained exceeds the additional cost of serving more subscribers. _Managed competition is about creating such price elasticity_" (emphasis added) ("Managed Competition," p. 32). In other words, marginal revenue must exceed marginal cost for any price reduction to be rational. Enthoven's emphasis on price elasticity reflects an implicit assumption that marginal costs of additional subscribers are relatively constant.

131

business away from higher-priced plans by cutting premiums more. The lowest-priced plan must be able to widen the gap between its price and the next lowest by cutting price. Premiums of course are quoted in the context of the annual enrollments. The sponsor sets its contribution after the health plans have submitted their quotes.[53]

The rules of the annual bidding process can have a significant impact on the prices that plans quote, and the selection of the rules involves numerous trade-offs. On the one hand, if the initial quotations of higher-priced plans are binding for the entire year and cannot be adjusted in response to the realization that a plan is significantly above the lowest-priced plan, all plans would have an incentive to place their lowest bid first. Under this scenario, the lowest-priced plan would have a significant advantage in attracting additional subscribers. This type of arms-length bidding would seem to preclude the type of "jawboning" envisioned by Starr and Zelman and others but also would serve as an enforcer of any price-fixing arrangements. That is, once the bids are made, the prices listed by the HIPC would be set for one year. It would be difficult to cheat on the HIPC price.[54] On the other hand, if the higher-priced plans are allowed to revise their quotations after the lowest-priced plan's number is revealed, the advantages of being the lowest-priced plan—and thus the incentives to place the lowest bid—are reduced significantly. The HIPCs' jawboning strategy, then, which would probably dictate some type of postbidding adjustments, jeopardizes the bidding process.

A second problem with the bidding or bargaining process involves the *willingness* of the HIPCs to negotiate or impose the lowest possible rate. The motivation of HIPCs to be diligent managers of health care requires an analysis of the governance and incentives faced by HIPC managers.[55] As mentioned earlier, it is almost impossible to divorce an HIPC board from political influence because so much of what determines the success of the HIPC depends on the federal and state

---

[53]Ibid.

[54]For an analysis of how sealed-bid selling to the government facilitates collusion, see Armen A. Alchian and William R. Allen, *Exchange and Production: Theory in Use* (Belmont, Calif.: Wadsworth Publishing, 1969), p. 405.

[55]For the managed-care planners' version of the incentives facing HIPC managers, see Zelman, "Who Should Govern the Purchasing Cooperative?" *Health Affairs*, vol. 12, supp. (1993), pp. 49–57; Paul Starr, "Design of Health Insurance Purchasing Cooperatives," *Health Affairs*, vol. 12, supp. (1993), pp. 58–64.

governments. Moreover, the potential for regulatory capture by health care plans or providers is always a threat to the HIPCs' proconsumer functions envisioned by managed-competition planners. Finally, not-for-profit institutions are notorious for pursuing agendas inconsistent with the stated purpose of the institution.

A third problem with the bidding or bargaining process involves the *ability* of the HIPCs to negotiate or impose the lowest possible rate. Even if an HIPC governance mechanism could be established to ensure that HIPC managers tried to minimize costs and protect consumers, it is not clear that HIPCs would be able to achieve those goals, especially when they must operate under the constraint of a global budget. In this regard, Starr and Zelman, for example, assume that the HIPCs would use their dominant role as purchasers to control prices, but the analysis presented here suggests that a global budget substantially reduces the bargaining power of HIPCs.

Consider the impact of the annual national global budget–setting process on the relationship between HIPCs and the plans. The proponents of managed competition within a global budget envision a top-down rate-setting process in which the global budget for a region would be determined by "the benchmark premium times the total number of enrollees."[56] In effect, after the initial benchmark premium is determined, subsequent capitation rates will be based on determinations by "the president and Congress on the advice of economic advisers and the National Health Board"[57] about permissible annual rates of increase in the global budget. All the plans will be aware of the rate of increase approved by Congress and allocated to the HIPCs through the states. As a consequence, the HIPCs would lose all credibility if they tried to keep premium increases below the congressionally approved rate of increase. Thus, the plans will collectively refuse to be jawboned into accepting lower capitation rates, and the *global budget ceiling becomes the floor.*

A similar anticompetitive result emerges if HIPCs rely on a sealed bidding process without postbidding jawboning. The economics of cartels teaches us that collusion is more likely to occur in markets with relatively uniform products and a relatively small number of competitors. Those structural characteristics are created by managed competition: the benchmark plan is certainly a uniform product, and there is widespread agreement that managed competition will result in dramatic reductions in the number of competitors in the health

---

[56]Starr and Zelman, "Bridge to Compromise," p. 32.

[57]Ibid., p. 19.

plan market. In addition to these collusion-enhancing structural changes, the annual rate-setting process by an HIPC is an iterative game in which the participant bidders are likely to learn how to predict the behavior of their competitors and tacitly collude on price. Thus, even if no information about the national rate of increase in the global budget is announced, the bidding process is likely to lose any semblance of a competitive process over time.

If, however, the annual rate of increase is announced at the national level (and it is difficult to imagine such a decision being kept secret), the public decision-making process for the annual increase in the benchmark price would allow the competitors to know in advance the minimum amount of increase that they can expect to receive. This public information would reinforce the information learned from earlier bidding processes, serve as a signal point for bids, and thus result in tacit collusive setting of rates. Managed competition within a global budget is likely to lead to tacit collusion among plans in the pricing of the benchmark plan. Once again, the global budget ceiling becomes the floor.

The impact of managed competition on industry structure also suggests an additional way in which a global budget will corrupt the HIPCs' pricing mechanisms. The imposition of managed competition could result in a very concentrated health plan industry that would be effective in bargaining with the HIPCs.[58] With concentration on both sides of the market, it is difficult to predict the outcome of any bargaining process because prices under bilateral monopoly are indeterminant within a certain range. As was explained above, however, the national global budget-setting process and the annual benchmark pricing process provide plans with very strong price signals. That is, unlike the traditional bilateral monopoly story, there is an obvious solution—the ceiling should be the floor. Once again, the interaction of managed competition and a global budget will derail the HIPCs' cost-containment efforts by reducing their bargaining power.

The anticompetitive impact of global budgeting on the bidding also feeds back into the political process. The collusion-enhancing aspects of the bidding process give health plans and providers an even greater incentive to lobby for higher annual increases because the collusion makes it more likely that they will capture the gains from their rent-seeking activities. In other words, because the process

---

[58]For example, Starr and Zelman predict that the imposition of managed competition with a cap will "produce extensive consolidation"; ibid., p. 13.

turns the global budget ceiling into a floor, interest groups will lobby to have the ceiling increased.

As with any cartel, the more successful the price-fixing plan, the greater the incentive to cheat by reducing price or increasing output. Managed competition, however, provides the mechanisms for discouraging cheating. The politicalization of the health care industry, which will undoubtedly result in the capture of state regulatory boards and HIPCs in at least some states, will help enforce cartelization and reinforce rent-seeking incentives. The problem of free riders, for example, is a threat to the stability of all cartels (or other collusive arrangements). If managed competition reduces the number of firms, either cheating on the collusive price or free riding on the political activity of other firms will be less likely. Firms that refuse to cooperate with the collusive pricing or attempt to be apolitical will be likely targets for state regulatory boards. It is not inconceivable that political pressure will arise to decertify plans that undercut the cartel price—in fact, attacks on low-quality price cutters are common in medical markets now. Thus, the presence of a global budget raises the stakes and forces all industry participants to be politically active at both the state and the federal level. And, as mentioned above, rent-seeking expenditures are a waste of society's scarce resources.

These incentives influencing the pricing of the benchmark benefits package—when combined with the earlier concerns about political battles over the content of the benchmark package and the fact that Congress does not bear the full cost of its decisions on contents or rates of increase—suggest that a global budget will be under continued pressure for increases. Rather than complementing managed competition, a global budget guarantees that managed competition will not work. Thus, Enthoven's assessment that "it is altogether possible that a very efficient competitive system could get us back to 9 or 10 percent"[59] from the current 14 percent of GDP is threatened by the anticompetitive institutional shackles created by a global budget.

The Role of the States. Most managed-competition proposals include an important role for the states in the administration or management of competition.[60] HIPCs will be chartered by states and subject to

---

[59]Enthoven, "Managed Competition," p. 40.

[60]See, generally, Kronick, "Where Should the Buck Stop." The allocation of authority to the states is also part of the Starr and Zelman proposal: "The states, on the other hand, would be given direct authority to supervise the purchasing cooperatives and license health plans. As we

state governance. The global budget will be determined nationally and then allocated through the states. To some extent, the reliance on the states is an administrative convenience adapted from Medicaid—the joint federal-state program to provide health care to the poor. After Congress sets Medicaid benefits and provides partial funding, the states administer the benefits and provide the rest of the financing. The reliance on the states is recognition that the administration of the program is too big a job for the federal government to handle. An additional benefit of state administration is that it allows for experimentation with and comparison of different management techniques.[61] In this section, an alternative interpretation of the role of states is presented: states are relied on because they facilitate the rent-seeking competition that naturally results from managed competition within a global budget.

States have a well-documented history of interest-group influences in health care and other areas of regulation.[62] In health care, for example, the proliferation of mandated services under state regulation of health insurance indicates the role of interest groups in affecting political outcomes. Moreover, in general, the pattern of interest-group legislation varies across states in predictable ways that reflect differences in demand and supply in political markets. Thus, to the extent that interest groups differ across states in their organization and effectiveness, the granting of authority to state regulators facilitates market segmentation across states and price discrimination in the selling of special-interest legislation.

In this regard, the allocation of regulatory authority under managed competition within a global budget appears to facilitate rent-seeking behavior. To begin with, Paul Starr and others have recognized substantial differences in health care markets across the country.[63] The allocation of regulatory power so that differences in author-

---

conceive them, the HIPCs most likely would be state-chartered public corporations; their boards would be designed to represent the purchasers—that is, consumers and employers in their region" ("Bridge to Compromise," p. 12).

[61]See Kronick, "Where Should the Buck Stop," p. 89.

[62]See, for example, Starr, "Health Insurance Purchasing Cooperatives": "Past experience suggests caution because of the dominant influence of provider interests in state health policy" (p. 62).

[63]See, for example, Kronick, "Where Should the Buck Stop": "There are substantial variations across the country in the ecology of the medical care delivery system and the preferences of providers, patients, and politicians." (p. 88). Starr also notes: "Another reason to rely on the

ity match with underlying market differences makes for a more responsive public-interest apparatus. The interest-group theory of government, though, teaches us that the allocation of regulatory authority along these lines may result in a system more responsive to interest groups than to consumers.

The reform proposals based on managed competition would likely create a well-designed rent-seeking and rent-extraction deal between federal and state legislators. The federal government could preempt the entire health care system if it wanted to, but the task of dividing the country into different geographic regions for rent extraction purposes exceeds the abilities of even the most entrepreneurial federal legislators and regulators.[64] Local regulators and legislators have specific information about local market conditions—such as the relative organizational strength of different interest groups—that can be exploited efficiently only by granting them the authority to make important local decisions. There is a great deal of truth in the saying that "all politics is local."

Thus, the allocation of regulatory authority to the states for better response to different conditions may segment the market in a way that allows state legislators to collect rents that would not be available—to either federal or state legislators—if the federal government controlled the administration of the entire system. Managed-competition proposals suggest that the federal government should leave some authority to the states, but an interesting question concerns the areas to be taken over by the federal government and those delegated to the states. Under most proposals for managed competition within a global budget, the federal government preempts two major decisions that are bound to be subject to continuous interest-group pressures. First, the decision about the contents of benchmark health benefits plans will force many interest groups that have heretofore concentrated on state capitals to centralize their operations in

---

states is the regional diversity of health-care organizations and the difficulty of prescribing a single solution for the entire country. Successful reform will have to involve devolution—that is, moving many decisions about health insurance downward in the federal system. Devolution does not have to compromise the fundamental goals of reform. Even in Canada each province has its own health-insurance system, operating within the framework of national guidelines. In the United States, primary responsibility should also belong to the states" (*The Logic of Health-Care Reform*, p. 68).

[64]See, generally, Henry N. Butler and Jonathan Macey, "The Myth of Competition in the Dual Banking System," *Cornell Law Review*, vol. 73 (1988), p. 677.

Washington. Second, the annual decision concerning the rate of increase in the global budget will be made in Washington.

The states are left with more than table scraps, however. First, the states will control the HIPCs, and it is up to the states to decide how many HIPCs should operate in each state. But regardless of how many HIPCs are in each state, the HIPCs will not compete with one another—they are granted exclusive geographic territories. An exclusive geographic territory means that HIPCs are not only monopsonists (as the exclusive buyers of health plans) but also monopolists (as the exclusive marketers of health plans). If the HIPCs are captured through the state political process by health care providers, the potential monopoly rents allocated through rent seeking are enormous.[65] Moreover, because states start with a segmented market (by state boundary) and can then divide them up further to reflect organizational differences among interest groups, the state legislators are more efficient rent extractors than federal legislators could be under a highly centralized system. In fact, the geographic division of states may help the formation of interest groups.

A second way that states facilitate the rent-seeking process is their role as administrator and enforcer of the anticompetitive pricing scheme discussed in the preceding section. Every administrative mechanism that can be justified to help administer a managed-competition plan can be used by entrepreneurial legislators and bureaucrats to extract rents from the health care industry. The consumer protection role of the state in certifying plans for marketing through an HIPC, for example, can be manipulated into a cartel enforcement mechanism. Providers or plans that refuse to participate in the political process may be subject to administrative harassment or even decertification.[66] The large size of the U.S. health care market makes it very difficult for national legislators and national bureaucrats to segment markets, discriminate on price, punish cheaters, and reward players. In most managed-competition proposals, however,

---

[65]Starr explicitly recognizes this problem with state control and uses it to argue for a stronger federal role in monitoring and disciplining state-chartered HIPCs. See Starr, "Design of Health Insurance Purchasing Cooperatives," p. 62. The problem with his solution is that it merely shifts the interest-group battle to Washington.

[66]Robinson suggests giving an extraordinary degree of discretion to HIPCs—for example: "If the HIPC is not convinced that the premium demanded by a particular plan is justified and if a lower rate cannot be negotiated, then the HIPC can refuse to contract with that plan" ("A Payment Method," p. 66).

the federal government maintains backup authority to decertify HIPCs that ostensibly fail to control costs, but in practice this may be a way to punish plans and providers that fail to play the political game.

As a final point about the important role of the states in this elaborate rent-seeking system, managed competition within a global budget plan does nothing to diminish the role of states as the primary regulator of entry into the health care professions and related services.[67] Despite all the rhetoric about too many doctors or too many specialists, in fact, much of the spiraling increase in health care costs is due to subsidized demand through the tax code and restricted supply as a result of state regulations on entry.

In summary, the role of the states is more than that of benign administrators. The states play an important role in the organization of the rent-seeking and rent-extraction system created by the allocation of regulatory authority to states and the quasi-governmental HIPCs. The states have demonstrated that they are proficient in allocating favors.

Summary. Managed competition within a global budget creates powerful incentives for all health care providers and all health care plans to be politically active. From political battles over the coverage of the benchmark benefits plan to the creation of an anticompetitive pricing mechanism through HIPCs to selected delegation to the states, the combination of managed competition within a global budget is a dream come true for lobbyists, legislators, and bureaucrats. In fact, if federal legislators set out to design a system to cartelize an industry by market segmentation, they could hardly come up with a more creative and effective plan than the one at the heart of the basic managed-competition model. The imposition of a global budget on top of this regulatory apparatus is genius—the annual national debate over rate of increase in the global budget is an effective way to convey price-fixing information while giving the public the false impression of meaningful and open competition. This analysis suggests that managed competition within a global budget cannot be

---

[67]See, for example, Stephen S. Hyde, "The Last Priesthood: The Coming Revolution in Medical Care Delivery," *Regulation* (Fall 1992), p. 74: "Today's medical profession is perhaps the last priesthood that operates according to the principles of the medieval guild. That is, it enjoys state-enforced monopoly, requires excessively long education and apprenticeship, employs arcane language, and exhibits a circle-the-wagons mentality (to mix my metaphor) when faced with any threat."

sustained, but in the interim before collapse, the rent-seeking frenzy that would accompany it would result in tremendous waste and misallocation of resources.

Final Thoughts

The analysis presented in this chapter suggests that a congressional commitment to a specified global budget will be about as durable as Gramm-Rudman-Hollings and other nonconstitutional constraints on congressional spending. But the problems with a global budget are much larger than the false promise of cost containment. I am skeptical about the ability of managed competition to delivery on its promoters' promises. I am confident that a global budget makes managed competition unworkable. And I am concerned about the long-term consequences of the collapse of a plan based on managed competition with a budget, a point that needs some explanation.

The trend toward more and more government control of health care suggests that the system that emerges after the failure of managed competition within a global budget will involve even more extensive government control. Proponents of managed competition are rightly concerned that global budgeting will be the downfall of managed competition. Although I am not a proponent of managed competition, it seems to me that its proponents should fight to make sure it is given a reasonable chance without the added burden of a global budget.

I am constantly frustrated by the argument that market-based reforms should not be adopted because the health care market has failed, when in fact the market has not been given a chance. After a few years of managed competition within a global budget, proponents of managed competition may be faced with an analogous situation of arguing with proponents of nationalized health care who would say that we have tried managed competition and it has failed. In other words, proponents of nationalized health care can take a big step in that direction by insisting on the imposition of a global budget on any managed-competition plan. But from the perspective of the typical American consumer of health care, this would surely be a mistake.

If we have learned anything in the past fifty years, it should be that consumers must be involved in making their own tough choices. The predictable behavior of politicians is not a good substitute for the predictable behavior of consumers. Paul Starr and Walter Zelman attempt to sell their global budget proposal as a bridge to compromise, but a consideration of the predictable behavior of politicians suggests that their proposal is merely a bridge along the road to ruin of the American health care system. Any reform proposal that fails to recognize and address the limitations and perversions of political decision making will not work. Finally, although President Clinton appears committed to a program of managed competition within a budget, I feel compelled to use his words in response: "We can do better than that."

Commentary on Part Two

Martha Phillips

The conventional wisdom in budget circles in the 1980s was that we had to do something about entitlements if we wanted to do something about the deficit. Since entitlements were the problem, we were told, we should tackle entitlements. So we tackled them, over and over, from with the first grand reconciliation bill in 1980 to all the subsequent ones almost every year thereafter. Medicare and Medicaid reductions were large parts of those bills.

After we tackled entitlements, the problem turned out to be not entitlements in general but health care entitlements in particular. To deal with the federal deficit, we were told, we had to tackle Medicare and Medicaid—not entitlements for government employee retirement, agricultural payments, pension benefit guarantees, or other entitlement funds.

After we took on Medicare and Medicaid, we were told that was not the answer either. We had to deal with the total health economy embedded in the economy of the country. We were told that federal health expenditures could not be controlled until total national health care costs were controlled.

So we said we would wait until after the election and then take on health reform. Only now we are told that this will not reduce the federal deficit. We now hear about $50–90 billion of increased federal spending that could very well increase—not reduce—the federal structural deficit.

The question is whether we need both managed competition and a global budget in order to get sufficient control over our expenditures, be they economywide or federal governmentwide.

That question reminds me of the fellow who got a telegram saying that his mother-in-law had died and asking what he wanted done with the remains: cremation or burial. He cabled back instantly, "Take no chances. Do both."

The mother-in-law is gone, but health care is very much alive and with us, and we will have to deal with it for a long time. Should we take no chances and do both?

From the budgeting perspective, the question boils down to the same dynamics that pertain to all federal budgeting: to reduce the federal budget deficit, we have to spend less and tax more. For health care reform, it is probably the same. We either persuade people to accept less in services or we make them pay more, or we do some of each.

The problem then gets to be a political one, and I am fascinated with Stuart Butler's analysis. People think they will get better services, more services, and quicker services, and that these will cost them less.

At the very least, people are hoping that we can cover some of those who do not have care now, while the rest of us continue getting all the services we currently get and pay nothing more.

Public opinion shows that people are willing to pay *a little* more, not much more, to reform this system. So if we do not have more taxes, what will we do with the models?

There are no doubt various medical system equivalents to our favorite old budget game. In the budget world, if we cannot bring ourselves to make tough choices on spending and we do not want to raise taxes, then we cut "waste, fraud, and abuse." We have done it over and over. In budget summit negotiations and in reconciliation bills, when we are down to the last margin and we need deficit reduction of one or two billion dollars more to make our target, we just stick in a slug of waste, fraud, and abuse elimination. It is usually called management efficiency, or better administration of the tax system by the IRS. Something comparable in the health care area will be dredged up.

The other thing we are hearing about is setting an entitlement cap. President Clinton established a target for federal health care costs; he wants to hold them to the rate of population growth plus the rate of inflation plus 2 percent. He calculated the deficit over a ten-year period, showing the deficit coming down, with his restraint on federal health care spending.

Some in Congress say, Why not take him at his word and enact a cap on federal health care spending? A third of this Congress, new to Washington, came here hell-bent to change the system. They want to go further than anybody has gone before toward reducing deficit spending.

But the problem with the cap is that no one has determined how to accomplish it. We can enact formulas, but until we have a plan for applying them, they are not worth much.

Norman J. Ornstein

When we tamper with one-seventh of the economy and affect everyone's lives, many people will find ways to get around changes and return to practices with which they are comfortable. Furthermore, to try to change the system in one fell swoop involves untold headaches and unintended consequences. Through cycles of reform in government, the rule is, the larger the change, the greater the headaches and unintended consequences. The proposed health care reform is greater than anything we have dealt with before.

If ever we had a reason to move to federalism as our mainstay and let fifty flowers bloom as empirical experiments, this is it. It is unfortunate that the experiments the states have wanted to try in the past were quashed, or we would have some better information now.

One essential question is, What will work substantively? We have to determine what will actually restrain health care costs so that we can avoid these problems at the individual, governmental, and societal levels as health care continues to move forward.

A second question is, What is feasible politically? We can talk about global budgets and managed competition, but we must consider what is actually possible to pass and implement. That is different from the theoretical models.

Far more national focus has been placed on the so-called special interests than on the public. An implicit assumption holds that the public has been crying for change and is the driving force pushing for dramatic health care reform. I think that is misstated.

Public opinion on health care involves three elements. One is the public's view of its own situation. The reality, of course, is that most people are quite satisfied with their own physicians, with delivery of their health care services, and with the protection and coverage they have. They are worried about losing this protection. About 70–80 percent like what they have.

The second element is the public's view of the system. An increasing number of Americans do think the system is in deep trouble. Those of us who have watched the Congress for many years recognize a familiar paradox. People love their congressmen and hate their Congress. Similarly, people love their physicians and hate their medical system, because they keep hearing and reading that it is a terrible system and has gone out of control. But if they like what they get, their first concern will be to keep what they like. And if we turn what they have upside down as we change the system, we risk unleashing a tremendous amount of wrath.

A recent CBS-*New York Times* poll asked people what they were willing to sacrifice to make the system better. They were least willing to sacrifice the new technologies and the expensive treatments currently available to them. At the top of the list of medical care that people wanted in their basic package was mental health care. According to 80 percent, that absolutely has to be there. In effect, almost any change that we want to make will strike at what people like.

The almost universal public definition of health reform is more services for less money. The universal expert definition is fewer services for more money. And in addition to the paradox that people love their doctors and their own health care but hate the system, we have another paradox: to reduce costs, we have to provide some discipline at the individual level, at least in the short term. Individuals will have to pay more, whether it be in dollars or in discomfort, in order to try to restrain total costs.

Perhaps this should be done with the promise that the pain today will result in great pleasure tomorrow. It is doubtful how that will work in a political system where the phrase "trust me," coming from a politician, will be met with gales of laughter.

The third element in public opinion is the public's view of other players in the system. In our society today there is no epithet worse than "special interest." We have been taught that the major problem with the health care system is the rapacious physicians, insurers, and drug company officials who are earning billions of dollars while manipulating the political process through their political action committees and their control of politicians. If only we got rid of these, according to the received wisdom, we would have no problem.

Why do people believe that health care reform can mean more services for less money? Because we have taught them that if doctors would drive Mecurys instead of Mercedeses, that would solve the problem. In other words, we can bring pain to the people who are making out like bandits in this system and not affect other people's lives in any deleterious way. Indeed, they can get better coverage and more services for less money.

But it will not work that way. Politicians who push this concept of scapegoating are playing with fire. They are raising expectations that cannot be met.

That leads to the broader paradox that to make something sell in a political system geared against dramatic change, one has to help oneself. One has to convince people that they will get something enormous in return for the sacrifices or short-term bumps in the road they will have to endure. Yet in the process of overselling it, one must create expectations that cannot be met and can lead to an enormous backlash. Once we get past the complex question of how to impose enormous change on one-seventh of the economy without suffering these unintended consequences, if we can come up with a reasonable solution we will have to sell it to a public that will expect something very different.

Is this public willing to make some sacrifices? Yes. The level of sacrifice people are willing to tolerate is increasing. President Clinton has been effective in convincing people that some collective sacrifice will be necessary both in the budget and in the health care area. The focus has been on the uninsured.

But if 37 million Americans are uninsured and 215 million are insured, the biggest concern for the latter will not be the former. It will be themselves.

A recent Harris poll asked, "Would you be willing to pay an extra $20 a month or an extra $50 a month so that everybody in this society could have basic medical coverage?" The answer is not what one would expect from a society inclined toward great sacrifice. Between 20 percent and 25 percent said they would be willing to pay those relatively nominal amounts to serve that particular purpose.

I will end with a story about three fellows sitting around at the wake of a good friend who was known for his charitable works and devotion of time and resources on the less fortunate. They decided that as a symbol of their solidarity with him, when his casket was lowered into the ground they would each throw a hundred-dollar bill on top of it. The first two threw their hundred-dollar bills down with great flourish. The third man took out a check for $300, put it down there, and took the two hundred-dollar bills.

Sacrifice, by many, is defined along those lines.

PART THREE

Managed Competition

6

Killing with Kindness

Why Some Forms of
Managed Competition Might Needlessly
Stifle Competitive Managed Care

Mark V. Pauly

The idea of using competitive markets in health insurance plans to achieve efficiency, responsiveness, and responsibility in medical markets is currently popular. The popularity is deserved, and much of the credit for it goes to Alain Enthoven and Paul Ellwood, who have worked tirelessly, for decades, in promoting what is fundamentally a valuable and sound idea: it is the only alternative to collective choice and collective management of decisions about citizens' use of medical care.

The viability of allegedly market-based solutions (to anything) in the political hothouse is, however, always delicate: such ideas can either wilt away or mutate into entwining bureaucratic growths. The delicate design of government-market structures, the careful calibration of market and political incentives, and the need to be ever vigilant for the hidden agenda, the weak reed, or the tiny tyrant in search of a bureaucratic sinecure are all challenges that must be addressed if this good idea is to turn into good policy. The purpose of this chapter is to warn about some risks—some political and some technical—that might otherwise smother this healthy organism and to suggest a strategy that may ensure its robust growth.

Definitions and a Cautionary Tale

The fundamental concept of competitive solutions to the problem of efficiency in health care markets has two and only two essential ideas:

- Competitive insurance plans should offer citizens the opportunity to purchase a wide variety of insurance and financing arrangements, where the arrangements differ along many dimensions, including the type of device or method used to determine the style, intensity, and convenience of care.
- There should be no subsidies to the purchase of health plans, no monopolies or oligopolies, and buyers should be properly informed.

The first idea defines the product: "coverage by a health plan." The second idea says that it should be sold in competitive markets. Some citizens may need transfers to help them afford a minimum basic level of benefits, but above this minimum people can choose what they want and spend as much as they want, as long as they are well informed, are paying prices that cover costs, and are spending their own money.

Which kind of health plan will or should people choose? It is likely that most Americans would prefer to choose a health maintenance organization (HMO) or managed-care type of plan, if given proper markets and proper information. Nothing in the logic of competitive health markets, however, dictates that the HMO must be favored, or subsidized as the only "rational" type, or that such plans should somehow be favored in comparison with conventional insurance coverage. There is no basis for saying that such plans necessarily have more rational structures or incentives than do indemnity insurance plans that cover providers who bill fee for service. What is true is that fee-for-service arrangements will often be more costly than the typical HMO, even while being more trouble free. The fundamental concept of a competitive market is that no one product is intrinsically "better" than any other product, but only that there are trade-offs.

Proposals for managed competition are not the first time the use of HMOs has been advocated as the centerpiece of a health reform strategy. In the early 1970s, largely because of the advocacy of Paul Ellwood, the HMO became a key theme in the Nixon administration health reform strategy. Our experience during that episode suggests many parallels with the current discussion of managed competition.

The most general historical message is as follows: the HMO act was ostensibly intended to foster the growth of the HMO type of insurance, but few policies temporarily slowed the growth of HMOs more than did the HMO act. Accounts of motivation differ somewhat, but most analysts agree on the cause: the act so loaded HMOs with regulatory baggage that initiation and operation of plans were made extraordinarily difficult, especially for HMOs that sought federal qualification.[1] The HMO form experienced explosive growth only after the Reagan administration, through a combination of deregulation and benign neglect, greatly reduced the regulatory burden on HMOs.

Most, if not all, of the regulations in the HMO act were based on good intentions. Many of these good intentions are shared with the approach to managed competition proposed by the Jackson Hole group.[2] And yet the message is that, by trying to do too much with regulation of managed care, policy makers run the risk of defeating the very objectives they seek. It is rarely a mistake to err on the side of too little regulation, especially if consumer information and fundamentally correct incentives are in place. The primary good intention in 1973 in the Jackson Hole deliberations and in some of the emanations from the Clinton task force, is a desire for "reassurance," a desire to be sure that all the potentially good effects of market competition and none of the potentially bad effects are achieved. What are we afraid of, and how much courage do we need?

Who Needs to Be Reassured about What?

The "management" that advocates of managed competition think needs to be added to competition has as its motivation the fear that unmanaged or unregulated competition cannot be guaranteed to do the right thing. Advocates of managed competition do, however, profess to trust one outcome: they are certain that the rate of growth in medical care spending that will be achieved under managed competition will be acceptably low (at least to themselves), with only a few extra limits on specific technologies needed. Prominent policy makers, however, do not share even this degree of confidence. They think that additional controls on competition need to be added to guarantee a low enough level of spending and spending growth and propose an additional regulatory device—in a large variety of potential forms—as a way of achieving this guarantee: governmentally imposed spending limits. In contrast, managed-competition advocates, confident that their policy has the potential to control costs,

---

[1]Harold Luft, *Health Maintenance Organizations* (New York: Wiley, 1981).

[2]Paul Ellwood, "The 21st Century American Health System," *Interstudy* (1991–1992).

are much more apprehensive than policy makers that governmental regulation of spending growth will make things worse.[3]

Behind all policy proposals that require competition to be managed is distrust: fear of markets and fear of government. In no case is there certain evidence that these fears are justified, but in every case there is circumstantial evidence that they have some foundation. And yet the great risk, as in the case of the original HMO act, is that devices intended to protect against risk may bring about the failure—if not the total collapse—of the concept that they seek to support.

Make no mistake about it: formulating policy for health care reform is a betting game, and the most one can hope to do is to improve the odds of good outcomes. My own observations, therefore, will necessarily be in terms of possibilities and likelihoods, not cinches. I will, however, try to reduce the total uncertainty by discussing three related issues: (1) How likely, based on the evidence we currently have, are the bad outcomes against which competition must be managed? (2) Are there better ways—to increase certainty or avoid side effects—of dealing with the more likely potential bad outcomes? (3) How can one design a system that offers policy makers, and citizens, greater assurance of good outcomes; are there ways of reassuring the fearful, without hobbling the confident? Finally, I will turn to the fundamental trade-off: can we still sleep nights and yet give competitive markets in medical care enough room (or enough rope) that they can achieve what we all hope?

In what follows, I will address five of the regulatory objectives of managed competition:

- premiums that achieve *fairness* because they do not depend on the illness level of the family unit
- *avoiding distorted competition,* in which insurers compete on the basis of risk selection rather than efficiency
- the need for buyers of health insurance to have *bargaining power* relative both to sellers of health insurance and to health providers
- the need to *standardize benefit packages* to permit comparison shopping across insurers
- compelling employers to offer *multiple insurance choices* to all employees

Competition and Variations in Expected Expenses

Most of the regulations embodied in Jackson Hole–style managed competition aimed at offsetting risk-related premiums that might

---

[3]Alain Enthoven, "The History and Principles of Managed Competition," *Health Affairs,* supp. (1993), pp. 24–28.

occur under unregulated competition. The fear is plausible enough: any competitive market, insurance included, will result in prices that depend on the costs producers expect to incur when they produce the output. For insurance plans, managed care or otherwise, the main component of cost is the costs of the medical services expected to be rendered. If insurers expect these costs to be different for different customers, they will charge them different prices. In itself, there is nothing inefficient about this arrangement: in fact, inefficiency arises when insureds whose use of a given nominal insurance policy will be greater cannot be charged a higher premium (either because of law or incomplete information). Insurers then get swamped by higher risks who snap up a favorable bet at bargain prices, and the "death spiral" of *true* adverse selection ensues.

What is troubling about a world of efficient risk-rated insurances is two things. First, it seems unfair that people with the bad luck to have a serious illness should be subject to higher subsequent insurance premiums. Second, but for the grace of God, we all are potentially subject to the risk of serious illness, somehow losing insurance coverage (and perhaps a job in the process) and then finding that replacing coverage can be done only at substantially higher premiums, if at all. While some degree of premium variation might not be of great concern—it might be modest enough to be ignored as part of the lifetime variation in any person's fortunes or it might serve as an incentive for individuals to maintain good health—policy makers may reasonably want to reduce large and random variation in lifetime premiums.

The greatest part of the regulatory structure embodied in managed competition is therefore directed at the objective of making transfers from the lucky to the unlucky, from the population as a whole to those with costly and chronic illnesses. The approach is classic Posnerian "taxation by regulation."[4] Persons for whom insurance will be more costly than average are to be charged the same premium as everyone else; the shortfall between the premiums collected from them and their costs is to be made up by charging (taxing) those with average or good risks a premium above their costs. Thus, the transfers to high risks are, in effect, financed by an excise tax on insurance purchased by others, a tax that is proportional to the premium at any risk level but that is imposed at a higher rate the lower the risk. This tax is not collected by government but by

---

[4]Richard Posner, "Taxation by Regulation," *Bell Journal of Economics and Management Science*, vol. 2, no. 1 (Spring 1971), pp. 22–50.

regulated insurers and therefore does not appear on any government budget.

Since such mandatory community rating would ordinarily set in place a process of adverse selection—a kind of created or "inessential" adverse selection caused by the requirement that insurers not use information about different risk levels even when they have it—there needs to be a set of rules to prevent the better risks from opting out of the tax-and-transfer mechanism in some way.[5] Since they might do so by purchasing less extensive coverage, it becomes necessary to require uniform coverage, or at least prohibit cost-reducing deductibles and coinsurance because these devices might also serve to make such insurance less attractive to high risks. Since good risks will prefer that those who sell them insurance try to avoid selling the same insurance to high risks, because doing so would raise good-risk premiums, it is also necessary to prohibit underwriting based on illness levels. Since some small insurance plans might, by chance alone, sign up a nonrandom slice of the population, it is necessary to limit the number of plans to ensure that these plans become large (whatever the consequences for efficiency or marketing). At a minimum, it is necessary to subsidize the community-rating plans (by giving higher tax subsidies to them); it will probably be necessary to forbid self-insured plans eventually.

These efforts to engineer transfers cause a number of inefficiencies. As already noted, the use of cost sharing, shown by the RAND Health Insurance Experiment to be nearly twice as effective at controlling health care costs as HMOs alone, is abandoned. Tailoring coverage to the needs of people at specific risk levels—even to the needs of high risks—has to be forbidden. And an extraordinarily complex structure needs to be set up to regulate the community-rating process. Indeed, Paul Starr and Walter Zelman suggest that even all this effort may not be enough: a mechanism for measuring the average risk levels of the people who sign up with various plans and for making explicit transfers across plans may be needed.[6]

The unfairness of risk rating is so apparent to most policy makers—and the apparent belief that if one requires community rating it will be the rich insurers, rather than the middle-income persons of average risk, who will pay—that two crucial questions

---

[5]Kathryn Langwell and Mark Pauly, "Research on Competition in Financing and Delivery of Health Services: Future Research Needs," USDHHS, NLHSR, Pub. No. 83-3328-2, October 1982.

[6]Paul Starr and Walter Zelman, "Bridge to Compromise: Competition under a Budget," *Health Affairs*, supp. (1993), pp. 7–23.

have gone unasked and unanswered. First, how serious *is* the problem of risk rating and its consequences? If the entire medical care financing and delivery system is to be regulated to make the transfers in question, how large an enemy is it for which these howitzers are being wheeled out? Second, are there alternative and better ways of making transfers to high risks that involve less regulation and distortion?

What do we know about the amount of harm risk rating does? There are two kinds of harms that advocates of regulated managed care discuss: risk rating causes insurers to put excessive effort into identifying different risk levels, and (as already noted) some individuals may pay higher lifetime health insurance premiums than others or may go without insurance altogether.

The first argument is that, when risk rating is permitted, insurance plans put their effort into trying to pick off good risks, rather than into trying to hold down medical expenses.[7] Such behavior, one should note at the outset, would not be consistent with profit maximization by insurers. The profit-maximizing insurance firm would be just as happy to sell insurance to above-average risks as to below-average risks, as long as it could identify them and charge higher premiums to the riskier insureds. In addition, whatever effort is put into underwriting and selection, it still pays to engage in the cost-minimizing amount of effort to control costs once the insurance is sold. The profit-maximizing firm does not have a limited stock of "effort" that it must use up in targeting good risks and so has none left over for managing care; it can hire inputs to perform both tasks.

This much having been said, inefficiencies can still occur when risks differ. Using real resources to identify different risk levels is wasteful from a social point of view if all it does is redistribute income. Moreover, adverse selection can in theory be a problem, though the main adverse consequence of adverse selection is too little insurance for *good* risks who are priced out of the market—not at all the burden of the laments about cream skimming harming the chronically ill.

There is a more fundamental issue when managed competition is combined with mandated universal coverage, an issue that, as far as I am concerned, suggests that adverse selection should be a matter of minor worry. Consider the form of universal coverage needed to be required for a middle-income family. For a family of average risk,

---

[7]Alain Enthoven and Richard Kronick, "A Consumer-Choice Health Plan for the 1990s," *New England Journal of Medicine*, vol. 320, nos. 1 and 2 (1989).

there is no need to forbid it from choosing a policy with substantial cost sharing—perhaps up to 10 percent of income as the maximum out-of-pocket payment in any year but with year-to-year limits. The family would not be *required* to buy only such limited coverage; it could choose an HMO with more nominal out-of-pocket payments or a more generous indemnity insurance if it was willing to pay the higher premium. The fear of advocates of managed competition, however, is that the average and good risks might be attracted by a policy with high out-of-pocket-payments, while the strongly risk averse and the moderately above-average risks would prefer (and be willing to pay for) the more generous coverage.

Initially, adverse selection does make low-deductible indemnity coverage costly. Adverse selection might, under the worst scenario, kill off generous indemnity coverage. But should we shed a tear? Such coverage pushes up total medical spending, and, although it might be needed for perfect efficiency with regard to very risk-averse persons, it is not obvious that a small reduction in welfare for these persons, and a small (surely less than 5 percent of premiums) addition to insurance administrative costs for underwriting, is a matter of enough concern to justify forbidding ordinary people to buy coverage with efficient levels of cost sharing. If only high risks would have voluntarily purchased generous indemnity coverage, and if such a purchase was efficient (in the sense that the value of the coverage exceeded its cost), then those persons should continue to purchase coverage even after community rating disappears.

Might permitting some cost sharing also kill off comprehensive HMOs? The great bulk of our recent experience suggests that, relative to indemnity plans with cost sharing at conventional levels (for example, $400 deductible, 20 percent coinsurance, and no coverage for routine office visits), the results are quite the contrary: if anything, it is the HMO benefit policies that differentially attract good risks, not indemnity insurance. This kind of adverse selection against indemnity insurers in favor of HMOs does not occur for all HMOs; in the RAND Health Insurance Experiment, the Group Health Cooperative of Puget Sound apparently attracted a random slice of the population.[8] But the main point is that, at the current cost-sharing level (approximately, on average, about 25 percent of personal health expenditures paid out of pocket), there is no basis for fearing risk sorting. If removal of the tax subsidy increased the level of cost

---

[8]Willard Manning et al., "A Controlled Trial of the Effect of Prepaid Group Practice on the Use of Services," *New England Journal of Medicine*, vol. 310 (June 7, 1984), pp. 1505–10.

sharing, there might be a problem, but it appears that there is some leeway before HMOs would stop selecting good risks.

To put it bluntly, there might still be a little adverse selection in the market for insurance that supplements or adds to the basic minimum socially required coverage, but who cares? While the omnipotent, welfare-maximizing economist might want to make all markets work efficiently, once everyone has basic minimum coverage, producing efficiency in this supplementary coverage market is probably not high on the list of any realistic person's set of priorities.

More formally, if coverage at some level of cost sharing is thought adequate, then permitting such cost sharing to be purchased will not lead to a segmentation of risks unless high risks are actually better off purchasing more generous coverage and paying a rate appropriate to their risk levels than they would be if they bought the high cost-sharing coverage at a pooled rate. That is, high risks always have the option of joining low risks and purchasing the high cost-sharing coverage; if they do so, the break-even premium for such coverage will be a community rate. If they choose to purchase some other more generous policy, that policy will have to carry a rate based on the experience of high risks. If high risks choose to pay such a rate, they must be better off by doing so.

It is true that high risks will not be as well off, in either equilibrium, as they would have been when purchasing generous coverage at a pooled rate. It is not obvious, however, that subsidizing high risks to purchase more coverage than is necessary is a desirable social objective.

The main point then is that purchasing less generous coverage cannot be inconsistent with social objectives. What about purchasing more generous coverage? Can addition of a benefit not in the standard package cause risk segmentation? The answer depends on whether there is some subclass of medical services for which persons with generally lower risk are nevertheless at above-average risk. Such cases are not so easy to find, but they are possible.

Suppose a plan offers to pay for high-intensity aerobics and other fitness services. Reasonably, the healthy might be at higher "risk" to use those services than the frail. If an extra premium is charged to cover the cost of such services, it is possible that the new package may appeal to low risks (who would value the extra benefits at more than the extra premium) but not to high risks (who attach little value to the benefit), relative to the initial pooled standard package. The initial pooled policy may then not be at equilibrium, and premiums for the standard package will rise as high risks are drawn to the health club insurance. There are two equilibria possible: high risks

157

may still stay in their separate policy but prefer paying its (higher) premium, or they may join the low risks in the health club policy, sharing the cost of this benefit. If the new policy must charge a pooled rate, it paradoxically "over charges" high risks.

Most fundamentally, it is hard to believe that this type of risk selection, by offering more generous coverage, can amount to much. The worst that can happen to a small number of high risks is that their premium rises a little as they share in the cost of benefits they do not use. This transfer must be small compared with the transfer they receive through community rating.

On balance, there seems to be virtually no case for regulating packages above the minimum benefit package. As long as the minimum coverage is still decent, high risks can purchase it and avoid adverse selection.

If adverse selection among moderate risks is not a matter of serious concern, however, unusually large premiums for unusually high risks are. How many such persons are there? Surprisingly, we apparently have no answer to this critical question: *we do not know how serious the problem of high premiums for high risks is.* We do have a host of anecdotes and newspaper stories.[9] We do have some evidence that the level of coverage has declined among small firms, but it is virtually certain that this decline has less to do with risk rating and much more to do with high administrative costs and the growth of total premiums for insurance relative to the value of the "free" insurance available to all who become bad debts.

The problem of unexpected jumps in premiums does not exist for the high percentage of the population who receive their insurance from large firms (above 100 workers), since such firms are not medically underwritten. There can be a problem for the person who loses his job, but this is obviously a small proportion of high-risk families among employees of large firms.

For those who buy their insurance as individuals or as members of small groups, the relevant question can be posed as follows. Define what is regarded as an unusually high premium—say, above 150 percent of the average. Then, take a sample of 1,000 persons who work for small firms or buy insurance on their own. Ask how many such persons, over the next year, would find that insurers would charge them premiums above 150 percent of the average. Note that this is not the same thing as asking what proportion would have high medical expenses, since insurers do not know beforehand who will

---

[9]Gina Kolata, "New Insurance Practice Dividing Sick from Well," *New York Times*, March 4, 1992.

get sick and who will not. We ask only what proportion would insurers *forecast* to have unusually high expenses. This is important: to deal with risk rating, policy does not have to know who in fact will have high expenses; it needs to know only as much as insurers know (or are willing to act on).

As we have noted elsewhere, only about 3 percent of the population report themselves to be in fair or poor health.[10] The percentage of the under–sixty-five population estimated to be uninsurable is typically about 1 percent. In addition, requiring that chronic conditions be truly chronic, by imposing limited-term guaranteed renewability (as discussed below) effectively removes the insuree characteristic that accounts statistically for high expected future medical expenses.[11] In addition, even when insurers could use objective indicators of risk, that information is costly.[12]

By all accounts, the actual number of unusually high anticipated risks has to be a small proportion of all families. While a more careful investigation of the number and characteristics of people who would be charged substantially higher-than-average premiums would be warranted, we know what the outcome has to be. It is virtually a tautology to say that people or small groups who would be quoted much above-average premiums because their expected expenses are unusually high are a small fraction of the population. If they were a large fraction, their expenses and premiums could not be much above average, because the average would be high. I conjecture that 5 percent or less of the population would exceed the 150 percent limit within any demographic category.

Heavily regulating the insurance and care purchase of the 95 percent or more who do not fall into the high-risk category cannot be the best policy: it is like burning the haystack to find the needle. A better strategy, in my view, is one that permits insurers to charge high premiums to those they identify as high risks but then make transfers to those individuals in sufficient amounts to keep insurance affordable for them. The task for public policy is made immensely easier because insurers have already done the hard work of identify-

---

10Mark Pauly, Patricia Danzon, Paul Feldstein, and John Hoff, *Responsible National Health Insurance* (Washington, D.C.: AEI Press, 1992)

11Susan Marquis, "Adverse Selection with a Multiple Choice among Health Insurance Plans: A Simulation Analysis," *Journal of Health Economics*, vol. 11 (August 1992), pp. 129–51.

12Frank Sloan, "Adverse Selection: Does It Preclude a Competitive Health Insurance Market?" *Journal of Health Economics*, vol. 11, no. 3 (October 1992), pp. 353–56.

ing the high risks. It is then only necessary to make transfers or credits available to those persons so identified, with credits financed by efficient and fair taxes (rather than the inefficient and inequitable excise tax embodied in community rating).

Identification of high risks is easily accomplished by permitting those who have been quoted unusually high premiums to claim credits that cover almost all (but not quite all) of the above-average premiums. There cannot be 100 percent offset, because then individuals and insurers will have an incentive to conspire to be falsely designated as high risks in order to receive a subsidy. Administratively, the transfer could be accomplished in one of two ways: by permitting higher transfers based on certification of risk status and the premium charged or by permitting identified high-risk people to purchase insurance from a subsidized high-risk pool in which (net) premiums are set somewhat above the levels available to average risks. The two are not mutually exclusive; both options can be made available. We have experience with high-risk pools, and we know that they are feasible. The main advantage of the explicit individual credit approach is that it allows the high-risk market to benefit maximally from competition—since high-risk pools must regulate their insurers' coverage to some extent.

For many policy makers, the great defect of such an explicit tax-and-transfer mechanism is precisely its transparency: would the citizenry tolerate being taxed to subsidize insurance for high-risk people, or isn't it better to require community-rated insurers to cover such persons and pretend that it is the insurer, not the other insureds, who are paying? I know of no easy answer to this question, other than to express my own preference for informed voter choice, as opposed to letting the ends justify the means.

The task of offsetting risk-rated premiums for a tiny minority of the population is a formidable one for public policy, and there is no doubt that implementing it would add a layer of administrative complexity. The challenge could be mitigated by requiring insurers to offer contracts in which, over some period of time, they promise not to raise premiums because of temporarily high expenditures by a particular individual or small group. Such limited-term guaranteed renewability at standard rates is surely the kind of feature a rational buyer of insurance would choose in any case, since no one would want to risk having one's premium jump significantly during a spell of illness. The rationale for the design of mandated coverage—mandate the minimum protection a properly informed risk-averse person, at any income level, would choose—suggests that requiring guaranteed renewability for three or four years should be part of the mandate and should not, in a world where all are obligated to purchase insurance, cause serious problems for insurers.[13] Insurers now in fact offer such guaranteed renewability features—even if I pay my premiums quarterly, my insurer guarantees my premiums, and the issue of insurance, for one year. Since there is nothing special about twelve months (compared, say, with thirty-six months), it seems feasible to extend the period of at least partial premium guarantees.

The other observation is that the alternative mechanism for subsidizing high risks (that is, requiring some type of community rating—even if within demographic categories) also gets administratively complex very quickly. Even large insurers or health plans can, by chance or intent, end up with a nonrandom slice of the population, based on where their facilities are located, what kinds of doctors they hire, and the like. Then, as policy analysts have recognized, it will be necessary to have a mechanism to measure the risk levels at each insurer or plan and make transfers across plans.[14] That is, it will be necessary for government or some quasi-governmental agency such as a health insurance purchasing corporation (HIPC) to collect medical underwriting data, exactly the same data needed to implement risk-adjusted tax credits. The need to measure risk levels is still present under community rating.

Bargaining Strength and Insurer Regulation

It is beyond doubt that, historically, the U.S. private health care system conferred monopoly power on hospitals and doctors in various ways. It is less generally recognized that some of the most beloved forms of government intervention were the vehicles for conferring this power: licensure of physicians and chartering and awarding privileges to physician-and-hospital-owned Blue Cross and Blue Shield coverage. What Charles Weller has called "guild free choice" was, for the greater part of this century, the conventional way of organizing and paying for medical care.[15] The revolution that

---

[13]Mark Pauly, Patricia Danzon, Paul Feldstein, and John Hoff, "A Plan for Responsible National Health Insurance," *Health Affairs* (Spring 1991), pp. 5–26.

[14]J. Robinson, "A Payment Method for Health Insurance Purchasing Cooperatives," *Health Affairs*, supp. (1993), pp. 65–75.

[15]Charles Weller, " 'Free Choice' as a Restraint of Trade in American Health Care Delivery and Insurance," *Iowa Law Review* (July 1984), pp. 1351–92.

has virtually wiped out the insurance that pays for what the doctor and patient agree on, regardless, has surely eroded this market power. What is less sure is how much remains and whether some of that power, having been taken from venal providers, might simply be transferred to greedy health plans. How much control is needed to allow the consumer, as the ultimate buyer of and payer for health insurance, the ability to purchase at prices that equal marginal cost, that is, in a competitive market?

The argument that "health care has historically been characterized by strong providers and weak purchasers" is not historically correct.[16] A typical hospital has revenues of less than $100 million per year and in a large metropolitan area will capture less than 10 percent of the market. It usually faces a Blue Cross plan with a market share of approximately one-third of private business or a commercial insurer or large self-insured firm, with revenues in the billions of dollars. Even an HMO can often match the market share and exceed the revenue. What is true, historically, is not that purchasers were weak but that they behaved weakly. That is, for a number of reasons, they chose not to use such market power as they possessed.

The key issues are, as usual, the numbers of buyers and sellers. In most metropolitan areas, there are sufficient numbers of hospitals and doctors to suggest that a health plan with a reasonably large number of members should be able to negotiate prices close to cost. Indeed, in some cases, because hospital managers often think that their fixed costs are higher than they are, the price may fall below both average cost and marginal cost. If a hospital does not have market power, then surely the physician, competing with hundreds of other physicians, does not.

It is sometimes said that small firms and individual buyers need help to get lower prices. But, of course, there is no connection between the size of the employment group and the size of the insurer; it is possible (and it often happens) that a large insurance plan can be assembled out of sales of insurance to small firms. Then the large plan can negotiate low prices with providers as the agent of the individual buyers as well as the benefits department of a large corporation can. Conversely, it might be imagined that there would be difficulty for small buyers if they must buy from a large health insurance plan. But this should not be a problem if there are many such plans, each competing for the customer's business. The pre-

---

[16]Paul Starr, "Healthy Compromise: Universal Coverage and Managed Competition under a Cap," *American Prospect* (Winter 1993), pp. 42–52.

mium will be bid down close to cost (although there may still be animosity and suspicion).

Moreover, another alleged advantage for forming larger purchasing groups for small firms—lower administrative cost—is largely illusory. Starr and Zelman, for instance, claim that the administrative cost is twenty-five cents out of every premium dollar for firms with 25 to 49 employees. (This estimate appears to come from a table that represents a consulting firm's guesswork, which then became "official" when it was included in a study by the Congressional Research Service.[17] Starr and Zelman also misread the table, since the table says that administrative costs are 25 percent of *claims*, not premiums; this works out to one-fifth of premiums going for administrative costs.) It is, however, surely wrong to imagine that most of these administrative costs will go away just because the small employers are amalgamated. The higher per employee administrative cost in a set of ten 25-employee firms, as compared with a single group of 250, arises because each firm must be sold insurance, each firm must receive a premium bill, and each firm must be serviced. With ten 25-person firms, each one of these tasks must be done ten times, rather than once as in the 250-person firm, and yet the cost per task per firm is about as high (and sometimes higher) if the firm is small as if it is large. But combining the ten firms into one HIPC does not change the number of sales, bills, or services required; you cannot make a giant just by rounding up a passel of midgets.

It is possible to reduce administrative costs by limiting the variety of plans or by mandating employer (or employee) payment. But then the basis of the cost reduction is the new rules, not the new structure.

The strongest rationale for cost reduction by grouping small firms in HIPCs is that doing so may help to avoid a risk premium, which insurers are alleged to add when they must insure small groups. This add-on to the basic premium does not reflect real resource cost but rather the idea that, in offering to insure a small group, the insurer takes the risk that it might guess wrong in classifying that risk. If its underwriting and risk-rating procedures are off, it can undercharge many small groups and run the risk of large losses.

If insurers are owned by investors who themselves can pool risk by owning a diversified portfolio, the stockholders will not want their firm to sacrifice market share by jacking up premiums to reassure nervous management. More generally, it does not seem plausible

---

[17]U.S. Library of Congress, Congressional Research Service, *Insuring the Uninsured: Options and Analysis* (October 1988).

that insurers offering coverage to small groups conventionally charge premiums that exceed both medical benefits and explicit administrative costs by 5 percent or more, just to offset the risk of big losses in the year they got the ratebook and underwriting manual wrong. The strongest evidence against this view is that selling small group insurance is not usually profitable. I am not aware of evidence that such insurers on average earn high profits to offset the more risky character of investment in firms with volatile earnings. The case that HIPCs will cut costs by cutting the return required by risk-averse investors, by making HMO and insurance stocks a safe bet, seems implausible, especially since HIPCs (and reform in general) will surely add *political* risk, government not always being a reliable partner for private sector cooperation.

Of course, if either providers or insurers collude, a competitive outcome will not arise. In some cities, there have been tales of such collusion or of HMOs' "shadow pricing" of conventional insurers. But these sound like temporary way stations on the path to competitive equilibrium. This behavior may also have been caused by some features of the HMO act, such as the requirement that large employers offer an HMO to their employees, whether that HMO was shadow pricing or not.

Smaller cities with only a few hospitals may face more of a problem. But because there will also tend to be fewer health plans, the negotiations between providers and plans should still work reasonably well. But there may be too few plans for perfect competition. In many ways, the problem with health plan competition in smaller cities is no different from the problem citizens of these cities face for other products: the selection will not be quite as good, and the prices not quite as low. But let prices float too high, and a Wal-Mart (or its health plan analogue) will come to town. There is likely to be strong discipline from potential entry, and the amount of time it takes to organize an independent practice association–type of plan is not long.

In rural areas, managed competition will not work well, with or without regulation. If such areas are thought to be hotbeds of expenditure growth, perhaps they might be treated to a dose of direct price controls, which are not needed in the rest of the country. For reasons described below, however, even that might not be necessary.

The conclusion is that we have no evidence of the need to organize, in an artificial way, aggregates of buyers into health plans; there is no obvious need for HIPCs. Probably, competition alone can work as well as could a system burdened by an entirely new, poorly organized, and poorly motivated bureaucratic structure. (As I will note below, there are some crucial functions HIPCs are to perform.)

Nevertheless, it is the doubt, the fear that such markets will not work well, that gives the HIPC concept its great appeal. With an HIPC, one does not have to trust the shadowy operations of markets; one can see a structure, staffed by employees whose job it is to do the right thing—no matter if they do not know for sure what the right thing is, how to do it, or why it is in their interest to do so. So some further reassurance may be needed.

Making Buyer Choice Work

The shining vision of competition among health care plans is that individual citizens themselves would choose, with full information, among a set of health plans that offer them varying combinations of quality and rate of improvement in quality, with varying premiums and rates of growth in premiums. The fear of advocates of managed competition is, however, that real consumers might not be allowed by their employers to make such choices and, if they were so allowed, they might not choose intelligently. Accordingly, regulations are proposed to require employers to let individual employees choose and to simplify the set of insurance policies so that they can make those choices without making mistakes.

Employers are to be required to make fixed-dollar contributions toward the costs of all plans and permit employees individual choice among plans, paying the differential premium. Such an arrangement, without consideration of administrative cost, does offer ideal incentives to properly informed workers. The puzzle is why, if this is so, employers have to be ordered to implement such an arrangement. If employers are simply misinformed, communication of recommendations should do the trick. They may choose not to implement this system because they fear adverse selection; other changes that limit adverse selection should make them alter their financing behavior. Less benignly, employees may sometimes prefer that employers make the choice for them; they treat the employer as their agent, whom they trust to help them avoid the cost of choice. There seems to be no good reason to forbid this behavior.

The outstanding example of confusion in choice among health plans is the Federal Employees Health Benefit Plan, which offers so many choices that "the eyes quickly glaze over when confronted with page after page of coverage variations among alternative plans."[18] FEHBP offers many more plans than private insurers choose, for a

---

[18]Linda Bergthold, "Benefit Design Choices under Managed Competition," *Health Affairs*, supp. (1993), pp. 99–109.

simple reason: the federal government must be sensitive to political pressures to keep a plan in the set of options, which private employers can and do resist. There is a certain irony in others' using this example of a highly political choice to illustrate why private markets will not work well. In any case, when all is said and done, it is not even clear that federal employees would prefer to have their choices limited in FEHBP: glazed eyes may be a small side effect they are willing to tolerate.

The other issue specifically concerns individual employee-citizen choice. What is needed to permit people to make good choices? The easiest answer to give, but perhaps the hardest to implement, is the provision to buyers of information that describes different health plans. Variations in the extent of indemnity coverage can be confusing to buyers, but fortunately there is an easy way to eliminate the confusion, without resorting to requiring a standard benefit package: require every insurer to state its loading or administrative cost percentage. This tells how much each insured gets back of what is put in, which is the true cost of insurance. We do not really need to look at the details of coverage to get a good idea of what we will pay.

Paradoxically, it is much more difficult to provide similar comparative information on HMOs, even though they all provide the same benefit package. Information on administrative costs will help a little. The real problem, however, is that all HMOs will promise to deliver the medical services the person needs, but they have different rules for deciding what is needed in a given setting and different nonmonetary prices (waiting, travel, inconvenience, choice of provider) that are much harder to communicate. What the buyer wants to know is either what health *and* convenience outcome is achieved or what rationing rule is followed. If we can measure all or most relevant outcomes accurately, with perfect adjustments for initial severity, all our problems are solved. HMOs, however, are just beginning a very rudimentary technology of outcome measurement, which has no claim, other than self-definition, to represent all the things that matter to consumers. Alternatively, we could imagine that some HMOs would set priorities by means of cost-effectiveness analysis; each HMO could then tell consumers what they need to know by telling them its threshold cost per quality-adjusted life year (QALY). The HMO that will produce QALY as long as they cost less than $100,000 will have a higher premium than the one that requires that cost to be below $50,000 before sacrificing one statistical life year, but consumers can presumably judge what quality of life and life expectancy are worth to them.

Information will never be perfect, but it can surely be improved.

A useful role for an HIPC—or some other marketwide association of potential insurance buyers—is to provide that information. Because of the public-good nature of information, there will need to be an element of compulsion or tax financing. In addition, this sponsor can make sure to avoid those plans that are poor value for the money— so that the buyer can compare only plans that fall at different points on the cost-quality trade-off. Here again, perfection is neither to be expected nor sought, and it is inevitable that some buyers will make mistakes. Regulatory bodies can prohibit types of insurance that do harm, at any income level, so that the worst consequence of a mistake in buyer choice will be paying too much for health care, not adverse health outcomes. It might also be useful to set up a public program to grade health plans—as "aggressive," "conservative," "high tech," "super convenient," and so forth—and plans could choose which label best fits their management and marketing philosophy. Many of these product types are neither higher nor lower quality, just different, and so such information is important to improve the match between buyers and sellers.

A further problem with a politically chosen standard benefit package is that politics will intrude. This process is already apparent as various advocacy groups (some of which I belong to) lobby to make sure that coverage of their service or the particular disease is generously included in the benefit package. Political definition of the minimum benefits to be provided to low-income people for whom the government will be paying the bill is inevitable, as is the intrusion of politics. But we can keep the tumult down to a dull roar by making this package truly the minimum (in terms of services included) and permitting cost sharing, but for a wide range of services, for the nonpoor. That is, it becomes feasible to cover a wide range of services if one does not require their cost to be covered in full for the nonpoor.

What Employers Should Do

Health insurance is currently rather tightly tied to employment, and proponents of managed competition have mixed feelings about that tie. On the one hand, they believe that employers often make mistakes in the types of plans they provide to workers and that the link of coverage to continued employment can lock workers into bad jobs. On the other hand, since they seem almost universally unaware that employer payments ultimately come out of workers' wages, they tend to blame employers for spending their money irrationally.

The regulatory solution generally has two parts. First, it requires the employer to "pay" a majority of the premium, at least a majority

167

of the premium of a minimum or benchmark plan. Second, it requires the employer to make the payment independent of the health plan chosen (for example, by requiring a fixed-dollar contribution) and to let employees choose from a variety of plans. These rules have two rationales: to make sure that employers continue to "pay" for insurance and to give employees choice among plans.

The rules may be unnecessary. Both economic theory and recent empirical work are definitive and unequivocal: employer "payments," by far the greatest part, come out of what would be workers' money wages.[19] The worker pays for his health insurance whether he pays part of the premium directly or has it taken from his wages. This means that rules about employer contributions are irrelevant at best and misleading at worst. Moreover, such rules tend to create wholly artificial distinctions among employees of large firms, employees of small firms, and the self-employed. Starr and Zelman, for instance, are at a loss over how to treat the self-employed once they have proposed a rule that requires that the employer "contribute" most of the benchmark premium. They offer the vague suggestion that the self-employed should receive (larger?) subsidies. But since, as the recent controversy over the attorney general nomination showed, a given worker can be labeled either an employee or an independent self-employed contractor, tying subsidies or rules to the presence or absence of an employment contract is sure to be distortive. If the self-employed get subsidies, or can avoid regulatory rules imposed on the employment contract, there can be a serious distortion in the labor market and an incentive for workers to be "de-employed." Similar comments apply to part-time workers or workers in small rather than large firms. The ideal policy makes subsidies and regulations independent of the type of employment and dependent only on total household income.

Even so solid an economist as Henry Aaron is unnerved by the question of how to treat employer payments.[20] He first asserts that they fall on workers but then ends up advocating mandated employer payments as politically realistic. But since "employer payment" is

---

[19]See Mark Pauly, "The Incidence of Health Insurance Costs: Is Everyone out of Step but Economists?" IRRA proceedings of the forty-first annual meeting, New York City, December 29, 1988, pp. 387–410; and U. Reinhardt, "Reorganizing the Financial Flows in American Health Care," *Health Affairs*, supp. (1993), pp. 172–93.

[20]Henry Aaron, "Employer Mandates: The Only Practicable Option," paper presented at the annual meeting of the National Academy of Social Insurance, January 28, 1993.

really just compulsory *employee* payment, he winds up endorsing regressive taxation.

How do employers decide what to pay for health insurance and what set of insurances to offer? The answer in theory is straightforward enough—they offer whatever sells in the labor market. If their employees (or, more precisely, those whom they would like to be and remain their employees) want to have the option to choose among a variety of plans, employers will offer choice. If employees prefer to have fewer or no choices—because offering many plans raises the premium cost or the subjective cost to the employee of choosing—employers will offer no choice. Starr and Zelman, for instance, decry employers who "impose managed care, often depriving employees of a choice of plan or physician."[21] In fact, few employers impose a single HMO, although there is a tendency to offer point-of-service HMO plans that attach a financial penalty to out-of-network use, but do not deprive. Still, suppose an employer did require all workers for his firm to belong to one HMO. That would happen only if the employer believed that doing so would increase the attractiveness of working for his firm, either because it was a good HMO or because the lower premium cost would permit the employer to pay higher money wages. Since we have little evidence that, on average, employers shoot themselves in the foot in designing benefits packages (although some surely do), there seems to be little reason to regulate what they should do, save for regulation intended to prevent deception.

What we do not understand very well is how employers set the premium differences among options when they offer multiple options. The managed-competition regulations on this score are clear and sensible: they envision requiring the employee to pay the full difference between plans with after-tax dollars, so that, as Starr and Zelman observe, "the system implicitly asks consumers whether plans other than the benchmark plan are worth the extra cost."[22] Why would an employer ever choose to distort this choice by, for example, paying a proportion of every premium? One possible answer is to reduce or manage risk rating and adverse selection. In virtually all multiple-choice settings, employers do not permit plans to charge risk-rated premiums, even though such premiums could easily be related to employee age and family size, if not to health. Indeed, it can be shown that an employer can choose the set of plans

---

[21]Starr and Zelman, "Bridge to Compromise."

[22]Ibid.

and cross-subsidized premiums to deal optimally with adverse selection if it is a problem.

Policy here needs to walk a fine line. On the one hand, it seems impractical to jettison the existing apparatus for choosing and paying for health insurance in connection with employment. On the other hand, we want to avoid introducing further distortions and rigidities by enshrining the employment nexus as the only way of obtaining health insurance. I continue to believe that the approach we took in *Responsible National Health Insurance* is the right one: construct neutral incentives so that employment can serve as the way of obtaining insurance for those firms and individuals for whom it is best, but not necessarily for all.[23] One important point about responsible national health insurance is often (willfully, I sometimes suspect) misinterpreted: responsible national health insurance does *not* require persons to get their insurance as individuals. After all, individual insurance is expensive. What it does do is permit employees to work for firms in which the employer writes out all or part of the check for health insurance and arrange the coverage (that is offer group insurance), if doing so is sufficiently attractive or efficient to make it a good labor market strategy. Employers and employees, however, are not required to do things this way.

Global Budgets

The final set of regulations, proposed by the Clinton administration and by some proponents of managed competition but opposed by others, is some form of global budgeting. I do not want to go into great detail here to explore the reasons for global budgets, other than to say that many of the reasons offered—high health care costs will bankrupt the country, or high costs mean that no one can afford health care—are economic nonsense, at least in a world where tax subsidies are removed. In such a world, competition will tie plan premiums to actual cost, and well-informed individuals will choose higher-cost plans only if the extra benefits from those plans are worth the extra cost. Indeed, the fact that people do pay those ballooning costs means that they can afford them and prefer to spend their money on health care rather than on other things.

This does not settle the issue, of course: rising costs generated by the willingness of the middle class to buy new health technology may price poorer people out of the market (the "gentrification" of

---

[23]Pauly, Danzon, Feldstein, and Hoff, *Responsible National Health Insurance.*

170

health care), and rising costs cause problems for atherosclerotic government budgetary processes. Moreover, a sine qua non of managed competition—that managed-care plans be permitted to refuse to deliver beneficial technology that they judge not to be worth the price and that negligence law not be permitted to override these choices— must be achieved. Finally, global budgets are not objectionable and really ought to be required for those insurances that the government administers—Medicare and, at least at present, Medicaid.

The real issue is applying spending limits to citizens' expenditures of their own private funds—making it a crime to spend your own money on your own medical care. The bottom line is that if one really accepts the managed-competition paradigm and has the required amount of faith, neither total global budgets nor partial budgetary limits in the form of technology boards are required.

The problem, for most people, is that they really cannot be reassured that competition will bring prices down to costs and that citizens will really make reasonable choices. They do not have faith that, even under undistorted competition, the rate of growth in medical spending will be the right rate. The truth be told, the main weapon for cost containment in managed competition does seem to be a fairly anemic one: remove the tax subsidy, we preach, and people will become more cost conscious, cost conscious enough to tame the medical inflation dragon. For someone who wonders how the Internal Revenue Service can engineer a fall in the real rate of growth of medical spending enough to stablize the share of GNP— which requires cutting the growth rate by at least half—reliance on tax incentives seems a risky bet.

One can try to reset expectations. It is not necessary to freeze the share of GNP going to health care, and there is nothing bad about a growing share if people prefer to spend a disproportionate amount of real productivity growth on their health as opposed to their home appliances. After all, the services sector share of GNP has been growing for more than a century, fueled in part by productivity growth in manufacturing and agriculture. But people still wonder whether competition will work and whether it will be enough to break the back of health care cost inflation. Advocates of spending limits, therefore, view these limits as a fail-safe mechanism. Starr and Zelman use the analogy of equipping an aircraft with a second engine, in case the first one fails. Why not have a backup?

Enthoven and some market-oriented commentators argue vociferously against such limits. They prefer to imagine spending limits as analogous to equipping a single-engine Cessna with an auxiliary steam engine, pointed at an oblique angle, that at a minimum will

171

make it hard to get off the ground and may force the craft off course and down in flames. Governmentally enforced global budgets can be manipulated politically, can impede what some managed-competition firms are trying to do, and are unnecessary. Still, the citizenry may want a life preserver. Isn't there a way to design one that is effective but not obstructive?

Budget Limits and Competitive Markets

I believe there is a way to have budget limits along with competitive markets: it comes in the form of a device that will be needed for health care reform in any case. The best way to assure people of the opportunity to control medical costs is to use a fallback or publicly designated insurer as the vehicle. Let me first describe how this idea would work in RNHI and then discuss it in a more generic context.

If all Americans are to have access to health insurance, there needs to be an insurer of last resort to cover those who are not conventional employees or who have no access to the usual forms of coverage. This insurer has to offer the basic or minimum acceptable benefit package, and the net premium paid for this coverage must be judged to be fair. Obviously, the government has to select the fallback insurer, though it may either contract out its management or run it itself. As part of specifying the policies of that insurer, it can specify what its premium will be next year: the insurer will then have to deliver as much care as can be obtained from that amount.

If the government wishes to limit the rate of growth in spending to some level it judges appropriate, it can begin by limiting the rate of growth in premiums for the fallback insurer. If it wishes to limit the rate of growth in medical spending to GNP growth plus 2 percent, for instance, it can specify that the premium for a comprehensive fallback insurer can increase by at most only GNP plus 2 percent. Competitive bidding should guarantee that the insurer will deliver the maximum amount of care (and new technology) that can be purchased with that amount of money. Since fallback coverage must be available to every citizen, it follows that every citizen has, as an option, choosing an insurer whose premium is rising at the rate that collective choice deems to be appropriate and delivering the services it can deliver for that amount of money. The mixture of services can also be guided by the government.

Note the dramatic change this makes. Each American has the *option* of obtaining an insurance, for an equitable premium, that provides the set of services judged collectively to be appropriate and growing at the appropriate rate. If the government in fact chooses as most citizens would prefer, customers should beat a path to the door of the fallback insurer (or to other firms that copy it). Thus, all Americans can be *guaranteed* the chance to keep their health care costs under that degree of control the government deems appropriate.

The fear that many advocates of managed competition have, however, is that the government may not choose the right rate of growth in cost or in the forms of coverage or new technology. The collectively chosen rate may be wrong for everyone (either too high, because of political pressures, or too low, because of fiscal pressures). Or it may be right for many but still wrong for some whose valuation of new medical services differs from the average. The fallback insurer plan, however, guarantees against such mistakes, since it offers the *option* of purchase of other insurance, at prices reflective of their cost. Suppose, as Enthoven has warned, that timid politics may make the budgetary target too high. Then competitive insurers offering plans that undercut the target will be more attractive to consumers. Or suppose (to keep Medicare from looking bad financially) the collective spending limit is set too low. Then, despite their higher price, people will prefer more costly private insurance options that offer higher quality, convenience, technology, or humane treatment.

Many believe that the current health care system is shot through with inefficiency. They believe that it ought to be possible to carve improvements in efficiency out of a $900 billion system that would allow universal coverage and low rates of growth in spending, at least for a long while. The empirical evidence on the amount of waste is contradictory, confusing, and inconclusive. What if there isn't enough inefficiency? But the strategy I have suggested here avoids having to bet the farm on the existence of massive inefficiency. If such inefficiency is present, both the fallback insurer and other competitive plans should be able to identify it, weed it out, and offer an attractive insurance package at lower premiums than could be charged by more complacent insurers. If there is little inefficiency, no one will be constrained.

In effect, the fallback insurer proposal amounts to offering full, 100 percent socialized medicine: insurance chosen by the government, run by the government (or its contractor), and financed by the government. Private alternatives, however, are permitted. These alternatives are not, it should be emphasized, supplementary coverage—they are *substitute* plans. When people do choose such higher-cost options, they will not ordinarily be opting for cosmetic surgery but rather for quicker access to new technology, greater use of possibly but not certainly beneficial tests (for example, mammography for women under age fifty), or greater convenience and choice.

This proposal actually echoes, in a more transparent way, some proposals that have been made by others. California Insurance Commissioner John Garamendi proposed, if I understand his ideas correctly, to make a Medicaid-like option available to all citizens; the fallback proposal here simply generalizes that public insurance option.[24] Less obviously, Starr and Zelman, though ostensibly endorsing effective budgetary limits, seem willing to settle for a cap on a benchmark premium. If there is a fixed proportion of employer and employee payments, and if only employer payments to the benchmark premium are excluded from taxation, the effect of such a rule is to set a limit on the rate of growth of the dollar amount excluded from taxation. Since the key incentive issue is the marginal tax rate, such a policy in effect limits the dollar amount of premium that would be tax subsidized and is virtually no different—other than in symbolic value—from simply eliminating the tax subsidy.

One should probably not denigrate the symbolic value of a premium limit. Having a particular rate of premium growth endorsed by some type of public body should prompt buyers to ask any plan that wishes to raise its premium further to provide an explanation; this may be an effective way of eliciting information on just what people can expect to get for their money if they choose a plan whose premium is growing faster than the benchmark premium.

Starr and Zelman believe that such a mild cap "ordinarily should be sufficient." They offer the somewhat cryptic and ominous comment that the regulators should "keep an eye on various forms of out of pocket spending that might signal a problem" but then move on without saying what should happen if a problem is spotted.[25] My judgment is that, if all consumers have the option of a fallback insurer that is toeing the spending cap line, then their willingness to pay more than the cap in out-of-pocket payments—as long as they pay with their own money, with no subsidies—means no problem at all.

Not only does the presence of a fallback insurer keep other managed-care firms honest when it comes to rates of premium growth, this insurer can also be the guarantee on the issues of risk spreading, bargaining, and employee choice discussed in the previous sections. The fallback insurer is permitted to risk rate, but it—of all entities—should be relied on to give the government the correct

---

[24]John Garamendi, "California Health in the 21st Century: A Vision for Reform" (Sacramento: California Department of Insurance, 1992).

[25]Starr and Zelman, "Bridge to Compromise."

information on who is a high risk to trigger an offsetting credit. The fallback insurer should have enough presence—and enough motivation, if it wants the government contract next year—to bargain with providers and to furnish a spending-constrained option for every citizen, even those condemned to live in rural areas. And while the fallback insurer is a single choice, it is a decent plan, so that no one can rightfully complain about being in the government's good hands.

Conclusion

It is too soon at this point to predict what type of health reform will emerge. For any proposal, all sorts of possible bad consequences can be imagined, and there is a strong political dynamic to build in lawyerly regulations to protect against the possible, or the undesirable behavior (this being a big country) that is sure to happen to some Americans. In my view, the best policy is not to give in to this lust for certainty, because it can never be satisfied. Instead, a good strategy is one of creating and offering a model public plan, as a kind of safe harbor for those Americans (few, I suspect, but I run the risk of being wrong) unwilling to make market choices for themselves. That would allow others to select the efficient level and type of spending on this most personal of services.

Market-oriented economists are fond of singing the praises of unregulated competition, and I am usually happy to join in for the chorus. In situations in which there is uncertainty about market performance, however, there is an alternative to the stifling embrace of heavy regulation, for the market's own good. It is a wholly new paradigm—the planned entry of a collectively chosen and publicly managed competitor. The presence of such a plan, in effect, puts the market to the market test. And may the best institution win.

7

The Effectiveness of Managed Competition in Reducing the Costs of Health Insurance

Roger Feldman and Bryan Dowd

Managed competition is the central feature of several proposals to restructure the health care system in fundamental ways that would address the dual concerns of rising health care costs and the large number of Americans who are not covered by health insurance. Although many individuals are associated with managed competition, this theory has been articulated most recently by Alain Enthoven and Richard Kronick.[1] Their proposal includes mandated employer-provided health insurance, premium contributions from all employers and employees, a limit on tax-free employer premium contributions, and public sponsors to structure and manage the demand side of the health insurance market. Enthoven and Kronick

We would like to thank Brenda Byron, insurance plan manager for the University of Minnesota, and Dennis Mackey, health financial analyst at the Minnesota Department of Employee Relations, for providing data used in this study. John Klein, manager of the Minnesota Public Employees Insurance Plan, offered helpful advice. The study was funded by the Agency for Health Care Policy and Research. The opinions expressed in this chapter are solely those of the authors.

[1]Alain C. Enthoven and Richard Kronick, "Universal Health Insurance through Incentives Reform," *Journal of the American Medical Association*, vol. 265, no. 19 (May 15, 1991), pp. 2532–36.

argue that this proposal will give people the opportunity to choose an economically responsible health insurance policy. Given this opportunity, people will choose "value for money," they believe, selecting health insurance plans that offer the best quality of service at the most reasonable price.

Most elements in Enthoven and Kronick's prescription were included in a bill introduced in the 102d Congress by Representative Jim Cooper (H.R. 5936). Managed competition may be the centerpiece of President Clinton's proposed health care reforms, and it certainly will be debated by policy makers regardless of the president's specific proposals.

Despite the popularity of the managed-competition theory, there is surprisingly little agreement about how managed competition might work in practice—partly because managed competition has never been tried on a national scale. As Robert Reischauer, director of the Congressional Budget Office, testified before the House Ways and Means Committee on February 2, 1993: "Little information from either the United States or abroad is available on the time that it would take for all the changes to occur or on the magnitude of the impacts of these changes once they were fully implemented and all behavioral responses had occurred."

While agreeing that managed competition has never been tried on a national scale, we nevertheless believe that certain large employers have experimented with this concept long enough to assess its potential impact as a cost-control strategy. The experience of these employers may be of considerable value in judging the likely impact of managed competition as a national strategy. We were recently awarded a grant by the Agency for Health Care Policy and Research to analyze data from large employers that may provide insights into two critical elements of the managed-competition strategy. First, will employees switch health insurance plans when they are faced with higher out-of-pocket premiums? Second, are total premiums lower at a point in time, and do they rise more slowly for employers who manage the demand side of the health insurance market?

This chapter presents the results of our analysis of employees' choice of health plans. The analysis uses data from the State of Minnesota Group Insurance Program, which covers almost 57,000 state employees. This group is ideal for examining the effects of out-of-pocket premium differences on employees' choice of health plans. The state pays a fixed amount of the health care premium for every employee, based on the premium of the low-cost health insurance carrier in each county. Employees must pay 100 percent of the additional cost if they choose a plan more expensive than the low-cost carrier. Thus, employees have a strong financial incentive to choose the best value for their money, as recommended by Enthoven and Kronick.[2] In addition, starting in 1988, the out-of-pocket premiums of some plans have increased substantially, thus creating the setting for a natural experiment with health plan choice. Based on our analysis of Minnesota data from 1988 to 1993, we conclude that employees are sensitive to differences in out-of-pocket health plan premiums. Observed changes in health plan enrollment match the predictions from an econometric model quite closely in some instances. Even where the model's predictions do not exactly fit the data, our analysis may provide useful insights into the dynamics of health plan competition that might arise in a national system of managed competition.

The second section of the chapter describes the theoretical model that we used to predict how employees would change plans. The third section provides an overview of the Minnesota State Health Insurance Program, focusing on the program's evolution into a competitive system. The fourth section describes data and methods. The fifth section presents the results of our analysis. Finally, the sixth section summarizes the findings and their implications for the effectiveness of managed competition.

Model of Health Insurance Choice

The extent to which managed competition achieves savings in total health care costs will depend on how successfully it induces consumers to choose less comprehensive indemnity insurance (leading to fewer consumer-initiated requests for care) or else to enroll in cost-effective managed-care plans. Furthermore, the tax policy proposals of managed competition—taxing employer-paid health insurance premiums wholly or partly and reducing or eliminating the "section 125" exemption for employee-paid premiums—would substantially increase the cost of more expensive health plans compared with less expensive plans. The managed-competition theory assumes that these changes in tax policy will induce consumers to choose less comprehensive indemnity insurance or managed care.

In a previous empirical study, we found that employees are sensitive to differences in out-of-pocket premiums in firms that offer multiple-choice health insurance programs.[3] We also found, however,

---

[2]Ibid.

[3]Roger Feldman, Michael Finch, Bryan Dowd, and Steven Cassou, "The

that employees do not consider all health plans offered by their employer to be equally close substitutes. In particular, they regard independent practice associations (IPAs) and fee-for-service (FFS) plans as close substitutes for one another. These plans are distinguished by wide choice of doctors and hospitals with relatively few restrictions on patients' freedom to choose among them. Staff, group, and network model health maintenance organizations are also close substitutes. Staff and group HMOs are organized around a single physician group practice (the HMO unit controls the group practice in the staff model and contracts with it in the group model). Network HMOs contract with two or more group practices. Patients can obtain covered health care services without a referral only from these groups. Not surprisingly, there is much less substitution between these two classes of health plans.

The notion of close substitution can be formalized by the "nested logit" model of health plan choice. Suppose the employee has a choice of health plan classes or "nests" indexed 1,2, . . . ,N and health plan alternatives 1,2, . . . ,K_i within nest i. Our empirical study identified two nests: plans with unrestricted choice (IPAs and FFS plans) and plans with restricted choice (group, staff, and network HMOs).

McFadden has shown that the probability of choosing a particular plan can be represented by a two-stage process.[4] In the first stage, employees compare the value of every plan with the value of other plans in the same nest. If they were going to choose nest i, for example, the probability of selecting plan ij in this nest is

$$Q_{j|i} = \exp(\beta' X_{ij})/\exp(I_i) \qquad (7\text{--}1)$$

The numerator of equation (7–1) represents the value of plan ij to the consumer, based on its observed characteristics, which are represented by a vector of X variables. Some of these characteristics (for example, short waiting time to obtain appointments and full coverage of inpatient and outpatient services) add to the value of the plan, while others, such as a high out-of-pocket premium, reduce the plan's value. The values per unit of plan characteristics are represented by β', a row vector of regression coefficients. The denominator

Demand for Employment-based Health Insurance Plans," *Journal of Human Resources*, vol. 24, no. 1 (Winter 1989), pp. 115–42.

4Daniel McFadden, "Modelling the Choice of Residential Location," in A. Karlquist et al., eds., *Spatial Interaction Theory and Residential Location* (Amsterdam: North-Holland, 1978), pp. 75–96.

of equation (7–1) represents the value of all plans in this nest, that is,

$$I_i = \ln[\sum_{k=1}^{K_i} \exp{(\beta' X_{ik})}] \qquad (7\text{–}2)$$

Equation (7–2) is called the "inclusive value" of the nest.

In the second stage of the choice process, employees compare the value of each health plan nest. The probability of choosing nest i, for example, is

$$Q_i = \exp(\alpha' Y_i + \lambda I_i)/ \sum_{n=1}^{N} \exp(\alpha' Y_n + \lambda I_n) \qquad (7\text{–}3)$$

Observed characteristics that vary only by nest (for example, freedom to choose the doctor) are denoted by Y, and α' is a row vector of coefficients for these characteristics. The coefficient of the inclusive value, λ, provides an estimate of the similarity of choices within each plan type or nest. If $\lambda = 0$, consumers care only about characteristics of the health plan nest. This represents the lowest degree of substitution—in fact, a plan in nest i could reduce its premium without attracting any new enrollees from plans in other nests. A value of $\lambda = 1$ would indicate that all plans are equally close substitutes.

The probability of choosing plan ij is the product of the conditional probability given in equation (7–1) times the probability of choosing nest i from equation (7–3). In other words,

$$Q_{ij} = Q_{j|i} * Q_i \qquad (7\text{–}4)$$

Data for estimating this model were collected in 1984 by the Institute for Health Services Research at the University of Minnesota and the Minnesota Coalition on Health Care Costs. Working together, these organizations conducted a survey of employees in twenty Twin Cities firms. To participate in the study, firms had to be willing to pay part of the survey cost. The surveyed firms employed 7.2 percent of the Twin Cities work force and thus represented an important, if nonrandom, sample of employers. Within each firm, employees were selected randomly with different sampling probabilities. Altogether, 10,798 employees were surveyed, and 5,161 (47.8 percent) responded.

We were forced to drop two companies because of a defect in the survey design. Another small company that offered only an FFS plan was also dropped from the analysis of health plan choice. The remaining seventeen companies each offered at least one health care plan in the "freedom-of-choice" nest and at least one group, staff, or network HMO. Altogether, the seventeen firms offered thirty-five health plans in the freedom-of-choice nest and thirty-four group, staff, or network HMOs.

We selected single employees without dependents for our primary data set, and we assumed that they wanted only single-coverage health insurance. There were 900 employees in this group. We also analyzed a second group of employees: single-parent families and married workers whose spouse was not covered by health insurance through his or her job. These workers were assumed to want only family-coverage health insurance policies. Both assumptions were confirmed by examination of the data.

Estimation of the nested logit model showed that the coefficient of the inclusive variable, λ, was .304 and that it was significantly different from both 1 and 0. This finding indicates that consumers view health care plans in the two nests (FFS plans and IPAs; and group, staff, or network HMOs) as limited substitutes. In addition, the coefficient of the employee's out-of-pocket premium (measured in cents per month) was negative and statistically significant. We simulated the change in single-coverage health plan enrollment for a $5 monthly increase in out-of-pocket premiums and the change in family-coverage enrollment for a $10 monthly premium increase. Employees were quite sensitive to premium increases of $5 or $10. We concluded that employees will drop a high-cost plan if they have to pay part of the cost.

Our study suggests that managed competition may substantially reduce health care costs by inducing employees to change from more expensive to less expensive health plans. Several issues must be addressed, however, before the results of this study can be used to make predictions for a national managed-competition program. In the first place, the premium effect in our study is larger than that found by several other studies of health plan choice.[5] We have explained in detail why these differences arise and why the results of our analysis may be more reliable than those of other studies.[6] Ours was the only study to identify the plans that each employee actually

---

[5]Pamela Farley Short and Amy K. Taylor, "Premiums, Benefits, and Employee Choice of Health Insurance Options," *Journal of Health Economics*, vol. 8, no. 3 (December 1989), pp. 293–311; and W. P. Welch, "The Elasticity of Demand for Health Maintenance Organizations," *Journal of Human Resources*, vol. 21, no. 2 (Spring 1986), pp. 252–66.

[6]Roger Feldman, Bryan Dowd, Michael Finch, and Steven Cassou, *Employer-based Health Insurance*, National Center for Health Services Research and Health Care Technology Assessment, DHHS Publication No. (PHS) 89-3434, June 1989.

considered. Single employees without dependents, for example, will choose *only* from the single-coverage plans offered by their employer. Other studies used arbitrary assumptions to select the plans to be analyzed. We also used statistical tests to demonstrate that the nested logit model was the right way to analyze the data. The studies that we reviewed did concur on the general finding that employees will drop more expensive plans if they have to pay higher out-of-pocket premiums.

Second, conditions in the health plan market have changed significantly since 1984. At that time, premiums were heavily subsidized by employers, with most employees in our study paying less than $10 out-of-pocket per month for single coverage. Family coverage was also heavily subsidized. Since 1984, employees have had to pay a larger share of health plan premiums. It is not clear whether they will become more or less sensitive to premium changes as a result of this trend toward greater cost sharing. Another market-level change is the evolution of fee-for-service health plans from "old-fashioned" coverage of all doctors and hospitals into more tightly managed preferred provider organizations. None of the FFS plans in our study had a preferred provider network. Today, it is unusual in the Twin Cities to find an old-fashioned FFS plan. A similar decline in enrollment in conventional FFS plans without utilization management occurred at the national level.[7]

Because there are several different estimates of the demand for health plans and because conditions in the market have changed since 1984, it is important to have more studies of health plan choice. Replication of our study in a similar setting would be extremely useful. Unfortunately, a replication study is not feasible in the short run because of substantial data collection costs and the time required to analyze the data. There is an alternative way to validate our findings, however: this is to apply them to a multiple-plan employer where out-of-pocket premiums recently increased for some plans. Did employees leave these plans, as our model predicts? If they did, this provides an important verification of the model.

To make this test, we assembled data on out-of-pocket premiums, enrollment, and plan characteristics for single- and family-coverage health plans offered by the Minnesota Group Insurance Program. We predicted the change in enrollment for each health plan offered by the state program to employees in the Minneapolis–St. Paul metro-

---

[7]Cynthia B. Sullivan, Marianne Miller, Roger Feldman, and Bryan Dowd, "Employer-sponsored Health Insurance in 1991," *Health Affairs*, vol. 11, no. 4 (Winter 1992), pp. 172–85.

politan area from 1988 to 1993. Most of the employees covered by the state program live in this area. We repeated the same calculations for employees of the University of Minnesota in the Twin Cities from 1990 to 1993. These employees are covered by the state program, but data from the university were available only for four years. The following section of the chapter describes the Minnesota Group Insurance Program, the setting for this natural experiment in health plan choice.

Health Plan Contracting Methods Used by the State of Minnesota

The State of Minnesota Group Insurance Program provides health benefits for almost 57,000 employees. With dependents and retirees, the program covers approximately 144,000 people, making it the largest employer-based health insurance group in the state. Unlike most employers, who have employees in relatively few locations, Minnesota has employees working in every county, and the state is a major employer in many counties. The state's health benefits program must, therefore, serve the needs of people in urban and in rural areas and in areas with and without HMOs.

Before 1986, the cornerstone of the state's approach to health plan contracting was a fee-for-service plan offered through Blue Cross and Blue Shield of Minnesota. This was the original plan in the program before the advent of HMOs and the only plan available statewide. During most of the 1980s, this plan had half or more of the total group enrollment.

A state law allowed any HMO that wished to be offered into the program. As a result, the state offered a large number of HMOs—at times as many as ten. HMOs were available only in certain parts of the state, however, with the largest number in the Twin Cities. Under the same law, the state's contribution toward the cost of health insurance was tied to the FFS premium—100 percent contribution for employee coverage, 90 percent for dependent coverage. Employees did not receive a rebate for choosing an HMO that cost less than the FFS plan; however, they had to pay the difference if they chose a more expensive plan. HMO rates tended to cluster near the FFS rate. The rates submitted by the HMOs and Blue Cross and Blue Shield were not examined critically by the state.

Although the full extent of change did not become apparent for several years, 1985 was a watershed for the health benefits program. During this period, the state consolidated its HMO offerings and changed the basis for determining its premium contribution. These changes eventually led to significantly increased competition among the insurers and HMOs that participate in the state's program. From a high of ten HMOs, the state began 1990 with six. This reduction occurred for a variety of reasons, including:

- 1985 repeal of the law requiring an open-door policy toward HMOs
- HMO attrition and mergers
- rejection of applications to join the plan from HMOs that did not meet the state's criteria and objectives
- departure of an HMO that could not maintain reasonable premium rates
- no longer allowing an insurer or HMO to offer more than one option to employees or to add plans at its own initiative

Having fewer HMOs simplified the competitive dynamics among the state's health plans. Fewer HMOs meant that the remaining plans had a better chance of gaining a significant market share and more to gain from offering an attractive, well-managed plan. It also diminished the prospects for biased selection and for gaming the system, such as by adding plans to undercut a competitor's position or to "shore up" an existing plan.

But perhaps the most significant reform during this period was changing the formula for determining the employer contribution. Through collective bargaining with ten unions that represent state employees, the state replaced the formula based on the FFS plan to one based on the low-cost carrier serving a given county. Under the new formula, which was adopted in October 1985 for the 1986 contract year, the state continues to contribute 100 percent for employee coverage and 90 percent for dependent coverage, but the contribution is now based on the low-cost carrier rather than on the FFS plan. In the first several years after the low-cost carrier formula was introduced (from 1986 through 1988), the FFS plan continued to have the lowest rate and remained the basis for the employer contribution. As cost containment became increasingly difficult in the FFS plan, however, the HMOs were able to offer lower rates despite having better coverage. Beginning in 1989, seven different HMOs have been the low-cost carrier in at least some part of the state.

Introduction of the low-cost carrier formula led to striking changes in the pattern of health plan premiums. Table 7–1 traces these changes from 1988, the last year before the formula began to have an impact, through 1993. As the table shows, HMO premium rates in 1988 still tended to cluster around the FFS rate. Premiums for the four largest HMOs (Group Health, Share, MedCenters, and Medica Choice) averaged 112 percent of the low-cost FFS plan spon-

TABLE 7-1

ANNUAL PREMIUM FOR FAMILY HEALTH COVERAGE IN THE MINNESOTA GROUP INSURANCE PROGRAM, 1988–1993

(dollars)

	1988	1989	Per-cent In-crease	1990	Per-cent In-crease	1991	Per-cent In-crease	1992	Per-cent In-crease	1993	Per-cent In-crease
Group Health (staff model HMO)	2,315	2,662	15.0	3,050	14.6	3,492	14.5	3,715	6.4	3,919	5.5
First Plan HMO (network model HMO)	2,228	2,759	23.8	3,182	15.3	3,822	20.1	4,257	11.4	4,450	4.5
Medica Primary (network model HMO)	2,394	2,848	19.0	3,273	14.9	3,665	12.0	3,891	6.2	4,274	9.8
Central MN Group Health (network model HMO)	2,293	3,031	32.2	3,343	10.3	3,834	14.7	—	—	—	—
MedCenters Health Plan (network model HMO)	2,363	2,834	19.1	3,655	29.0	4,087	11.8	4,537	11.0	4,603	1.5
HMO Gold (network HMO with out-of-net coverage)	2,400	3,241	35.0	—	—	—	—	—	—	—	—
Medica Choice (IPA model HMO with out-of-net coverage)	2,481	3,398	37.0	3,909	15.0	4,405	12.7	4,790	8.7	5,422	13.2
Mayo Health Plan (IPA model HMO)	2,397	3,655	52.5	—	—	—	—	—	—	—	—
Blue Cross and Blue Shield (fee-for-service plan)	2,128	3,461	62.6	—	—	—	—	—	—	—	—
State Health Plan (PPO with out-of-net coverage)	—	—	—	4,037	—	4,263	5.6	4,477	5.0	4,710	5.2

— = Indicates that a plan was not offered.
SOURCE: State of Minnesota Group Insurance Program.

sored by Blue Cross and Blue Shield. The low-cost carrier formula, however, created a substantial incentive for plans to submit the lowest possible rate regardless of the FFS rate. Any plan now has a chance to be the basis for the employer contribution and to attract more enrollees as a result. The competitors also know that it is better to stay "within range" of the low-cost carrier, since employees must pay 100 percent of the premium differential if they choose a higher-cost plan. Finally, the new formula enhances regional competition among HMOs—even if a plan is not the low-cost carrier in the Twin Cities, it may be low-cost in another area.

Plans with the greatest structural ability to control health care costs, such as staff model HMOs, have submitted the lowest premium rates. Since 1989, Group Health has been a low-cost carrier, with premiums sometimes $1,000 per year below those of competing plans. In contrast, IPA-model HMOs with open networks, and plans that allow out-of-network coverage, have had the highest premium rates. This pattern was not evident until the low-cost carrier formula took effect.

It remains important for employee and union perceptions that a single plan be available on a statewide basis with uniform benefit levels and premium rates—criteria that no HMO has been able to satisfy. Blue Cross and Blue Shield played this role before 1990, with its statewide fee-for-service plan. Tremendous cost increases, however, forced the Group Insurance Program to drop the fee-for-service plan in 1990. To offer a statewide plan, the state and the unions negotiated reforms that substituted a preferred provider organization administered by Blue Cross and Blue Shield. Aggressive management of the new PPO held its premium increases to 5.60 percent, 5.0 percent, and 5.2 percent in 1990–1991, 1991–1992, and 1992–1993. These percentages compare favorably with premium increases posted by other plans, including HMOs. Many state employees, however, were dissatisfied with the PPO's limited provider network, and for a time it appeared that the University of Minnesota might pull out of the Group Insurance Program to form its own health insurance program. The university eventually decided to stay with the state program.

The change in the statewide plan has had beneficial effects in rural areas. In converting this plan to a PPO, the state limited the number of health care providers in the network. As a result, in some rural areas employees had to change physicians or incur the higher costs of going out of network. This change was controversial but necessary in the judgment of the state and the unions. Rather than risk the loss of long-term patients, some physicians who were not in the new PPO sought to join an HMO plan. In the fall of 1989, initiatives of this kind led to the availability of an HMO plan in eleven rural counties where employees previously had no choice of plans. In other words, aggressive management of the statewide plan led to reduced premiums and created a stimulus to rural HMO development that otherwise would not have occurred. The expansion of HMOs in rural areas will reduce the state's health insurance costs in future years through competition encouraged by the low-cost carrier formula.

Data and Methods

Data. We obtained data on out-of-pocket premiums and enrollment by county for all health plans offered by the State of Minnesota from 1988 to 1993. As we explained in the previous section, only the State Health Plan (the PPO option) is offered statewide. Since every plan is not available in every county, it would be inappropriate to pool the data for an analysis of health plan choice. If health plan ij is not available in county X, for example, the premium for plan ij is not relevant for these employees.

Therefore, we narrowed our attention to the seven-county Twin Cities metropolitan area (Minneapolis, St. Paul, and their suburbs). Approximately 19,000 state employees in this area were covered by the Minnesota Group Insurance Program each year from 1988 to 1993. Throughout this period, these employees had a choice of five health plans: the State Health Plan, Group Health Plan, MedCenters Health Plan, Medica Choice, and Medica Primary. Coordinated Health Care, a small network HMO, operated in the Twin Cities in 1988 only, and a network HMO (with out-of-network coverage), HMO Gold, was available in 1988 and 1989. Tables 7–2 and 7–3 show the annual enrollment in each plan, as well as the percentage of total enrollment and the monthly out-of-pocket premium, from 1988 to 1993.

We also collected data on approximately 15,000 University of Minnesota employees in the Twin Cities from 1990 to 1993. This group had access to the same health plans as other state employees and paid the same premium. Enrollment data for the University of Minnesota employees are shown in table 7–4. Our two experimental groups make up about three-fifths of the employees covered by the state program.

Methods. Our methods can be described simply: we used the nested logit model of health plan choice to predict the percentage of enroll-

187

TABLE 7-2

SEVEN-COUNTY METRO-AREA YEARLY ENROLLMENT AND MONTHLY OUT-OF-POCKET PREMIUMS FOR MINNESOTA STATE EMPLOYEES WITH SINGLE-COVERAGE HEALTH PLANS, 1988–1993

Health Plan	1988	1989	1990	1991	1992	1993
State Health Plan						
Enrollment	3,259	2,114	1,050	1,040	1,079	1,201
Percent of total	42.53	23.49	12.01	11.97	12.19	13.65
Premium (dollars)	0	40.06	46.76	39.72	40.16	41.88
Group Health Inc.						
Enrollment	1,894	3,320	3,900	3,936	4,178	4,180
Percent of total	24.72	36.89	44.59	45.31	47.20	47.51
Premium (dollars)	0.48	0	0	0	0	0
Medica Choice						
Enrollment	1,082	1,391	2,006	1,997	1,879	1,653
Percent of total	14.12	15.46	22.94	22.99	21.23	18.79
Premium (dollars)	2.22	19.58	22.88	24.10	28.98	42.48
MedCenters						

Enrollment	586	1,022	990	946	893	917
Percent of total	7.65	11.36	11.32	10.89	10.09	10.42
Premium (dollars)	0	2.92	19.08	18.70	26.68	22.00
Medica Primary						
Enrollment	290	722	800	767	823	848
Percent of total	3.78	8.02	9.15	8.83	9.30	9.64
Premium (dollars)	3.18	2.18	2.78	0.54	0.28	5.80
Coordinated Health Care[a]						
Enrollment	114					
Percent of total	1.49					
Premium (dollars)	4.28					
HMO Gold[b]						
Enrollment	437	431				
Percent of total	5.70	4.79				
Premium (dollars)	4.28	24.86				
Total enrollment	7,662	9,000	8,746	8,686	8,852	8,799

a. Did not operate after 1988.
b. Did not operate after 1989.
SOURCE: State of Minnesota Group Insurance Program.

TABLE 7-3

SEVEN-COUNTY METRO-AREA YEARLY ENROLLMENT AND MONTHLY OUT-OF-POCKET PREMIUMS FOR MINNESOTA STATE EMPLOYEES WITH FAMILY-COVERAGE HEALTH PLANS, 1988–1993

Health Plan	1988	1989	1990	1991	1992	1993
State Health Plan						
Enrollment	4,452	2,757	1,526	1,618	1,733	1,957
Percent of total	41.88	23.60	13.81	14.47	15.37	17.10
Premium (dollars)	9.96	79.82	97.28	81.58	81.90	85.30
Group Health Inc.						
Enrollment	3,064	4,837	5,576	6,798	6,020	6,221
Percent of total	28.25	41.41	50.46	51.84	53.39	54.37
Premium (dollars)	25.52	13.18	15.10	17.32	18.42	19.44
Medica Choice						
Enrollment	1,284	1,122	1,669	1,538	1,384	1,113
Percent of total	11.84	9.60	15.10	13.75	12.27	9.73
Premium (dollars)	39.40	74.62	86.62	93.44	107.98	144.70
MedCenters						

Enrollment	665	1,427	1,284	1,267	1,170	1,210
Percent of total	6.12	12.22	11.62	11.33	10.38	10.57
Premium (dollars)	29.58	27.54	65.56	66.94	86.92	76.42
Medica Primary						
Enrollment	384	813	996	963	968	942
Percent of total	3.54	6.96	9.01	8.61	8.59	8.23
Premium (dollars)	32.12	28.72	33.64	31.80	33.08	49.02
Coordinated Health Care[a]						
Enrollment	190					
Percent of total	1.75					
Premium (dollars)	27.66					
HMO Gold[b]						
Enrollment	717	726				
Percent of total	6.58	6.21				
Premium (dollars)	32.66	61.46				
Total enrollment	10,846	11,682	11,051	11,184	11,275	11,443

a. Dropped out of system after 1988.
b. Dropped out of system after 1989.
Source: State of Minnesota Group Insurance Program.

TABLE 7-4

SEVEN-COUNTY METRO-AREA YEARLY ENROLLMENT OF UNIVERSITY OF MINNESOTA EMPLOYEES, 1990–1993

Health Plan	1990		1991		1992		1993	
	Single	Family	Single	Family	Single	Family	Single	Family
State Health Plan								
Enrollment	1,339	1,668	1,181	1,569	1,205	1,609	1,213	1,705
Percent of Total	17.36	21.53	16.31	20.56	15.85	20.71	15.99	21.73
Group Health, Inc.								
Enrollment	3,623	3,834	3,494	3,886	3,945	4,185	4,041	4,336
Percent of total	46.98	49.50	48.28	50.92	51.88	53.85	53.28	55.26
Medica Choice								
Enrollment	1,639	1,167	1,581	1,118	1,511	987	1,358	796
Percent of total	21.25	15.07	21.85	14.65	19.87	12.70	17.90	10.14
MedCenters								
Enrollment	668	605	592	607	527	547	542	576
Percent of total	8.66	7.81	8.18	7.95	6.93	7.04	7.15	7.34
Medica Primary								
Enrollment	443	472	389	451	416	443	431	434
Percent of total	5.74	6.09	5.38	5.91	5.47	5.70	5.68	5.53
Total enrollment	7,712	7,746	7,237	7,631	7,604	7,771	7,585	7,847

SOURCE: University of Minnesota, Office of Human Resources.

ees who chose each health plan from 1988 (or 1990) to 1993. Next, we calculated a 95 percent confidence interval around each prediction and determined whether actual enrollment percentages fell within this confidence interval. If they did, we cannot reject the hypothesis that the data were generated by the model. If actual enrollment percentages are outside the 95 percent confidence interval, however, this is not consistent with the model. We also counted the number of times that predicted enrollment and actual enrollment changed in the same direction from year to year. To be useful, the model should predict when enrollment is rising or falling.

As described earlier, the nested logit model predicts which health plan an enrollee will join, based on the value of that plan and the nest to which it belongs. The value of plans depends on characteristics such as the out-of-pocket premium, waiting times for an appointment, and the like. Employees with different personal traits may place different values on plan characteristics. Employees with large families, for example, may prefer plans with a limited number of deductibles compared with plans where every family member must pay a deductible. Employees may also place different values on characteristics of health plan nests. Most important, our study showed that older employees preferred health plans with freedom to choose medical providers.[8]

For our model to predict health plan choice, it would be ideal to have data on individual employees. Then we could include interactions between personal traits and health plan characteristics in the model. Individual data for state employees were not available, however, nor were aggregate data (for example, average age). Thus, our predictions are limited to information based on health plan characteristics, which is available for all plans in the state program. We selected seven characteristics of single-coverage policies: the monthly out-of-pocket premium; the deductible, coinsurance rate, and stop-loss limit for inpatient care; and the deductible, coinsurance rate, and stop-loss limit for outpatient care. The stop-loss limit is the maximum amount of money an enrollee must pay for covered services before the plan pays 100 percent. None of the HMOs in the state program had any enrollee cost-sharing for services during the period from 1988 to 1993.

For the analysis of family-coverage choice, we measured the out-of-pocket premium and other plan characteristics on a per family member basis. We also included the maximum number of inpatient and outpatient deductibles per family, thus making a total of nine

---

[8]Feldman et al., "The Demand for Employment-based Health Insurance," pp. 115–42.

characteristics that were used to determine the value of each plan.

Several plan characteristics in our model (for example, deductibles) are measured in dollars. A deductible of given size becomes a less important barrier to obtaining medical care and, therefore, a less negative element of plan value, as medical care inflation increases the cost of covered services. A $100 deductible, for example, that represented three physician visits in 1984 might represent only two visits in 1990. We converted all deductibles and stop-loss limits into units of constant value by multiplying times the ratio of the medical care component of the consumer price index (M-CPI) in 1984 to the M-CPI in each study year. The constant value of a $100 deductible in 1990, for example, was $100 times (103.9/162.8) = .65602, because the M-CPI increased from 103.9 in 1984 to 162.6 in 1990.

An out-of-pocket premium of given size becomes less burdensome over time because of general inflation in the economy. Therefore, we converted all dollar premiums into units of constant purchasing power using the ratio of the consumer price index (CPI) in 1984 to the CPI in each study year. In 1989, the Minnesota program introduced a change that significantly reduced the cost of choosing expensive health plans. In this year, the employer added medical and dependent care reimbursement accounts through which employees can pay health and dental premiums with before-tax dollars. Reimbursement accounts can also be used to pay for unreimbursed health care expenses (for example, coinsurance, deductibles, and some services not covered by the plan). These accounts, which are authorized by section 125 of the Internal Revenue Code, shelter eligible expenses from federal and state income taxes and the employee's portion of the FICA (social security) tax.

Fortunately, the state and the University of Minnesota were able to provide aggregate data on average employee salaries per year. We assumed that single employees and employees choosing family coverage had the same average salary, because the data did not separate these two groups. Next, we added the marginal federal income tax, state income tax, and FICA tax rates in each year for employees with salaries at the average state and university levels. In 1989, the combined marginal tax rate for both state and university employees was 43.51 percent. This rose to 43.65 percent from 1990 to 1993. The introduction of section 125 accounts reduced out-of-pocket health insurance premiums by these percentages. A health plan that cost $10 out of pocket in 1988, for example, would cost only $5.65 in 1989. We adjusted all premium data from 1989 onward by the section 125 tax subsidy. Subsequent studies using individual data can make specific adjustments for each employee depending on that individual's income and tax status.

Since our interest was in predicting *changes* in enrollment due to *changes* in premiums, we wanted the model's predictions to match the actual enrollment percentages in 1988. This would allow us to compare actual changes against predicted changes in enrollment from 1989 onward. We knew, however, that the model would not exactly predict enrollment shares in the state program. It was estimated with individual data from seventeen employers (not including the State of Minnesota), and therefore it would not be sensitive to any unmeasured features of state employees or the state program. To make predicted and actual enrollment equal in 1988, we added a plan-specific constant to the value of each plan. These constants give each plan exactly the right value to be chosen by the percentage of employees who actually selected that plan in 1988. Details of the method for calculating the constants are given in the appendix. The base year for predicting changes in enrollment for University of Minnesota employees was 1990.

Finally, our analysis is based on the type of coverage (single or family) actually chosen by state and university employees. This differs from our 1989 study, in which we were able to determine which type of coverage each employee considered without having to look at their actual choices.[9] The 1989 study divided all employees into three categories: those choosing only among single-coverage policies, those choosing only among family-coverage policies, and others.

This categorization was based on both fact and theory. The fact was that employees in the sample of firms were not permitted to turn down coverage entirely—each employee had to choose at least a single-coverage policy. The theory was that employees would not choose redundant coverages, nor would family members be allowed to go without insurance, if the family had no other source of employment-based health insurance. Therefore, we predicted that single employees without dependents would choose only single-coverage policies. We also predicted that families with dependent children and married employees whose spouse was not eligible for health insurance through the spouse's place of employment would choose only family coverage. We tested the first prediction by looking for instances of single employees without dependents who chose family policies. Only six employees of this type were found out of 920

---

[9]Ibid.

responses, a fraction so small that it could be due to coding errors. The second prediction was tested by looking for instances of employees with a family (dependent children or spouse) and no other source of health insurance who did not choose family coverage. The number of these employees in our data was also small enough to be explained by coding errors. Together, the employees that were categorized as "single-coverage only" and "family-coverage only" account for approximately three-fifths of the employees in our sample.

The "other" category refers to married employees whose spouse is offered health insurance through the spouse's place of employment. These employees have the option of choosing either single or family coverage. If there are children, one of the parents will need to choose family coverage. Even if there are no children, one employee may choose single coverage (perhaps the low-cost plan), and the spouse may choose family coverage from a plan with generous benefits or a broad provider network. If both employees have access to both types of plans, their decisions may depend on the employers' premium contributions to the various options.

The "other" category poses a problem because the statistical model that we used for our analysis requires a complete description of all choices considered by those making the decisions. Employees whose spouses have health insurance through their place of employment have more choices than those offered by the firms where the surveyed employees work. We did not have the resources needed to confirm all the choices faced by spouses of employees in the "other" group. These missing data will result in incorrect estimates of health plan choice probabilities for employees in this group.

Suppose, for example, that Mr. and Mrs. Jones work for different companies that offer multiple health plans. They have a dependent child, so one of them must choose family coverage. Mr. Jones (the employee in our survey) currently chooses family coverage from plan A because his employer pays a greater portion of the family premium than Mrs. Jones's employer. She chooses single-coverage from plan B. If the out-of-pocket premium for his family plan increases, he might change to single coverage, and Mrs. Jones would change to family coverage. They might even move to another insurance carrier.

The Joneses also might change plans if Mrs. Jones's employer offers another option that was not previously available. We would observe plan switching without any premium changes in this case. This example shows that the probabilities of health plan choice will change, depending on the options offered to the spouse. The Joneses' "mixing and matching" health plans causes trouble in using our estimates to explain plan switching at the aggregate firm level.

We estimated separate health plan choice equations for the two groups for whom the choice set was correctly defined: employees choosing only among single-coverage policies; and employees choosing only among family-coverage policies.

Our estimates apply only to individuals or families that meet the same requirements as the sample on which the estimates were based. To use our estimates to explain plan switching at the firm level, the analyst must be able to describe all the choices for the family unit. The family unit must also choose only one plan from the single- or family-coverage offerings. These requirements would be met by health insurance purchasing arrangements that restrict the choices to plans offered by one sponsor and require all family members to choose the same plan.

Unfortunately, these requirements are not met if the data include family units in the "other" category. Some employees in the Minnesota Group Insurance Program must fall into the "other" category. We do not have data that indicate the category to which individual state employees belong. All we know is the total proportions of employees choosing single and family coverage. Our estimates for "single-coverage only" and "family-coverage" employees, then, may not explain historical trends in enrollment for health plans offered by the State of Minnesota.

An alternative approach is to estimate the model using the "incorrect" sample, that is, to estimate the single-coverage choice equation for every employee who chose a single-coverage plan in the original data. Feldman and others presented the alternative estimates to illustrate the penalty of using deficient data.[10] The premium coefficient for the "incorrect" sample was biased toward zero, but the bias was not large because approximately three-fourths of the sample was selected correctly. The bias, however, might be larger for other data sets. We did not estimate the "wrong" model for all employees who chose family coverage in the original data.

We used the "right" equations to predict single- and family-coverage health plan choice. The predictions for single-coverage employees using the "right" equation will be compared with predictions using all single-coverage employees. By performing this sensitivity analysis, we can determine whether the bias from using the wrong model is significant for state and university employees. The next section presents the results of this analysis and other predictions.

---

[10]Ibid.

Results, Sensitivity Analysis, and Policy Applications

Results. The results of our analysis are presented in figures 7–1 through 7–6. A complete list of predictions can be found in table 7–5. Each figure shows the predicted and actual enrollment percentages for a health plan and the type of coverage (single or family) in all study years. As we explained earlier, predicted and actual enrollment are made to be equal in 1988. Surrounding each prediction is a shaded area that represents the 95 percent confidence interval. The mathematical formula for calculating this confidence interval is derived in the appendix.

Each figure also shows a line representing the premium for the plan in question versus the State Health Plan. If this line is falling, the plan is becoming relatively cheaper, compared with the State Health Plan. Other things equal, the plan should gain enrollment. We caution that all health plans compete with each other to some extent, so the premium for each plan must be compared with *every* other premium to make a prediction. The State Health Plan, however, competed directly with other plans in the freedom-of-choice nest. And because it was the largest plan in the base year, its premium also had an important effect on enrollment in the network HMO plans. Thus, we selected the premium for the State Health Plan as an interesting, but not complete, indicator of competition among plans.

Figure 7–1 shows the results for Group Health single-coverage enrollment. In 1989, this option became drastically cheaper than the State Health Plan. Our model predicts that Group Health's enrollment should have increased from 24.72 percent of all single-coverage state employees in 1988 to 43.45 percent in 1989. Actual enrollment increased by a lesser amount, to 36.89 percent, but it was inside the confidence interval allowed by our model. In fact, actual enrollment was inside the confidence interval for every year except 1993, when our prediction was too high to be allowed by the model. Even so, Group Health had become the dominant plan in the state program by 1993, with almost half of all single-coverage enrollment. In other words, Group Health's enrollment percentage *doubled* from 1988 to 1993, a direct consequence of becoming the low-cost plan in 1989 and remaining in that favorable position to 1993.

Figure 7–1 dispels a myth about health plan switching in a managed-competition program: the myth is that employees react slowly to premium changes. In fact, enrollees moved rapidly into Group Health from other plans, with actual enrollment swelling in 1989 and 1990. Actual enrollment would have been below the confidence interval for 1989 and 1990, if switching had occurred slowly.

TABLE 7-5

PREDICTED YEARLY ENROLLMENT OF STATE OF MINNESOTA EMPLOYEES IN SIX DIFFERENT HEALTH CARE PLANS IN THE SEVEN-COUNTY METRO AREA, 1989–1993

(percent)

Health Plan	1989 Single	Family	1990 Single	Family	1991 Single	Family	1992 Single	Family	1993 Single	Family
State Health Plan	3.03[b]	4.11[b]	2.16[b]	8.22	5.90	12.86[b]	8.72[b]	14.22[b]	16.69[b]	15.66[b]
Group Health, Inc.	43.45[b]	50.31[b]	50.33[b]	71.59[b]	47.57	68.02	49.90[b]	69.86[b]	59.89[b]	73.68[b]
Medica Choice	27.04[b]	24.02	35.70[b]	9.67	31.94	7.48[b]	26.47[b]	5.46[b]	12.92[b]	2.05[b]
MedCenters	8.14[b]	8.34[b]	1.29[b]	3.21[b]	1.40	3.39	0.62[b]	1.92[b]	1.35[b]	3.11[b]
Medica Primary	9.64[b]	5.56[b]	10.53[b]	7.31[b]	13.19	8.25	14.28[b]	8.55	9.15	5.49
HMO Gold[a]	8.69	7.67								

a. Dropped out of system after 1989.
b. Actual and predicted enrollment changed in the same direction from prior year.
SOURCE: Authors.

199

FIGURE 7–1

ENROLLMENT OF MINNESOTA STATE EMPLOYEES IN THE TWIN CITIES
AREA IN THE GROUP HEALTH PLAN WITH SINGLE COVERAGE,
1988–1993
(percent)

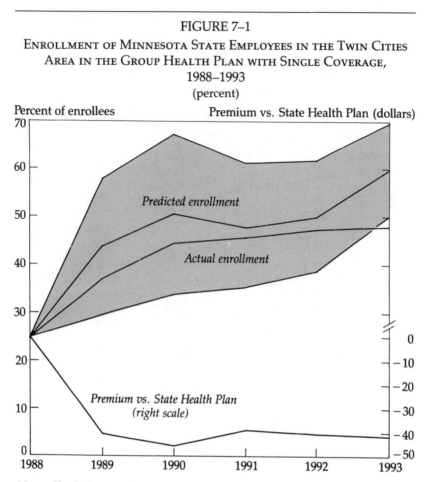

NOTE: Shaded area indicates the 95 percent confidence interval.
SOURCE: Authors.

Although we are not sure why actual enrollment was below the confidence interval in 1993, we think the dynamics of competition may change when one plan has a large share of total enrollment. By 1992, Group Health had 47.2 percent of total single-coverage enrollment. The following year, the out-of-pocket premium for Medica Choice increased from $28.98 to $42.48 per month. Other premiums stayed fairly constant. The model predicts that employees would leave Medica Choice. Many would join the State Health Plan, which is in the same nest as Medica Choice, but some would join Group Health. By 1993, however, Group Health had a large share of total enrollment. We suggest that state employees who remained in other plans had strong attachments to their current medical care providers. The premium difference needed for these employees to switch to *any* plan that does not cover their current providers may be greater than the difference needed for employees to switch in earlier years. In other words, the model's predictions may tend to "overshoot" actual plan switching when one plan in the system becomes very large. This problem could be overcome if we had data on individual employees in the state program.

Figure 7-1 shows the most important result for single-coverage employees in the state program, because it describes the plan that almost half of them had joined by 1993. What was happening to the other single-coverage plans? Figures 7-2 and 7-3 present the results for the State Health Plan and Medica Choice. In 1988, Blue Cross AWARE Gold Limited, the predecessor to the State Health Plan, was the largest plan for state employees in the Twin Cities, with 42.53 percent of all single-coverage enrollees. In 1989, however, the out-of-pocket premium for this plan jumped from $0 to $40.16. Our model predicts a large drop in AWARE Gold Limited enrollment and increased enrollment for Medica Choice, the "choice" plan with about one-seventh of total single-coverage enrollment in 1988. Actual enrollment in AWARE Gold Limited did fall, and Medica Choice did gain enrollees, but actual changes were less than predicted changes in both plans.

From 1989 through 1993, the State Health Plan's premium stayed at about $40 per month, whereas Medica's premium increased from $19.58 to $42.48. Our model predicts that the State Health Plan should have won back some of its original losses and that Medica's enrollment should have fallen (as shown by the "hump-shaped" prediction in figure 7-3). Again, actual enrollment moved in the same direction as these predictions but to a smaller degree.

Figures 7-2 and 7-3 indicate that our model is somewhat oversensitive in predicting enrollment shifts between plans in the same nest, such as the State Health Plan and Medica Choice. According to the model, consumers are extremely sensitive to premium differences between plans in the same nest. In practice, however, enrollees may have unmeasured personal characteristics that create stronger attachments to their existing plans than the model predicts.

One explanation for our model's sensitivity is that conditions in the health plan market have changed since 1984. In 1984, plans in the "choice" nest had broader provider networks with access to most physicians and hospitals in the Twin Cities. Freedom of choice has been restricted since 1984. The State Health Plan, for example, has

FIGURE 7–2

ENROLLMENT OF MINNESOTA STATE EMPLOYEES IN THE TWIN CITIES
AREA IN THE STATE HEALTH PLAN WITH SINGLE COVERAGE, 1988–1993
(percent)

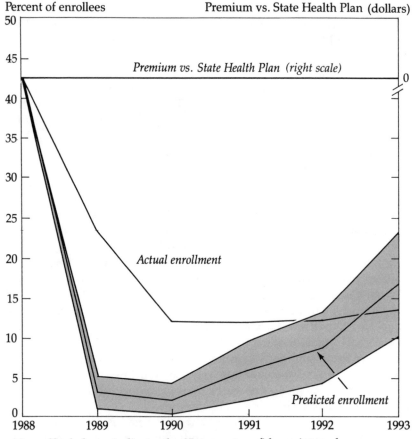

Percent of enrollees   Premium vs. State Health Plan (dollars)

NOTE: Shaded area indicates the 95 percent confidence interval.
SOURCE: Authors.

evolved from an old-fashioned FFS organization into a PPO.

Figures 7–4 through 7–6 present the results for family-coverage health plans. Group Health Plan gained enrollees, but not as many as predicted. Enrollment in the State Health Plan fell and then bounced back slightly—a pattern that is similar to single-coverage enrollment and is in the direction predicted by our model. Medica Choice enrollment shows a strange pattern, moving against the

FIGURE 7–3

ENROLLMENT OF MINNESOTA STATE EMPLOYEES IN THE TWIN CITIES
AREA IN MEDICA CHOICE WITH SINGLE COVERAGE, 1988–1993
(percent)

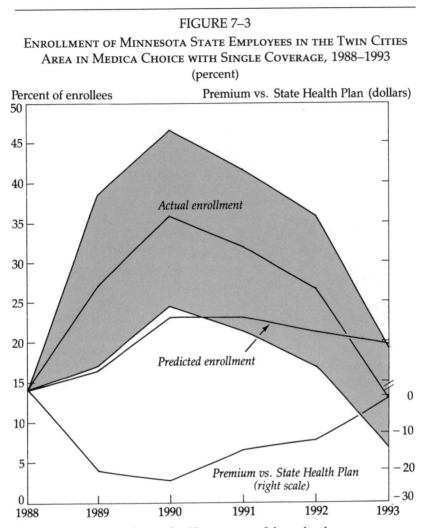

NOTE: Shaded area indicates the 95 percent confidence level.
SOURCE: Authors.

model's predictions in 1989 and 1990. In 1989, Medica's premium
increased from $39.40 to $74.63, but the State Health Plan premium
increased even more—from $9.96 to $79.82. The model predicts that
Medica Choice enrollment should have increased (Medica Choice is
like the lesser of two evils). Some enrollees, though, must have
decided that neither the State Health Plan nor Medica Choice was
worth staying in for these large premium increases. Our explanation

FIGURE 7-4

Enrollment of Minnesota State Employees in the Twin Cities
Area in Group Health with Family Coverage, 1988–1993
(percent)

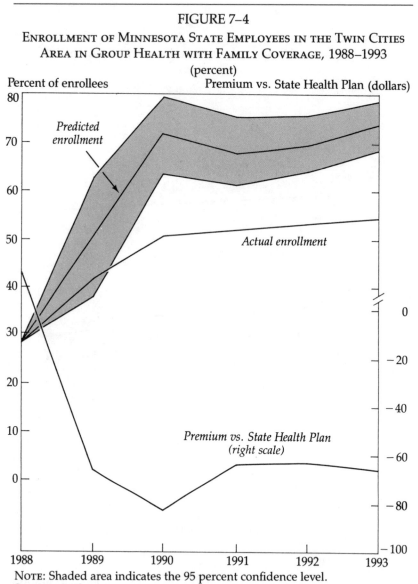

NOTE: Shaded area indicates the 95 percent confidence level.
SOURCE: Authors.

of the unexpected bounce back in Medica Choice enrollment for 1990
is that many employees reacted unfavorably to the introduction of
the State Health Plan in 1990. This plan had a more restricted provider

FIGURE 7–5

Enrollment of Minnesota State Employees in the Twin Cities Area in the State Health Plan with Family Coverage, 1988–1993

(percent)

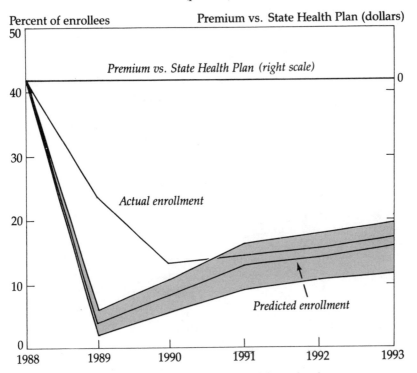

Percent of enrollees   Premium vs. State Health Plan (dollars)

NOTE: Shaded area indicates the 95 percent confidence level.
SOURCE: Authors.

network than the AWARE Gold Limited plan that it replaced, and this may have driven some employees into Medica Choice.

The state program includes several smaller health plans (for example, Medica Primary and MedCenters). We did not prepare separate figures for the small participants in the state program. A complete list of results can be found in table 7–5, which shows predicted enrollment by plan, year, and type of coverage. Cases where predicted and actual enrollment changed in the *same direction* from the prior year are noted.

Of the fifty-two predicted changes in enrollment, our model was

FIGURE 7–6

ENROLLMENT OF MINNESOTA STATE EMPLOYEES IN THE TWIN CITIES
AREA IN MEDICA CHOICE WITH FAMILY COVERAGE, 1988–1993

(percent)

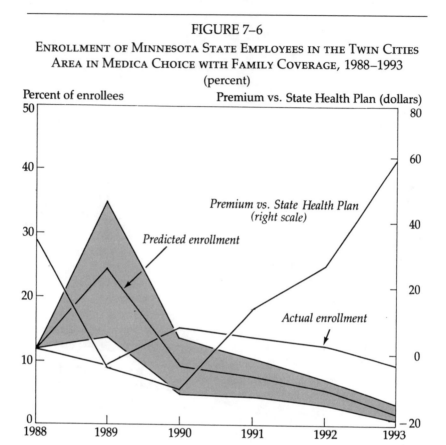

NOTE: Shaded area indicates the 95 percent confidence level.
SOURCE: Authors.

right in thirty-six cases and wrong in sixteen. The chances of obtaining this many successes with simple guesswork are less than 5 in
100.[11] It appears that the model was more likely to be right in 1989,
the first year of large changes in out-of-pocket premiums, and less
likely to be right in 1991. We suggest that the large premium increases
of 1989 had been absorbed by 1991 and that competition may have
shifted to other dimensions (for example, provider networks). By
1993, however, the model was again accurately predicting enrollment
changes.

---

[11]John E. Freund, *Mathematical Statistics*. 2d ed. (Englewood Cliffs, N.J.:
Prentice-Hall, 1971).

We had enrollment data for University of Minnesota employees only from 1990 to 1993. Using 1990 as the base year, we predicted the enrollment in each plan and type of coverage in 1991, 1992, and 1993. To conserve space, these results are shown in figures 7–A1—7–A6 in the appendix (for example, figure 7–A1 shows single-coverage enrollment by university employees in Group Health Plan). From 1991 to 1993, most out-of-pocket premiums were fairly stable in relation to Group Health, the low-cost plan. Therefore, both predicted and actual enrollment in most plans were fairly stable. Medica Choice, which experienced large premium increases for both single and family coverage, is an exception. Medica Choice lost both single and family members, as predicted by our model. The losses, however, were smaller than predicted by the model. This suggests that University of Minnesota employees remaining in Medica Choice may have strong attachments to their current medical care providers.

Sensitivity Analysis. We performed three analyses to test the sensitivity of our predictions to different assumptions. First, as mentioned, the model used to predict single-coverage enrollment was based on single employees without dependents, who had no reason to consider any other type of coverage. We also had a single-coverage model, however, that was based on all employees who chose single-coverage health policies. To test the sensitivity of our predictions, we used the second model to predict state employees' enrollment in single-coverage plans from 1989 to 1993. The results of this analysis showed that the two sets of predictions were similar. Therefore, in this case, it does not matter whether we use the "right" model or the model based on all employees who chose single coverage.

Second, in our original data the coefficient of out-of-pocket premiums was estimated with much greater precision than the coefficients of plan characteristics (for example, deductibles and coinsurance). Moreover, none of the HMO plans in the state program had any cost sharing for covered services from 1988 to 1993, and these characteristics changed little for the FFS plans (the only significant change was a decline in the real value of deductibles and stop-loss limits due to medical care inflation). Thus, we created a "short version" of the model that included only one variable—the employee's out-of-pocket premium. Predictions from this model matched those from the "long version" (with seven variables for single coverage and nine variables for family coverage) closely. Therefore, in the Minnesota program, shifts in plan enrollment from 1989–1993 were caused primarily by changes in the employee's out-of-pocket premium, not changes in other plan characteristics. We caution, however, that this finding might not apply to other programs (for example, where the FFS plan introduces a large deductible).

Third, we have noted that two small plans dropped out of the state program in 1989 and 1990. We tested the sensitivity of our predictions to the withdrawal of these plans by excluding them in the base year. All enrollment percentages were recalculated using the number of enrollees in other plans in 1988. Then, we repeated the predictions using only the plans that stayed in the program from 1988 to 1993. The results were similar to those in figures 7–2 through 7–6. Based on these three tests, we conclude that our predictions are not sensitive to the choice of models, exclusion of plan characteristics, and exclusion of two plans that dropped out of the state program.

Policy Applications. One of the key elements of managed-competition proposals is a limit on tax-free employer contributions to health insurance policies.[12] There is surprisingly little evidence, however, on how this proposal might affect employees' choice of health plans. Our prediction model can be used to provide some insights into the effects of ending or curtailing this tax subsidy.

Under the present tax system, 100 percent of the employer-paid premium for any health plan is tax-free to employees. Now suppose that the tax subsidy was "capped" or limited to the premium for the low-cost plan. Employees should have an incentive to choose the low-cost plan. A similar effect should occur in the Minnesota program if the health care spending accounts, through which employees can pay for health and dental premiums with before-tax dollars, were eliminated.

To simulate the effect of limiting the tax subsidy, we added it back into the premium for all single-coverage plans except the Group Health Plan. As the low-cost carrier in the state program from 1989 to 1993, Group Health was available to all employees at no out-of-pocket cost. Capping the tax subsidy would have increased the out-of-pocket premiums for all other plans by 43 percent.

Figure 7–7 presents the results of this simulation for Group Health single-coverage enrollment. The line reproduced from figure 7–1 shows predicted Group Health enrollment under the present system, which subsidizes the premiums for all competing single-coverage plans. The second line shows predicted Group Health enrollment if employees paid out-of-pocket premiums with after-tax dollars. Our model predicts that capping the tax subsidy would substantially increase Group Health's enrollment: predicted enroll-

---

[12]Enthoven and Kronick, "Universal Health Insurance," pp. 2532–36.

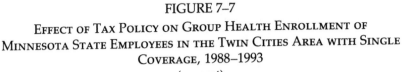

FIGURE 7–7

EFFECT OF TAX POLICY ON GROUP HEALTH ENROLLMENT OF
MINNESOTA STATE EMPLOYEES IN THE TWIN CITIES AREA WITH SINGLE
COVERAGE, 1988–1993
(percent)

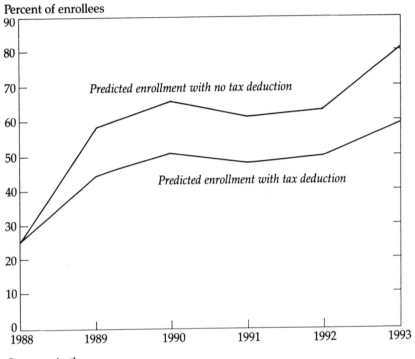

Percent of enrollees

SOURCE: Authors.

ment *with* the tax subsidy is about 50 percent in most years; *without* the subsidy, predicted enrollment jumps to about 60 percent.

We caution that figure 7–7 relies on a comparison of two predictions. Actual enrollment was less than predicted enrollment with the tax subsidy, so it might also be less than predicted enrollment if the tax subsidy were capped. Nevertheless, we believe that capping the tax subsidy would increase enrollment in the low-cost plan in Minnesota's program by *some* amount and possibly by as much as ten percentage points. Thus, our simulation supports the argument that the tax policy proposals of managed competition would encourage enrollees to choose low-cost health plans.

The second policy application is an estimate of the savings to the State of Minnesota program due to employees' changing health plans

TABLE 7–6

SAVINGS FROM HEALTH PLAN CHOICE BY STATE OF MINNESOTA
EMPLOYEES IN THE SEVEN-COUNTY METRO AREA, 1988–1993
(dollars)

| | Coverage and Premium | | | |
| | Single coverage | | Family coverage | |
Year	Actual dollars	No switching	Actual dollars	No switching
1988	940	940	2,257	2,257
1989	1,245	1,341	2,975	3,141
1990	1,400	1,558	3,406	3,661
1991	1,563	1,695	3,811	4,008
1992	1,670	1,805	4,065	4,263
1993	1,786	1,920	4,302	4,534

NOTE: "No switching" means that employees stay in the same plan and
coverage option (single or family) that they chose in 1988.
SOURCE: Authors.

from 1989 to 1993. To make this estimate, we calculated the total
premium cost to the program in 1988 for employees in the Twin Cities
area. Then we used the 1988 enrollment percentages to calculate costs
from 1989 to 1993, assuming that enrollment had stayed constant.
These fixed enrollment weights were multiplied times actual premiums in each year to calculate predicted costs in the absence of plan
switching.

We caution that this is only an estimate of the savings from
changing health plans. Actual premiums may have been influenced
by the low-cost carrier system that was responsible for health plan
switching. On the one hand, if the low-cost carrier system forced
plans to compete to become more efficient, then our estimate of the
savings from plan switching would be too small, because it does not
include any savings from competition.

On the other hand, the low-cost plans (for example, Group
Health) may have enjoyed favorable risk selection compared with
high-cost plans such as Medica Choice and the State Health Plan.
Then our estimate of the savings from plan switching would be too
large, because it would include favorable selection as well as efficiency. In the second part of our study, we are comparing total
premiums for employers who manage the demand side of the health
insurance market, compared with employers who do not manage the

demand for health insurance. Those results will provide a better measure of the total savings from managed competition.

In the interim, however, estimates of savings from health plan switching are shown in table 7–6. Starting in 1988, the actual cost of health insurance was $940 for single coverage and $2,257 for family coverage for State of Minnesota employees in the Twin Cities, excluding Coordinated Health Care and HMO Gold (the two small plans that dropped out of the system). The predicted cost of health insurance without employee health plan switching is higher than the actual cost in every year from 1989 to 1993. Much of the savings occurred in 1989, when the low-cost carrier formula began to have an impact. In 1993, health plan switching was responsible for saving $134 per single-coverage contract and $232 per family-coverage contract. On an enrollment base of 8,799 single-coverage employees and 11,443 family-coverage employees, the total savings in 1993 was $3,833,842. Savings would have been larger if employees did not receive a tax subsidy for choosing more expensive health plans.

Summary

The State of Minnesota operates a health insurance program that has most of the features of managed competition: the state is an active sponsor that offers several health insurance plans and uses a low-cost carrier formula to determine the employer's premium contribution. Except for the tax shelter for employee-paid premiums, this program might be a working model of managed competition.

In this chapter, we focus on one critical aspect of managed competition: the effectiveness of out-of-pocket premium differences in encouraging employees to switch to low-cost health plans. Starting in 1989, employees have faced large out-of-pocket premiums for some plans in the Minnesota program. Using an economic model of health plan choice, we predicted the change in enrollment for single- and family-coverage health plans offered to state and university employees in the Twin Cities area. In most cases, actual changes in enrollment moved in the same direction as our predictions. It is especially noteworthy that Group Health Plan substantially increased its share of both single- and family-coverage contracts. This is a direct consequence of Group Health's becoming the low-cost carrier in 1989. Several high-cost plans, particularly the State Health Plan and Medica Choice, lost enrollment. We conclude from this analysis that employees will switch health plans when they have to pay higher premiums. We conducted several sensitivity tests of this result, and we are

211

confident that our results depend on premium differences, not on other variables in the model.

We used the model to investigate two important policy issues. The first is the effect of removing the tax subsidy for health insurance premiums. Our calculations indicate that tax policy reform would substantially increase enrollment in low-cost health plans. Second, we estimated the cost savings due to employees' changing health plans from 1989 to 1993. We estimate that these changes saved $3.8 million for state employees in the Twin Cities in 1993. The savings represents 5.9 percent of actual health care premiums for these employees in 1993. The findings from this natural experiment indicate that managed competition will reduce health care costs by encouraging employees to choose low-cost health care plans.

Appendix 7–A

Calculating Baseline Enrollment Values. Predicted enrollment in plan ij, conditional on choosing nest i, is

$$Q_{j|i} = exp(\beta' X_{ij})/exp(I_i) \qquad (7\text{–A1})$$

Predicted conditional enrollment for plan K (the last plan in the same nest) is

$$Q_{K|i} = exp(\beta' X_{iK})/exp(I_i) \qquad (7\text{–A2})$$

If we take the natural logarithm of (7–A1)/(7–A2), it is clear that the denominators will difference away:

$$\ln Q_{j|i} - \ln Q_{K|i} = \beta' X_{ij} - \beta' X_{iK} \qquad (7\text{–A3})$$

The natural logarithms of enrollment in equation (7–A3) are *predictions*. As explained in the text, these predictions will not equal actual enrollment. We can, however, add a constant to the right-hand side of (7–A3) that will give it enough value to make predicted enrollment equal actual enrollment:

$$\ln AQ_{j|i} - \ln AQ_{K|i} = \beta' X_{ij} - \beta' X_{iK} + C_{ij} \qquad (7\text{–A4})$$

where AQ stands for actual enrollment. There will be a similar equation for each plan in the nest, including plan K, which is used as the comparison for the other equations.

Since the only unknown variable in equation (7–A4) is C_{ij}, we can solve for C_{ij}. Likewise, we can solve for the constants that will make predicted enrollment equal actual enrollment for every other plan in this nest. C_{iK} must equal zero because all the other terms in the equation for the comparison plan will difference away. A similar set of constants can be found for plans in the other nest. This nest also will have one comparison plan for which the constant term equals zero.

To make predicted enrollment equal actual enrollment for the two health plan nests, we take the natural logarithm of Q_i/Q_N and solve for the constant that satisfies the following equation:

$$\ln AQ_i - \ln AQ_N = (\alpha'Y_i + \lambda I_i) - (\alpha'Y_N + \lambda I_N) + C_i \quad (7\text{--}A5)$$

The constant term for nest N, the comparison nest, must be zero.

Confidence Intervals of Predictions in the Nested Logit Model. We will start with some basic notions and develop these to fit our model. In general, the predicted value of enrollment, given a single health plan characteristic and its estimated coefficient, can be written as $Q(\beta X)$. The expected value of enrollment is $Q(BX)$, where B stands for the expected value of the coefficient. Treating the estimated coefficient as a variable, take a first-order Taylor series expansion of $Q(\beta X)$ near $Q(BX)$:

$$Q(\beta X) - Q(BX) = \partial Q(\beta X)/\partial \beta * (\beta - B) \quad (7\text{--}A6)$$

Square both sides of (7–A6) to obtain the variance of the prediction:

$$VAR(Q(\beta X)) = (\partial Q(\beta X)/\partial \beta)^2 * VAR(\beta) \quad (7\text{--}A7)$$

In a multivariate model, the formula becomes

$$VAR(Q(\beta'X)) = (\partial Q(\beta'X)/\partial \beta)' * \Sigma * \partial Q(\beta'X)/\partial \beta \quad (7\text{--}A8)$$

where Σ is the variance-covariance matrix of the estimated coefficients. This is premultiplied by a row vector of derivatives of the predictions with respect to the estimated coefficients, and postmultiplied by a column vector of the same derivatives.

Our model has three types of estimated coefficients: β, α, and λ. The data available for this study, however, did not include personal characteristics of employees, the variables that are related to the α coefficients. We had only two types of variables: those measuring plan characteristics (related to β); and the inclusive value (related to λ). Thus, to calculate equation (7–A8), we need to find the derivatives of predicted enrollment with respect to β and λ, but not α.

What is the derivative of predicted enrollment in plan ij with respect to one of the β's, for example β_n? We differentiated the nested logit demand function to find the answer:

$$\partial Q_{ij}/\partial \beta_n = Q_{ij}\{X_{ijn} - (1-\lambda) * \sum_{k=1}^{K_i} Q_{k|i} * X_{ikn}$$
$$- \lambda \sum_{i=1}^{N} \sum_{k=1}^{K_i} Q_i * Q_{k|i} * X_{ikn}\} \quad (7\text{--}A9)$$

213

FIGURE 7–A1

Enrollment of University of Minnesota Employees in the Twin Cities Area in Group Health with Single Coverage, 1990–1993
(percent)

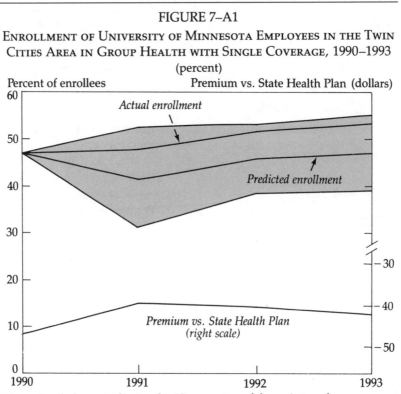

NOTE: Shaded area indicates the 95 percent confidence interval.
SOURCE: Authors.

X_{ijn} is the value of characteristic n for plan ij. Each plan characteristic has a derivative similar to (7–A9). The model of single-coverage choice has seven plan characteristics; the model of family-coverage choice has nine characteristics.

The derivative of predicted enrollment in plan ij with respect to λ is

$$\partial Q_{ij}/\partial\lambda = Q_{ij} * (I_i - \sum_{i=1}^{N} I_i Q_i) \qquad (7\text{–}A10)$$

We calculated these derivatives according to equations (7–A9) and (7–A10) and substituted them into equation (7–A8). The variance-covariance matrix from Feldman and others was also substituted into (7–A8). This equation gives the variance of a prediction in the nested

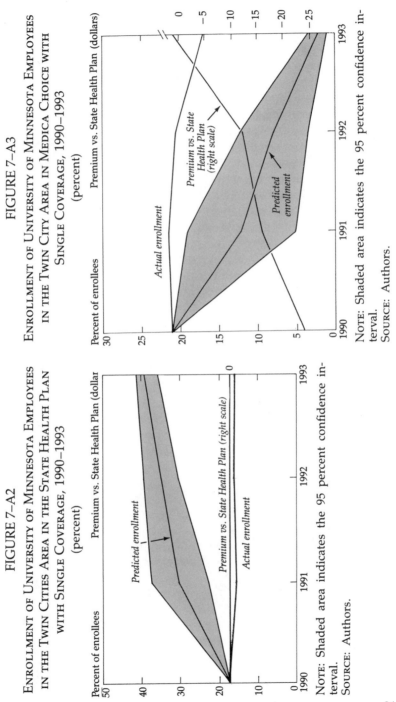

FIGURE 7–A2

ENROLLMENT OF UNIVERSITY OF MINNESOTA EMPLOYEES
IN THE TWIN CITIES AREA IN THE STATE HEALTH PLAN
WITH SINGLE COVERAGE, 1990–1993
(percent)

NOTE: Shaded area indicates the 95 percent confidence interval.
SOURCE: Authors.

FIGURE 7–A3

ENROLLMENT OF UNIVERSITY OF MINNESOTA EMPLOYEES
IN THE TWIN CITY AREA IN MEDICA CHOICE WITH
SINGLE COVERAGE, 1990–1993
(percent)

NOTE: Shaded area indicates the 95 percent confidence interval.
SOURCE: Authors.

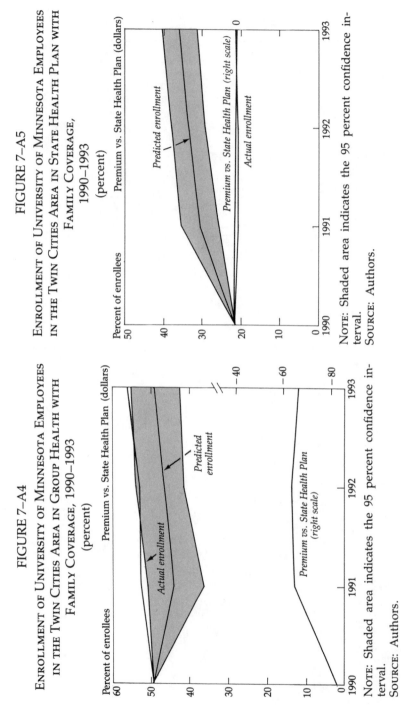

FIGURE 7–A4
ENROLLMENT OF UNIVERSITY OF MINNESOTA EMPLOYEES
IN THE TWIN CITIES AREA IN GROUP HEALTH WITH
FAMILY COVERAGE, 1990–1993
(percent)

NOTE: Shaded area indicates the 95 percent confidence interval.
SOURCE: Authors.

FIGURE 7–A5
ENROLLMENT OF UNIVERSITY OF MINNESOTA EMPLOYEES
IN THE TWIN CITIES AREA IN STATE HEALTH PLAN WITH
FAMILY COVERAGE,
1990–1993
(percent)

NOTE: Shaded area indicates the 95 percent confidence interval.
SOURCE: Authors.

FIGURE 7–A6
Enrollment of University of Minnesota Employees in the Twin Cities Area in Medica Choice with Family Coverage,
1990–1993
(percent)

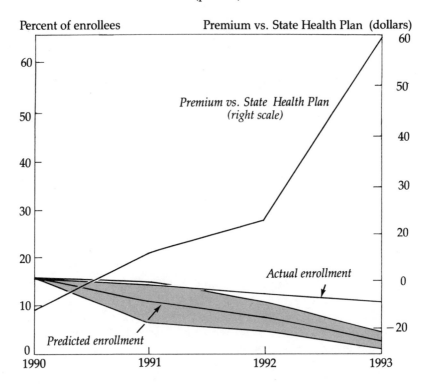

NOTE: Shaded area indicates the 95 percent confidence interval.
SOURCE: Authors.

logit model. A confidence interval for the prediction can be found by choosing an appropriate type-1 error (for example, we chose 5 percent for a two-tailed test of significance). Thus, we multiplied the variance times $Z_{.05} = 1.96$ to calculate the confidence intervals in our report.

8

The Effects of Managed Competition

Theory and Real-World Experience

Alain Enthoven

It is unusual for me these days to find myself positioned out in left field: my reactions must be readjusted a bit. A few weeks ago, a friend who this year is serving with the Council of Economic Advisers was back home for the weekend with her husband, describing what was happening with the Task Force on National Health Reform. Her husband sat back and said, "I wonder how Alain is going to feel, being known as the father of American socialized medicine."

Mark Pauly's chapter almost makes me understand what that comment meant. While he and I are both economists who prefer individual freedom and decentralized private markets to coercion and government command and control regulation, we do have some differences in our world view. Mark Pauly is still thinking of insurance with the insurance function separate from the organization and provision of medical care, while I am confidently looking forward to the day of integrated financing and delivery systems that systematically match resources used to the needs of the population served, that choose efficient methods of production, that do continuous quality improvement, and so forth. To some extent, what one sees as appropriate rules and structures depends on that world view.

I am not certain that the rate of growth in medical care spending that will be achieved under managed competition will be acceptably low. If we set up the market properly, doesn't that market have to produce the right answer? I have said the contrary. If a new health care system is a Jackson Hole–like market-reform model, like any kind of health care, about half will be taxpayer financed. Even with a competitive model, some features or some decisions that formed it may lead to costs that are too high in the judgment of the taxpayers who are paying for half of it.

We may need to make responsible collective decisions to buy less—for example, we may need to include less in the tax-subsidized benefit package and to increase the cost sharing. The Jackson Hole group is not opposed to any cost sharing at all. But cost sharing at the point of service is not the primary incentive to economical behavior. When an injured child is bleeding on the operating table, whether the parent must pay a $10 copayment for each stitch does not help in making good decisions about care.

But the managed-competition system that is set up may cost too much money perhaps because we will have decided to buy too much technology. Think of drugs like Ceredase, for people with Gaucher's disease: recommended enzyme doses cost $360,000 a year. If many such conditions are included in the benefit package, we might have an extremely expensive version of managed competition, costing too many tax dollars, and a national health board may have to reconsider those decisions and to set more restrictive standards about what technologies are covered. A decentralized private market cannot deal effectively with such situations. If some health plans cover Ceredase and some do not, guess which will get all the Gaucher's patients?

Mark Pauly says that the central idea behind policy proposals that require competition to be managed is distrust, fear of markets, fear of government—as if we have nothing to fear but fear itself. In the case of government, my views are not based on distrust or fear; they are based on knowledge. Having spent the 1960s as point man for Robert McNamara in trying to bring efficiency and cost-effectiveness to the Pentagon, I know that government is fundamentally antiefficiency. I learned that the ideal weapon system is built in 435 congressional districts. The central idea is not distrust; it is a conviction based on experience and on the knowledge that our system of government was simply not designed to allocate resources efficiently.

Because of this knowledge, I do not trust government to offer the Mark Pauly government health insurance fallback. Government cannot do that with efficiency and effectiveness, and even if it could, I fear it would act the way Medicare acts—that is, it would wire all the rules to favor and protect the company plan. Government and private employers offering competing managed-care plans need to be honest brokers. To do that, they cannot have their own company plan to protect.

Market Performance

The central idea is not fear of markets, either. Although I prefer markets, private markets in their present configuration (with much distortion created by government) have not produced acceptable results. There seems to be a consensus that this year we are spending too much money on health care relative to other things and that there is much waste.

Pennsylvania, for example, reported recently on coronary-artery bypass graft surgery performed in thirty-five hospitals. The charges ranged from Reading, at $21,000 per case, which had a significantly better-than-average mortality rate, to the University of Pennsylvania Graduate Hospital, at around $84,000 a case. The statewide average was $44,600. If we take as waste the difference between $44,600 and $21,000 and multiply it by nearly 15,000 cases, we find more than $350 million worth of waste for one procedure in one state in one year because of an extremely inefficient coronary-artery bypass graft surgery industry. (This assumes charges approximate costs, which is not the case. We need data on actual costs.)

Price-inelastic Demand

As it has been configured, the market is not working. The causes of failure need to be analyzed, and the incentives have to be restructured. There are two main reasons why the market has been failing; one is price-inelastic demand, with a lack of any incentive for health plans to cut price and cost. Also, it is more rewarding for them to select among the wide variation in health risks than to manage care efficiently.

Why is demand price inelastic? We can find many reasons. One is that most employers pay all or most of the cost of the fee-for-service plan. We have all deplored the unlimited exclusion of employer contributions from taxable income. Another reason is that nonstandard benefit packages make value-for-money comparisons difficult or impossible. People will not switch from plan A to plan B to save $20 a month in premiums because of a fear of tricky exclusions in the fine print that they will discover only when they are seriously sick.

There is also a lack of good information on comparative quality because of the organized efforts of the provider community to prevent the collection of such information. There is uncompensated risk selection. There is a lack of individual choice of plan in the large part of the market consisting of small employment groups.

Managed competition does not imply a fear of markets. There are many different possible market configurations. Managed competition seeks to redesign and to restructure the market in such a way as to create price-elastic demand so that there will be powerful incentives for health plans to cut prices and costs.

Redesign will include an annual open enrollment for everybody with side-by-side comparisons and premium price–conscious choice (which Roger Feldman and Bryan Dowd discussed), a limit on tax-free employer contributions, a standardized benefit package, risk-adjusted premiums, a program of consumer information on quality, and individual choice of plan. This series of interventions will be designed to take us from inelastic demand to elastic demand within a functioning market.

Risk Selection

The other problem is how to prevent insurance firms from competing for the best risks rather than cutting costs and improving the quality of care. Joseph Newhouse observed that in the RAND experiment, 1 percent of the patients in any given year accounted for 28 percent of the costs. He likened the situation to the game of hearts, where everyone tries to pass off the queen of spades. The best way for an insurance firm to increase its profit is to pass the most expensive clients—the queen of spades—to someone else rather than to figure out how to improve care.

Annual health expenditures are concentrated in a few high-cost patients. Because of avoidance by insurers and free-riding by healthy people, many people are without coverage. There are outright refusals to cover, as well as exclusions of care for costly conditions, exclusions of coverage for preexisting conditions, and so forth. A major part of managed competition is to design a system with the incentives focused on improving the quality and economy of care, rather than on selecting risks. The design should include a single point of entry, contracts for each health plan to accept all members of a sponsored group, guaranteed continuity of coverage, inclusion of persons with preexisting conditions, community rating within the sponsored group, a standardized benefit package, and risk-adjusted premiums.

Rules in health care should be designed to create the right incentives. The motivation is not the fear of markets but the recognition that any market system must have particular rules. To date, we have chosen a particularly bad set of rules, which has produced unsatisfactory results.

Mark Pauly thinks that adverse selection is a minor problem, in which fewer than 5 percent of the population have small-group premiums more than 50 percent above the average in any demographic category. That is not my impression, nor is it the impression widely held in the industry. Good published data on premium variations are hard to find. I have heard of five- to tenfold variations for small employment groups. In the debate on reform last year, the insurance industry proposed reforms permitting tenfold variations in the premiums in small groups as if that were a great reduction.

In trying to get information on small groups with high-cost patients, part of the problem is what happens that truncates the data. The insurer may refuse to renew the policy of the whole group or of individuals within it, such as those with cancer. If the policy is cancelled, the employer may get another policy elsewhere, but with exclusions on preexisting conditions, so that the ones who were diagnosed with cancer find themselves uninsurable.

The exclusions of preexisting conditions may be permanent. One policy says it will never pay for treatment of anything to do with breast cancer because a young woman's mother had breast cancer. Coverage of people with AIDS may also be dropped. There are myriad techniques for truncating the sample. When we leave the world of insurance and enter the world of competing integrated systems, the incentives for health plans are not to be effective in treating costly chronic conditions, like cancer, but to attract healthy young people and not older people. The older I get, the less I like that idea.

A reasonably good set of risk adjustors combined with standardized benefits need not be complex. But a goal of managed competition is to create a system that is not destabilized by different risks enrolling in different plans. Managed competition focuses on rewarding cost cutting and improving the quality of care and not on all the myriad ways in which health plans seek to avoid risks.

Collective Action

The reason for health insurance purchasing cooperatives (HIPCs) is that groups of one hundred or less are too small to achieve economies of scale in administration. Mark Pauly objects to a limited study from the Congressional Research Service showing that the administrative costs in small firms of one to five employees are about 40 percent of claims. People in the insurance industry seem to think that is roughly right.

There is a comparable cost for employers with less than one hundred employees. Someone has to figure the right policy for a firm; the employer may pay a broker an 8 percent premium to do so. There are many costs on both sides of the market.

These small groups are too small to acquire and process information needed for a sophisticated understanding of how to buy. They are too small to spread risk. Thus, we have wide variations in the premiums among small employment groups. They are too small to manage competition, and they are too small to offer individuals a choice of plans. A small company with twenty-five or thirty people cannot offer a choice among all health maintenance organizations in town. But to create price-elastic demand, everyone in that group should be able to choose among all of them.

The California Public Employers Retirement System (CALPERS) has a health benefits program for employees, retirees, and dependents of the state and of 800 local government agencies. As an HIPC, it does solve these problems well, by spreading the risk widely. There are great economies of scale in administration, expertise on the demand side, and individual choice of plan. Even for those of us who do like markets and want to rely on markets, there is a rational basis for a set of rules and an HIPC, a purchasing cooperative, to do this with economies of scale.

In CALPERS, where 890,000 people are cared for, our purchaser-side administrative costs are one-half of 1 percent of premium. That is much better than small employers get in the free market, with brokerage fees of 8 to 15 percent of premiums.

Why should employers be required to offer choices and level-defined contributions? Why make them all do what the state of Minnesota and Stanford Universities do? Typical employer behavior—offering a fee-for-service plan and paying the whole thing—is hard to explain in rational terms. Because employers have been doing that for a long time, there is now inertia, along with a fear of upsetting employees. When Stanford made the change from employer-pay-all—it now offers employees three HMOs and the fee-for-service preferred provider organization plan—there was a large, angry demonstration. Five hundred furious people came to a big auditorium to hurl insults at Donald Kennedy, Stanford's president, Barbara Butterfield, our vice-president of human resources, and me, as chairman of the benefits committee. I can understand why other employers have not been eager to walk this plank. By the way, after a few weeks, we heard no more complaints.

As I pointed out at Stanford, if we change to an economically rational model with premium price conscious choice by employees while other employers stay in the open-ended system, we will achieve limited savings in terms of reduced shadow pricing. But we will not get a reformed cost-effective health care delivery system. There is a collective-action problem. Our premiums are probably $1 million–2 million a year less than they would be if Stanford had stayed with our old system. We will not have a cost-effective health care system until a critical mass of employers in our area do the same. As Roger Feldman and Bryan Dowd have shown, one employer cannot reform the whole health care system.

Other Variables

There are also problems of short-term pain versus long-term gain. There are problems of unions, which can make rational purchasing of health care difficult. There are problems because the executives, the professors, and others want the wide-access plan but are not willing to pay its extra cost with their own money.

At the University of California, the benefits committee is made up of professors who want to be sure that they have the fee-for-service wide-access plan. They know that if the university made level contributions, the wide-access plan would not stand up in competition. Too few people would want it, and they would lose it, and so they want to make the university subsidize it. Top executives in many companies lack understanding of the situation. Health care has the power to cloud people's minds.

Why standardize the benefit package? That sounds heavy-handed and un-American, although we did just that at CALPERS and at Stanford. One reason is to combat product differentiation, and another is to combat market segmentation. Plan A has wonderful vision care and no podiatry, and plan B has wonderful podiatry and no vision care: people with bad feet and good eyes join plan B, and people with good feet and bad eyes join plan A. Nobody is willing to switch from one to the other to save $10 a month in premium.

To create a system in which people will move to save $10 a month in premiums, the coverage has to be standardized. Otherwise, the people with bad eyes and good feet will not switch. To create price-elastic demand, the risk-selection games must be eliminated. As we found, all our HMOs covered outpatient drugs, but one, in the fine print, did not cover the delivery system for insulin. That makes the plan unattractive to people with diabetes.

Nonstandard benefit packages are shot through with fear of air pockets. Standardization, again, may sound left wing to Mark Pauly, but coverage contracts are complex. Most people do not understand their own coverage contracts. Do they cover transplants? If so, do they cover liver transplants for other than biliary atresia? If so, do they cover the cost of harvesting and transporting the organs? When CALPERS introduced standardization, it found that one plan said in bold print that it covered transplants but in the fine print said that it did not cover the cost of harvesting and transporting the organ. In our experience with CALPERS, nobody really understood what was in the benefit packages of multiple-choice plans. There were too many variations.

Regarding the employer mandate, what the employer ostensibly pays, the employee actually pays. We all know that. It is like an individual mandate administered through the employer. Among the reasons for continuing to do so are its continuity and its administrative efficiency. We are used to it. Since incrementalism is one of the first laws of our democracy, that is what we are doing.

I disagree that an employer mandate is regressive. It is "normal", unless you want to argue that the purchasing of most goods and services is considered regressive and that it would be better if we made everything "progressive," in which case there would be no incentive to work.

I do not want to see another $300 billion—the current cost of our private health insurance premiums (augmented by coverage for the uncovered)—loaded onto the progressive income tax. Individual income tax revenues for 1993 are about $520 billion. Do we want to load $300 billion more on that? President Clinton has figured out how to raise taxes higher than most of us want to see them.

Feldman and Dowd's research once again shows us that many of the best ideas and practices come from Minnesota. They show that Minnesota doctors and health economists are statistically significantly above average. They have clearly written the best empirical paper on the subject of health plan competition. I am particularly impressed by the analysis of the section 125 effect.

Managed competition is a list of many interventions to promote price-elastic demand. As Feldman and Dowd noted, even more could be done than has been done in Minnesota so far to increase the price sensitivity of demand: standardizing benefit packages, for example. But to get full system benefits, to get health plans to change the way they practice medicine and greatly improve efficiency, we need at least a critical mass of Minnesota employers in managed competition.

225

What Minnesota has, important and valuable as it is, is not a full test of what could be done if it were applied to the total health economy of the state.

Maintaining the Integrity of Managed Competition

Finally, managed competition is a concept to improve efficiency; as such, it has integrity. It can be fine-tuned, but some changes that might be proposed in the political process or in the congressional sausage grinder would destroy the plan's integrity. The resulting plan would not work. It would be like designing an airplane and then leaving off a wing. The process must be reasoned through, with microeconomic analysis.

We need, for example, premium price–conscious subscriber choice and, therefore, defined contributions that do not exceed the low-priced plan. We need a limit on tax-free employer contributions, so that people are using 100-cent dollars, rather than 60-cent dollars, at the margin. Managed competition will not work without a tax cap.

We cannot have voluntary health insurance that people can postpone buying until they are sick. Spirals of adverse selection will result. Voluntary HIPCs will not be possible. Unfortunately, in California and in Florida, where the idea is being tried, people think that the insurance plan can be voluntary.

Some time ago, Milton Friedman said to me that if purchasing cooperatives were a good idea, they would have happened in the private sector. I often agree with that idea, but not in this case. When there is a wide variation in the costs and the health risks among small employment groups, high-cost sick groups want to be pooled and all healthy low-cost groups want not to be pooled.

What about indemnity insurance as one competitor? I rather doubt that this can be reconciled with managed competition. Indemnity insurance means no contract between a carrier and providers, and that means no defined provider group for quality accountability. And without a contract with providers, the insurance may not be paid in full. Indemnity payment schedules, as in the Federal Employees Health Benefits program, are great tools for risk selection. They just pay poorly for services associated with chronic conditions. The employee association plans in the Federal Employees Health Benefits Program provide a textbook for how to create a risk-selecting scheme. It is difficult to design properly for risk management with indemnity insurance.

I offer these ideas to those who think that we can have indemnity insurance or self-insurance or no tax cap and still have managed competition. Some basic notions must be included, however, to make health reform work.

Commentary on Part Three

Stan Jones

I would like to describe what I, through my consulting, have seen in employer and in insurer practices in managed-competition settings, particularly with big employers offering choices to employees with competing plans in that framework. They are the prototypes that we need to apply the ideas on managed-competition that we are discussing. A big issue in the current policy process is how to move from what might work to something that will work. I will offer three examples.

• An employer decides that health maintenance organizations could save money or at least offer young families more benefits for the dollar. After making some calls, he signs on several HMOs. Then, the local physicians ask that their new HMO also be offered. He complies; after all, competition is good, he tells the consultant. Other HMOs also sell him. At the end of five years, he has one strong group model, one aggressive independent practice association (IPA), and four fee-for-service plans with slick brochures.

At no point does he evaluate the potential of the HMOs to contain costs, based on the literature or common sense. His employees distribute themselves fairly evenly among the five HMOs.

This is not unusual. I suggest that we could end up this way with the health insurance purchasing cooperatives, if the criteria for certification are low enough and if the HIPC is obliged to buy from all providers.

• In another example, the employer decides HMOs have the potential to save money or at least offer his young families more benefits for the dollar. So he offers several.

After a number of years, he finds his average premium per employee going up faster after starting multiple choices than before he offered them. He decides the HMOs must be the problem, because they are new. He eliminates them in favor of the faltering indemnity plan, which offered to cover all his employees with a less comprehensive benefit for less per employee. Employers all over the country are reaching this conclusion because they are looking at their costs per capita, which, in fact, are going up faster than before.

• In a related model, the employer offers several HMOs, one a tough staff model, along with the self-insured indemnity plan.

He sees his indemnity plan's cost going up inexorably, year to year, because, someone tells him, the HMOs are getting the good risks. The claim might be made that the HMOs are competing unfairly with the company plan.

So he adopts the strategy of forcing the HMOs to cut benefits, jiggling the formula to reduce the employer's premium share to make the HMOs less attractive and give the company plan a better chance of getting its "fair share" of good risks. He looks at the more efficient HMOs as competitors of the company plan, rather than as tools to be used to lower costs over time.

On the insurance side of this equation, we find a more sophisticated set of sellers.

In the Madison Avenue approach to risk selection, an insurer finds his indemnity plan premium going up in competition against a strong new HMO competing for the same employees and the same employer. In an unaccountable moment of insight, he becomes analytical. He hires a well-known survey firm to interview a list he provides of the low users and the high users who left his plan during open season to find out, first, why they chose this new HMO, and what distinguished the reasons of the high users from those of the low users.

He finds low users worried about this new thing called an HMO. But they overcome their concern. High users did better research and did not worry as much; they knew what they were getting into. In the next open season, he advertises with the theme "stay with us— you know who we are," and virtually stops the outflow of low users from his plan. He changes nothing in benefits, nothing except the presentation and advertising of his plan. He gets religion and invests big bucks each year in surveying and is now well into the favorable selection zone and going strong.

He has learned the following things about low users and high users and movement in response to premium changes, after many millions of dollars of investment and research.

First, high users stay with you to the bitter end. They think your plan is worth it even if premiums are raised, because you paid out so much for them last year. And they and their doctors, to whom they seem to be joined biologically, are used to your forms and procedures, so you may as well learn to live with these high users. It may even be worth trying to manage their care, if only you do not have to work too closely with physicians.

The low users, however, believe you are too expensive, however low your premium is. As they see it, they have nothing out of it. People do not understand buying protection against risks: they think they have gotten nothing for their money.

If you raise your premium more than others in your pack, these low users will shop seriously for a new plan. If you raise deductibles and coinsurance, one of the few things they clearly understand on your coverage brochure, even the low users will get mad. They will say on surveys, "I've been paying premiums all these years and have gotten nothing for it, and now they don't even want to pay all the bill if I do get sick."

Certain benefits or services really get the attention of low users. A happy, pretty, responsive, well-baby unit in the right part of town, for example, is a great thing to have for low users. Insurers also learn some ways of keeping away high users. You certainly do not want to be known for your good treatment of AIDS patients, for example, or for having good coverages for AIDS patients.

Low users do not have a doctor, and they will go for a select panel without even looking at the list of participating providers, if it keeps their premiums down. High users, by the way, look carefully at that list, so pick your list with that in mind.

Most low users do not even shop for a new plan or open a brochure unless an employer does something to wake them up, like raising premiums or cost sharing too much. Your strategy becomes to keep your own low users quiescent. Disturb the low users in your competitor's plan and do nothing radical to attract high users. You have enough already.

These observations are based on research and common knowledge and are used as practice in a successful plan. I would like for people to apply their model and skills to these kinds of data. The industry is way ahead in some respects on this kind of research.

As a final example, we have a very efficient plan—perhaps a staff model HMO or an indemnity plan with a good catastrophic case management program. It takes care of certain chronic conditions in a way less costly and more satisfactory to the patient, as confirmed by surveys. The plan has been perfected and now offers the new coverages and terms to its subscribers who are diagnosed with the condition. But the plan does not advertise its new service or add it to the open-season brochure. If it did, it might attract many or most of the employees with this condition.

AIDS is an excellent case in point. No matter how efficient a plan is, too many AIDS patients would push premiums to levels where this plan could not be competitive with the other plans. The employers do not seem to understand what they are losing by this behavior.

I was glad to have pointed out the disincentive to adapting coverages to the needs of special populations as one of the prices a plan might pay if it tries to standardize benefits or regulate too tightly. This is really a terrible and paralyzing trade-off. The real costs of keeping loose indemnity plans and a system where people keep enrolling in those plans may be the loss of a much more efficient way to take care of those with a chronic illness.

Harry Sutton, Jr.

It has been estimated that 5 percent of the population is responsible for 50 percent of total health costs. I suspect that even adjusting for age and sex, it is much higher than that. A recent study done by OTA, Office of Technology Assessment, introduced in Congress as information, showed that insurance companies that wrote individual health insurance modified 28 percent of the applications. About 8 percent of them were rejected.[1] The others either had higher premium rates—up to about 200 percent of the standard premium—and the others had waivers like a permanent limitation on preexisting conditions.

Now, these were individual policies, not group. Since most brokers and agents will not submit an application if they know it will be rejected, those applications should have been screened for obvious rejections ahead of time. So it is hard to figure out why the numbers are so high.

---

[1]Testimony of Jill Eden, senior analyst, Office of Technology Assessment, U.S. Congress, before U.S. Congress, House Committee on Energy and Commerce, Subcommittee on Commerce, Consumer Protection, and Competitiveness, September 19, 1990.

I think that the number of modifications could be higher. Let's look at Minnesota, where I am from. We have a high-risk pool with 32,000 people who have to be uninsurable to get in. That is only about three-quarters of 1 percent of our population. Enrollment over the past five years, however, has shown a 30 percent turnover a year in this pool, with people coming in and going out. We have probably covered 2 or 3 percent of the population over a five-year period.

Some people lose jobs and come into the pool, or their employer discontinues retiree benefits and they can come in. A company goes bankrupt, and the former employees can come in with no limits on preexisting conditions, and so on. The experience of this group is about 300 percent of normal premium. These 32,000 people lose $32 million every year in premium adequacy. In other words, the loss ratio is well over 200 percent of premium, and they are supposed to be charged 125 percent of standard premium. Here we have 1 or 2 percent of the population that runs at 300 percent or so of average cost.

One reason for this is that we have so many medical interventions. A $1 million claim, for example, might include a $350,000 drug bill for a certain disease. If a company is to pay for treatment, the risk of a catastrophic loss is fairly high. The carriers are much more likely to reject an applicant today who is perceived as a high risk. When I started in the health insurance business in 1952, we sold daily benefits in the hospital of $10, because that is what the average semi-private room rate was in the early 1950s.

I believe in the structure of managed competition but would suggest three or four things that have to be done, though they are politically unpalatable.

First, we should try to lower the expectations and demands of a population for excessive coverage. Everybody thinks that he can do whatever he wants and somebody—the government, the employer, or whoever—will pay to give him a new heart, a new liver, or whatever. He thinks he should not have to pay anything for it, mostly because he has no idea what his employer is paying. When his contribution goes from $10 a month to $20, he is furious because his premium just doubled, when actually he is paying less than 5 percent of the cost.

I see three ways to lower expectations—ways not antipathetic to managed competition. All the employer's contributions to health insurance should be taxable income with a tax credit, so that low-income people would not pay anything. Then, at least on the W-2 form, the employee will see the $5,000 a year that his employer is paying.

The bigger employers should offer multiple options and use the lowest-cost plan that will save money and create incentives.

In addition, in the base benefit plan there should be at least some modest coinsurance, deductibles, copayments, or the like, to make people aware that health care costs money. Perhaps for those below the federal poverty level, this requirement could be waived because we do not want to block the poor from getting health care.

This proposal is probably unacceptable because Congress would never permit anybody to pay taxes on his health insurance premiums. Nevertheless, it is one of the ways of bringing to people's attention what health care costs.

Second, a lot of the health care inflation is caused by the increase in high-tech medicine. I insure organ transplants in my daily business, and I see, for example, our rate of autologous bone marrow transplants is doubling and quadrupling every year. In our little company, we had twenty-five of them submitted for claims on our reinsured population in the first quarter of 1993.

Unfortunately, if we have a standardized benefit plan in the health insurance purchasing cooperative approach, often the government will decide what we pay for and what we don't. We cannot have coverage of catastrophic events varying among different plans. Moreover, one plan cannot pay for bone marrow transplants for breast cancer while another one claims the procedure is not medically sound: someone at the top must make the decision about what will and what will not be paid for and under what conditions.

This approach would prevent the courts from mandating that the health plan pay for something that is not medically warranted. The exclusion of experimental medicine is beaten to death by courts and beaten to death by the good will of state legislatures, who never saw a benefit they did not like.

Third, we underestimate the expense of running an HIPC. Bringing together a number of employers with ten employees each and getting a thousand employees in a plan does not incur the same administrative cost as enrolling a single employer with a thousand employees.

I agree that the administrative cost for small groups is too high. Maybe half the administrative costs for a small group goes for marketing and commission overhead. Now, if coverage is mandated and everyone has to have it, a lot of marketing and overhead should be eliminated. But in the HIPC program in California, there are about twenty HMOs, each paying 5 percent commissions. They all do not operate in all six regions of the state. To educate the individual employee of the small employer, a book sixty pages long, printed on glossy paper, explains all these HMO options, with a separate rate page for each region in the state. This book is costly to produce. Moreover, maybe an agent should explain to the individual or the small employer what the various options are and which HMOs are in his territory.

The problem of administration is quite complex. Eventually, individuals, unemployed people, and maybe Medicaid recipients, with subsidies for small employers and additional subsidies for individuals with low incomes, will come under state administration.

Will individuals be billed at home? Will the premiums be collected through their bank accounts? How will half be collected from the individual and half from the state? Who will guarantee that the premium is paid? If the premium is late, will the individual's coverage be canceled for nonpayment?

When a Medicaid recipient gets a job and goes off Medicaid, the state will not pay. Then he has to pay, or the federal government pays part of it. If he goes back into Medicaid, the state owes the whole premium. How will these people be signed up and readjusted? How will their premiums be reallocated to the financers, and how can the money be collected without a terrible administrative hassle?

I think we have underestimated the cost of managing the HIPC, not just for small employers but for complex subsidized products or partially subsidized premiums from various taxing entities. After we explained this problem to the people in Minnesota, they said the state would pay the premium for low-income persons and then try to collect their portion of the premium from them at home or from their job—but good luck.

My final topic is high technology. In Ohio, we had a case for which we needed a heart transplant, and the state refused to pay for it unless the procedure was done at Ohio State University. But the school would not negotiate a deal. We could have bought the heart transplant at fifty cents on the dollar elsewhere. We could have sent the patient to the Mayo Clinic or some other place at half the price that Ohio State wanted to charge: it just would not negotiate.

I am concerned that with a state budget, the state will lock all the care within the state. We operate on a global basis. We try to find the best providers for these very complex procedures that can run $300,000–400,000. If we want to send patients to Houston, to the Mayo Clinic, or to the Cleveland Clinic, we should be able to. Providers have different specialties. Some medical centers, unfortunately, seem to be willing to try anything on any patient without consideration of the likely outcome.

We currently will not use the services of such centers, but we are concerned that we will face constraints and not be able to get the best care where we want to get it. We are in a global health environment. We want to be able to use the best service where it is. Transportation or bringing the family along is not a major expense when the medical costs are hundreds of thousands of dollars.

Robert Waller

Will there be tremendous pressure by the government to subsidize a managed-competitive care plan, as described by Mark Pauly, and, in direct ways, to make the subsidy more attractive by having it come from the taxpayers who were in other plans? Might it attract more healthy people who do not anticipate needing any health care and, thus, drive up the average cost of all other plans?

Roger Feldman and Bryan Dowd have examined the response to premium changes by the Minnesota state employees' plan. They certainly have demonstrated that consumers will respond to a competitive marketplace. Managed competition will allow consumers to evaluate competing plans on the basis of quality.

The goal under discussion in the Minnesota state legislature and in the governor's office is to reduce the rate of growth in health care spending by approximately 10 percent per year over the next five years; this would bring in managed competition (this is called an integrated service network in Minnesota, instead of an accountable health plan). Managed competition would then be allowed to govern the system.

If one takes the annual growth rate of approximately 10 percent of health care spending per capita—and we can debate whether that is correct—and extrapolates the national data from the Minnesota target, one would see that in year 1, there would be a 9 percent rate of growth; year 2, 8.1; and so on. The real question is, Is this possible?

At the Mayo Foundation, we have about 1,500 physicians and 17,000 other employees. We are the largest multispecialty group practice in America and the first one, begun 129 years ago. All ingredients of our organization bring to mind many negatives. We are predominantly fee-for-service. Seventy-five percent of our physicians are specialists. We have an increasingly ill patient population, as judged by the case-mix index from 1988 to 1992. In the past five years, we have invested an average 10.6 percent in research and education. We are a perfect setup for a high-cost provider. But is that in fact the case?

Growth in national health care expenditure per capita has been 9.6 percent; growth in gross domestic product per capita has been close to 3.8 percent in the past five years. The Mayo rate of growth in revenue per patient registration in the past five years has been approximately 4.8 percent. This is not a perfect measure, but these are the best data of this sort that we have. If the target is health care spending per capita equal to the growth of per capita gross domestic product, we were close to meeting this target in the past five years.

Why is this happening? If the data are correct, then Mayo is the integrated health care delivery system that Alain Enthoven and Paul Ellwood have been envisioning. Inpatient and outpatient services are integrated. We have merged with our hospital systems. We have one governing body, which looks at resource allocation and utilization of outpatient and inpatient services. We have a unified medical record. We have continuous peer accountability. The research and education programs are integrated with the practice. How are we organized, and how do we pay ourselves? We have fixed salaries. We have no special perks. How much are we paid? Mayo invests $100 million in research and education each year, buys the tools for the practice, builds the buildings to practice in, and *then* pays our salaries: that sequence gives an idea of how compensation relates to some other segments.

Who is ultimately responsible for how Mayo physicians are paid? The ultimate authority is in the public domain. The public trustees of the Mayo Foundation decide the compensation schedules. Thus, we are an integrated delivery system, which provides the infrastructure for managed competition.

Can we further reduce the rate of growth in revenue per patient? Absolutely. It is an essential requirement for the future. We have made the commitment to do so, and we are taking the position that, regardless of the health care reform scenario that evolves, we all must be more efficient. We have defined efficiency as providing more quality care and using fewer resources, which usually means fewer services per patient.

Our approach to building the more efficient, integrated-service network is complex. It involves merger with family physicians in Decorah, Iowa; in Eau Claire, Wisconsin; and a new experiment with the John Deere Corporation in the Quad Cities, 200 miles away.

Is there any way that a tertiary care center and a corporation can develop a new relationship with one another to raise quality and reduce costs? The key words in managed-care contracts are *vertical integration* and *managed care*.

236

Every health care reform option must look at how to support research and education and continuously improve systems. Price controls are incompatible with this system. Price controls impede addressing the underlying causes of increased health expenditures. Our top three causes of rising costs are the lack of constraint in the provision of care, the lack of constraint on patient demand, and the absence of adequate health insurance reform.

In summary, at Mayo we are strong proponents of managed competition. We are strong proponents of integrated health care delivery systems. We are one of several examples of integrated care. These systems are the substratum or infrastructure of managed competition. We all need to be about the business of refining the definition of managed competition.

PART FOUR

Competition in a Changing Market

9

California Providers Adjust to Increasing Price Competition

Jack Zwanziger, Glenn A. Melnick, and Anil Bamezai

In June 1982, California became the first state to enact legislation encouraging insurance plans to contract with selected providers. This legislation spawned the development and growth of numerous and various types of managed-care plans. The legislation allowed the state's Medicaid program, MediCal, to contract with a subset of hospitals to which it would channel its beneficiaries in return for price concessions. At the same time, private insurance plans were explicitly provided with the same right. Enrollment in the insurance plans that resulted, known as preferred provider organizations, has grown explosively. In addition, the restructuring of health insurance accelerated the growth of health maintenance organizations, particularly those that contract for hospital services. By 1990, the insurance market in California had been transformed, with more than 85 percent of beneficiaries enrolled in PPOs or HMOs.

The resulting market behavior is similar in some respects to the behavior that managed competition would attempt to create. Important buyers are increasingly sensitive to price so that hospitals are competing on a price basis for contracts with PPOs and HMOs. Hospitals facing these binding constraints on their revenue have reduced the rate of increase in costs. The insurance industry in California, which had been extremely fragmented, has begun to consolidate. Similarly, providers have begun to organize themselves into more coordinated units, with the creation of local hospital chains, the rapid growth of physician groups, and the cultivation of relationships by hospitals with admitting physicians, particularly those providing primary care.

Following the introduction of the managed-care law, California's health care managers radically restructured their approach to cost management as well as to patient services. Hospitals, changing from a largely fixed-cost operation, increased the proportion of their variable costs—with staffing (the largest element of hospital costs) adjusted up or down from day to day depending on fluctuations in the daily census. The approach of flexible staffing has become the standard throughout the industry.

In this chapter, we draw on our own research and that of others into the effects of the California managed-care system. We also describe how the findings of this policy experiment may be used to help guide reform of the health care system on the national level.

We first describe the conceptual framework for our study. Then we examine how cost, utilization, and staffing trends changed in California following the passage of selective-contracting legislation. The data show that after 1982 California hospitals reduced the rate of growth in total costs relative to the U.S. experience. We found that these trends are not mere accounting anomalies: a dramatic divergence has developed since 1982 between continued staffing growth in the United States and stability in California. Finally, we will discuss our study, updating the results of our statistical analysis of hospital costs to identify the separate effects of selective contracting and the competitiveness of the physician market.

Conceptual Framework

Competitive dynamics in hospital care are shaped by the parties to the transaction, namely, the physician, the patient, and the insurer. Each player has different criteria for selecting or guiding the selection of a hospital. The nature of hospital competition within a market depends on each party's relative ability to influence this choice. Theory suggests that in some hospital markets the choice is largely under physician control and in others, insurers. The focus of competition differs dramatically in these two types of markets.

In physician-dominated markets, hospitals compete for patients largely through efforts to attract physicians. Since physicians are generally not price sensitive, the demand for hospital services is mainly determined by a comparison of the quality and amenities it offers with those offered by its competitors. The availability of technically sophisticated services, a modern hospital building, and convenient parking are some of the critical dimensions of competition among hospitals. As a result, hospital competition in physician-dominated markets will tend to increase hospital costs. The parties most damaged are the third-party payers, employers that pay premiums, or taxpayers when the patients are beneficiaries of publicly financed insurance programs.

In insurer-dominated markets, in contrast, hospitals compete on price as well as on quality. Through their ability to channel beneficiaries to selected providers, selective-contracting insurance plans may be able to extract price concessions from hospitals during negotiations. In market areas where such insurance plans have a substantial share of the market, hospitals and insurers play a complex competitive game. Hospitals must still attract patients by competing for the favor of admitting physicians, but they must also compete first for inclusion in insurers' preferred-provider networks. Price now becomes a much more important factor in attracting and retaining a patient base. As a result, hospitals that can control their costs are in a much better position to secure contracts. Although possession of a contract alone does not guarantee an increased flow of patients, a contract channels patients by creating a cost gap so that patients' out-of-pocket costs are lower in contract hospitals. A hospital's failure to win a contract will generally all but eliminate HMO or PPO subscribers as patients.

In California, the locus of control has shifted notably over the past decade from primarily physician-dominated markets to a greater degree of insurer control. This situation has created an ideal environment in which to research some of the expected results of managed competition.

A Comparison of the Hospital Trends in California and the United States

The profile of a profound change in hospital behavior can be drawn from data in the 1992 *Hospital Fact Book*, published by the California Association of Hospitals and Health Systems. These data are drawn from the annual survey of hospitals of the American Hospital Association. We compared California and United States hospitals on a variety of measures for two periods: 1975–1982, to capture the preselective trend, and 1982–1990, for the post–selective-contracting period.

The most inclusive measure of the change in total hospital expenditures (inpatient plus outpatient) is the proportion of total per capita income those expenditures consume (figure 9–1). The propor-

FIGURE 9–1

PER CAPITA HOSPITAL EXPENSE AS A PERCENTAGE OF PER CAPITA
INCOME FOR THE UNITED STATES AND CALIFORNIA,
1975, 1982, AND 1990

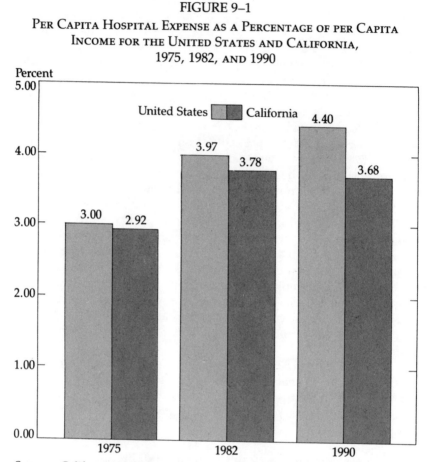

SOURCE: California Association of Hospitals and Health Systems, *1991–1992 Hospital Fact Book*, 16th ed. (Sacramento: CAHHS, 1992).

tion of per capita income for hospital expenditures increased by approximately the same amount between 1975 and 1982 for California and the United States (.86 versus .97). Between 1982 and 1990, this proportion continued to increase for the United States, although by a somewhat smaller amount (.43), but actually declined in California by 0.10. Thus, on average, U.S. citizens continued to pay an increasing proportion of their income for hospital expenses, at the same time that Californians actually reduced the proportion of income accounted for by hospital expenses.

The other aggregate measure of burden imposed by hospital

FIGURE 9–2

AVERAGE ANNUAL PERCENTAGE CHANGE IN PER CAPITA HOSPITAL
EXPENSE, IN THE UNITED STATES AND CALIFORNIA, 1975–1990

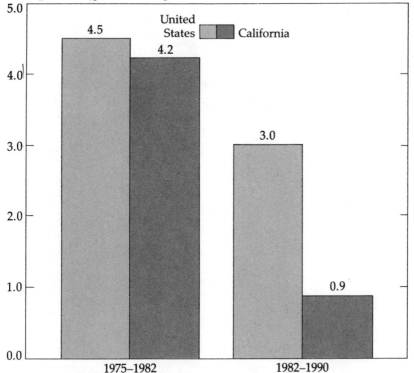

Average annual percent change

NOTE: Deflated by the hospital market basket.
SOURCE: California Association of Hospitals and Health Systems, *1991–1992
Hospital Fact Book*, 16th ed. (Sacramento: CAHHS, 1992).

expenditures, real per capita hospital expenditures, shows the same
trend reversal (figure 9–2). Per capita expenses in California increased
at a slightly lower rate between 1975 and 1982 (4.2 versus 4.5 percent
annually), whereas in the later period, there was a large difference in
the rate of growth (0.9 versus 3.0).

This difference was not caused to any substantial extent by a
slower rate of growth in hospital output—that is, inpatient days and
outpatient visits (figure 9–3). Per capita inpatient days dropped more
slowly in California than in the United States (−3.3 versus −3.5), at
the same time that outpatient visits grew at a lower rate (0.4 versus
1.5) (figure 9–4). Combining both inpatient and outpatient outputs,

245

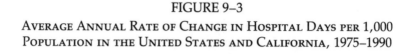

FIGURE 9–3

AVERAGE ANNUAL RATE OF CHANGE IN HOSPITAL DAYS PER 1,000
POPULATION IN THE UNITED STATES AND CALIFORNIA, 1975–1990

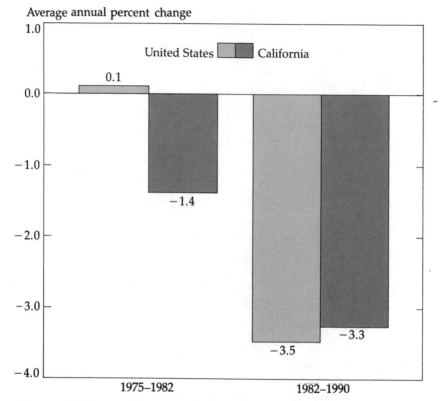

SOURCE: California Association of Hospitals and Health Systems, *1991–1992 Hospital Fact Book*, 16th ed. (Sacramento: CAHHS, 1992).

these two approximately offsetting trends show that the differences in cost trends that we have observed are not due to differences in output changes.

The lower rate of increase was caused primarily by an increase in efficiency (figure 9–5). Whereas hospital expenses per adjusted discharge, probably the best measure of the cost of a unit of hospital output, increased much more rapidly in California during the 1975–1982 period (5.6 versus 4.0), it increased at a substantially lower rate after the introduction of selective contracting (2.4 versus 4.2). This lower rate of growth in expenses is associated primarily with lower resource use, so that California hospitals have had a much lower rate

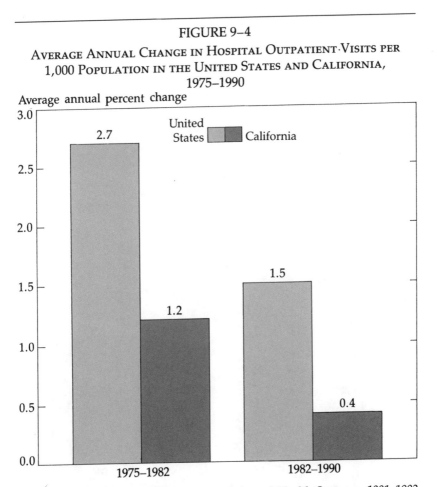

FIGURE 9–4

AVERAGE ANNUAL CHANGE IN HOSPITAL OUTPATIENT·VISITS PER 1,000 POPULATION IN THE UNITED STATES AND CALIFORNIA, 1975–1990

SOURCE: California Association of Hospitals and Health Systems, *1991–1992 Hospital Fact Book*, 16th ed. (Sacramento: CAHHS, 1992).

of increase in the number of hospital full-time–equivalent personnel per adjusted day (figure 9–6).

We see that trends in California showed a dramatic change in 1982. We will now demonstrate that this change is the result of selective contracting rather than some other factor.

The Effects of Competition and Managed Care in California

In the previous section, we presented some descriptive time series data comparing the performance of California with the United States as a whole. In this section, we review some of the empirical evidence

247

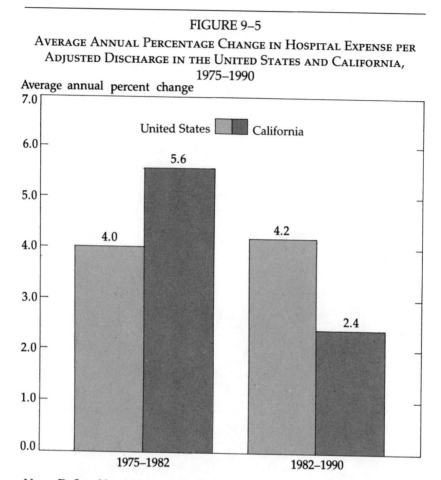

FIGURE 9–5

AVERAGE ANNUAL PERCENTAGE CHANGE IN HOSPITAL EXPENSE PER
ADJUSTED DISCHARGE IN THE UNITED STATES AND CALIFORNIA,
1975–1990

NOTE: Deflated by the hospital market basket.
SOURCE: California Association of Hospitals and Health Systems, *1991–1992 Hospital Fact Book*, 16th ed. (Sacramento: CAHHS, 1992).

on hospital behavior within California that compares hospitals based on the competitiveness of their market.

Here, we focus on both the broader roles of market forces and economic incentives in the health sector and the more specific findings relating hospital costs, prices, and efficiency. The primary conclusion we draw from our work is that by changing the economic incentives to encourage health care providers to compete on the basis of price, health care costs and prices can be lowered. The evidence indicates that prices themselves, as opposed to the rate of cost increases alone, can actually be deflated. Hospitals, when faced with

FIGURE 9–6

AVERAGE ANNUAL RATE OF CHANGE IN FULL-TIME EQUIVALENT
HOSPITAL PERSONNEL IN THE UNITED STATES AND CALIFORNIA,
1975–1990

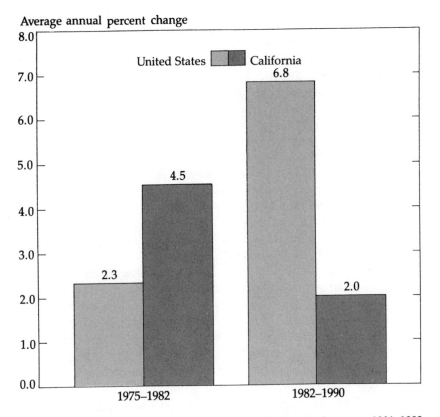

SOURCE: California Association of Hospitals and Health Systems, *1991–1992
Hospital Fact Book*, 16th ed. (Sacramento: CAHHS, 1992).

the need to compete for managed-care contracts, will cut their costs
both substantially and quickly. Such cost cutting as a result of price
competition, however, may exacerbate the access problems of the
uninsured, underscoring the need to expand coverage to the entire
population. Some of the specific empirical results are presented
below.

Effects of Competition on Hospital Expenses. We used several approaches to study the immediate effects of selective contracting on

hospital costs. We chose to focus on costs for two reasons. First, we expected any effects of selective contracting to show up first in hospital costs, with managers changing their behavior in anticipation of the new competitive environment. Revenues, though, would not be affected to any significant degree until enough beneficiaries had switched into the insurance plans that contract selectively to affect hospital revenue noticeably.

We expected selective contracting to have little effect in very concentrated markets, since in such markets insurance plans have no ability to threaten to divert patients to a competitor. We used several approaches to compare hospital cost trends in markets at different intensities of competition[1] These studies all found that after 1982, hospital costs were growing slower in more competitive markets, a finding confirmed by J. C. Robinson and Harold Luft, who used an entirely different methodology.[2]

Using a multivariate regression model, we estimated the effects of the hospital market structure, MediCal contracting, and the Medicare prospective payment schedule program on total hospital costs before and after the introduction of selective-contracting legislation.[3] In the period before selective contracting (1980–1982), hospitals located in more competitive markets had higher costs. This is consistent with previous findings pertaining to nonprice competition among hospitals. In the period following the introduction of selective contracting (1983–1985), the positive cost differential for hospitals in more competitive markets eroded as a result of increased price competition under selective contracting. In another analysis that expanded the set of dependent variables, we provided a more comprehensive picture of the various effects of increased hospital price

---

[1]Glenn A. Melnick and Jack Zwanziger, "Hospital Behavior under Competition and Cost-Containment Policies," *Journal of the American Medical Association*, vol. 260 (1988), pp. 2669–75; Glenn A. Melnick, Jack Zwanziger, and T. Bradley, "Competition and Cost Containment in California: 1980–1987," *Health Affairs* (Summer 1989), pp. 129–36; and Jack Zwanziger and Glenn A. Melnick, "The Effects of Hospital Competition and the Medicare PPS Program on Hospital Cost Behavior in California," *Journal of Health Economics*, vol. 7 (1988), pp. 301–20.

[2]J. C. Robinson and Harold S. Luft, "Competition, Regulation, and Hospital Costs," *Journal of the American Medical Association*, vol. 260 (1988), pp. 2676–81.

[3]Zwanziger and Melnick, "Effects of Hospital Competition and the Medicare PPS Program."

competition on hospital costs, revenue, and utilization for the period 1980–1985.[4]

Using an analysis of variants (ANOVA) model to control for hospital market structure and Medicare's PPS, we found numerous significant changes in hospital behavior. The rate of growth in both total and unit costs slowed dramatically for hospitals located in competitive markets following the introduction of selective contracting. The rates of growth in both revenue and use also slowed, but the differences between hospitals located in high-competition and low-competition markets were not statistically significant.

Using a similar ANOVA model but extending the time frame by two years, we examined trends in the rates of growth of total hospital revenues and total hospital expenses for 1980–1987.[5] During 1986 and 1987 the costs of hospitals in highly competitive markets began to climb at rates similar to those in less competitive markets, suggesting that the pressure of price competition might be lessening. Hospitals in highly competitive market areas, however, experienced relatively low rates of growth in hospital net revenue (after adjusting for inflation), suggesting that contracting activities were beginning to constrain the rate of growth in hospital revenues.

There are several striking features of these results. First, the change in trend quickly followed enactment of the selective-contracting legislation in 1982. By 1983, hospitals were responding, and this response depended on the competitiveness of their markets and led to a substantial drop in the rate of growth of hospital costs (see figure 9–7). Hospital administrators, anticipating the competitive pressure from selective-contracting plans, began to control their costs, with the stringency of their efforts depending on the competitiveness of their markets.

Long-Term Cost Containment. To determine the effects of the 1982 policy changes on the California hospital market, we estimated a multivariate model of total hospital expenses. Variables included discharges and outpatient visits as measures of hospital outputs, input prices, and a variety of other hospital characteristics, such as ownership. Also included were factors that influence the demand for hospital services, such as the percentage of the area's population

---

[4]Melnick and Zwanziger, "Hospital Behavior under Competition and Cost-Containment Policies."

[5]Melnick, Zwanziger, and Bradley, "Competition and Cost Containment in California."

FIGURE 9–7

PERCENTAGE DIFFERENCE IN TOTAL CALIFORNIA HOSPITAL EXPENSES
SHOWING THE COMPETITION EFFECT, 1980–1985

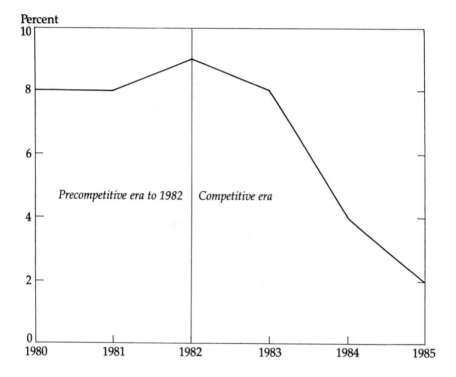

SOURCE: Authors' calculations using the California Office of Statewide Health Planning and Development annual discharge data, 1983–1988, and the quarterly hospital data, 1980–1990.

over age sixty-five or with a household income below the poverty line. Finally, we included variables that measure the effects of selective contracting, the Medicare diagnosis-related group–based prospective payment system, and MediCal selective contracting.

To isolate the effects of policy variables, we simulated their predicted impacts on total expenses. All the numbers indicate the ratio by which either low or high is different from the average. We used 1980–1982 as the base period and examined all time trends relative to it. For the simulations, we have contrasted how average hospital costs among the top and bottom 20 percent of hospitals compare with the average for each comparison category. So, for

FIGURE 9–8

COMPARISON OF HOSPITAL COSTS IN HIGH-COMPETITION VERSUS LOW-
COMPETITION MARKETS IN CALIFORNIA, 1980–1990

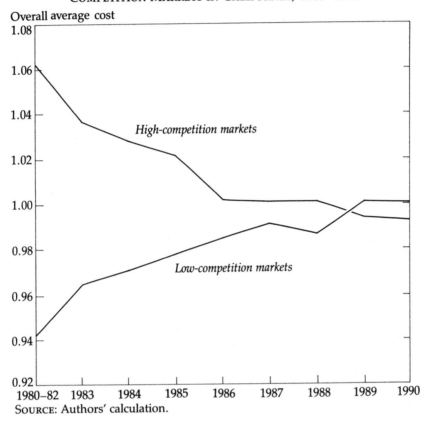

Overall average cost

SOURCE: Authors' calculation.

example, we compared costs for the average concentration of the most and least competitive 20 percent of hospitals. We then divided these costs by the average cost for each year.

Our data from California indicate that the managed-care policy has successfully controlled cost increases on a sustained basis through the end of 1990. Figure 9–8 presents data comparing the costs of hospitals in high- and low-competition markets over time in California. In the base period, 1980–1982, before the introduction of California's managed-care legislation, hospital costs in highly competitive markets were approximately 12 percent higher than the costs for hospitals located in less competitive markets. This finding—that greater competition leads to higher hospital costs—is consistent with

253

FIGURE 9–9

COMPARISON OF HOSPITAL COSTS IN HIGH- AND LOW-PHYSICIAN
PER CAPITA MARKETS IN CALIFORNIA, 1980–1990

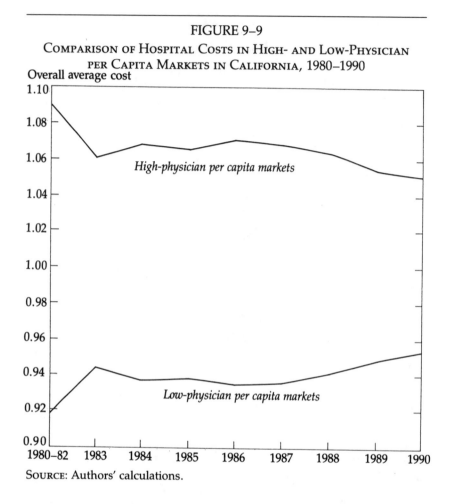

SOURCE: Authors' calculations.

all previous studies of hospital competition. Following the introduction of the managed-care law in California, this gap narrowed, but hospital costs in competitive markets still remained above those in less competitive markets, at least until the 1989–1990 period. By the end of 1990, hospital costs in less competitive markets actually exceeded those in more competitive markets. The policy lowered expenses at high-competition hospitals by almost 14 percent relative to those at low-competition hospitals. These findings demonstrate that the observed cost reductions are long term, rather than a one-time effect, a distinction of critical importance with regard to any cost-containment program.

Physician concentration, as measured by the number of physi-

254

cians per 1,000 population in the hospital's market, had a substantial effect on hospital costs (figure 9–9). This result is consistent with the tendency of areas of high physician concentration to have a greater concentration of specialists as well and therefore for the practice of a more intensive style of medicine. The difference in expenditures between the least and the most concentrated hospital markets was reduced during the 1990s, presumably under pressure from managed-care plans. By 1990, the difference had shrunk steadily to 10 percent from more than 17 percent. Thus, the effect of physician concentration on hospital costs diminished, but did not disappear, during this period.

Leveraging Competition and Market Power to Lower Prices

While the previous section presents evidence that hospital costs can be reduced through competition pressure, it does not speak to the ability of managed-care plans (or consumers) to share in these cost savings. This section reviews the evidence on the ability of managed-care plans to capture some of these cost savings in the form of lower prices paid to hospitals.

Following the introduction of California's managed-care legislation, there was a rapid growth in the formation and adoption of PPO and HMO plans. Fueling this growth was the belief by employers and insurance carriers that excess capacity and competitive market conditions could be leveraged to negotiate lower prices with health care providers. The ability to assemble preferred provider networks endows third-party payers with the potential power to channel patients away from more expensive providers. By using this approach, known as selective contracting, payers seek to extract price discounts and other concessions from providers. This thinking is a cornerstone of the proposed formation of health insurance purchasing cooperatives, or large health insurance purchasing pools, which would confer substantial buying power in the market on managed-care plans.

We recently completed a study to provide a partial test of the ability of the selective-contracting process to control hospital prices.[6] The primary objective of this analysis was to measure the independent effect of hospital market structure and the relative strength of Blue Cross vis-à-vis each hospital on the price paid by Blue Cross in its PPO. To investigate this effect, we examined prices obtained in

---

[6]Glenn A. Melnick, Jack Zwanziger, Anil Bamezai, and R. Pattison, "The Effects of Market Structure and Bargaining Position on Hospital Prices," *Journal of Health Economics*, vol. 11 (1992), pp. 217–33.

different types of markets by the largest PPO in California. We found that lower prices were obtained in the more competitive markets. Our results indicate that managed-care plans can leverage both competitive market conditions and their own market power to extract price discounts from providers.

An important finding of that study is that the competitiveness of the hospital market has a substantial effect on the price paid by Blue Cross to its network hospitals. After controlling for product differences, Blue Cross pays higher prices to hospitals located in less competitive markets. In addition, we estimated the effects of two market-position variables as a measure of the relationship between Blue Cross and member hospitals. The results suggest countervailing forces at work. The higher the percentage of a hospital's total patient days accounted for by Blue Cross, on the one hand, the greater the leverage Blue Cross has with the hospital. This leverage permits Blue Cross to obtain greater discounts. On the other hand, the larger the share of Blue Cross patients accounted for by a hospital, the greater the hospital's leverage and the higher the price. Further, as competition declines in the market, the sharper the increase in the price that Blue Cross pays. Both market structure and the market position have big impacts on negotiated prices.

In addition, we found that tight occupancy rates affect providers' bargaining power. Hospitals with high occupancy rates operating in markets with a small excess capacity were able to negotiate significantly higher rates.

Our results indicate that prices paid to hospitals in the Blue Cross of California PPO network, after controlling for hospital product differences, are strongly influenced by the competitive structure of the hospital market. Hospitals located in less competitive markets are able to secure higher prices. Relative bargaining position was assessed in terms of both the importance of each hospital in the payer's network and the importance of the payer to each hospital's patient base. Hospitals that serve a larger share of the Blue Cross market in their area are generally able to negotiate higher prices, while those serving in less competitive markets are able to negotiate even higher prices. These results show that actual hospital prices are lower in more competitive markets. The policies encouraging selective contracting have proved effective in transforming the structure of the private insurance industry and, in turn, producing changes in the nature of hospital competition.

Conclusions and Policy Implications

We have observed sustained changes in California over a nine-year period, but after national health system reform we would expect to observe a far more rapid rate of change partly because health insurance purchasing cooperatives would have more market power than insurance plans in California, with its highly competitive insurance industry, and partly because HMOs and PPOs typically have greater penetration than was the case in California initially. Finally, utilization management technology is now far more developed with its utilization review programs and organizations than in 1982. As a result of these features of the present health system, an environment amenable to reform and conducive to accelerated cost containment would evolve.

The cost savings we observed have several sources: partly from reductions in utilization (reduced admissions, average length of stay tests, and other services) and partly from increased provider efficiency in reducing the cost-to-unit output. Initial studies have shown that in California, competition has generally had a more significant effect on unit costs than on utilization.[7] This observation suggests that much of the savings from selective contracting is independent of the stringency of utilization review on the part of the managed-care plans. It is not utilization reductions but efficiency gains that appear to dominate cost containment.

An important aspect of a managed-competition program is that it has its greatest impact where enough competing providers have enough excess capacity to generate competitive pressure in the market. To the extent that some areas do not have sufficient alternative providers to generate competitive pressure, the cost savings from managed competition will be less. While a substantial majority of the U.S. population lives in areas with competing health care providers, it may be necessary to combine some elements of regulation with managed competition in less populated areas. Even here, we could design policies to transfer the efficiency gains from competitive to regulated areas. At present, for example it is difficult to assess the efficiency of hospitals in noncompetitive areas. Standards obtained from hospitals operating in competitive markets may be used as benchmarks by which to compare cost-containment efforts in noncompetitive areas.

Greater hospital competition for selective contracts tends toward lower prices. This effect decreases substantially as the importance of a hospital to an area PPO increases. It is crucial to cost-containment efforts, therefore, that competitive markets are not made uncompeti-

---

7Jack Zwanziger, Glenn A. Melnick, J. Mann, and L. Simonson, "How Hospitals Practice Cost Containment with Selective Contracting and PPS," working paper, 1992.

tive through mergers or acquisitions. One aspect of managed competition, though, is that providers consolidate into networks ("accountable health plans"). These observations suggest a simple conceptual criterion for assessing such reorganizations: any consolidation that significantly reduces the options available to the population living in an area is anticompetitive and, therefore, undesirable.

In summary, the advent of selective contracting has changed the nature of competition in California from a cost-increasing to a cost-decreasing force. Competition prior to selective contracting was cost increasing because of the nonprice nature of the competition. With selective contracting, we see that hospitals have restrained the rate of increase in costs over a nine-year period. By the end of the period, a 15 percent shift in relative costs had taken place. The available evidence from California's ten-year experience (as the most developed managed-care sector in the country) suggests that price competition can encourage health care managers and health care providers to change their behavior. Behavioral change is a necessary requirement of any successful health care reform program to manage health care resources and meet health care needs in a more cost-effective manner.

10

Collective Purchasing and Competition in Health Care

Sean Sullivan

The advocates of regulating health care prices like to claim that competition has been tried in health care but has failed. Their conclusion is wrong, because their premise is false: competition has not failed in health care, because it has not really been tried.

Competition is possible only where a market exists. There has not been a genuine market in health care, however, because the prerequisites for one—information, proper incentives, and sufficient buying power on the demand side of the market—have been lacking. Information on which to base rational purchasing decisions has been nonexistent, while the incentives in the health care system have pointed precisely in the wrong direction—toward the use of ever more services with little concern for how much they cost or whether they produce successful results. And purchasers have lacked the power to bargain successfully with providers even if they had the information.

The critics of competition are right about one thing—there has been market failure in health care. But they wrongly conclude that such failure is built into the nature of health care markets and cannot be corrected. Evidence is mounting from various corners of the country that, armed with good information about the product and being willing to change the perverse incentives that encourage over-use of services, purchasers can aggregate their buying power to get better value in health care. Much of this evidence is coming from the

259

growing business coalition movement, as employers pursue collective purchasing in communities small and large.

The Value Test

Since the late 1970s, employers have been organizing coalitions to find ways to contain their rising health care costs—but for nearly a decade they did little. Some of them began to realize, though, that without good information about the health care services they were buying, they had no way to judge the value of those services. In this sense, health care was unique. Everything else that businesses purchased was subjected to a value test: if one supplier of a good or a service delivered greater value than another, that supplier got more orders.

In health care, however, there was no value test. To determine the value of health care services, we must know both their cost and their quality. (Responsible employers are not interested in cost alone; they also want good quality care for their employees.) While business purchasers knew that their costs were rising all too rapidly, they had no idea what they were getting in return—whether those expenditures were buying better quality or just paying higher prices for more services of questionable value. In short, they were buying blind.

Purchasing Power

Not only were employers blind, but also in most instances they were weak when pitted against large health care providers in a community. While a few large employers could cut themselves better deals, most controlled too little patient flow to make hospitals or physicians bother to notice them. This lack of bargaining power relegated them to the role of price takers—and blind ones, at that.

This individual weakness in the marketplace should have made coalitions a natural vehicle for collective bargaining with providers, but employers were not organized or determined enough yet to pursue this course until much later. Part of their weakness came from the fact that many coalitions started out as broader-based entities, with providers and insurers often sitting around the same table. These communitywide coalitions were premised on the idea that getting all the actors together in the same room would lead to collective action in the best interests of all. Unfortunately, this was not an idea whose time had yet come.

Gradually, business purchasers began to see that it would take something more than merely reasoning together to slow accelerating costs. This realization led some to form separate coalitions of purchasers only, excluding the providers and insurers of health care that were increasingly seen as part of the problem rather than part of the solution. The trend toward coalitions made up exclusively of purchasers spread; today nearly all the new groups being formed are built on this model. Now constituted to do collective purchasing, these coalitions have already altered the balance of power in their own health care marketplaces. Providers can no longer ignore groups that control a large flow of patients, and individual employers no longer need to be price takers. Bargaining relationships have emerged, and health care "markets" have begun to function.

Blind Markets

These new purchasing groups were able to negotiate better prices than they had been paying by giving providers the incentive of continued or even increased business. They were still buying blind, however—unable to judge the value of services being provided or the caliber of medical practitioners providing them. Yet lacking were reliable data on the quality of health care—the necessity or appropriateness of services and their effectiveness compared with their cost. Without being able to tell who did what best at the lowest cost, businesses only could assume that they were saving money. Discounts may actually cost more if those who give them perform unnecessary procedures or have to correct their own mistakes for lack of skill.

The need for good—or even any—information on the quality of care eventually created a market of its own. Medical entrepreneurs rushed to meet this need, developing systems to measure the comparative performance of hospitals and doctors in achieving good medical outcomes at a reasonable cost. Purchasers and providers had been learning from the work of medical researchers like Dr. John Wennberg that enormous variations in medical practice often had no correlation with clinical results or health. When measurement systems such as MedisGroups and Iameter became available to document the relationship between quality and cost for many procedures, buyers were no longer blind in the market for medical services.

Coalitions and Market Competition

A new model for market-based competition is emerging in health care, led by the actions of employer coalitions around the nation. It derives from the often overlooked fact that health care is a quintessentially local industry, with services delivered and used locally. For the market to perform its historical role of enabling competitive forces to maximize consumer welfare in health care as well, purchasers must have good information about what they are buying and then use it to "buy smart"—to buy the best value available to them in the relevant marketplace. In health care, this marketplace tends to be a well-defined community, and coalitions of local employers are ideally suited to make competition work by overcoming the existing fragmentation on the demand side of the market. Such coalitions can then impel the improvement of quality and efficiency that will increase the value of health care and maximize consumer satisfaction—while reducing costs for them, the purchasers.

Community-based market reform occurs when three things happen:

- Purchasers work with providers to develop agreed-on measures of quality and cost-effectiveness that enable them to determine the value of health care services.
- Purchasers agree to buy from those providers that deliver good value and continue to improve, thereby establishing accountability for performance.
- Purchasers reward those providers that deliver better value, with more patients and better payment.

These fundamental principles of community-based market reform were first put forth by Dr. Walter McClure of the Center for Policy Studies. McClure provided the crucial insights that form the basis for true market reform in health care:

- Individual communities are the health care marketplaces within which reform must occur.
- Reform must occur within each such market in response to the actions of purchasers and providers in that community.
- Purchasers must drive reform by seeking and rewarding providers that deliver the best value.

Using these principles, community-based coalitions are now leading the movement to make the market work in health care, to the ultimate benefit of consumers.

Making Community-based Reform Work

The coalitions and their employer-members in the vanguard of community-based market reform are leading a movement that is only now coming to the attention of many health care analysts. The policy establishment has had its gaze fixed on the grand designs of expert groups and the debates among legislative proponents of everything from the health care systems in Canada or Germany to medical savings accounts. In the meantime, coalitions have quietly been going about their work of effecting real changes in their own health care marketplaces. It is past time for their accomplishments to be celebrated and for their experience to be shared with those who are still working on grand designs.

Examples of Success

The next sections relate the two most notable examples of real successes in making health care markets work as they should to lower costs and improve quality. The success of the Memphis Business Group on Health is already well known from earlier press attention. Now the Employers Purchasing Alliance of Central Florida is emerging into the spotlight because of its critical role in driving larger public policy reforms recently enacted in that state. Several other coalitions also are mentioned more briefly, to give a fuller picture of how collective purchasing by business groups around the country is becoming the leading edge of serious health care reform, using market principles of information and incentives to achieve greater efficiencies and ensure more consistent quality.

Memphis. The oldest and best-known story of coalition success is in Memphis. There, in 1987, the Memphis Business Group on Health decided to seek bids for hospital care for 25,000 employees of member companies. Memphis, at the time, was a bastion of the old world in health care—health maintenance organizations were nonexistent—and the market was dominated by several of the largest hospitals in the world. The challenge to the old order began when eleven companies led by Federal Express, the largest in Memphis, decided to cure themselves of market blindness. In a study of hospital charges that they commissioned, they found that some hospitals charged as much as 80 percent more than others for the same service. Armed with these findings, the group called a press conference and released the results, ranking the hospitals by name. It then announced its intention to have the hospitals bid competitively for its business. Not surprisingly, these hospitals largely ignored the effort by purchasers to create a competitive market.

Baptist Memorial, the largest nonprofit hospital in the world, submitted the only bid. It offered discounts of up to 20 percent in return for the companies' promise of more patients. Under the contract, the companies agreed to steer their employees to Baptist and an affiliated network of physicians by requiring the employees to pay more of their own money if they went elsewhere. The result was dramatic, shaking up the rigid old order in a city where the health care industry is the largest employer. Two years later, every hospital responded to the coalition's request for bids.

At the time of the first contract in 1987, Baptist had about half the coalition members' inpatient business. In 1993, its share stands at 80 percent of a much larger number, since the business group now includes more than thirty companies with well over 100,000 employees and dependents—about 20 percent of the entire private sector market in Memphis. As the group's chief executive put it, "It's really taken a lot of dollars away from the other facilities." The president of Methodist Health Systems, the second largest provider in town, acknowledges that "it's a very significant block of business."

The coalition's members count their savings from the contract with Baptist in the tens of millions of dollars. Even more important, though, is the effect that the whole experience has had on the other providers. Methodist, Baptist's chief rival, has held its own prices steady for the past three years and last year won the contract for the city's employees. When Methodist discovered that its costs were 15 percent to 20 percent higher than Baptist's, it launched a productivity drive in response. New information systems revealed how widely doctors varied in their use of medical resources to treat the same conditions, yet with similar results. St. Francis Hospital, the city's third largest, formed its own physician network to compete for contracts and has been submitting everything it does to a quality improvement program.

The managing director for employee benefits at Federal Express concludes, "There's no doubt we've had an influence on the way hospitals are doing business in this town." The hospitals acknowledge that the business group's actions were a wake-up call for them to pursue changes that other market factors were already making necessary. Now the coalition is working with all the hospitals to establish a communitywide information system that would process and record every health care transaction in Memphis, using the electronic technology from automated teller machines. More important, the system would be used to create a database of performance reports on cost and quality on all hospitals and doctors, which purchasers and patients could use to help select providers. This system would be a complete cure for the chronic blindness of the health care market.

The Memphis Business Group on Health has been a trailblazer

in collective action by business to change the marketplace—or, rather, to create a marketplace—in health care. The group has leveraged the power of large companies like Federal Express and First Tennessee National to win bargaining power and cost savings for smaller employers like Seesel's, a local supermarket chain that has seen its health care bill decline for three successive years. Now the coalition is working to develop an insurance product for even smaller companies that have not yet been able to take advantage of collective power, because they are not self-insured.

Central Florida. The story in central Florida has developed in a different way from Memphis, reflecting the differences among communities that lie at the heart of the community-based approach enunciated by McClure and pursued by the coalitions. The Central Florida Health Care Coalition is a consortium of forty-five private and public employers in the Orlando area. Its approach has been to put an information system in place that measures the comparative performance of area hospitals and then to move to collective purchasing on the basis of those measures. Interestingly, the Florida Gulf Coast Health Coalition in nearby Tampa started with collective purchasing much like Memphis, and the two coalitions now have joined forces in the Employers Purchasing Alliance to pursue information-based purchasing for much of central Florida.

From its beginning, the Orlando coalition knew that it needed good data to manage costs and ensure quality at the same time—to determine the *value* of services being purchased. Although a 1986 analysis of hospital claims data showed large differences in costs per admission and average length of stay, there was no way to adjust for relative severity of cases treated to make valid comparisons of results. The next step, then, was to establish a measurement system that would make such adjustments, so that costs could be compared with medical outcomes. For this purpose, the coalition chose the Medis-Groups II system, which uses information from patients' actual medical charts instead of claims forms to compute a severity-of-illness score before and after treatment, making possible valid comparisons of the effectiveness of care.

An initial analysis of the area's twelve hospitals showed wide variations, both among themselves and compared with state and national norms in the MedisGroups database. These findings opened the eyes of the hospital administrators and of the employers to potential areas of large cost savings. Given the receptivity of hospital leadership (a different situation from Memphis), coalition members agreed on a joint initiative to improve quality continuously against

265

measurable standards and to reduce costs by improving efficiencies at the same time. In the spirit of cooperation, the coalition agreed that initial negative results would not be used against the hospitals; in the future, though, managed-care contracts would reward improvement. Since the coalition includes Disney as well as General Mills, GTE, and the school district in Orlando, these contracts will represent a large share of the market for the hospitals.

The results to date from installation of the MedisGroups system in the hospitals have been nothing short of startling. In 1992, the two largest providers, Orlando Regional Healthcare System and Florida Hospital Medical Center, actually reduced their expenses per admission by 2 percent and 4.2 percent, respectively (at Orlando Regional, this reduction came on the heels of a sharp drop in the rate of increase the year before, from 9 percent to 1.4 percent). These savings are being realized from the combined effect of reducing average lengths of stay and use of ancillary services such as laboratory tests and X-rays.

Florida Hospital targeted high charges for treating respiratory illness. Study groups recommended changes in the management of patient care that reduced costs by more than a million dollars annually, and the hospital is redefining the national MedisGroup's benchmark for treatment of simple pneumonia. Orlando Regional reports that it is now breaking even on Medicare after losing $12 million annually before, so that these costs are no longer being shifted to private purchasers. The savings are being shared with purchasers even before any selective contracting is done. The school district has seen its average employee hospital bill drop 11 percent and spent a million dollars less on health benefits in 1992 than in 1991. For private purchasers like General Mills, bills are running as much as 25 percent below a year ago.

The Employers Purchasing Alliance that includes coalitions in Orlando, Tampa, and now Sarasota expects to save $50 million annually on its members' health care bills once the MedisGroups system is in place throughout the region. The alliance now covers twenty-six counties and more than 700,000 persons. When the Florida Health Coalition in Miami is integrated into the alliance, coverage will expand to more than 2 million individuals, and savings will multiply further.

Looking farther ahead, the alliance plans to establish a communitywide database on quality and costs that will include physicians as well as hospitals, extending cost-saving efforts to outpatient care. Smaller employers are being recruited actively to make an affordable insurance product available to them. And efforts are under way to sign affiliation agreements with other coalitions across the country to give their members access to the alliance network of providers in Florida.

The most telling point of the Florida story is how much money can be saved without even using collective purchasing power to do selective contracting—if the providers are receptive to pursuing quality improvement and sharing the savings that result from it. Value-based purchasing, the next step in Orlando, will bring more savings to the purchasers as they seek out the providers that deliver the best value. Gains are already being realized from collective purchasing in Tampa, which will now be adding the power of information to increase savings for employers. As the coalition in Miami joins the alliance effort, most of the state will soon be a competitive marketplace driven by the concept of value.

Other Coalitions and Markets. Other coalitions are creating competitive marketplaces for health care in their communities, though few have as much data on cost savings to share. The Colorado Health Care Purchasing Alliance based in Denver is statewide in scope. Many of its more than a hundred members have fewer than a hundred employees, and they share in savings gained from collective purchasing for more than 100,000 covered individuals. The alliance contracts with a network of hospitals, physicians, and ancillary providers, using comparative information on their prices and utilization patterns. It also offers its members an exclusive provider option that allows them to realize even greater savings for such services as obstetrics and open-heart surgery; the average charge for heart surgery through the exclusive contracting arrangement is $29,400, compared with $35,000 for other purchasers at the same hospital and a community average charge of about $42,000. The alliance is particularly noteworthy for giving many smaller employers access to the savings that usually only larger businesses can obtain.

The Madison Area Employers Healthcare Coalition in Wisconsin created a separate arm called the Alliance to do collective purchasing for employers with more than 60,000 covered persons—a good-sized share of the local market. Members include local government bodies as well as private sector employers. Successful in keeping its members' cost increases below the average, the Alliance is now serving as a model for the state's newly announced version of managed competition just as the Orlando and Tampa coalitions have been a model for Florida's version. The Health Care Network of Greater Milwaukee has had similar success in negotiating collectively for a large group of employers in that city.

267

Other collective purchasing coalitions are making competition work for their employer members in Nashville, Tennessee; Richmond, Virginia; Savannah, Georgia; and Des Moines, Iowa. Group purchasing by coalitions is clearly on the rise, with new initiatives being launched in major cities like Seattle, San Francisco, and Houston as well as in smaller communities across the United States.

Summary and Conclusion

A new, community-oriented, market-based model for health care reform is springing up around the nation. Driven by coalitions of employers working together, this model is creating competitive marketplaces in health care where they did not exist before. This new model is based on these principles:

- Health care services must be purchased on the basis of their measurably superior value.
- Purchasers must contract with providers that deliver demonstrably better value.
- Consumers must be given information and incentives to use these providers.

As these principles are followed in more communities, competitive forces will bring the cost of delivering health care services under control even as the quality of those services is improved. This is happening already in some communities, and it can happen eventually in all.

11

The Political Economy of the Federal Employees Health Benefits Program

Walton Francis

Because the way in which markets achieve results is both indirect and seldom understood, it is not surprising that more direct techniques of social intervention are usually chosen.

CHARLES SCHULTZE
The Public Use of Private Interest

While the nation debates the merits of President Clinton's national health care proposal, a seminal health program is enjoying great success. Run by the federal government for its employees, annuitants, dependents, ex-employees, and former spouses, the Federal Employees Health Benefits Program embraces most of the tenets economists believe are essential to a cost-effective health care program. Over the past decade, benefits have improved, and costs to the employee have risen much less than inflation. These impressive accomplishments were an accident. Yet, the FEHBP was the original

---

The views I present are only my own. Some portions of this paper have been modified from an article I wrote for the *Washington Post* ("Shopping for a Health Plan," November 17, 1992) and a talk I gave at the Heritage Foundation (published in "Open Season for America?" November 9, 1992).

model for the managed-competition proposal made by Stanford professor Alain Enthoven, subsequently elaborated in the Jackson Hole initiative, and endorsed by candidate Clinton.[1] Under the managed-competition idea, and in the FEHBP, a sponsor or manager arranges for a number of health plans to compete for enrollment on the basis of cost and quality. Because consumers bear, on the margin, the full amount of a plan's cost in excess of the employer's or government's contribution, they face substantial incentives to make frugal choices, and plans that control costs better gain market share.

The federal government was a laggard in providing health benefits for its employees. Most large private employers added health benefits during World War II as a simple way of getting around wage controls to attract workers. Lacking employer help, unions and employee organizations representing federal workers set up group coverage for their members. In 1959, when the government proposed a single plan for its employees, unions and employees resisted abandoning their own plans. A compromise was struck. The existing plans would be allowed to survive and to compete for members in an annual open season. The government role would be limited to enforcing financial solvency safeguards, setting enrollment procedures, and creating minimal plan standards. The government would contribute a set amount for each employee, with the employee paying the difference between that amount and the cost of the plan he wanted to join. And so a system of choice was born.

Every year some 4 million Americans, representing 9 million family members, make a choice among health plans. During the month-long open season, they decide which of two dozen to three dozen health plans (the number depending on where they live) will best protect them against the cost of illness for the coming year. During open season, they get advice from plan advertising, newspaper columns, and health fairs. Some even read a book of consumer advice. Most talk to colleagues in the workplace, in much the same manner as most of us talk to friends and neighbors about their automobile experiences when we consider buying a new car.

In each open season, most of these people simply stick with the health plan they chose the previous year. If the benefits are not worse, if the premium has not risen much faster than inflation, and if service has been acceptable, why bother to change? On average, however, about 5 percent change plans each open season. Although

---

[1]Alain C. Enthoven, *Health Plan* (Reading, Mass.: Addison-Wesley, 1980), and "The History and Principles of Managed Competition," *Health Affairs*, supp., 1993, pp. 24–48.

only one in twenty enrollees switches plans, some individual plans lose half or more of their enrollment, and some plans drop out each year. Each plan must take any eligible employee *without regard to a preexisting condition* (a few plans, however, are allowed to restrict enrollment to employees of a particular kind, for example, foreign service or secret service).

How successful has the program been, and why? In what follows, I analyze the actual performance of the FEHBP and the political factors that condition and affect that performance. I focus on the program as a whole, with the health care system setting the environment within which the program performs and which the program influences only to a modest degree. Within this context, I compare the costs, benefits, and managerial responsiveness of the federal employee program with the other two large, sponsored programs for which data are available, Medicare and large private employer insurance.

Program Performance

It is commonplace among economists that the health care marketplace has been fatally flawed by departures from normal market characteristics. The flaws most often cited are the lack of consumer information (in choosing among both procedures and providers) and the role of insurance in destroying the link between consumption and cost to the consumer. At the most fundamental level, the argument for competition among managed-care plans is an argument for creating a workable market. Thus, the jargon term *managed competition* expresses both an empirical prediction and a normative view that with some seemingly simple changes in health care markets, we can achieve radical improvements in efficiency. This view, presumably, encompasses improving allocative efficiency (consumer decisions based on their own preferences), improving efficiency in the use of resources (reduction of costs through more sensible purchasing decisions), and reducing X inefficiency (the sheer waste that occurs in monopolistic markets).

There is no nation in the world in which managed competition is used on a large enough scale to create the kinds of market pressures that might radically improve industry performance.[2] What might

---

[2]Recent testimony by the Congressional Budget Office dismissed managed care as likely to save only one year's increase in health care spending and asserted that "it probably would not affect the long-term growth of those costs" (statement of Robert D. Reischauer, director, CBO, March 2,

happen to the practices of the medical profession if, say, 90 percent of the customers got services only from doctors who have shown themselves willing and able to meet norms of performance, enforced by managers who regularly run statistical profiles to see who may be an outlier compared with disciplined doctors? What might happen to hospital dynamics if a flat payment such as the diagnosis-related group system were to be used by *all* payers, and costs could not be shifted to private insurers still paying "cost plus" prices? What would happen if the tax exemption for employer-paid health insurance were repealed or capped? No one can predict for certain, but a health care system in which prices go up *less* than the consumer price index for a decade or more would be a likely outcome if several such reforms were instituted.

Regardless of the possibilities for a radically improved health care market, what are the possibilities within the market as we find it today? Here we face only bounded outcomes. A program shaving off a few percent of costs compared with its competitors may be doing all that can be done.

In analyzing the performance of the FEHBP, there are two obvious points of comparison within the present health care financing system: other government programs and other (private) employer programs. The other major government programs covering millions of lives are Medicare, Medicaid, CHAMPUS (Civilian Health and Medical Program for the Uniformed Services), and the public hospitals run by most cities and counties. Medicaid and public hospitals together might be thought of as the American equivalent of the British health care system, missing only an explicit guarantee. Regardless of one's perspective, their problems and niche are so unique as to be a diversion from the purpose of this chapter. CHAMPUS, unfortunately, is a program on which reliable cost and other data are nonexistent, reflecting the reliance of its covered population on military facilities for much care on a space-available basis.

This leaves Medicare and private employers as the best points of comparison. Dimensions of performance on which these systems might be compared include costs, benefits, consumer responsiveness, equity, and management responsiveness to emerging problems. Before turning to evaluative measures, however, let us review some simple data on the FEHBP.

1993, before the Subcommittee on Health of the House Ways and Means Committee). This testimony is accurate so far as it goes, but it neglects the possibility that dynamically growing cost savings could arise if managed care dominated and transformed the market.

Program Structure and Trends. It is useful to think of the Federal Employees Health Benefits Program as one in which the government pays a basic dollar amount toward the cost of health insurance, with the employee paying the difference between the government contribution and the cost of the plan. As a result, if a plan operates with above-average efficiency, the employee can gain by paying a lower premium or by enjoying higher benefits for the same premium. The government lets many plans compete for this business on the condition that they offer group rates, provide reasonable policy coverage, meet various requirements for financial solvency, and admit any eligible employee or annuitant who signs up in open season.

The law creating the program was enacted in 1959. As shown in table 11-1, the program started operation in 1961 with some twenty-eight plans, of which fifteen were available to the one-third of government employees in the Washington, D.C., metropolitan area.[3] Because health maintenance organizations were rare and concentrated in a few areas of the country, most federal employees could choose from among slightly under a dozen fee-for-service plans available on an unrestricted basis. The program grew slowly for many years, from twenty-eight plans in 1961 to about forty a decade later. Then, as now, the government generally allowed new HMOs to join without any barrier but, by law and regulation, generally prohibited new fee-for-service competitors (a major fee-for-service expansion occurred in the middle 1980s, after Congress bowed to union pressures to begin new plans).[4]

Although it is tempting—and for many purposes useful—to think of the program as a voucher system, in which the government certifies any willing and able competitors, the fee-for-service competitors were franchised on a first-come–first-served basis. In fact, as discussed below, the government has been slow to force existing plans out even after they prove themselves market failures.

The program has been criticized for reimbursing fee-for-service

---

[3]For a history of the early program and its creation, see Odin Anderson and J. Joel May, "The Federal Employees Health Benefits Program, 1961–68: A Model for National Health Insurance?" in *Perspectives* (Chicago: Center for Health Administration Studies, University of Chicago, 1971).

[4]Since then, most new union plans have folded, victims of adverse risk selection and other failures. The two most successful new plans, Beneficial Association of Capitol Hill Employees and Secret Service, made the key strategic decision to limit enrollment to employees rather than retired annuitants, thus getting a free ride unavailable to most other plans. Allowing this restriction was a major management mistake from the managed-competition perspective.

TABLE 11–1
Growth and Decline in Number of FEHBP Plans, 1961–1991

Year	National			D.C. Metro Area		
	Fee-for-service	HMO	Total	Fee-for-service	HMO	Total
1961	15	13	28	13	2	15
1970	18	21	39	16	2	18
1975	26	33	59	24	4	28
1976	24	41	65	22	4	26
1977	22	47	69	20	4	24
1978	19	65	84	17	5	22
1979	18	70	88	16	5	21
1980	24	86	110	22	6	28
1981	24	100	124	22	6	28
1982	24	101	125	22	6	28
1983	23	114	137	21	7	28
1984	23	162	185	21	8	29
1985	28	200	228	26	10	36
1986	31	294	325	29	13	42
1987	35	404	439	33	13	46
1988	33	478	511	31	18	49
1989	30	421	451	28	18	46
1990	26	378	404	24	20	44
1991	19	372	391	17	19	36

Note: Each high and low option is counted as a separate plan. Even in the D.C. area, the number of plans available to any particular employee is lower, because some plans are restricted to particular agencies. The table does not indicate preferred provider options. These have emerged since 1990 and are now available in almost all fee-for-service plans.
Sources: Office of Personnel Management, annual insurance report and other documents.

plans on what amounts to a cost-plus (experience-rated) basis. In effect, this criticism goes, a plan cannot lose money (and hence has little incentive to save money), because if its costs go up, it can simply raise premiums the next year to make up the difference. The actual incentives, however, are more complex. First, if the plan loses both money and enrollees, it may be unable to make up the difference before being driven out of business. This is a real possibility: some plans have cost their unhappy union sponsors millions of dollars before exiting the program. Second, if a plan raises premiums to make up for prior deficits, it will lose substantial business on the margin, and it may give up market share, a loss that it can never recover.[5] Since the government allows fully allocated overhead costs to be included in the premium, a company can give up substantial profits (in an economic sense) on the margin if it is forced to leave the program, even though its accounting profits are small. Thus, in economic terms, the program presents real business profits and risks, even if these are not shown in government budget data. Third, the great majority of HMOs participate in the program on a community rating basis, subject, in most cases, to no adjustments other than age of enrollees. These HMOs make real (economic) profits and losses.

Because of the government's free-entry policy for HMOs, the national explosion in the number of HMOs in the late 1970s and early 1980s translated into immediate growth in the FEHBP HMO participation. As shown in table 11–1, the number of plans zoomed from fewer than 100 during the program's first two decades to a peak of more than 500 in 1988.[6] Since then, industry shakeout and consolidations have reduced both the national number and the number participating in this program. Regardless, in excess of four-fifths of all the nation's HMOs did, and do, participate in the FEHBP.[7]

Not shown in table 11–1 is the recent emergence of preferred provider organization options in the program. For the past three years, starting with the 1990 open season, four fee-for-service plans

---

[5]For a presentation of data on the dramatic enrollment changes that can and do occur, and why, see Walton Francis, "HMO Customer Service," *Health Affairs*, Spring 1986, pp. 173–82. As a tool for my use of quit rates as a measure of HMO service quality in Walton Francis, CHECKBOOK's *Guide to Health Insurance for Federal Employees* (Washington, D.C.: Washington Center for the Study of Services), I run a regression analysis every year on influences on HMO enrollment. Premium, change in premium, and changes in number of competitors are powerful predictors that explain about half of the variation in quit rates among plans.

[6]Other descriptions of this program have sometimes cited much lower numbers of plans than cited here. I treat as a separate plan any policy that varies either in benefits or in premiums from another, even if both are offered by the same corporation. In the jargon of this program, sometimes a single company offers a high and a low option; I treat these as the entirely separate offerings they are. I have not, however, counted as separate plans either the preferred provider organization or Medigap variations that individual fee-for-service plans now typically offer within their structure.

[7]This is one of many program dimensions in which the FEHBP outperforms Medicare. Only about 100 HMOs, and none at all in many major markets such as the District of Columbia, participate in Medicare.

TABLE 11–2

ENROLLMENT TRENDS IN THE FEHBP, 1975–1992

(persons in thousands; excludes dependents)

Year	Total	Fee-for-Service	HMO	% in HMO	Annui-tants	% of Annui-tants
1975	3,147	2,904	243	8	858	27
1976	3,226	2,952	274	8	920	29
1977	3,298	3,007	291	9	985	30
1978	3,393	3,076	317	9	1,046	31
1979	3,491	3,156	335	10	1,138	33
1980	3,598	3,239	359	10	1,214	34
1981	3,684	3,302	382	10	1,330	36
1982	3,558	3,149	409	11	1,282	36
1983	3,593	3,150	443	12	1,364	38
1984	3,670	3,148	522	14	1,397	38
1985	3,760	3,167	593	16	1,440	38
1986	3,832	3,203	629	16	1,489	39
1987	3,901	3,181	720	18	1,517	39
1988	3,950	3,066	884	22	1,567	40
1989	4,001	3,013	988	25	1,593	40
1990	4,035	3,041	994	25	1,583	39
1991	4,073	2,966	1,107	27	1,644	40
1992	4,114	2,957	1,157	28	1,656	40

SOURCES: Office of Personnel Management, annual insurance report, spring head count, and other documents.

offered significant PPO options within the structure of their plans.[8] In the first several years, even these options were marginal in potential enrollee savings and in geographic coverage, but they now appear to be economically significant—relying on national networks with substantial discounts.

As shown in table 11–2, HMO enrollment took off in the 1980s, rising from 10 percent to 25 percent of total enrollment. This is particularly striking growth in the light of the 40 percent of enrollees who are annuitants. Older and sicker Americans are notoriously less

[8]That is, by enrolling in a plan such as the American Postal Workers Union, the employee can have unrestricted freedom of choice at the regular deductible and coinsurance rates or get a significantly better deal by using preferred providers. The employee can use both preferred and non-preferred providers in the same year, even concurrently.

willing to join HMOs (a result that may reflect their lack of market options, such as plans fully covering winter sojourns away from home, rather than the motives commonly assumed). Eighteen percent of federal annuitants belong to HMOs, despite the fact that more than half of them are now receiving Medicare and most of these get little financial advantage from an FEHBP HMO.[9]

Costs. Table 11–3 presents information on the relative ability of Medicare, FEHBP, and private employers to control health insurance costs over time. These data seem to show that Medicare and the FEHBP program do about equally well and that both do substantially better than private employers in holding down costs. In fact, with an adjustment for monopsonistic cost shifting, the FEHBP would surge to the front, and both Medicare and private employer plans tie for a distant second. Before explaining this result, let us consider the data with some care.

Authoritative published time series on private insurance costs are nonexistent.[10] The Labor Department publishes survey data, the Health Insurance Association of America publishes survey data, and many benefits consulting firms publish such data, but all of these sources fail to present a simple time series of raw (let alone adjusted) data on average costs. The best source may be a little-known series developed by the Hay/Huggins Company, an employee benefits consulting firm, for a major study of the FEHBP prepared by the Congressional Research Service several years ago.[11] To extend the

---

[9]In the FEHBP, in most fee-for-service plans, enrollees who are also Medicare clients get 100 percent wraparound coverage for a premium lower than most HMOs charge.

[10]For a depressing discussion of the paucity of reliable data on private insurance costs, see Jon R. Gabel, "Perspective: A Look at Insurance Data," *Health Affairs*, Winter 1992, pp. 186–90. In a recent study, the Government Accounting Office relied on Foster Higgins data for a 1987–1991 comparison. These data provide almost identical results to the Hay/Huggins data for the four years in which they overlap. See U.S. General Accounting Office, "Employer-based Health Insurance: High Costs, Wide Variation Threaten System," GAO/HRD-92-125, September 1992, p. 23.

[11]U.S. Congressional Research Service, *The Federal Employees Health Benefits Program: Possible Strategies for Reform* (Washington, D.C.: Government Printing Office, May 24, 1989), p. 256. This series was expanded to cover 1991 and cited in a recent study by Lewin-ICF: Allen Dobson, Rob Mechanic, and Kellie Mitra, *Comparison of Premium Trends for the Federal Employees Health Benefits Program to Private Sector Premiums and Other Market Indicators* (unpublished report prepared for Blue Cross and Blue Shield, November 12, 1992), tables 1 and 2.

TABLE 11-3
Cost Control over Time by Medicare, Private Employer Plans, and FEHBP, 1975–1993

Year	Medicare Benefits Paid			Private Premiums Paid			FEHBP Premiums Paid		
	Total cost per enrollee ($)	Annual increase (%)	Ten-year average increase (%)	Total cost per enrollee ($)	Annual increase (%)	Ten-year average increase (%)	Total cost per enrollee ($)	Annual increase (%)	Ten-year average increase (%)
1975	488						557		
1976	661	35					694	25	
1977	834	26					789	14	
1978	968	16					828	5	
1979	1,103	14					902	9	
1980	1,237	12		900			1,021	13	
1981	1,454	18		1,053	17		1,263	24	
1982	1,670	15		1,232	17		1,384	10	
1983	1,887	13		1,562	27		1,485	7	
1984	2,103	11		1,676	7		1,548	4	

1985	2,320	10	17.1	1,740	4		1,543	0	11.0
1986	2,422	4	14.0	1,789	3		1,909	24	10.9
1987	2,561	6	11.9	1,942	9		2,029	6	10.2
1988	2,700	5	10.9	2,271	17		2,284	13	10.9
1989	2,923	8	10.3	2,725	20		2,472	8	10.8
1990	3,269	12	10.3	3,202	17	13.8	2,801	13	10.9
1991	3,405	4	8.9	3,602	12	13.3	2,960	6	9.1
1992	3,793	11	8.6	3,965	10	12.6	3,197	8	8.9
1993	4,162	10	8.3	NA	NA	NA	3,485	9	9.1

NOTE: Cost per enrollee is per person for Medicare and per employee (including family) for the other programs. Costs are in dollars of that year.

SOURCES: Private increase data through 1991 from Hay/Huggins Benefits Survey, as reported in U.S. Congressional Research Service, *The Federal Employees Health Benefits Program: Possible Strategies for Reform* (Washington, D.C.: Government Printing Office, May 24, 1989), and Allen Dobson, Rob Mechanic, and Kellie Mitra, *Comparison of Premium Trends for the Federal Employees Health Benefits Program to Private Sector Premiums and Other Market Indicators* (unpublished report prepared for Blue Cross and Blue Shield, November 12, 1992); for 1992 data from Foster Huggins survey, see U.S. General Accounting Office, "Employer-based Health Insurance: High Costs, Wide Variation Threaten System," GAO/HRD-92–125, September 1992; total cost extrapolated back from 1992. FEHBP data from the Office of Personnel Management, annual *Insurance Report* and other documents. Medicare data from U.S. Congress, House Ways and Means Committee, annual *Green Book*, updated in 1992 and 1993 from the latest Department of Health and Human Services budget. Some early years are interpolated.

series, I added the 1992 percentage change (10 percent) from the survey by another benefits consulting firm, Foster Higgins. For an absolute measure, I used the Foster Higgins estimate of about $3,965 as an average 1992 premium cost, which I then extrapolated backward using the Hay/Huggins factors.[12] These data cover large corporate sponsors of health insurance.

Interestingly, the Foster Higgins estimate of $3,965 in per employee premium costs is more than one-fifth higher than the FEHBP figure of $3,197 for 1992. Some of this difference reflects the slightly better benefit structure of the largest private programs. This is largely or perhaps completely offset by the large number of federal annuitants without Medicare. The balance implies that the Fortune 500 have not been able to figure out how to save the 20 percent that the federal government has been achieving without even trying vigorously to reduce costs.

The Medicare and FEHBP data are much more straightforward and utterly reliable. They simply reflect actual accounting data as to total costs incurred and total premiums paid (in the case of Medicare, however, I had to interpolate a few of the older years).[13] Particularly for FEHBP, individual year-to-year changes have considerable variability on the margin due to accounting vagaries, as reserves are reduced and then replenished to reflect difficulties in predicting the course of health care costs (the 1993 rate was set in the summer of 1992, reflecting primarily data from the previous winter). The FEHBP data also reflect a significant benefit cutback in 1983 (since then this has been more than completely restored) and have not been adjusted for a major rebate from excess reserves in the mid-1980s. These and other idiosyncrasies in these series do not affect the main conclusions significantly, so long as one does not focus on a one-, two-, or three-year period.

Over time, these data show that Medicare and the FEHBP have been able to bring annual cost increases down from the double-digit levels of the 1970s to the single-digit range. Private employers once appeared to have achieved similar success but have lapsed in recent years. Cumulatively, the results of whatever forces and factors have been at work appear to have led to a compound annual growth rate

---

[12]See "The Price of Worker Health Care," Milt Freudenheim, *New York Times*, March 2, 1993, sec. D, p. 1.

[13]The Medicare data come from U.S. House of Representatives, Ways and Means Committee, *Green Book: Overview of Entitlement Programs* (Washington, D.C.: Government Printing Office, various years). This is a 2,000-page compilation of useful data on programs within the jurisdiction of the House Ways and Means Committee, published annually.

in Medicare costs of around 8 percent to 9 percent a year (depending on just what years one chooses to include in the computation), a growth rate for the FEHBP of about 9 percent a year, and a growth rate for private employers distinctly higher, at around 12 percent a year.

What explains these similarities and differences? There are myriads of factors, most not susceptible to simple measurement. The FEHBP, for example, has seen a distinct aging of the federal work force and annuitant pools, with attendant heavy pressure on costs. But, starting in 1984, all new federal annuitants became Medicare-eligible once they reached age sixty-five. Since Medicare pays first, this saves the FEHBP money. (Most annuitants, however, are not covered by Medicare: all those aged fifty-five to sixty-four, and the several hundred thousand old and costly persons who retired before 1984 without Medicare coverage.) Considering that the model retirement age is fifty-five, the first wave of these fully Medicare-covered annuitants is just about to benefit the FEHBP. On the Medicare side, these data show dramatically the effect of the prospective payment system in reducing growth in hospital costs in the middle and late 1980s and the attenuation of this source of savings in recent years.

One factor penalizes the FEHBP. As discussed below, improvements in real benefit levels have not occurred in Medicare or the private sector. In contrast, real benefit increases have occurred in the FEHBP. They have probably not affected cost levels, however, more than a few hundred dollars or rates of cost increase more than a fraction of 1 percent.

Three factors, however, clearly stand out as important. First, Medicare has had the ability to exercise monopsony power. Most dramatically in the prospective payment system and also in dozens of lesser initiatives, Congress has by fiat set below-market prices for providers of services. At present, according to the Congressional Budget Office and the Prospective Payment Assessment Commission, Medicare is paying hospitals $10 billion a year below the cost of serving Medicare clients.[14] This translates into a saving of about $300 a year per enrollee, about 7 percent of total costs.

Second, the FEHBP runs a competitive program, and enrollees have been voting with their wallets for lower cost plans. As shown, HMO enrollment rose from 10 percent to 25 percent of total enrollment in the 1980s and almost 30 percent today. Table 11–4 shows that both ten years earlier and today HMOs had about a 20 percent cost

---

[14]See statement of Robert D. Reischauer, director, CBO, before the Committee on Ways and Means, March 2, 1993, p. 20.

TABLE 11-4

FEHBP PREMIUM CHANGES FOR HMO AND FEE-FOR-SERVICE PLANS, 1983–1992

	A Total premium	B Enrollee premium	C Enrollee out-of-pocket	D Total cost to enrollee (B + C)	E Total cost (A + C)	F Out-of-pocket as % of total cost
1983 HMO self-enrollment	727	224	205	429	932	22
1992 HMO self-enrollment	1,868	467	260	727	2,128	12
% of increase in decade	157	108	27	69	128	
1983 fee self-enrollment	941	426	455	881	1,396	33
1992 fee self-enrollment	2,062	552	596	1,148	2,658	22
% of increase in decade	119	30	31	30	90	
1983 weighted (for 12% in HMOs)	915	402	425	827	1,340	32
1992 weighted (for 28% in HMOs)	2,008	528	502	1,030	2,510	20
% of increase in decade	119	31	18	25	87	

NOTE: These calculations average the five plans of each type with the largest enrollment in the indicated year. In all instances except 1992 HMO data this accounts for the majority of program costs. Costs are in dollars of that year.

SOURCES: All data except enrollee out-of-pocket costs come from Office of Personnel Management, *Insurance Report*, 1983 and 1992 editions. Out-of-pocket costs are from Walton Francis, *CHECKBOOK's Guide to Health Insurance for Federal Employees* (Washington, D.C.: Washington Center for the Study of Services).

advantage over fee-for-service plans (in column E, the 1992 total self-only cost of an average HMO was $2,128, compared with $2,658 for an average fee-for-service plan). Therefore, simply shifting hundreds of thousands of people to a lower cost set of plans was sure to save the program much money and lower the rate of cost increase. Likewise, enrollees have been shifting to lower-cost plans within the fee-for-service group, ameliorating cost increases there. Interestingly, the data show that HMO premiums have risen faster than fee-for-service premiums. Nonetheless, HMOs are so much less costly that the program has still done well. Total cost, an arguably better measure than premium cost because it takes into account changes in out-of-pocket exposure, has risen far less rapidly than premium cost. It has also risen less rapidly than the cost of either type of plan, as is common when people shift from a high-cost system to a low-cost system.

Third, as a byproduct of Medicare's payment rate controls, substantial costs have been shifted from Medicare to private plans, that is, to the FEHBP plans and other employer plans. CBO estimates (reproduced as table 11–5) show that, as of 1990, private plans were paying some $23 billion and 28 percent a year more than the actual costs they incur because of the savings forced on hospitals by Medicare, Medicaid, and other programs. In a competitive private market, such cost shifting would be impossible—but hospital care is evidently only imperfectly competitive. Taking into account cost shifting, the quasi-private FEHBP soundly outperforms Medicare in controlling costs, and the private plans probably match Medicare.

Taken together, these three factors suggest two obvious conclusions. First, absent coercive power, Medicare has done little or nothing effective to control costs. This need not remain merely a logical deduction. The concept of managed care is alien to Medicare, despite much lip service and some real efforts defeated by the political system. The percentage of Medicare clients in HMOs has remained stuck at 3 percent for years (fewer than one in five HMOs even bothers to do business with Medicare, in part because of bizarre reimbursement and enrollment systems).[15] Medicare does not run a

---

[15]Medicare allows its clients to disenroll from an HMO at will. In the federal employee system and most private employer programs, an HMO election is binding until the next open season. Medicare refuses to pay HMOs adjusted community rates, or experience rates, but instead forces them to accept arbitrarily shifting geographic payment rates based on complex formulas rooted in the false assumption that managed-care costs vary substantially from place to place in proportion to differences in fee-

TABLE 11–5
HOSPITAL REVENUES AND COSTS, BY PAYER OR OTHER SOURCE, 1990

Payer or Other Source	Revenues		Costs		Ratio of Revenues to Costs
	In billions of $	As % of total	In billions of $	As % of total	
Total	210.6	100.0	203.2	100.0	1.04
Medicare	69.8	33.2	78.0	38.4	0.90
Medicaid	18.4	8.7	23.0	11.3	0.80
Other government payers	3.4	1.6	3.2	1.6	1.06
Uncompensated care[a]	2.5	1.2	12.1	5.9	0.21
Private payers	104.1	49.5	81.6	40.1	1.28
Nonpatient sources[b]	12.4	5.8	5.5	2.7	2.25

a. Uncompensated care is defined as charity care plus bad debt. The revenues shown are operating subsidies from state and local governments.

b. This includes operating revenues and costs from sources other than patient care, such as profits from cafeterias and gift shops, plus nonoperating revenues such as contributions, grants, and earnings on endowments.

SOURCES: Table reproduced from March 2, 1993, testimony of Robert D. Reischauer, director, Congressional Budget Office, before the Subcommittee on Health, Committee on Ways and Means, U.S. House of Representatives. CBO estimates are based on data from Prospective Payment Assessment Commission, *Medicare and the American Health Care System: Report to the Congress* (June 1992). The underlying data are from the American Hospital Association, *Annual Survey of Hospitals*, 1990. They correspond to hospitals' fiscal years ending during calendar year 1990.

PPO. Medicare does not even use large-case management. Instead, Medicare relies on those initiatives that command the support of congressional leaders and that someone argues will save money.[16] Many dozens of large and small schemes aimed at saving money have been enacted in the past decade. A few of them (for example, mandatory second surgical opinions) have been repealed when it was found that they cost more than they saved.

Second, competition works. The FEHBP has greatly outperformed the one-size-fits-all system of both the private sector and Medicare. It has done so despite far less attention to cost-saving management initiatives than either Medicare or most private sector payers. Simply through political accident, the government has created what may be the most cost-effective health insurance system in America.

Benefits. Over the past decade, the federal employee program has progressively improved its benefit coverage. As recently as 1987, there were five fee-for-service plans with significant loopholes in their catastrophic guarantees.[17] Today, there are none. Almost all the guarantees hold out-of-pocket costs to $3,000 or less (plus premium). In contrast, the rise and fall of the Medicare Catastrophic Coverage Act has already generated thousands of pages of learned analysis. Interestingly, the CHAMPUS program has only a $10,000 catastrophic guarantee. This is perceived as so inadequate by most families that a substantial market for supplementary plans has developed. In fact, in the last year an association of military wives has proposed that CHAMPUS be abolished and that military dependents join the FEHBP instead. Medicare has provoked an extensive supplemental market for Medigap plans.[18] In contrast, the supplemental market for FEHBP is negligible.

---

for-service costs. HMO executives, like any others, prefer some stability in their business.

[16]One recent law makes it illegal for doctors to own shares in laboratories. The theory is that they will overtest their patients to earn extra money. The law, however, exempts 95 percent of all laboratories: those right in the physician's office and used in high volume every day in conjunction with patients visits. Why it is bad to own a laboratory down the hall but not in the office has never been explained. It is rumored that Congress plans to expand this law soon to cover other ancillary services, such as orthopedic doctors selling crutches and splints to their patients.

[17]Francis, CHECKBOOK's Guide to 1987 Health Insurance Plans for Federal Employees, p. 12.

[18]According to the House Ways and Means Committee, 1992 Green Book

285

For routine coverage (including most but not all catastrophically large bills), Medicare has remained a consistently good but unchanged payer for decades. For the expenses it covers, enrollees paid 16–17 percent over the past two decades.[19] Medicare does not pay at all for outpatient prescription drugs or dental expenses (subject to minor exceptions, such as injectable cancer drugs administered by physicians). Calculated on a larger base, Medicare enrollees pay perhaps one-fourth of all bills.

The private sector is diverse, but for the large-employer segment covered in the major surveys most plans have coverage slightly better than the FEHBP. A decade ago, most of these plans had much better coverage (for example, a $100 deductible when $200 was common in the FEHBP). Regardless, private employers apparently have cut back coverage in recent years at a rate slightly in excess of inflation, so that inflation-adjusted benefits have been modestly reduced.[20]

Surprisingly, federal employee benefits have improved. Table 11–4 shows that out-of-pocket costs (column C) have risen much less rapidly than inflation and have decreased from one-fifth to one-tenth of total costs of insurance for HMOs and from one-third to one-fifth for fee plans and for the program as a whole.[21] Considering that the FEHBP covers major categories of expense excluded from Medicare coverage, and that these figures include dental expenses, clearly the federal employee program significantly betters Medicare in benefits.

Management Responsiveness. The FEHBP responds to market forces in roughly the same way as any competitive system—rapidly when viewed over a period of a decade, or even several years, but surprisingly slowly in any shorter period. This responsiveness, however, is limited to those problems that can be fixed without legislative intervention.

In contrast, Medicare moves with glacial slowness. In the recent past, the makers of fancy reclining chairs discovered a loophole

---

(p. 262), about two-thirds of Medicare enrollees have supplemental coverage, half at their own expense and half provided by employers.

[19]House Ways and Means Committee, *1992 Green Book*, p. 253.

[20]G. Jensen et al., "Cost Sharing and the Changing Pattern of Employer-sponsored Health Benefits," *Milbank Quarterly*, vol. 65, no. 4 (1987).

[21]The out-of-pocket costs are estimates taken from the pertinent editions of Francis, CHECKBOOK's *Guide to Health Insurance for Federal Employees*. They include the effects of coverage exclusions, deductibles, copayments, and coinsurance on hospital, doctor, other medical, drug, and dental costs.

through which they could get Medicare to pay for these chairs if a doctor would certify that a patient needed assistance to stand. A $50 million a year industry was born, complete with late-night television advertisements explaining how to take advantage of this loophole. The Office of Management and Budget discovered this problem within a year and in a budget "passback" ordered Medicare to close the loophole by revising its regulations. In theory, this should have been easy—changing the coverage provision from "seat lift chair" to "seat lift mechanism" (an assistive mechanism can be purchased for less than $100). The regulatory process, however, usually takes years. In exasperation, Congress finally banned the purchase of the chairs, several years and more than $100 million dollars after the problem began.

Private payers, like the FEHBP, have no problem resolving such problems within weeks. They have been extraordinarily slow, however, in learning how to use HMOs to reduce costs, in raising deductibles to levels that discourage spending, and in other major reforms. It is notorious that large corporations, by paying a fixed percentage rather than fixed amount toward the premium of both fee-for-service and HMO plans, have fostered risk selection and excess expenditures on health care. The higher-cost employees have tended to stay with the fee-for-service plan, and HMOs have been able to price their products at levels that do not reflect the better risks that they have attracted. Management can prevent this from happening—but often has not.

Equity. All health insurance contains gaps and exclusions that are inequitable to at least some persons. Virtually no plans, for example, pay for certain forms of dental surgery that are extremely expensive. Of the three programs under discussion, Medicare has a surprising number of seemingly arbitrary exclusions and such major gaps as its failure to cover prescription drugs or to provide a catastrophic guarantee. Most large-employer plans and all FEHBP plans have few consequential gaps. The most important of these, in an insurance sense, is that only a handful of FEHBP plans (and only one fee-for-service plan) cover more than twenty-five outpatient psychiatric visits. This is a common limitation in the private sector. Medicare was, until recently, even more restrictive.

The FEHBP fails to manage risk selection well, as discussed below. This creates, as a byproduct, one unfortunate and arguably unfair program characteristic. At any point, several plans (the best-known is Blue Cross high option) have a premium cost well in excess of actuarial value. This occurs simply because each plan must cover the costs of those enrolled, and this plan is used primarily by older persons without Medicare. *CHECKBOOK's Guide to 1993 Health Insurance for Federal Employees* calculates the Blue Cross high option and the Blue Cross standard option at virtually equal actuarial value, yet the premium cost to single enrollees is only $540 for the standard option and $2,040 for the high option.[22] The $1,500 difference may be, in effect, an ignorance tax paid by those who do not understand, or who are afraid to leave, a plan that was once by far the largest in the program and still retains the strongest benefits for all services other than dental.

An economist could well argue that if consumers choose to buy a Mercedes plan at quadruple the cost of a Ford, they are entitled to make that choice. Peace of mind may be worth the premium difference to some. But many people involved are afraid or unwilling to change (about nine-tenths are annuitants), if for no other reason than the erroneous belief that higher price means higher quality. Yet, some join to get the best outpatient mental health benefits in the program. Regardless, the problem could be readily solved by simple premium adjustments, which the government has been unwilling to consider seriously.[23] This is a major but correctable flaw of the program.

Employee Cost and Employee Benefits. The analysis above assumes implicitly that total cost or total premium is the best measure of cost control. And so it is. But there is another dimension of cost: who pays. From an economist's point of view, this is a value question about which different people are entitled to hold diametrically opposite views. It may also be a moot question, since economic theory tells us that few things are more certain than that the employee pays both the employer share and the employee share of any fringe benefit—it is all compensation regardless of how the accountants and legislators label it.

Regardless, some would regard it as relevant that the government pays distinctly less of the premium bill than is common in large corporations.[24] In theory, the government pays 60 percent (this is

---

[22]P. 16. This estimate is for general schedule and other non-postal employees.

[23]Walton Francis, "How to Reform, and How Not to Reform, the Federal Employees Health Benefits Program," unpublished testimony presented to the Office of Personnel Management at a hearing on FEHBP reform, July 26, 1988 (revised 1991), p. 6.

[24]According to the Health Insurance Association of America survey, employers pay on average about 85–90 percent of the cost of self-only

what the law seems to say and what the drafters intended). Because of the combined effects of risk selection and an arbitrary formula that bases the government contribution on the cost of the six largest plans in the FEHBP ("Big Six"), not the entire program, the government share has risen over the past decade to slightly more than 70 percent of the total premium, on average, for both self and family coverage. This leads to the interesting result shown in table 11–4: while the total premium for single enrollees has risen about 119 percent over the past decade, the enrollee share has risen only about 31 percent. As a result of this and of the improved benefit coverage, total cost to enrollees has risen only about 25 percent in ten years, far less than inflation.

These data have another implication. About 15 percent of federal employees do not enroll in this program at all. Some are young, low-wage employees for whom immortality and cash mean more than insurance and who know perfectly well that they will get treatment if they need it (like a large fraction of the 37 million uninsured). And most have spouses who get a better deal from their employer, such as 90 percent of premium. There is some danger, however, that the FEHBP might improve to the point where fewer would elect the private employer option. The potential cost to the government would be on the order of a half billion dollars annually if the government share were to reach the common private sector level. This particular effect of the program is little known and was not a factor in establishing the cost-sharing formula.

Risk Selection. This program enrolls three distinctly different sets of people: employees, annuitants with Medicare, and annuitants without Medicare (this latter is really two groups, one aged fifty-five to sixty-five, the other mostly in their seventies and eighties). Annuitants with Medicare cost the program about the same as employees, because Medicare is the primary insurer in almost all cases and this offsets on average their much higher health bills. The other annuitants are several times as costly as employees.

The recent history of this program has seen the first two groups fleeing the plans with disproportionate shares of annuitants without Medicare. This has had a number of unfortunate consequences, including the demise of well-managed, low-cost plans that suffered a death spiral from adverse selection. Many critics of the program have

---

coverage, and 70–75 percent of the cost of family coverage. See Cynthia B. Sullivan et al., "Employer-Sponsored Health Insurance in 1991," *Health Affairs*, Winter 1992, p. 180.

asserted (though with little evidence, even anecdotal) that the plans have subtly skewed benefits to attract the young and healthy rather than sick and old. If true, much of the advantage of competition has been lost. This is a criticism made by persons as wise as Alain Enthoven and as silly as the benefit consultants hired by the Office of Personnel Management and Congress, who fail to understand, let alone appreciate, the benefits of consumer choice and competition.

The criticism of skewing is arguably either wrong or misplaced. First, as an empirical matter the weaker plans have been improving benefits. Some of this improvement has come at the prodding of OPM staff, but regardless of motive, it has happened. Second, this program has been outperforming the competition handily. Conceivably it could have performed even better, but that is a hypothetical gain compared with the bird in hand. Third, the problem is readily correctable. The main reform needed is to have the high-cost annuitants carry an extra premium contribution with them as they move among plans. The net effect need be no real-world change at all in the government subsidy taken as a whole, but the appearances are to the contrary and the prospect unsettling to unions and retiree groups.

As a technical matter, what is particularly interesting about the program is how slowly it responds to risk-selection forces. Over the past decade, profound enrollment shifts have occurred. Hundreds of plans have entered and left the program. Yet, only 5 percent of enrollees a year have changed plans. If all federal employees were the economists' hypothetical rational man, even more plans would have died a decade ago. Instead, evolution has been gradual. This has major implications for the health reformers worried about developing risk adjustors to guarantee that every premium minimizes risk selection. The problem is insoluble. We can predict that an eighty-year-old will cost five times as much as a thirty-year-old, but among the eighty-year-old group, we will never be able to predict which ones will cost zero and which ones $50,000. The good news, from the FEHBP, is that perfect risk adjustors are not needed.

There is another whole category of risk selection involved in the FEHBP. People deliberately join particular plans to get particular benefits. In the D.C. area, for example, all the plans with really first-rate dental coverage are HMOs. The rational man will, nature permitting, save up his dental problems until he is ready to join an HMO with a high dental benefit for a year, get his teeth fixed, and perhaps then leave. Premiums reflect this excess usage. People with greater-than-average dental problems congregate in certain plans, pay the higher premiums, and let the rest enjoy a lower premium. I know of no economic argument against this arrangement. It does not lead to market instability or create any obvious administrative or other problem. There is a weak ethical line of argument against this practice, best answered by asking the critic, Do you object, then, to charging different premiums for single people and families?

Yet, presumably to prevent employee self-selection into plans they prefer (just as people choose the kind of car they prefer, even if it means spending more), the current theology of managed competition insists that all plans have identical benefits.[25] As discussed in the "The Strange Politics of the FEHBP," this has major adverse political consequences.

Geographic Competition. There are three interesting geographic aspects of health care for which the FEHBP experience has considerable relevance.

First, how well can rural areas be served? A recent article on the demographic limitations of managed competition[26] concludes that more than a third of the American population live in areas too small to support the sophisticated medical centers for the three competitive plans deemed necessary for workable competition by the authors. The article, for example, estimates that Connecticut, Rhode Island, Delaware, and North Carolina, lacking cities of more than 1.2 million in population, cannot support effective competition. The article concludes with a plea for what amounts to local monopolies run by government to serve vast areas composing the great majority of the American land area.

Time does not permit a full empirical analysis here of the extent to which the FEHBP's HMOs serve these allegedly impracticable remote areas. Suffice it to say that they do so quite handily. Among

---

[25]See, for example, Linda Bergthold, "Benefit Design Choices under Managed Competition," *Health Affairs*, supp., 1993, pp. 99–109. Although it is not my intent to enter the debate over national health insurance reform in this chapter, I cannot refrain from observing that the supposedly prochoice advocates of managed competition seem to distrust the ability of consumers to make choices among complex products. Substituting the word *automobile* for *health insurance* in such articles, particularly where they discuss confused consumers and the need for health experts supervised by politicians to design *the* benefit structure, leads to a chilling vision of the government-designed automobile that we all must buy, choosing only among different prices.

[26]Richard Kronick et al., "The Demographic Limitations of Managed Competition," *New England Journal of Medicine*, vol. 328, no. 2 (1983), pp. 148–52.

HMOs, six plans serve Connecticut, five plans serve Rhode Island, three plans serve Delaware, and five plans serve North Carolina. These plans offer benefits and premiums that are, on average, fully competitive with other HMOs centered in large cities.[27]

How can the FEHBP solve this problem? It is quite simple. The Kronick article makes a number of artificial assumptions that do not fit the real world. Even if, say, Delaware cannot support three tertiary care centers, each employing at least one doctor in every specialty, Philadelphia is just a short distance away. There are potential market entrants, which provide pressure to keep costs and prices down even if only one provider is present now. Why assume that every HMO must be a vertically integrated staff model, running its own hospital? Regardless, we need not be either agnostic or artificial in modeling certain aspects of managed competition: we have a real model to observe and to analyze.

Second, how well can a program of this kind deal with geographic differences in costs? The literature of health economics seems to be obsessed by geographic variation in costs. Many proposals for cost controls of the global-budgeting school assume explicitly that there will have to be area-specific budgets to reflect differences in costs. "Everyone knows" that medical practice varies widely from one town to another and one region of the country to another. How can a premium subsidy be fair if the same amount, or the same percentage, applies both to North Carolina and New York?

The FEHBP provides interesting data on this topic. Program data, summarized in table 11–6, demonstrate that while there is substantial variation among HMO costs in the same city and from year to year for the same HMO (undoubtedly reflecting good and bad luck with rare cases), geographic variation across cities is quite low. Table 11–6 is based on total premium, plus estimated unreimbursed costs, to control for variations in plan coverage. It measures the actual cost of delivering all types of health care (except custodial nursing care) to about 1 million enrollees and more than 2 million persons. It shows that among the 42 metropolitan areas served by three or more HMOs this year, the costs of two-thirds are within 8–9 percent of the national average. The city with the highest cost is only about 30 percent higher than the city with the lowest cost (a multiyear analysis would significantly reduce even these disparities). This is not a particularly profound or surprising finding. Why should one expect managed care to differ in one place from another? It happens,

---

[27]There are, however, no FEHBP HMOs serving Alaska, Montana, or Wyoming (see Francis, *CHECKBOOK's Guide to Health Insurance for Federal Employees* [1993], pp. 56–77).

however, to contradict our preconceptions.

These data contradict some research findings. A recent article finds that Medicare physician costs are about twice as high in Miami as in San Francisco and displayed almost equally broad differences among many other cities.[28] Yet, in the FEHBP, the average cost of an HMO enrollment in the two cities is only 5 percent apart, with Miami actually *lower*. Another recent study alleges equally large intercity variations, though many are inconsistent with the Welch study.[29] To be sure, some of these fee-for-service differences may be precisely what managed care is all about reducing. Regardless, the FEHBP data strongly suggest that interarea problems in a system emphasizing managed care may be, if not negligible, quite small enough to ignore.

Third, the FEHBP tells us something about plan boundaries. They are messy. Some plans, for example, serve only San Diego, some serve only Los Angeles, and some serve both; likewise for Washington and Baltimore. And in a given metro area, some plans may serve only one portion (for example, Westchester or Long Island or Manhattan but not all three). The Harvard Health Plan recently expanded to cover parts of four states and most of New England. These differences are not just arbitrary but reflect differential success in organizing providers and a host of other factors, such as mergers and consolidations. The FEHBP and the HMO system it supports operate quite well with complex boundaries that do not neatly fit into cookie cutter shapes. Again, some of the rhetoric on managed competition seems to take on an aura of unreality, assuming that health insurance purchasing cooperatives will have monopsony powers, be run by state or local government, and fit local political boundaries.[30] It is hard to imagine what the Johns Hopkins/ Prudential, Harvard, and Kaiser plans will do if they must simultaneously obey the edicts of two or three government agencies, each asserting jurisdiction over benefits, service areas, open-season pamphlets, finan-

---

[28]W. Pete Welch et al., "Geographic Variation in Expenditures for Physician Services in the United States," *New England Journal of Medicine*, vol. 328, no. 9 (1993), pp. 621–27.

[29]See appendix on differences in the cost of group health plans by location in U.S. General Accounting Office, "Employer-Based Health Insurance: High Costs, Wide Variation Threaten System," GAO/HRD-92-125, September 1992. The GAO study cites data showing that San Francisco and New York are high-cost cities, in contrast to the Welch finding that they are low-cost cities.

[30]See Walter A. Zelman, "Who Should Govern the Purchasing Cooperative," *Health Affairs*, supp., 1993, pp. 49–57, and Richard Kronick, "Where Should the Buck Stop: Federal and State Responsibilities in Health Care Financing Reform," *Health Affairs*, supp., 1993, pp. 87–98.

TABLE 11-6
AVERAGE COSTS OF FEHBP HMO ENROLLMENT BY METROPOLITAN AREA, 1993

State	Metropolitan Area	Self Only		Family	
		Enroll-ment	Average cost ($)	Enroll-ment	Average cost ($)
Arizona	Phoenix	5,615	1,970	10,144	5,420
Illinois	Chicago	10,333	1,970	15,992	5,300
Michigan	Grand Rapids	382	1,970	1,100	5,390
Minnesota	Twin Cities	6,760	1,970	11,657	5,370
New York	Buffalo	1,678	1,980	5,806	5,370
Pennsylvania	Pittsburgh	3,362	1,990	7,168	5,430
Pennsylvania	Harrisburg	2,819	2,000	4,320	5,140
Wisconsin	Madison	1,806	2,010	3,729	5,390
New Mexico	Albuquerque	3,739	2,020	7,794	5,190
Maryland	Baltimore	13,145	2,070	13,965	5,290
Colorado	Denver	12,382	2,080	20,301	5,260
Oklahoma	Tulsa	554	2,090	1,314	5,330
Florida	Tampa–St. Petersburg	1,600	2,110	2,572	5,600

Florida	Orlando	1,017	2,120	1,764	5,430
Kansas	Kansas City	3,300	2,120	5,464	5,630
Wisconsin	Milwaukee	2,768	2,120	5,015	5,500
Kentucky	Lexington	2,581	2,130	5,451	5,740
Michigan	Detroit	6,137	2,130	9,273	5,660
North Carolina	Triangle	1,350	2,150	2,799	5,450
Florida	Miami–Palm Beach	2,372	2,200	4,254	5,580
Florida	Jacksonville	2,130	2,230	3,492	5,850
Georgia	Atlanta	5,930	2,230	8,148	5,860
Oklahoma	Oklahoma City	3,545	2,230	6,966	5,630
District of Columbia		71,863	2,240	77,948	5,510
Hawaii	Honolulu	14,881	2,250	21,207	5,680
New York	New York City–Long Island	41,495	2,260	46,309	5,760
Oregon	Portland	6,971	2,260	11,204	5,430
Virginia	Richmond	1,475	2,260	2,237	6,030
Louisiana	New Orleans	1,049	2,270	2,067	5,880
New York	Albany-Schenectady-Valley	2,977	2,270	5,954	5,830
Pennsylvania	Philadelphia	16,143	2,270	26,766	5,870
Texas	Austin-Temple-Waco	5,241	2,290	8,114	6,060
Ohio	Columbus	1,770	2,310	2,508	5,800
California	San Francisco Bay Area	47,167	2,330	64,392	5,480
Ohio	Cleveland-Akron	2,897	2,390	5,034	5,850

(Table continues.)

TABLE 11-6 (continued)

State	Metropolitan Area	Self Only		Family	
		Enrollment	Average cost ($)	Enrollment	Average cost ($)
Virginia	Tidewater	4,936	2,390	9,173	5,830
California	Los Angeles–San Diego	31,766	2,410	43,469	5,990
Texas	Dallas–Forth Worth	3,251	2,410	8,478	6,050
Missouri	St. Louis	4,946	2,450	8,386	5,870
Massachusetts	Boston	8,665	2,710	6,426	7,250
Washington	Seattle–Puget Sound	13,763	2,740	21,147	6,290
Connecticut	Hartford	2,978	2,790	2,978	6,950
Average		9,040	2,220	12,670	5,700
Median		3,360	2,230	6,970	5,630
Maximum		71,860	2,790	77,950	7,250
Minimum		550	1,970	1,310	5,140
Standard deviation of population		17,140	200	19,320	470
Standard deviation as % of average		190	9	152	8

NOTE: Ranked by average cost for self only for 1993.
SOURCE: The table is based on the full-premium cost analysis presented in the table on "Cost and Special Features of HMOs by State," Walton Francis, CHECKBOOK's Guide to 1993 Health Insurance Plans for Federal Employees (Washington, D.C.: Washington Center for the Study of Services, 1992), pp. 56–77. The data on each HMO are weighted by 1992 enrollment in calculating the metropolitan average. Only cities with three or more HMOs competing in 1993 were included, to reduce variations caused by outlier HMOs.

cial reserves, and the like. Regardless, as on so many other topics, the FEHBP offers a rich and as yet virtually unstudied experience from which much can be learned.

The Strange Politics of the FEHBP

The FEHBP is so familiar and comfortable that few federal employees realize just how unusual it is to have an open season in which to make a choice among health plans. Ironically, this freedom arises under a federal government that sets all other pay and benefit policies by law and regulation. In sharp contrast to the FEHBP, the government treats the most minute details of health insurance for the elderly under Medicare as matters for only government decision. Similarly, in the large corporate environment, health insurance details are set by fiat, on a take-it-or-leave-the-company basis. To persons from corporate America, used to the company plan, the FEHBP often seems an aberration beyond belief.

Every few years a few of these private sector "experts" or sometimes Medicare "experts," recommend abolishing the program: the most common proposals would replace it with a single fee-for-service plan modeled along the same lines as Medicare and old-fashioned private sector plans.[31] The precise motive for these reformers is not clear, but some may be reflecting the common Washington insider assumption that the government can manage anything better than the market. As recently stated by Congressman Pete Stark chairman of the House of Representatives subcommittee through which the Clinton health plan will have to pass: "This is some dream of people who say competition and free enterprise can do better than any government can do. That's not true. [The government] can run circles around [private insurance]."[32] Even private sector experts may

---

[31]See John J. Creedon et al., *Report on Federal Employees Health Benefits Program*, Serial No. 102-6 (Washington, D.C.: Government Printing Office, May 1992), for the Committee on Post Office and Civil Service, U.S. House of Representatives; Towers, Perrin, Forster, and Crosby, *Study of the Federal Employees Health Benefits Program* (Washington, D.C.: April 1988) for the Office of Personnel Management; and U.S. General Accounting Office, "Federal Health Benefits Program: Stronger Controls Needed to Reduce Administrative Costs" (Washington, D.C.: Government Printing Office, February 1992). Each of these studies argues implicitly or explicitly for replacing the present FEHBP with a single-plan program modeled along the same lines as Medicare. Not one of them attempts a systematic comparison of program costs or benefits with either Medicare or the private sector.

[32]Quoted by Dana Priest, "Key Home Democrat Attacks 'Managed Competition' Health Plan," *Washington Post*, May 14, 1993, p. A18.

simply be so used to the single-plan model that they cannot conceive what purpose competition might serve.

Another set of critics are the managed-competition advocates. These advocates recognize the merits of the program but believe that a much better competitive program could be designed, building on the lessons learned from the FEHBP. Management willing and able to make sensible midcourse reforms could and would improve the program. But in government as in life, the best can be the enemy of the good. In the context of CHAMPUS (which just got its first HMO and discovered that it could save money if it gave up unlimited psychiatric benefits), Medicare, and the Fortune 500, the FEHBP arguably deserves close to an A on performance alone, and the rest of the competition a C.

Regardless of past performance, the FEHBP may also have some lessons for the brave new world of managed competition. The paradox of the program is that it is successful because it is relatively unmanaged. The riddle of the program is to understand how any government program can escape the endless tendency to create ever-expanding bureaucratic structures operating under ever-more complex rules, dictated and driven by the political system's peculiar obsessions and logic. The paradox for advocates of health reform is how to improve the management of health insurance while avoiding the seemingly inexorable tendencies of the American political system to redistribute wealth from the taxpayer at large into the congressional district or lobbyist's salary. In the ideal world of managed care and managed competition, hundreds of hospitals would be forced to close: would the preservation of these institutions replace the preservation of military bases as the next great preoccupation of American politicians?

Unfortunately, we lack a political model comparable in analytic or conceptual power to economic models even to give us a clear handle on how to explain what characteristics of the political process dictate the radically different processes and procedures, as well as outcomes, we observe in the FEHBP. Obviously, bargaining, coalitions, and the paraphernalia of the political process are at work; the question is how and why we get such different outcomes.[33]

---

[33]For an interesting effort attempting to delineate both conceptually and empirically the political variables influencing real-world successes and failures in health policy, see Frank J. Thompson, "Implementation of Health Policy: Politics and Bureaucracy," in Theodor J. Litman and Leonard S. Robins, eds., *Health Politics and Policy* (New York: Wiley, 1984), pp. 145–68. Unfortunately, Thompson's structure seems orthogonal to

Program Management in the FEHBP. It is hard for an outsider to comprehend how simple the FEHBP is in comparison with the Medicare model. A few statistics may help. The FEHBP is run by 150 government bureaucrats. Medicare is run by more than 3,000 bureaucrats (neither of these counts includes the people paying claims). To be sure, Medicare serves three times as many people, but the FEHBP runs three times as many plans (counting Medicare's 100 participating HMOs). As cited in one study: "The law creating the FEHBP is eight pages long, with sixteen pages of regulations and less than 100 pages of information and instructions. By contrast, the law creating Medicare is 142 pages long, with 400 pages of regulations and almost 11,000 pages of instructions."[34]

Perhaps the single most important reason that the program works well is that the government role is extremely limited. Consider the benefit structure set in law in Medicare. This structure is archaic and still retains many details—such as the rigid distinction between in-hospital (part A) and ambulatory (part B) benefits—that the health insurance industry has largely abandoned in recent decades. The FEHBP has no such legislated benefit structure. Because there are many plans, each with its own benefit structure, it is much harder for the political system to set particular details by fiat. Unlike Medicare, for example, there is no single deductible to set in concrete. Each plan, in response to competing customer demands, decides each year what deductible and associated premium will best attract customers. Proposals to change the Medicare deductible are so politically explosive that they are rarely advanced even by the most dedicated budget cutters. In the FEHBP, changes in deductible are frequent and attract or discourage enrollment changes in the open season, rather than political wars. Likewise, premium changes induce migration into more economical plans. The search is for bargains, not for lobbyists or votes in Congress.

Medicare and Micromanagement. The prospective payment system is the single most important reform in the history of Medicare. The basic idea is to create a marketlike payment approach by paying hospitals a going rate price rather than reimbursing them on a cost-plus basis. Hospitals that can perform the procedure for less make a

---

the problem at hand. He does, however, come tantalizingly close with a section on "The Perils and Potential of Precision" in drafting statutes.

[34]Robert E. Moffit, "Consumer Choice in Health: Learning from the Federal Employee Health Benefit Program," Heritage Foundation, November 9, 1992, p. 3.

profit; others have a tremendous incentive to cut costs. A problem arises, however, because one cannot reasonably ask a New York City hospital to accept a rural Kansas rate. Therefore, the program was designed to include a cost differential across geographic areas, based on a wage rate index calculated city by city. As a result, New York gets about 20 percent more than the national average, and rural Kansas about 20 percent less. There must, however, be boundaries separating the city from the rural area, so that each can get the proper indexed rate. Those boundaries are drawn around hundreds of cities.

Unfortunately, near many of those lines are hospitals on the "wrong" (low rate) side. Those hospitals are being treated unfairly, because they are just down the road from a well-paid hospital. But the boundaries have to be drawn, or New York would have to accept a rural rate. There is no escaping the dilemma that creating geographic boundaries necessarily harms some institutions. How does our political system respond to claims of unfair and irrational harm? With alacrity. In this case, Congress simply redraws the lines a little further out by "reclassifying" the disadvantaged hospital. But then another hospital is put near the boundary. The problem is insoluble: there is no stopping point. To date, about 900 of the nation's 6,500 hospitals have been reclassified, and hundreds of bureaucrats, researchers, consultants, and lobbyists have gained employment in dealing with reclassification issues.

How does Congress feel? It loves this kind of problem. After all, what helps a congressman more to be reelected than to help the local hospital against the unfeeling federal bureaucracy? And so it goes.

The FEHBP is not entirely immune from political pressures aimed at fine-tuning the system. A few years ago, for example, the statute was amended to require each plan to cover the services of clinical psychologists, clinical social workers, nurse-midwives, and nurse practitioners through self-referral. The statute was recently modified to cover ex-spouses and some other new categories of eligibles. The post office planned, until countered by the Office of Management and Budget and by Congress, to pull out of the system and finance benefits for current employees without the overhead of all those expensive annuitants. When one of the plans in the "Big Six" used to set premium contributions dropped out, Congress quickly created a phantom plan to prevent a drop in government premium contribution. And so on. But the entire list of FEHBP changes made over the past decade would not equal a single year's business for the Medicare program.

Lessons from Corporate America. Is there any reason to think that a company expert in making and selling widgets is likely to be expert in administering anything as complex as health insurance? The question answers itself. Under the currently prevailing model, each Fortune 500 company hires directly or by contract a handful of experts who advise it on such matters as how to set the deductible, how to set the employer contribution toward an HMO, and whether and how to self-insure. The model that is taken for granted is a single contract with a large insurance company, with grudging acceptance of PPO variations and an HMO or two on the side. The success of these experts can be measured not only by the past decade's performance in controlling costs of private health insurance but also by the knowledge that their recommendations are made largely in the context of labor management relations and what is now called human resource administration (whether or not actual union bargaining is involved).

Private employers have responded to the costly trends of the 1970s and 1980s by greatly increasing their willingness to make large and small changes in insurance arrangements for their employees. The tendency toward ever-increasing use of the tax subsidy for health insurance as a means of increasing employee compensation has been halted and slightly reversed, and self-insurance has enabled firms to escape costly state taxes on insurance premiums and state-mandated benefits.

In any event, even the largest corporations are hampered by the sheer size and complexity of the health insurance market. Even though the 150 OPM employees running the FEHBP are a mere handful by government standards and in comparison with the number running Medicare, it is hard to believe than any corporation could or would make a comparable investment to run its own consumer choice among competing plans system. Multiemployer systems have not developed, presumably because of the utter lack of interest of headquarters bureaucracy in cross-company collaboration.

Managing Health Insurance within Federal Government Constraints. The federal government faces unique constraints in managing its programs. Absent careful structural decisions aimed at preserving management flexibility, reform narrowly directed at the FEHBP or broadly directed at the nation may unintentionally reduce or eliminate, rather than ensure, competent management and flexibility. Three factors seem to be key.

First, *bureaucratic rigidity* reduces flexibility to make changes that must use normal bureaucratic processes and channels. Despite the superb skills of individual government managers, management throughout the federal government is ordinarily wooden and cautious, and innovation absent. As described in the 1983 report of the National Academy of Public Administration, *Revitalizing Federal Management*, federal managers are "captives of a series of cumbersome internal management 'systems' which they do not control."[35] These include personnel, procurement, and budget. It can and often does take two or three years, for example, to make a change by notice and comment regulations that a private insurance company could make in two or three weeks. These regulations severely constrain flexibility and the speed of decision making, even when there are no legislative constraints.

Second, *legislative constraints* can delay, or prevent, management initiatives. It is an inescapable feature of the federal government that it is usually difficult, and often impossible, to avoid legislative impediments to change. The Medicare law, for example, requires that insurance claims payment be contracted separately in each of the fifty states, despite the major inefficiencies this creates. The FEHBP's "Big Six" formula for setting premium contributions has cost the Treasury billions of dollars over the past five years, because legislative drafters years ago made the needless and heedless assumption that the biggest six plans would continue to enroll most employees into perpetuity. Legislative constraints operate asymmetrically. The legislative process creates a ratchetlike effect favoring enactment of provisions that give concentrated benefits to particular interests and impeding their repeal.

Third, there are *design-imposed constraints*. While these are not initially immutable, they become almost impossible to remove once set into law. Setting the Medicare program's part B premium as a percentage of cost, for example, makes every benefit increase a direct charge to the federal Treasury. In contrast, the FEHBP's quasi-fixed government contribution makes most benefit changes a matter of theoretical indifference to the Treasury.[36] In most cases, if a plan raises or lowers cost, it has no effect on government costs but directly

---

[35]NAPA, *Revitalizing Federal Management: Managers and Their Overburdened Systems*, A Report by a Panel of the National Academy of Public Administration (Washington, D.C., 1983), p. vii.

[36]Unfortunately, a linkage still remains: it is in the government's purely budgetary interest to prevent the "Big Six" from improving benefits—a $1 change in one of these plans leverages an additional $10 in spending for other plans. A fixed government contribution rising roughly at the rate of national health care spending and hence not tied to FEHBP plan decisions would solve this problem.

affects the enrollee's costs and choices.

Improving or Maintaining Flexibility. The federal government and the private sector both have many health reform choices. How does one improve or maintain flexibility for prudent managerial decisions that improve program performance? Three approaches seem to be both necessary and sufficient.

First, *decentralizing decisions* makes a big difference. On the surface, Medicare is a manager's delight, because all important decisions are theoretically made centrally. But because they are centralized, the manager cannot make any important decisions unilaterally. Too many other actors, from the Office of Management and Budget to the chairmen of key congressional committees have an interest and a voice. In the FEHBP, conversely, the initial responsibility for most decisions lies individually with hundreds of plans. The central manager seems impotent. But he can, if skillful, guide and steer by persuasion and pressure.

Second, a *menu of choices* is key. Quite apart from whether the decision is centralized or decentralized, are there options? The Medicare benefit package is detailed in law and regulation and presented to all enrollees on a take-it-or-leave-it basis. Therefore, in Medicare, a benefit change affects millions of people involuntarily. This brings into play the full panoply of bureaucratic and legislative forces that deal with issues of equity and fairness. In contrast, in the FEHBP, choices are exercised by both carriers and clients. A change in benefits in one plan is not a decision automatically affecting millions of people in predictable and involuntary ways. After all, they can always change plans, if they do not like the change in their present coverage.

Third, a *neutral structural design* greatly improves flexibility and responsiveness. In Medicare, benefit and coverage details are set forth in law and regulation, and claims are paid by bureaucracies that must follow those laws and regulations. Given this structure, every detail is subject to legislative, regulatory, budgetary, and contractual constraints. Medicare managers have the power to propose—but only subject to the rigidities, vetoes, and time delays imposed by bureaucratic and legislative processes. In the FEHBP, laws and regulations do not prescribe most benefit, coverage, and cost-containment details. Decisions must be reasonable under the circumstances but can be worked out through contract negotiations and other means.

All these principles apply equally whether the locus of decision is the federal government or the states. If the key decisions are made directly by political systems, the likely outcomes include rigidities of the same kinds that have plagued Medicare.

Conclusion

This accidentally created program, scarcely managed by government standards, has actually outperformed in both benefits and costs the most tightly controlled health insurance program operated by the federal government. Medicare is a good program, and thousands of dedicated and skilled bureaucrats in both the executive and the legislative branches continually seek to improve it. But Medicare operates under a crippling handicap; it is directly controlled by the meddlesome and creaky American political system.

Paradoxically, maintaining or improving management power requires diluting management authority. The FEHBP's greatest failures have tended to arise in areas where the program is constrained by law, for example, in the "Big Six" formula for premium levels, and the premium structure, which does not allow for providing differential contributions based on additional risk categories beyond family status.

Afterword

As of this writing, the informed expectation is that the Clinton administration will propose abolishing the FEHBP. How could this be? According to health care task force spokesman, Bob Boorstin, "We view the [federal employees' program] as a terrific system and we don't want to do anything that would hurt its effectiveness."[37] Apparently, however, the desire to avoid the appearance of a special system for a privileged elite weighs heavily in the political calculus: "I think you're going to see federal employees treated like everyone else."[38] Under the likely proposal, federal employees would be lumped into local health insurance purchasing cooperatives, along with the poor (Medicaid) and the uninsured. These cooperatives would provide a menu of health insurance choices similar to those offered under the FEHBP today. Large employers other than the federal government, however, would be allowed to opt out and run their own managed-competition systems.

Thus, in the ultimate paradox, the closest program to the managed-competition ideal—the original inspiration for the Clinton proposals and arguably the best-performing health insurance program in America—would be abolished because it was too good to be

---

[37]As quoted in "Clinton Weighs Dissolving U.S. Employee Health Plan," *Washington Post*, May 29, 1993, p. A6.

[38]Ibid., p. A1.

allowed to exist.[39] The federal government's own shining success would be terminated, while the antediluvian Medicare program would presumably continue unscathed so as to avoid offending the potent lobbies for the aged. But the 3½ million annuitants in the FEHBP might construct a different calculus. In that case, the impressive but accidental accomplishments of the Federal Employees Health Benefits Program might well continue.

Appendix 11–A:
How Does it Work?

The engine of consumer choice lies in the annual open season. For open season to offer a real choice among plans, preexisting-condition exclusions are banned. In the FEHBP, any employee or annuitant, no matter how ill, may join any plan. It is open-season competition that forces plans to respond to consumer preferences for benefits, service, and economy.

The government pays a set amount toward the premium cost. For calendar 1993, this amount is up to $1,675 annually for a single person and $3,630 for a family. The enrollee pays the rest—generally about one-half of the quoted amounts or one-third of total premium.

All plans must offer a solid core of comparable benefits. But on the margin, benefits are not identical among the plans. Most fee-for-service plans, for example, have a deductible of several hundred dollars. Most HMOs have no deductible at all. Thus, a given employee premium for HMO is a considerably better dollar buy than the same premium for a fee-for-service plan. There are numerous other benefit differences. Only some plans provide, for example, mail-order prescription drugs, chiropractic coverage, or dental coverage.

Enrollee share of premiums also varies widely, for three reasons. First, the government has not been willing to change the law to establish a separate premium pool, with higher government contribution, for annuitants without Medicare. Older people, on average, incur far higher medical expenses than younger people. As a result, younger and healthier employees have fled plans with a disproportionate share of these annuitants. Several plans have dropped out, because a concentration of older enrollees left them economically

---

[39]As a special irony, Senator William V. Roth, Jr., has for several years introduced legislation that would allow small businesses to buy into the FEHBP. Turning this proposal 180 degrees, the rumored Clinton plan would allow federal employees to buy into the plans set up for small businesses.

nonviable. Unfortunately, in this area, the FEHBP is not self-governing but subject to political stasis.

Second, these premium differences reflect differences in efficiency among the plans. Plans that control costs better, without alienating their customers, can charge a lower premium. Efficiency accounts for the ability of most HMOs to offer financial bargains. It has led to rapid growth in HMO enrollment over the past decade.

Third, each plan offers benefit variations. Some of these are substantial. Those plans offering dental coverage, for example, must charge higher premiums. Enrollees who want dental coverage have a choice whether to pay the higher premium to gain it. Dental coverage concentrates dental users in some plans, for which they pay higher premiums, but no one is harmed by this result. Likewise, those employees who want exceptionally strong mental health coverage can and do pay a hefty premium differential to join the Blue Cross high-option plan. In contrast, Medicare and most private sector plans offer virtually no dental coverage and highly limited mental health benefits.

Counting high and standard options as separate, ten national plans are open to all employees. (Seven others are open only to special groups, such as FBI agents, Capitol Hill employees, or foreign service officers). In almost all parts of the country, there are at least two or three HMOs. This makes a total of about a dozen choices. In the Washington, D.C., area, with its government concentration, employees can choose from sixteen HMO options and a total of twenty-six choices in 1993 (down from thirty-six just a few years earlier). That is a tremendous health insurance choice by the standards of the rest of the country. But for federal employees, it is a commonplace aspect of working life, rather than a source of confusion. Picking a plan is less interesting and challenging than selecting a new car or a new president, even though more complicated than deciding what to pick for lunch from the cafeteria menu.

The Office of Personnel Management helps minimize potential confusion. Unlike most private sector insurance policies, federal employee plans are required to explain their benefits in plain English. OPM insists on a standard format for plan brochures, so that each benefit category is presented in the same section and uses the same vocabulary. OPM also discourages confusing coverage limitations. These management practices facilitate plan comparisons. With such assistance, plus past experience in dealing with plans and advice from colleagues, consumers readily learn to choose easily from among plans.

It helps that in this program, as in any competitive market, only a small fraction of consumers have to be well-informed for market pressures to force all plans to be responsive. Federal employees grumble at complexity and red tape, but they grumble far less than retirees dealing with Medicare.

Commentary on Part Four

Stephen C. Schoenbaum

Jack Zwanziger and Glenn Melnick, Sean Sullivan, and Walton Francis have argued that competition among managed health care delivery systems blunts the rate of increase of health care cost and, perhaps, even can lead to lower costs in some instances.

Volume discount is one mechanism that managed care organizations like the Harvard Community Health Plan use to manage cost. We sign on vendors who are willing to get less profit per unit of business in return for guarantees of large units of business from us.

Second, some vendors see us as a marginal purchaser. That is, they would not have a full plate with all their other business if we were to leave. Therefore, they are willing to look at the marginal costs of servicing us and give us prices based on that.

Third, management of care seems to decrease unnecessary or wasteful care. Sean Sullivan gave an example of the large central-Florida hospitals that have decreased lengths of stay and use of ancillaries in response to community pressures. Presumably, those hospitals, acting as managers of care, were not cutting necessary care but rather care that simply did not have to be given.

Internally managed-care organizations have a number of incentives to lower use of unnecessary services. Most of our organizations use either salaried or capitated physicians. Therefore, the physicians do not have a financial incentive to do unnecessary procedures. It does not make a difference, for example, whether the ophthalmologist does ten cataract operations or one cataract operation.

Although these are important considerations, they deal with

only one side of the issue of cost management. In addition to the above, there is an enormous potential for cost savings through quality improvement. The notions that we have the best doctors, the best hospitals, the best nurses, the best health care are all challengeable. That is not to say that we do not have good doctors and so forth, but we do not have sound measurements to prove that we have the best achievable medical care.

First, there is too much art in medicine, along with too little skill and science. That may seem a strange statement when one considers how technically oriented medical care has become over the past few decades. But our skills are not well defined or calibrated, and that shows up as variability in performance.

Consider, for example, the phenomenon called observer variability. A group of radiologists or a group of pathologists will agree only about 80 percent of the time about the same slides or the same X-rays. We are not talking about subtle changes. They literally disagree on whether there is a fracture present if they are looking at an X-ray or a malignancy if they are looking at a pathologic slide. Observer variability is a major problem for the cost of services in that it leads to potential overuse of procedures because of overdiagnosis. That is wasteful. It can also lead to underuse of necessary services, which has its own associated cost. Underuse produces delays in diagnosis and treatment and ultimately more complications. To reduce the problems of under- and overuse, we will need to learn to calibrate our observations to a greater degree.

A second issue is our addiction to technology. We believe that more technology yields better results. Yet, few data prove that. In this country, for example, we have poorer results with pregnancy management than many countries where there is less available technology. We simply have not configured our health care delivery systems to be as comprehensive as they are in many other countries.

It is a fact that there are underserved populations in this country for high-tech procedures such as cardiac catheterization. Yet, as a recent study by Steve Udvarhelyi and Barbara McNeil[1] showed, the underserved populations, which tend to be women and blacks and low socioeconomic groups, do not have poorer survival rates from myocardial infarctions. There is dissonance between our use of technology and our outcomes.

1I. Steven Udvarhelyi, Constantine Gatsonis, Arnold M. Epstein, Chris L. Pashos, Joseph P. Newhouse, and Barbara McNeil, "Acute Myocardiac Infarction in the Medicare Population: Process of Care and Clinical Outcomes," *Journal of the American Medical Association*, vol. 268, no. 18.

In most instances, we do not have good data on the relationship between those processes and outcomes. Much of our care is unproved; we do not know what is truly necessary or unnecessary.

Uncertain indications for procedures, ones for which we do not know if the benefits exceed the risks, are not being managed forthrightly by the health care system. Currently, in such situations, the physician typically walks into the patient's room, states that in his opinion a procedure, for example, bypass surgery, is indicated, explains the risks of the procedure, and the procedure is done. Suppose, instead, I were to walk into a patient's room and say that in my opinion bypass surgery is indicated but that we do not have sufficient evidence from controlled trials to say that the benefits are greater than the risks. Patients would separate into two groups. Some patients would want to be aggressive, would go ahead with the procedure. Other patients would want to be conservative, not do the procedure. We could then have the populations on whom we could collect the outcome data to find out whether a patient actually does better as a result of a particular decision. This is an essential step for improving our future care, increasing its quality, and decreasing its cost. This step has not yet occurred.

We also have poorly thought-out processes of care that have grown up like Topsy. One should visit a sick relative or friend in a hospital room for a couple of hours and watch what seems like a random procession of people in and out of the room. Who could then tell me that hospitals have well thought-out processes of care and achieve all the efficiency that we can get in that system?

There are many errors in the process of care. There is the error of the wrong prescription leaving the pharmacy, something that the doctor did not intend for the patient. In hospitals, rates of error for prescriptions approach a few percent because of the multiple transactions over a hospitalization.[2]

Paul Cleary and his associates studied about 6,500 patients who were discharged from sixty-two medical-surgical hospitals chosen around the United States.[3] Thirty percent of the patients said that they were not told of the major complications from their discharge

---

[2]David W. Bates, Lucian L. Leape, and Stephen Petrycki, "Incidence and Preventabilty of Adverse Drug Events in Hospitalized Adults," *Journal of General Internal Medicine*, vol. 8 (1993), pp. 289–94.

[3]Paul D. Cleary, Susan Edgman-Levitan, Marc Roberts, Thomas W. Moloney, William McMullen, Janice D. Walker, and Thomas L. Delbanco, "Patients Evaluate Their Hospital Care: A National Survey," *Health Affairs*, Winter 1991, pp. 254–67.

medications. A similar percentage were not told when they should return to work. Patients reported about those same percentages for other instances of errors in care at the hospital.

The same pattern is developing in the ambulatory sphere. We are a subject of an unpublished study by the Harvard School of Public Health. This study is finding a 25 percent rate of error in returning laboratory results to patients. About 10 percent of patients say they never get results. Fifteen percent of patients say that results were not received for three or more weeks. This is inexcusable. Those of us who are managers in managed-care systems will have to do something about it. Solving these problems has cost implications; ultimately, the solutions will lower costs.

Purchasers can play a critical role in increasing the quality and the efficiency of the health care system. Purchasers, at least in our experience, have demanded accountability and value for dollars. Some important, large employers have been pushing us to provide them with data on what we do. Our ability to respond is at best rudimentary, but it is improving.

Those interested in purchasing cooperatives should realize that large numbers are necessary to provide good data, especially with younger populations. The events of interest to those who are outcome oriented do not occur commonly. Nevertheless, purchasers can obtain comparative data across plans that will be useful to them for their purchasing decisions and, interestingly, also important to us for quality improvement. Ultimately, we do not know how we perform unless we know that in relation to others. An argument can be made for obtaining comparative data for everyone's benefit.

Much money is spent on health care, but there is still little systematizing of the processes of care. Health care is still a cottage industry and must change. Obtaining data on care is an important first step in identifying what needs to be improved or systematized.

Finally, there are at least three dimensions to the delivery of health care to individuals. One is an information dimension: information is necessary for diagnosis, for treatment, for billing, for measurement. A second dimension is technical skills and procedures. That is the one we have worked on the most, over the years. But there is a need for knowing more about the technical aspects of what we are doing. The third dimension is personal service and delivery of services to people. It is an important dimension of care.

Those who would like to think of health care as an industry must also pay attention to the service dimension. Health care is a product made while the consumer is in the "factory." Satisfaction with care relates to experiences within the factory, not just the ultimate out-

311

come. There has been little work on improving transfer of clinical information and on engineering more efficient and satisfying personal services.

There are problems at every level of the system. Look at human resources, starting with physicians. Future physicians are chosen from a pool of individuals who are skilled at passing courses in calculus, physics, and inorganic and organic chemistry but are not required to understand statistics and developmental psychology or to have good interpersonal skills. These factors do not quite add up to a well-engineered system of health care.

Our information systems have been engineered to generate bills and to count services but not to provide the detailed information on the process and outcomes that we need to understand and to improve what we do.

The dichotomy in this country's discussion of the problems of cost of care and quality of care is remarkable. In an unpublished study of health benefits executives, 95 percent rated the cost problem as critical or crucial, and 50 percent of them rated quality as little or no problem. But the two go hand in hand. We cannot solve an underlying problem of cost until we have improved quality.

Jack Scanlon, Jr.

I would like to discuss the California selective contracting experience mentioned earlier, because this was the impetus for the procompetitive initiatives in health care in America.

In the summer of 1982, the governor, Jerry Brown, managed to convince the legislature that we could not deal with a $2 billion Medicaid Hospital budget; we had to save 10 percent. He convened a group of about nine or ten of us and gave us an imperative to save $200 million over the next twelve months.

We were fortunate enough to have as our leader the former president of Blue Cross of California, Bill Guy, who came to be known as the MediCal czar. Under his direction, our work was logical and businesslike. First, we put together a data base. When we began the selective contracting process for the governor's office, we discovered that MediCal had no idea how much it was spending on various providers. We then attempted to answer three basic questions: How much are we spending, to whom are the payments made, and for which types of illnesses?

Next, based on those data, we established negotiating targets—

not only price negotiating targets, but also service and access criteria, because the governor and the legislature viewed access as being as important as cost. We then negotiated with all the hospitals in California in approximately a nine-month period.

The success of the program revolved around two factors. One was our emphasis on price. When hospitals argued the old cost-to-charge magic, our line was, We care about your price, not your cost. This threw the hospital industry into quite a spin.

Second, we wanted to close a particular area to let the provider community know we were serious. We selected San Francisco and closed that area without two significant historical Medicaid hospitals. Needless to say, we had the attention of the entire provider community.

I think the successful implementation of the program was due primarily to an elegant simplicity: everyone understood the program. It was not complex, it was easy to administer, negotiations were straightforward, and we did not allow hospitals to carve out services. We insisted on all the services of a given hospital, and we would not, for example, negotiate with cardiovascular surgery here and intensive care and neonatal services at another place. We required hospitals to take all comers.

Finally, the concentration on a single per diem price was the other key ingredient. As I said, our approach revolutionized overnight the way the provider communities thought about the system. I might note that the system is still in place in California. I have heard many people asking, Why can't the states provide examples? I have often wondered why this clear success in California was never taken more to heart in Washington, D.C.

After we finished working in the governor's office, we went out and aggressively pursued the private sector for the next three years. We saw hospitals reconfiguring themselves before our eyes through that period. I would say Blue Cross, our firm, and several others made substantial market penetration in that time, signing up large corporate clients, insurance companies, and Union Trust Funds. In the early days, Union Trust Funds were some of the quickest sales, because the decision-making process is perhaps more streamlined in that environment.

By 1986, a whole range of other new entrants had come into the market, and by 1990, we had virtually saturated the California market, with the preferred provider organization as the prevailing option.

What is a preferred provider organization? Stripped to its bare essentials, a PPO is a volume purchasing business endeavor, analogous to other similar attempts to use business leverage to reduce the unit costs of the inputs required for production processes.

The structure requires that employers have access to these networks, and I would like to talk a bit about what makes a PPO successful. The difference between a PPO and an HMO is that an HMO offers singular choices. Either one goes to an HMO provider or not, and the benefits are all or none. In a PPO, people still maintain freedom of choice. The benefits are higher if you use a preferred provider organization, but a subscriber still has the option of going to a nonpreferred provider.

I identify three elements as key to a successful PPO. The first element is the level of competition. We classify markets into three zones. Zone 1 markets, which are the most competitive, are characterized by low occupany rates, redundancy of services, geographic proximity, and real quality alternatives. They are usually found in metropolitan areas. They are also the areas where the greatest savings are to be found.

Zone 2 areas are interesting: if any one of the conditions for a zone 1 is not met, it is a zone 2. That is, if the area has a higher occupancy rate, if we don't have a redundancy of services (for example, if only one hospital has an intensive care neonatal unit), if the providers are not geographically close, or if providers are dissimilar on a quality basis—we classify them as zone 2.

The zone 1 and the zone 2 markets provide most of the care in our benefit plans, as contrasted with the zone 3 markets. These are generally the rural and outlying markets, consisting of communities with, at most, two or three choices; some are sole providers. Negotiations here are more difficult.

I may have a slightly different view of the rural areas from what many people in Washington have. We have been successful in negotiating zone 3 areas. Certainly, we like to see high discounts and low per diem rates, but, in fact, in rural areas we cannot achieve them. We have to take what is there, and we rely instead on things like waiving bill audit. Many hospitals want to eliminate administrative burdens, so we will waive bill audit and guarantee quick pay discounts. For those reasons, the hospitals are able to make slight concessions.

When I look at that data empirically, I find less than 5 percent of a health plan's costs are incurred in zone 3 rural areas. In general, we find from patient origin studies that patients are receiving primary health care services in the rural communities. They are having babies, or they are going to the hospitals with broken limbs, appendicitis, and other relatively minor services. These are not high-cost problems in rural America. When our patients in rural America require high-cost services, they migrate to a zone 1 or zone 2 area to receive care from higher-level secondary and tertiary hospitals.

What has been the effect of our contracting effort? Nationally, during 1992, for hospital inpatient services, we are generating a 40 percent discount. These are not discounts off charges but per diem arrangements that translate to a 40 percent reduction from billed charges on the inpatient basis. For outpatients, we have generated savings of about 25 percent.

With regard to physicians, our unit cost savings are typically in the 20–25 percent range. Many in my company, however, including me, argue that unit cost savings should not be our sole focus. What is more important is to find the physician healers, those who can diagnose and treat an illness or injury, produce positive outcomes, without ordering or consuming excessive resources.

Savings on X-ray and laboratory services are phenomenal. In fact, we have been able to negotiate rates below the Medicare fee schedule.

In many cases in California, we have been able to drive the PPO indemnity plan rates down below the Kaiser HMO contribution levels. In my opinion, many Taft-Hartley clients have hired us as a counteroffensive measure. Kaiser in California is quite a dominant provider, and it pushes its weight around.

The second key element that determines the success of a PPO is the employer's benefit plan. The employer must take this seriously and channel patients into the preferred hospitals, or the whole notion of volume purchasing breaks down.

The third key element of the successful PPO is strong provider relations. We have tried to establish strong business relationships with our provider community.

The prognosis for PPOs is very strong. On the provider side, we see an incredible amount of competition, particularly for outpatients. In just the past few years, the new outpatient procedures are mind boggling: laparoscopic cholecystectomies, arthroscopies, and the myriad of other creative technologies. And frankly, it is a problem for us. The providers are creating these new technologies and delivery modalities faster than we can keep up with them. There is probably a six-month or one-year lag.

The other reason I say the prognosis for PPOs is strong is that employers are increasingly taking to heart the need to provide incentives for their employees to use preferred providers. Throughout the 1980s, employers were very timid about putting in severe benefit plan differentials. I would say only 10 percent differentiated a PPO from a non-PPO. With the low out-of-pocket stop-loss, there really was not

315

much effect. Therefore, PPOs did not have maximum penetration.

From now on, I predict we will see substantial coinsurance differences of 20 to 40 percent. But more important, we will see that the out-of-pocket stop-loss for nonnetwork utilization will be either very high or nil.

For transplant coverage, for example, in one of the plans in the Federal Employees Health Benefits Plan, if a patient does not go to a transplant center, his or her maximum for that procedure is $100,000, and the contingent liability a patient is exposed to would be very high.

People often ask whether PPOs have been successful only in California. I point to our nationwide enrollment of 1,300 hospitals and 75,000 physicians, and we are still growing. We are bringing in many small employers, some with as few as fifty employees, who take advantage of substantial negotiated rates based on the sheer volume of our business in a particular market.

In the future, I think we will see significant PPO activity in the whole reinsurance market. Workers' compensation is an area that we are deeply involved in and that is undergoing substantial change. Even the auto liability carriers are now turning more and more toward a preferred provider organization.

In summary, it has been my experience that selective contracting has worked for state government, as well as for the private sector. I feel somewhat remiss that the industry has not communicated better the true results and benefits of these programs. As an industry, we have failed to give our message to the policy makers in Washington. But I hope this failure will be remedied in the near future.

Arthur Lifson

I want to tell something about CIGNA and how we see our future. CIGNA is the largest investor-owned HMO company. It is one of the largest providers of employee benefits in the United States. It paid $777 million to acquire a little company called EQUICOR, which was a joint venture between the Hospital Corporation of America and the Equitable Life. It represents a commitment in the shift from an insurer to a health care deliverer. We see our future in health care delivery and now have an investment in that future of about $2 billion. We therefore take managed care and managed competition seriously: it is our future. Our stockholders are hoping that we do this right and that we know something about what we are doing. We own and operate staff-model health maintenance organizations, independent practice associations, and preferred provider organizations, and we still have a big book of indemnity business to manage.

Competition for satisfied customers has led us to this shift. In 1982, the rules changed in California, and we saw what happened there: corporate America took a look at health care costs and said, We can't afford the cost of these benefits. We have to find a different way of doing it, and we are going to do business with people who find ways of innovating and find ways of delivering employee benefits at prices that are producing real value for us.

Something else was going on too within corporate America: a recognition that quality is fair value and that high-quality service, in the long run, is the cheapest way to do business. It produces satisfied customers, it produces market share, and it does all sorts of other good things.

As corporate America declared its commitment to quality and continuous quality improvement, companies like GE and Xerox made clear their desire to do business with partners who had an equal commitment. And that attitude has led to a shift in companies such as my own that has changed tremendously the way we look at what we do, how we organize ourselves, how we perform various processes, and how we measure our performance—probably the biggest shift that I have seen.

We are now beginning to measure customer satisfaction with our performance, not just consultants' and brokers' satisfaction with our performance. It is important, particularly in the large employer market, to know whether the employees and their families are satisfied with our services. We recognize, in this brave new world of managed competition, that almost no matter how it comes out, we have to shift our perspective from wholesale to retail.

That shift puts a different light on things, on how we deliver services, to whom we deliver them, how we measure our performance, and how the marketplace measures our performance. Not many years ago, performance was measured on one thing and one thing only: retention. How much did it cost to process claims and do administration? For big customers, that was between 5 and 10 percent; for smaller customers it was more than that. Nobody paid attention to the 90 percent for claims. We have finally come around to recognize that we have to be concerned about the whole 100 percent.

The health care debate presents us, as a society, with some fundamental decisions. While we are looking for answers, though, we should realize that we will never have the perfect information we would like to make these decisions. We have heard about natural experiments that have gone on in places outside Washington; these give us some clues about what the answers to those questions might be. I have some observations to make:

First, health care really does respond to market forces. The conventional wisdom has always been that for health care, all the rules of economics—supply and demand and the like—are suspended. But one of the reasons that managed care is working—negotiating fee discounts, making different arrangements with people, steering people toward centers of excellence—is that we have an oversupply of physicians and an oversupply of hospital beds, creating competition for those services. The importance of price is clear from the chapter on California and its hospitals.

Second, according to conventional wisdom, the individual is incapable of making rational decisions about health care or lacks sufficient information to do so. That is probably true when someone is under the knife, or about to be, but the experience with FEHBP shows that when people are choosing among plans that meet certain minimum requirements for quality, they can make reasonable choices.

Third, it is important to keep the employer engaged in this debate. A lot of the innovation has come about because employers, especially large payers, have decided they need their suppliers to behave differently; the employers need a different product, and they want change. They had enough marketplace power, presence, and resources to force some of that change. Companies like Allied Signal, GE, and Xerox have put a lot of thought into how health insurance could be restructured and about how they would change their purchasing behaviors in the marketplace.

Some of the chapters in this book have considered regulation versus competition. The real topic is regulated competition and its benefits. I would juxtapose regulated competition against price fixing and regulation by government, with two examples from the chapters and my own experience. I have been involved in the Council on Health Care Financing in New York, which recommends how hospital rates will be regulated in the state. During the discussions of this council, I have concluded that the hospital administrators in New York State and their boards do not manage to their bottom line. They manage to Albany, because that is the only place where they can get approval for changing behavior.

In New York, only in recent years have HMOs been allowed to negotiate prices with the hospitals. Even though those prices have to be approved by the state, HMOs can negotiate their own deals. I asked one of the chief financial officers of a major New York teaching institution if he knew the marginal cost of providing a particular service. He did not—not because he is a bad person or an incompetent one. But his success was measured on Medicare cost reports and on beating the regulators in Albany on allocation decisions and convincing them to change base years and the like, not on what it really costs to produce the product.

In California, I am sure the accounting clerks know the marginal cost of delivering a whole host of services and whether or not a given institution will do well. I think competition really does produce a better result.

New York has always said it has about 5,000 excess beds, and as the state closes beds, the number still stays at 5,000. But every time someone tries to close a bed, it is a big political decision. We have claimed for a long time that we have had excess capacity of physicians and excess capacity of hospitals, which has induced its own costs. Yet we have not been able to squeeze out that excess capacity. From CIGNA's perspective, we are happy that excess capacity is out there now because we can cut deals with providers.

But over time, through competition, we will squeeze out that excess capacity, because the marketplace can allow people to fail and we can accept that failure. The state of New York, though, cannot accept the failure of an institution that maybe should fail.

Another thing I found interesting about California is that in a competitive market, it cost more to provide health services in 1982 than it did in a noncompetitive market. As I see it, the competition was not on price or on value but on bigger and better services. In 1992, the competitive market produces more value. That, I think, is a great lesson.

In Washington, D.C., a discussion is going on over whether HIPCs are active or passive. Are the HIPCs like Plato's philosopher kings who can make better decisions than the market over who should be a market participant and what prices they should charge? The FEHBP, for all its problems, shows that the more market entrants there are, the better off we are. If we just set the rules and let everybody play by them, we get a fairly good result. I would not want to try to second guess the results of the market.

I will conclude with an observation on what is happening in the marketplace itself, particularly with large employers. According to the data, they are experiencing a cost increase of 12 percent, Medicare is 9 percent, and FEHBP is 9 percent. In the 1980s, despite the rhetoric, employers were not requiring their employees to make hard decisions. I spent about six months with one employer who was

319

struggling over an increase in the employee contribution for family coverage from $5 a month to $10 a month. Employers have not been providing the incentives for people to get into the more managed plans.

A few did, companies like Allied. At Allied, 90 percent of the employees stay in the plan 100 percent of the time, and when asked, 95 percent say they are satisfied with the care they receive. There are some big disincentives for going out of network.

In the 1990s, we will see a stronger shift toward HMOs and more tightly managed plans. According to the Foster-Higgins data, those HMOs and tightly managed plans are producing services at about 60 percent of the increasing trend of pure indemnity plans.

As for innovation, I think it is in part what the health care reform debate will turn on: whether we freeze in place the world as we know it today or permit a world in which innovation can play an increasing role.

In Albuquerque and Santa Fe, New Mexico, for example, about 75 percent of the market is managed-care plans, all competing head to head. There are about six plans, one of which happens to be ours, Loveless. Competition has produced a number of different results. One is, because the market was saturated, Loveless had to go to rural areas to gain market share. The plans that had reached a saturation point in the Santa Fe and Albuquerque area moved to Los Cruces and Roswell and many smaller towns, and then farther out.

They found they had to innovate. There were not many primary care physicians out there, and whoever was there was really busy. They could not go to someone with twenty people waiting in the outer room and ask for a discount. They might even end up paying them more, as one of their innovations.

But we also started bringing in what we call mid-level practitioners—nurse-practitioners and physician assistants—to provide fundamental preventive and other services: we did triage, we put in place 800 numbers available to everybody, we got vans to move out into rural areas for immunizations, and we did many other things of that sort. The marketplace, not the government, required those measures for us to increase market share.

PART FIVE

Prospects for Health
Policy Reform

12

History and Politics

A Keynote Address

Bill Gradison

I approach health care reform with the strong conviction that we need comprehensive national action. It is useful, before looking forward, to look back. Health reform is not a new issue, and its history has not been one of extraordinary partisanship.

History of U.S. Health Care Reform

The first U.S. president to recommend national health insurance was Teddy Roosevelt. Franklin Roosevelt took a close look at it during the 1930s and originally considered including it in what became the Social Security Act. Harry Truman advocated national health insurance during his service in the White House, but he was unsuccessful in selling it to Congress.

Richard Nixon, of a different political persuasion, was the first president to recommend to the Congress in writing that employers be required to help pay for health insurance for their employees. Indeed, the major difference between that proposal and what we expect from President Clinton is that Nixon's plan would have required the employee to pay up to 35 percent of the cost, while Clinton will probably propose an 80 to 20 split.

President Carter was elected on a campaign pledge for comprehensive national health insurance. Once in office, Carter said it would be a mistake to extend access until costs were brought under control. He then sent Congress a hospital cost-containment bill, which was defeated. That Congress was by far more Democratic than the present one. The leader in opposition to President Carter's hospital cost-containment proposal on the House floor was a young Missouri congressman named Richard Gephardt.

Reasons for Past Failures

The history of health care reform thus demonstrates that if the approach becomes highly partisan, it is likely to fail. We have not had comprehensive action in the past for at least four reasons. First, there has been a striking unwillingness to compromise. The Nixon proposal, which today is the mainstream doctrine of the Democratic party, was not gratefully endorsed and passed when Nixon was president because Nixon *was* president, and also because the proposal was "insufficient." It did not go as far as some leaders in the Democratic party thought the nation should go.

Traditionally, second choice for a lot of people has been to do nothing. From a political point of view, you can vote against another plan and convince your constituents that you want something done about health care reform as long as you have a plan you are for.

The second obstacle has been a strong difference of opinion about whether change should be incremental or comprehensive. Our history has been one of incremental action. But many congressmen who favor a broad national comprehensive action absolutely oppose incremental action because they think it will resolve enough of the problem, and satisfy enough of the people to prevent their comprehensive plan from being sold to the public.

A third obstacle has been the question of how to pay for these things. The Stark-Gradison Catastrophic Health Insurance legislation was the first social insurance program in the history of the country to be repealed before it took effect. One reason was simply dollars and cents. The sleeper in that issue was the one-size-fits-all plan.

About 6 million people, or 20 percent of Medicare beneficiaries, had or believed they had coverage equivalent to that offered by the new catastrophic health insurance legislation. They asked, "Why should I pay for something I now get free?" Perhaps a 20 percent rule is at work here: if the proportion of the public that is already satisfied is high enough, it will be hard to come up with a plan that fits the entire society.

In a sense, we are victims of our success, because 85 percent of

Americans have health insurance. In the 1930s, only a small percentage were covered. So it is now harder to bring about effective change.

The fourth obstacle to change has been insufficient concern about the uninsured. Today there is new hope for action, because the middle class is worrying about the cost of health care and about losing coverage. These middle-class concerns have elevated health care to the top rung of salient political issues.

Current Voter Expectations

But a federal action is really not a slam-dunk. Data show that the public is paying attention to health reform as it never has before, but it has not focused on the specifics of the alternative plans.

Sometimes, I have concluded from reading health polls that the public wants national health insurance as long as the government has nothing to do with it. Or the public says, "Fix it, but don't send me the bill—I am paying too much for health care already."

The Democrats' Survey Results. One recent nationwide survey that sought public views on what is known of President Clinton's plan found that voters are cautious about change. They are satisfied with their own health care, though strongly critical of the national health care system. It is akin to disliking Congress but liking your own representative.

Voters in this survey were divided between concern that things would stay as they are and concern that change would go too far. A delicate balance has to be struck. Voters worry more about cost and quality under the current system and less about the health uninsured. The majority of respondents—59 percent—said they want national health care reform in order to get health costs under control. Only 24 percent believed that is the primary goal of the president's plan.

Their concern is that this plan focuses on the health uninsured. Those who have insurance are not sure the plan addresses their own concerns.

This survey suggests that voters would respond to any health care plan based on their own sense of gains and losses, not altruism, communitarianism, or the Judeo-Christian ethic.

There is a dangerous discrepancy in voters' thinking: 43 percent believe that the president's plan will cut health costs, but only 31 percent believe it will translate into health care savings for themselves.

At the same time, 70 percent of these respondents overwhelmingly believe the plan will increase their taxes. Although 64 percent think it will improve access to health care for all Americans, only 28 percent believe it will improve their own benefits, and only 26 percent believe it will improve the quality of their own health care.

This survey was done for the Democratic party and shared with Democratic members of Congress. It indicates what was said not by critics but by those who want to help the administration. The most important factor was whether the plan would reduce what the respondent pays for health care, which was twice as important as any other factor.

Respondents support reform because of what they believe it will do for them and their families, not for society in the aggregate. In fact, 44 percent of the respondents believe that national health care reform will increase the deficit; only 20 percent said it will decrease it.

They say it will increase the deficit because it will increase government spending. These respondents also believe that national health care reform will hurt, not help, the economy—respectively, 41 percent versus 27 percent. They think it will increase the burden on small businesses, taking more of their disposable income in taxes and restraining the health care industry itself, which is one of the major new employers in our society.

The Insurance Industry's Survey Results. We have just completed a nationwide survey of our own.[1] We found that 76 percent of Americans are paying close attention to the health insurance issue, but that no consensus has emerged about what the changes should be. A majority, however, supports limiting the role of government and fixing what is wrong in the system rather than changing the whole.

People are primarily seeking reassurance that they will keep their coverage and that the cost will be affordable. The elements that have the most support are the ability to choose one's own doctor and hospital, as we all knew, and also to choose one's own insurance company or plan. That is an interesting revelation.

Our survey also shows that the public wants a system in which nobody can be turned down for health insurance or can have his insurance canceled. Malpractice reform is strongly supported, as are price and wage controls. The latter shows up in virtually every survey I have seen, however, misguided it may be.

The survey respondents also favor the following features for a

---

[1]Voter/Consumer Research, "Coalition for Health Insurance Choices/ Health Insurance Association of America, National Survey, Health Care Reform," April 1993.

reform plan: a package of essential benefits for everyone; employee coverage for which employers will have to help pay; a government subsidy for companies that cannot afford to cover their employees; purchase of health insurance by individuals without an employer for themselves and their families, with a subsidy if necessary; and increases in sin taxes.

People do not want to be assigned to one of a few health plans or health maintenance organizations, where in effect they will be assigned to a physician. They also do not want the federal government to determine the amount of money to be spent on health care in a given region—so-called global budgets.

Constant Cultural Attitudes

Beyond these poll findings, Americans hold some deep-seated attitudes, which I call cultural factors. I doubt they will change quickly.

The first is that people like first-dollar insurance. If they do not have it, they try to get it. Medicare has premium deductibles and copayments; more than 80 percent of beneficiaries buy Medigap insurance to convert it into first-dollar coverage. The principal cause of labor unrest in this country is health care, and the principal cause of strikes is the attempt of employers to move away from first-dollar coverage.

The public has an idea about insurance for health care costs that is different from their ideas about other costs. No one suggests first-dollar coverage for a car or for fire insurance for a house—only for health insurance. That costs money for the system as well as for individuals. It will not be easy to make them pay a portion of their own health care costs.

A second deep-seated attitude of Americans is a preference for fee-for-service medicine. Ten years ago, we allowed Medicare beneficiaries to move into HMOs or competitive medical plans. The current market penetration of such capitated plans for Medicare is only about 5 percent. Of course, these people were not accustomed to capitated arrangements during their working years, and they were not told they would pay less if they were in a capitated plan.

Although I am convinced that managed care is the wave of the future, moving people there will be a slow process. If a plan is proposed that penalizes people who choose not to go into managed care, it will not be sellable.

A third social factor is American impatience. We in the health care field in this country point out redundant facilities—for instance, there are more magnetic resonance imaging (MRI) facilities in Tennessee than in Canada—and we see the phenomenon as a negative. But the public does not view it that way. To the public, it means there are no queues when someone needs a CAT scan or an MRI. Limitations imposed by government may make a lot of sense, but they will not be terribly popular.

The Unknowns of President Clinton's Plan

What is the benefit package that will be guaranteed to all Americans? How much will it cost? Apparently, the White House is considering a requirement that everybody have a plan in the eighty-fifth percentile of the plans currently in use in the private sector. This will create sticker-price shock on the part of "the good guys"—those below the eighty-fifth percentile. For those in these plans, health reform will mean paying more, unless the additional cost is offset by substantial reductions in cost shifting. That will not be easy to sell to the public. It is my impression that farmers, who by the nature of their work are accustomed to taking risks, purchase insurance with deductibles more often than the general public does. This is a way for them to keep costs down but protect themselves against catastrophic losses. Farmers, ranchers, hardware store owners, and other entrepreneurs, who now buy insurance on their own, will be required to pay for something substantially more comprehensive than they are accustomed to.

A related factor for an eighty-fifth percentile plan is the dramatic cost increase to the government. It is inconceivable that a benefit package would be offered to cover one's lifetime, right up to retirement or disablement, and another, lower benefit package would be provided under the government plan. So the desire to broaden benefits for the whole population is at war with the budgetary desire to hold down Medicare expenditures.

Perhaps because of my sixteen years on the House Ways and Means Committee, I talk too much about dollars and cents, but I think it is fundamental. The task force hearings held around the country have raised expectations to a high level. It seemed one day it would be long-term care, and the next day outpatient prescription drugs, and the next day unlimited mental health. I am not against them, but they have a price tag. Despite a lot of talk about their benefits, there was virtually no talk about how those things might be paid for.

Little has been said about the total cost of the program. The estimate of $30–90 billion came out of the task force. As an outsider, I assume that achieving the eighty-fifth percentile will bring us closer to the $90 billion than the $30 billion. This creates some serious difficulties, because it suggests that little money will be available to reduce the cost shifting the government is imposing on the private sector.

According to figures published in *Health Affairs*, Medicaid pays an average of 80 percent of hospital costs, Medicare 90 percent, and everyone else 128 percent. In other words, one reason health insurance is so expensive in the private sector is that government does not bargain; it just passes laws.

If all the available dollars are likely to be used for new benefits, none will be available for this cost shifting. Therefore, the pressures on the private sector will remain. Indeed, the latest budget presented by the president could, over the next five years, increase the cost shifting by another $50 billion or $60 billion for Medicare and Medicaid.

Another area we have not heard much about is the phase-in. Whatever is done will have to be phased in over time for many reasons. It will take time to implement these plans.

A fourth area is, of course, the source of financing. If someone will announce how much money is available, a group of knowledgeable people in an afternoon could figure out a fairly sensible way to spend the money to maximum advantage to improve our health care system. But I have the impression that this may be the last decision made.

If expectations of generous plans have been built up, they will require hefty financing. Sin taxes are not adequate to do this job.

The fifth factor that we look forward to learning more about is the role of the states. Over the past several years I have met with bipartisan groups of the nation's governors, and their message was clear: If Washington will not do anything soon about health care, why not let the states do it? They would speed up Medicaid waivers and begin to grant waivers to the Employment Retirement Income Security Act.

Neither of them is moving fast, although this administration has certainly moved more responsively than President Bush did on the Medicaid waivers. But the states are not waiting. Maryland has acted in a major way, and so has Florida. It will be more difficult, not less, to come up with a national plan.

It appears that the administration will suggest what we in the trade call exclusive health insurance purchasing cooperatives. We are using the HIPC term "local health alliances."

Florida has adopted a plan that has purchasing co-ops. They call them community health purchasing agencies, or CHIPPAs. Will the

Congress tell Florida, whose governor was recently a popular Democratic member of the Senate, that it cannot go voluntary? It will be difficult. The more states devise their own plans, the more general the federal plan will have to be, or it will cause real confrontation. If congressional action is possible this year, there could be another round of legislative sessions before it occurs.

Criteria for Evaluating a Health Plan

My experience convinces me that Congress is a responsive institution. Congressmen in a two-year term focus on survival. In closing, I will focus on some of the questions likely to be in the minds of the public and, therefore, of Congress.

In many ways, the most important role of a member of Congress is to ask good questions. These are questions members may be asking their constituents or hearing from them, in judging the president's plan or any competing plans that may be put forward.

Does the government police or run the system? A lot of polling data indicate that the public wants the government as the policeman, but not the administrator.

Is the greater risk for any family to be found in staying with the status quo or in adopting the change the plan proposes? This entails a delicate balance. People will reach judgments at different points in the spectrum. Exactly how will the plan deliver care, and exactly how will it work? It will be hard to rally public support for any plan without answering these questions in specific terms.

How will the proposal affect the individual family's out-of-pocket health costs, as opposed to the cost to the health care system as a whole? Would an individual have to change doctors or insurance plans? We will be told that we can follow our doctor into a health plan, but what if our primary care physician and pediatrician belong to different plans? What if we join the plan and then our pediatrician or family doctor drop out? Will the plan pay less for our health care if our personal physicians are not part of a government-certified plan approved by the purchasing co-op?

Will the plan cost the jobs of some in small business and in the health care industry? Will federal programs like Veterans Affairs, Medicare, and federal employees be treated like everyone else? An argument we used in the House against the Carter hospital cost-containment program was that it left out the VA hospitals. If this plan is so great for everyone else, why is the government unwilling to use it for its own programs?

Is the cost of the program shared fairly among the public in terms of age and lifestyle? Will there be a nonsmoker discount? Florida, for example, permits rating on four factors: age, gender, geography, and smoking. Once smoking is acknowledged, a lot of other factors might be taken into account.

Will the plan be financed by deficit spending or by new taxes? Will health care quality for my family improve or suffer? While all of us in the health care field focus on the macrolevel in this issue, the public and their representatives look at the microlevel and ask simple questions: How will this plan affect my family and what will it cost me?

My hunch is that no plan can be sold by generalizations like "peace of mind" or by pointing to scapegoats. This suggests that congressional action on health care reform will not occur overnight.

NATIONAL UNIVERSITY LIBRARY SAN DIEGO

Board of Trustees

Paul F. Oreffice, *Chairman*
Former Chairman
Dow Chemical Co.

Edwin L. Artzt
Chairman and CEO
The Procter & Gamble
  Company

Winton M. Blount, *Treasurer*
Chairman
Blount, Inc.

Vaughn D. Bryson

Joseph A. Cannon
Chairman and CEO
Geneva Steel Company

Raymond E. Cartledge
Chairman and CEO
Union Camp Corporation

Edwin L. Cox
Chairman
Cox Oil & Gas, Inc.

Christopher C. DeMuth
President
American Enterprise Institute

Malcolm S. Forbes, Jr.
President and CEO
Forbes Inc.

Tully M. Friedman
Hellman & Friedman

Christopher B. Galvin
Senior Executive Vice President
  and Assistant Chief Operating
  Officer
Motorola, Inc.

Robert F. Greenhill
Chairman and CEO
Smith Barney Shearson

M. Douglas Ivester
President
Coca-Cola USA

James W. Kinnear
Former President and CEO
Texaco Incorporated

Robert H. Malott
Chairman of the Executive Committee
FMC Corp.

The American Enterprise Institute
for Public Policy Research

Founded in 1943, AEI is a nonpartisan, nonprofit, research and educational organization based in Washington, D.C. The Institute sponsors research, conducts seminars and conferences, and publishes books and periodicals.

AEI's research is carried out under three major programs: Economic Policy Studies; Foreign Policy and Defense Studies; and Social and Political Studies. The resident scholars and fellows listed in these pages are part of a network that also includes ninety adjunct scholars at leading universities throughout the United States and in several foreign countries.

The views expressed in AEI publications are those of the authors and do not necessarily reflect the views of the staff, advisory panels, officers, or trustees.

George R. Roberts
Kohlberg Kravis Roberts & Co.

Edward B. Rust, Jr.
Chairman, President, and CEO
State Farm Mutual Automobile
  Insurance Company

Paul G. Stern
Forstmann Little & Co.

Wilson H. Taylor
Chairman and CEO
CIGNA Corporation

Henry Wendt
Chairman
SmithKline Beecham

James Q. Wilson
James A. Collins Professor
  of Management
University of California
  at Los Angeles

Charles Wohlstetter
Vice Chairman
GTE Corporation

Officers

Christopher C. DeMuth
President

David B. Gerson
Executive Vice President

Council of Academic
Advisers

James Q. Wilson, *Chairman*
James A. Collins Professor
  of Management
University of California
  at Los Angeles

Donald C. Hellmann
Professor of Political Science and
  International Studies
University of Washington

Gertrude Himmelfarb
Distinguished Professor of History
  Emeritus
City University of New York

Samuel P. Huntington
Eaton Professor of the
  Science of Government
Harvard University

D. Gale Johnson
Eliakim Hastings Moore
  Distinguished Service Professor
  of Economics Emeritus
University of Chicago

William M. Landes
Clifton R. Musser Professor of
  Economics
University of Chicago Law School

Glenn C. Loury
Department of Economics
Boston University

Sam Peltzman
Sears Roebuck Professor of Economics
and Financial Services
University of Chicago
  Graduate School of Business

Nelson W. Polsby
Professor of Political Science
University of California at Berkeley

Murray L. Weidenbaum
Mallinckrodt Distinguished
  University Professor
Washington University

Research Staff

Leon Aron
Resident Scholar

Claude E. Barfield
Resident Scholar; Director, Science
  and Technology Policy Studies

Walter Berns
Adjunct Scholar

Douglas J. Besharov
Resident Scholar

Jagdish Bhagwati
Visiting Scholar

Robert H. Bork
John M. Olin Scholar in Legal Studies

Michael Boskin
Visiting Scholar

Karlyn Bowman
Resident Fellow; Editor,
  The American Enterprise

David Bradford
Visiting Scholar

Dick B. Cheney
Senior Fellow

Lynne V. Cheney
W.H. Brady, Jr., Distinguished Fellow

Dinesh D'Souza
John M. Olin Research Fellow

Nicholas N. Eberstadt
Visiting Scholar

Mark Falcoff
Resident Scholar

Gerald R. Ford
Distinguished Fellow

Murray F. Foss
Visiting Scholar

Suzanne Garment
Resident Scholar

Patrick Glynn
Resident Scholar

Robert A. Goldwin
Resident Scholar

Gottfried Haberler
Resident Scholar

Robert W. Hahn
Resident Scholar

Robert B. Helms
Resident Scholar

Jeane J. Kirkpatrick
Senior Fellow; Director, Foreign and
  Defense Policy Studies

Marvin H. Kosters
Resident Scholar; Director,
  Economic Policy Studies

Irving Kristol
John M. Olin Distinguished Fellow

Michael A. Ledeen
Resident Scholar

James Lilley
Resident Fellow; Director, Asian
  Studies Program

Chong-Pin Lin
Resident Scholar; Associate Director,
  Asian Studies Program

John H. Makin
Resident Scholar; Director, Fiscal
  Policy Studies

Allan H. Meltzer
Visiting Scholar

Joshua Muravchik
Resident Scholar

Charles Murray
Bradley Fellow

Michael Novak
George F. Jewett Scholar in Religion,
  Philosophy, and Public Policy;
  Director, Social and
  Political Studies

Norman J. Ornstein
Resident Scholar

Richard N. Perle
Resident Fellow

William Schneider
Resident Fellow

William Shew
Visiting Scholar

J. Gregory Sidak
Resident Scholar

Herbert Stein
Senior Fellow

Irwin M. Stelzer
Resident Scholar; Director, Regulatory
  Policy Studies

Edward Styles
Director of Publications

W. Allen Wallis
Resident Scholar

Ben J. Wattenberg
Senior Fellow

Carolyn L. Weaver
Resident Scholar; Director, Social
  Security and Pension Studies

A NOTE ON THE BOOK

This book was edited by Ann Petty, Dana Lane, and Cheryl Weissman
of the publications staff of the American Enterprise Institute.
The figures were drawn by Hördur Karlsson.
The text was set in Palatino.
Coghill Composition Company of Richmond, Virginia,
set the type, and Data Reproductions Corporation,
of Rochester Hills, Michigan, printed and bound the book,
using permanent acid-free paper.

The AEI Press is the publisher for the American Enterprise Institute for Public Policy Research, 1150 17th Street, N.W., Washington, D.C. 20036; *Christopher C. DeMuth*, publisher; *Edward Styles*, director; *Dana Lane*, assistant director; *Ann Petty*, editor; *Cheryl Weissman*, editor; *Mary Cristina Delaney*, editorial assistant (rights and permissions).